**W9-BZA-709**

WITHDRAWN

FEB 2 7 2018 ✓

# Sports Injuries

## SOURCEBOOK

*Fifth Edition*

Ref
RD
97
.S736
2017

## Health Reference Series

### *Fifth Edition*

# Sports Injuries
# SOURCEBOOK

*Basic Consumer Health Information about Sprains, Fractures, Tendon Injuries, Overuse Injuries, and Injuries to the Head, Spine, Shoulders, Arms, Hands, Trunk, Legs, Knees, and Feet, and Facts about Sports-Specific Injuries, Injury Prevention, Protective Equipment, Children and Sports, and the Diagnosis, Treatment, and Rehabilitation of Sports Injuries*

*Along with a Glossary of Related Terms and a Directory of Resources for More Information*

## OMNIGRAPHICS

615 Griswold, Ste. 901, Detroit, MI 48226

Bibliographic Note

Because this page cannot legibly accommodate all the copyright notices, the Bibliographic Note portion of the Preface constitutes an extension of the copyright notice.

\* \* \*

*Health Reference Series*

Keith Jones, *Managing Editor*

\*\*\*

OMNIGRAPHICS

A PART OF RELEVANT INFORMATION

\*\*\*

Copyright © 2017 Omnigraphics
ISBN 978-0-7808-1528-5
E-ISBN 978-0-7808-1529-2

Library of Congress Cataloging-in-Publication Data

Names: Omnigraphics, Inc.

Title: Sports injuries sourcebook: basic consumer health information about sprains, fractures, tendon injuries, overuse injuries, and injuries to the head, spine, shoulders, arms, hands, trunk, legs, knees, and feet, and facts about sports-specific injuries, injury prevention, protective equipment, children and sports, and the diagnosis, treatment, and rehabilitation of sports injuries; along with a glossary of related terms and a directory of resources for more information.

Description: Fifth edition. | Detroit, MI: Omnigraphics, [2017] | Series: Health reference series | Includes bibliographical references and index.

Identifiers: LCCN 2017013733 (print) | LCCN 2017018554 (ebook) | ISBN 9780780815292 (eBook) | ISBN 9780780815285 (hardcover: alk. paper)

Subjects: LCSH: Sports injuries. | Sports medicine. | Wounds and injuries.

Classification: LCC RD97 (ebook) | LCC RD97.S736 2017 (print) | DDC 617.1/027--dc23

LC record available at https://lccn.loc.gov/2017013733

Electronic or mechanical reproduction, including photography, recording, or any other information storage and retrieval system for the purpose of resale is strictly prohibited without permission in writing from the publisher.

The information in this publication was compiled from the sources cited and from other sources considered reliable. While every possible effort has been made to ensure reliability, the publisher will not assume liability for damages caused by inaccuracies in the data, and makes no warranty, express or implied, on the accuracy of the information contained herein.

This book is printed on acid-free paper meeting the ANSI Z39.48 Standard. The infinity symbol that appears above indicates that the paper in this book meets that standard.

Printed in the United States

# Table of Contents

## Part II: Preventing Sports Injuries

## Part III: Head and Facial Injuries

## Part IV: Back, Neck, and Spine Injuries

## Part V: Shoulder and Upper Arm Injuries

## Part VI: Injuries to the Elbows, Wrists, and Hands

## Part VII: Injuries to the Trunk, Groin, Upper Legs, and Knees

## Part IX: Diagnosis, Treatment, and Rehabilitation of Sports Injuries

## Part X: Sports Injuries in Children and Young Athletes

## Part XI: Additional Help and Information

# Preface

## About This Book

Although the health benefits of participation in sports and exercise far outweigh the risks, sports injuries can occur in athletes of all ages and levels of experience and in many different activities. According to the Centers for Disease Control and Prevention (CDC), each year 38 million youth participate in organized sports and 170 million adults participate in leisure-time physical activity. Overuse and sudden, traumatic injuries often lead to short- and long-term consequences for athletes. With the proper training, warm-up, and equipment, many of these injuries can be prevented. Many others can be treated and rehabilitated.

*Sports Injuries Sourcebook, Fifth Edition* describes the basic types of sports injuries, including overuse injuries, tendonitis, heat illness, and skin disorders as well as traumatic injuries such as fractures, sprains, strains, spinal injuries, sudden cardiac arrest, concussion, and injuries to parts of the body, including the head, spine, torso, arms, hands, legs, and feet. The book discusses protective equipment and injury prevention strategies for specific activities and provides facts about nutrition and hydration, supplements, diagnosis and treatment, and specific risks and prevention strategies for children and young athletes. The book concludes with a glossary of related terms and a directory of resources for additional help and information.

## How to Use This Book

This book is divided into parts and chapters. Parts focus on broad areas of interest. Chapters are devoted to single topics within a part.

*Part I: Health and Sports* provides an introduction to basic sports injuries such as sprains, tendon injuries, overuse injuries, and sudden cardiac arrest, and it details the connection between sports injuries and breathing disorders, and also with skin disease. Sports nutrition and performance-enhancing substances are also discussed.

*Part II: Preventing Sports Injuries* offers guidance for injury prevention and first aid, along with facts about protective equipment and safety tips for a wide variety of team and individual sports and recreation activities. It also discusses safety when engaging in sports in various weather conditions.

*Part III: Head and Facial Injuries* details traumatic brain injuries, concussions, and injuries to the face, including the eyes.

*Part IV: Back, Neck, and Spine Injuries* offers facts about lower back pain in athletes as well as spinal and cervical injuries, degenerative conditions, and nerve damage.

*Part V: Shoulder and Upper Arm Injuries* discusses common sports injuries affecting the shoulder, including problems with motion loss, dislocation, and muscle and tendon injuries. It also offers details about collarbone fractures and biceps tendon injury.

*Part VI: Injuries to the Elbows, Wrists, and Hands* explores injuries such as sprains and fractures that can affect arms, hands, fingers, and elbows, as well as other sports-related conditions that have an impact on the hands and elbows of athletes.

*Part VII: Injuries to the Trunk, Groin, Upper Legs, and Knees* provides facts about trunk and groin injuries, injuries to the hip, and leg injuries such as fractures and hamstring injuries. It details injuries sustained by athletes to the knee cartilage, ligaments. Also, talks about patellar tendinitis and dislocated patella, as well as other painful knee conditions and injuries.

*Part VIII: Injuries to the Lower Legs, Ankles, and Feet* discusses Achilles tendon and other injuries, including sprains and fractures, that affect the lower legs, ankles, feet, or toes of athletes.

*Part IX: Diagnosis, Treatment, and Rehabilitation of Sports Injuries* offers details on tests used to diagnose sports injuries, medications used for the management of sports injuries, and treatments involving surgical procedures and physical therapies.

*Part X: Sports Injuries in Children and Young Athletes* provides specific details about the effect of sports injuries on young athletes, including details about sports physicals, prevention, and overtraining in youth sports programs. It details several growth conditions or injuries that specifically affect children and offers guidance on returning to play after an injury.

*Part XI: Additional Help and Information* contains a glossary of terms related to sports injuries and a list of resources providing information about sports injury topics.

## *Bibliographic Note*

This volume contains documents and excerpts from publications issued by the following U.S. government agencies: Agency for Healthcare Research and Quality (AHRQ); Centers for Disease Control and Prevention (CDC); Genetic and Rare Diseases Information Center (GARD); *Go4Life*; National Aeronautics and Space Administration (NASA); National Cancer Institute (NCI); National Institute of Diabetes and Digestive and Kidney Diseases (NIDDK); National Eye Institute (NEI); National Heart, Lung, and Blood Institute (NHLBI); National Institute of Arthritis and Musculoskeletal and Skin Diseases (NIAMS); National Institute of Biomedical Imaging and Bioengineering (NIBIB); National Institute of Neurological Disorders and Stroke (NINDS); National Institute on Aging (NIA); National Institute on Drug Abuse (NIDA); National Library of Medicine (NLM); National Oceanic and Atmospheric Administration (NOAA); Office of Disease Prevention and Health Promotion (ODPHP); Office on Women's Health (OWH); U.S. Consumer Product Safety Commission (CPSC); U.S. Department of Agriculture (USDA); U.S. Department of Health and Human Services (HHS); U.S. Department of Justice (DOJ); U.S. Department of Labor (DOL); U.S. Department of Veterans Affairs (VA); U.S. Food and Drug Administration (FDA); U.S. National Institutes of Health (NIH); U.S. Public Health Service Comissioned Corps (PHSCC); U.S. Social Security Administration (SSA); and Washington State Department of Labor & Industries (Washington L&I).

In addition, this volume contains copyrighted documents from the following organizations: American Academy of Orthopaedic Surgeons (AAOS); American College of Foot and Ankle Surgeons (ACFAS); American College of Sports Medicine (ACSM); American

Orthopaedic Foot and Ankle Society (AOFAS); American Orthopaedic Society for Sports Medicine (AOSSM) and Midwest Orthopaedics at Rush; The Nemours Foundation; and Osborne Head & Neck Institute.

It may also contain original material produced by Omnigraphics and reviewed by medical consultants.

## About the Health Reference Series

The *Health Reference Series* is designed to provide basic medical information for patients, families, caregivers, and the general public. Each volume takes a particular topic and provides comprehensive coverage. This is especially important for people who may be dealing with a newly diagnosed disease or a chronic disorder in themselves or in a family member. People looking for preventive guidance, information about disease warning signs, medical statistics, and risk factors for health problems will also find answers to their questions in the *Health Reference Series*. The *Series*, however, is not intended to serve as a tool for diagnosing illness, in prescribing treatments, or as a substitute for the physician/patient relationship. All people concerned about medical symptoms or the possibility of disease are encouraged to seek professional care from an appropriate healthcare provider.

## A Note about Spelling and Style

*Health Reference Series* editors use *Stedman's Medical Dictionary* as an authority for questions related to the spelling of medical terms and the *Chicago Manual of Style* for questions related to grammatical structures, punctuation, and other editorial concerns. Consistent adherence is not always possible, however, because the individual volumes within the *Series* include many documents from a wide variety of different producers, and the editor's primary goal is to present material from each source as accurately as is possible. This sometimes means that information in different chapters or sections may follow other guidelines and alternate spelling authorities.

## Medical Review

Omnigraphics contracts with a team of qualified, senior medical professionals who serve as medical consultants for the *Health Reference Series*. As necessary, medical consultants review reprinted and originally written material for currency and accuracy. Citations including the phrase, "Reviewed (month, year)" indicate material reviewed by this team. Medical consultation services are provided to the *Health Reference Series* editors by:

Dr. Vijayalakshmi, MBBS, DGO, MD
Dr. Senthil Selvan, MBBS, DCH, MD
Dr. Sivanandham, MBBS, DCH, MS (Research), PhD

## Our Advisory Board

We would like to thank the following board members for providing initial guidance on the development of this series:

- Dr. Lynda Baker, Associate Professor of Library and Information Science, Wayne State University, Detroit, MI

- Nancy Bulgarelli, William Beaumont Hospital Library, Royal Oak, MI

- Karen Imarisio, Bloomfield Township Public Library, Bloomfield Township, MI

- Karen Morgan, Mardigian Library, University of Michigan-Dearborn, Dearborn, MI

- Rosemary Orlando, St. Clair Shores Public Library, St. Clair Shores, MI

## Health Reference Series *Update Policy*

The inaugural book in the *Health Reference Series* was the first edition of *Cancer Sourcebook* published in 1989. Since then, the *Series* has been enthusiastically received by librarians and in the medical community. In order to maintain the standard of providing high-quality health information for the layperson the editorial staff at Omnigraphics felt it was necessary to implement a policy of updating volumes when warranted.

Medical researchers have been making tremendous strides, and it is the purpose of the *Health Reference Series* to stay current with the most recent advances. Each decision to update a volume is made on an individual basis. Some of the considerations include how much new information is available and the feedback we receive from people who use the books. If there is a topic you would like to see added to the update list, or an area of medical concern you feel has not been adequately addressed, please write to:

Managing Editor
*Health Reference Series*
Omnigraphics
615 Griswold, Ste. 901
Detroit, MI 48226

# Part One


# Health and Sports

# Chapter 1

# An Introduction to Sports Injuries and Exercise

In recent years, increasing numbers of people of all ages have been heeding their health professionals' advice to get active for all of the health benefits exercise has to offer. But for some people—particularly those who overdo or who don't properly train or warm up—these benefits can come at a price: sports injuries.

Fortunately, most musculoskeletal sports injuries can be treated effectively, and most people who suffer injuries can return to a satisfying level of physical activity after an injury. Even better, many sports injuries can be prevented if people take the proper precautions.

## What Are Sports Injuries?

The term "sports injury," in the broadest sense, refers to the kinds of injuries that most commonly occur during sports or exercise. Some sports injuries result from accidents; others are due to poor training practices, improper equipment, lack of conditioning, or insufficient warm-up and stretching.

This chapter contains text excerpted from the following sources: Text in this chapter begins with excerpts from "Sports Injuries—Handout on Health: Sports Injuries," National Institute of Arthritis and Musculoskeletal and Skin Diseases (NIAMS), February 2016; Text beginning with the heading "Benefits of Exercise" is excerpted from "Exercise: Benefits of Exercise," NIHSeniorHealth, National Institute on Aging (NIA), January 2015.

Following are some of the most common sports injuries:

- Muscle sprains and strains
- Tears of the ligaments that hold joints together
- Tears of the tendons that support joints and allow them to move
- Dislocated joints
- Fractured bones, including vertebrae.

### Sprains and Strains

A sprain is a stretch or tear of a ligament, the band of connective tissues that joins the end of one bone with another. Sprains are caused by trauma such as a fall or blow to the body that knocks a joint out of position and, in the worst case, ruptures the supporting ligaments. Sprains can range from first degree (minimally stretched ligament) to third degree (a complete tear). Areas of the body most vulnerable to sprains are ankles, knees, and wrists. Signs of a sprain include varying degrees of tenderness or pain; bruising; inflammation; swelling; inability to move a limb or joint; or joint looseness, laxity, or instability.

A strain is a twist, pull, or tear of a muscle or tendon, a cord of tissue connecting muscle to bone. It is an acute, noncontact injury that results from overstretching or overcontraction. Symptoms of a strain include pain, muscle spasm, and loss of strength. Although it's hard to tell the difference between mild and moderate strains, severe strains not treated professionally can cause damage and loss of function.

### Knee Injuries

Because of its complex structure and weight-bearing capacity, the knee is a commonly injured joint.

Knee injuries can range from mild to severe. Some of the less severe, yet still painful and functionally limiting, knee problems are runner's knee (pain or tenderness close to or under the knee cap at the front or side of the knee), iliotibial band syndrome (pain on the outer side of the knee), and tendinitis, also called tendinosis (marked by degeneration within a tendon, usually where it joins the bone).

More severe injuries include bone bruises or damage to the cartilage or ligaments. There are two types of cartilage in the knee. One is the meniscus, a crescent-shaped disc that absorbs shock between the thigh (femur) and lower leg bones (tibia and fibula). The other is a surface-coating (or articular) cartilage. It covers the ends of the bones where they meet, allowing them to glide against one another. The four major ligaments that support the knee are the anterior cruciate ligament (ACL), the posterior cruciate ligament (PCL), the medial collateral ligament (MCL), and the lateral collateral ligament (LCL).

Knee injuries can result from a blow to or twist of the knee; from improper landing after a jump; or from running too hard, too much, or without proper warm-up.

## Compartment Syndrome

In many parts of the body, muscles (along with the nerves and blood vessels that run alongside and through them) are enclosed in a "compartment" formed of a tough membrane called fascia. When muscles become swollen, they can fill the compartment to capacity, causing interference with nerves and blood vessels as well as damage to the muscles themselves. The resulting painful condition is referred to as compartment syndrome.

Compartment syndrome may be caused by a one-time traumatic injury (acute compartment syndrome), such as a fractured bone or a hard blow to the thigh, by repeated hard blows (depending upon the sport), or by ongoing overuse (chronic exertional compartment syndrome), which may occur, for example, in long-distance running.

## Shin Splints

Although the term "shin splints" has been widely used to describe any sort of leg pain associated with exercise, the term actually refers to pain along the tibia or shin bone, the large bone in the front of the lower leg. This pain can occur at the front outside part of the lower leg, including the foot and ankle (anterior shin splints) or at the inner edge of the bone where it meets the calf muscles (medial shin splints).

Shin splints are primarily seen in runners, particularly those just starting a running program. Risk factors for shin splints include overuse or incorrect use of the lower leg; improper stretching, warm-up, or exercise technique; overtraining; running or jumping on hard surfaces; and running in shoes that don't have enough support. These injuries are often associated with flat (overpronated) feet.

## Achilles Tendon Injuries

An Achilles tendon injury results from a stretch, tear, or irritation to the tendon connecting the calf muscle to the back of the heel. These injuries can be so sudden and agonizing that they have been known to bring down charging professional football players in shocking fashion.

The most common cause of Achilles tendon tears is a problem called tendinitis, a degenerative condition caused by aging or overuse. When a tendon is weakened, trauma can cause it to rupture.

Achilles tendon injuries are common in middle-aged "weekend warriors" who may not exercise regularly or take time to stretch properly before an activity. Among professional athletes, most Achilles injuries seem to occur in quick-acceleration, jumping sports like football and basketball, and almost always end the season's competition for the athlete.

## *Fractures*

A fracture is a break in the bone that can occur from either a quick, one-time injury to the bone (acute fracture) or from repeated stress to the bone over time (stress fracture).

**Acute fractures:** Acute fractures can be simple (a clean break with little damage to the surrounding tissue) or compound (a break in which the bone pierces the skin with little damage to the surrounding tissue). Most acute fractures are emergencies. One that breaks the skin is especially dangerous because there is a high risk of infection.

**Stress fractures:** Stress fractures occur largely in the feet and legs and are common in sports that require repetitive impact, primarily running/jumping sports such as gymnastics or track and field. Running creates forces two to three times a person's body weight on the lower limbs.

The most common symptom of a stress fracture is pain at the site that worsens with weight-bearing activity. Tenderness and swelling often accompany the pain.

## *Dislocations*

When the two bones that come together to form a joint become separated, the joint is described as being dislocated. Contact sports such as football and basketball, as well as high-impact sports and sports that can result in excessive stretching or falling, cause the majority of dislocations. A dislocated joint is an emergency situation that requires medical treatment.

*The Shoulder Joint*

The joints most likely to be dislocated are some of the hand joints. Aside from these joints, the joint most frequently dislocated is the shoulder. Dislocations of the knees, hips, and elbows are uncommon.

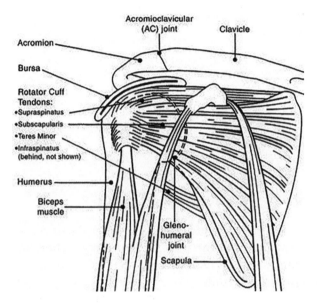

**Figure 1.1.** *The Shoulder Joint*

## What Is the Difference between Acute and Chronic Injuries?

Regardless of the specific structure affected, musculoskeletal sports injuries can generally be classified in one of two ways: acute or chronic.

*Acute Injuries*

Acute injuries, such as a sprained ankle, strained back, or fractured hand, occur suddenly during activity. Signs of an acute injury include the following:

• sudden, severe pain

• swelling

• inability to place weight on a lower limb

- extreme tenderness in an upper limb
- inability to move a joint through its full range of motion
- extreme limb weakness
- visible dislocation or break of a bone

### Chronic Injuries

Chronic injuries usually result from overusing one area of the body while playing a sport or exercising over a long period. The following are signs of a chronic injury:

- pain when performing an activity
- a dull ache when at rest
- swelling

## What Should I Do If I Suffer an Injury?

Whether an injury is acute or chronic, there is never a good reason to try to "work through" the pain of an injury. When you have pain from a particular movement or activity, STOP! Continuing the activity only causes further harm.

Some injuries require prompt medical attention, while others can be self-treated. Here's what you need to know about both types:

### When to Seek Medical Treatment

You should call a health professional if:

- The injury causes severe pain, swelling, or numbness.
- You can't tolerate any weight on the area.
- The pain or dull ache of an old injury is accompanied by increased swelling or joint abnormality or instability.

### When and How to Treat at Home

If you don't have any of the above symptoms, it's probably safe to treat the injury at home—at least at first. If pain or other symptoms worsen, it's best to check with your healthcare provider. Use the R.I.C.E method to relieve pain and inflammation and speed healing. Follow these four steps immediately after injury and continue for at least 48 hours.

- **Rest.** Reduce regular exercise or activities of daily living as needed. If you cannot put weight on an ankle or knee, crutches may help. If you use a cane or one crutch for an ankle injury, use it on the uninjured side to help you lean away and relieve weight on the injured ankle.

- **Ice.** Apply an ice pack to the injured area for 20 minutes at a time, four to eight times a day. A cold pack, ice bag, or plastic bag filled with crushed ice and wrapped in a towel can be used. To avoid cold injury and frostbite, do not apply the ice for more than 20 minutes. (Note: Do not use heat immediately after an injury. This tends to increase internal bleeding or swelling. Heat can be used later on to relieve muscle tension and promote relaxation.)

- **Compression.** Compression of the injured area may help reduce swelling. Compression can be achieved with elastic wraps, special boots, air casts, and splints. Ask your healthcare provider for advice on which one to use.

- **Elevation.** If possible, keep the injured ankle, knee, elbow, or wrist elevated on a pillow, above the level of the heart, to help decrease swelling.

## The Body's Healing Process

From the moment a bone breaks or a ligament tears, your body goes to work to repair the damage. Here's what happens at each stage of the healing process:

**At the moment of injury:** Chemicals are released from damaged cells, triggering a process called inflammation. Blood vessels at the injury site become dilated; blood flow increases to carry nutrients to the site of tissue damage.

**Within hours of injury:** White blood cells (leukocytes) travel down the bloodstream to the injury site where they begin to tear down and remove damaged tissue, allowing other specialized cells to start developing scar tissue.

**Within days of injury:** Scar tissue is formed on the skin or inside the body. The amount of scarring may be proportional to the amount of swelling, inflammation, or bleeding within. In the next few weeks, the damaged area will regain a great deal of strength as scar tissue continues to form.

9

**Within a month of injury:** Scar tissue may start to shrink, bringing damaged, torn, or separated tissues back together. However, it may be several months or more before the injury is completely healed.

## Who Should I See for My Injury?

Although severe injuries will need to be seen immediately in an emergency room, particularly if they occur on the weekend or after office hours, most musculoskeletal sports injuries can be evaluated and, in many cases, treated by your primary healthcare provider.

Depending on your preference and the severity of your injury or the likelihood that your injury may cause ongoing, long-term problems, you may want to see, or have your primary healthcare professional refer you to, one of the following:

* An **orthopaedic surgeon** is a doctor specializing in the diagnosis and treatment of the musculoskeletal system, which includes bones, joints, ligaments, tendons, muscles, and nerves.

* A **physical therapist/physiotherapist** is a healthcare professional who can develop a rehabilitation program. Your primary care physician may refer you to a physical therapist after you begin to recover from your injury to help strengthen muscles and joints and prevent further injury.

## How Are Sports Injuries Treated?

Although using the RICE technique described previously can be helpful for any sports injury, RICE is often just a starting point. Here are some other treatments your doctor or other healthcare provider may administer, recommend, or prescribe to help your injury heal.[1]

[1] *All medicines can have side effects. Some side effects may be more severe than others. You should review the package insert that comes with your medicine and ask your healthcare provider or pharmacist if you have any questions about the possible side effects.*

### Nonsteroidal Anti-Inflammatory Drugs (NSAIDs)

The moment you are injured, chemicals are released from damaged tissue cells. This triggers the first stage of healing: inflammation. Inflammation causes tissues to become swollen, tender, and painful. Although inflammation is needed for healing, it can actually slow the healing process if left unchecked.

To reduce inflammation and pain, doctors and other healthcare providers often recommend taking an over-the-counter (OTC) non-steroidal anti-inflammatory drug (NSAID) such as aspirin, ibuprofen, or naproxen sodium. For more severe pain and inflammation, doctors may prescribe one of several dozen NSAIDs available in prescription strength.[2]

Though not an NSAID, another commonly used OTC medication, acetaminophen, may relieve pain. It has no effect on inflammation, however.

[2] *Warning: Side effects of NSAIDs include stomach problems; skin rashes; high blood pressure; fluid retention; and liver, kidney, and heart problems. The longer a person uses NSAIDs, the more likely he or she is to have side effects, ranging from mild to serious. Many other drugs cannot be taken when a patient is being treated with NSAIDs, because NSAIDs alter the way the body uses or eliminates these other drugs. Check with your healthcare provider or pharmacist before you take NSAIDs. NSAIDs should only be used at the lowest dose possible for the shortest time needed.*

### *Immobilization*

Immobilization is a common treatment for musculoskeletal sports injuries that may be done immediately by a trainer or paramedic. Immobilization involves reducing movement in the area to prevent further damage. By enabling the blood supply to flow more directly to the injury (or the site of surgery to repair damage from an injury), immobilization reduces pain, swelling, and muscle spasm and helps the healing process begin. Following are some devices used for immobilization:

- **Slings**, to immobilize the upper body, including the arms and shoulders.

- **Splints and casts**, to support and protect injured bones and soft tissue. Casts can be made from plaster or fiberglass. Splints can be custom made or ready made. Standard splints come in a variety of shapes and sizes and have Velcro straps that make them easy to put on and take off or adjust. Splints generally offer less support and protection than a cast, and therefore may not always be a treatment option.

- **Leg immobilizers**, to keep the knee from bending after injury or surgery. Made from foam rubber covered with fabric, leg immobilizers enclose the entire leg, fastening with Velcro straps.

*Surgery*

In some cases, surgery is needed to repair torn connective tissues or to realign bones with compound fractures. The vast majority of musculoskeletal sports injuries, however, do not require surgery.

*Rehabilitation (Exercise)*

A key part of rehabilitation from sports injuries is a graduated exercise program designed to return the injured body part to a normal level of function.

With most injuries, early mobilization—getting the part moving as soon as possible—will speed healing. Generally, early mobilization starts with gentle range-of-motion exercises and then moves on to stretching and strengthening exercises when you can without increasing pain. For example, if you have a sprained ankle, you may be able to work on range of motion for the first day or two after the sprain by gently tracing letters with your big toe. Once your range of motion is fairly good, you can start doing gentle stretching and strengthening exercises. When you are ready, weights may be added to your exercise routine to further strengthen the injured area. The key is to avoid movement that causes pain.

As damaged tissue heals, scar tissue forms, which shrinks and brings torn or separated tissues back together. As a result, the injury site becomes tight or stiff, and damaged tissues are at risk of reinjury. That's why stretching and strengthening exercises are so important. You should continue to stretch the muscles daily and as the first part of your warm-up before exercising.

When planning your rehabilitation program with a healthcare professional, remember that progression is the key principle. Start with just a few exercises, do them often, and then gradually increase how much you do. A complete rehabilitation program should include exercises for flexibility, endurance, and strength; instruction in balance and proper body mechanics related to the sport; and a planned return to full participation.

Throughout the rehabilitation process, avoid painful activities and concentrate on those exercises that will improve function in the injured part. Don't resume your sport until you are sure you can stretch the injured tissues without any pain, swelling, or restricted movement, and monitor any other symptoms. When you do return to your sport, start slowly and gradually buildup to full participation.

## *Rest*

Although it is important to get moving as soon as possible, you must also take time to rest following an injury. All injuries need time to heal; proper rest will help the process. Your healthcare professional can guide you regarding the proper balance between rest and rehabilitation.

## *Other Therapies*

Other therapies used in rehabilitating sports injuries include:

- **Cold/cryotherapy:** Ice packs reduce inflammation by constricting blood vessels and limiting blood flow to the injured tissues. Cryotherapy eases pain by numbing the injured area. It is generally used for only the first 48 hours after injury.

- **Heat/thermotherapy:** Heat, in the form of hot compresses, heat lamps, or heating pads, causes the blood vessels to dilate and increase blood flow to the injury site. Increased blood flow aids the healing process by removing cell debris from damaged tissues and carrying healing nutrients to the injury site. Heat also helps to reduce pain. It should not be applied within the first 48 hours after an injury.

- **Ultrasound:** High-frequency sound waves produce deep heat that is applied directly to an injured area. Ultrasound stimulates blood flow to promote healing.

- **Massage:** Manual pressing, rubbing, and manipulation soothe tense muscles and increase blood flow to the injury site.

Most of these therapies are administered or supervised by a licensed healthcare professional.

## Tips for Preventing Injury

Whether you've never had a sports injury and you're trying to keep it that way or you've had an injury and don't want another, the following tips can help.

- Avoid bending knees past 90 degrees when doing half knee bends.

- Avoid twisting knees by keeping feet as flat as possible during stretches.

- When jumping, land with your knees bent.
- Do warm-up exercises not just before vigorous activities like running, but also before less vigorous ones such as golf.
- Don't overdo.
- Do warm-up stretches before activity. Stretch the Achilles tendon, hamstring, and quadriceps areas and hold the positions. Don't bounce.
- Cool down following vigorous sports. For example, after a race, walk or walk/jog for 5 minutes so your pulse comes down gradually.
- Wear properly fitting shoes that provide shock absorption and stability.
- Use the softest exercise surface available, and avoid running on hard surfaces like asphalt and concrete. Run on flat surfaces. Running uphill may increase the stress on the Achilles tendon and the leg itself.

## Benefits of Exercise

Exercise and physical activity are great ways to have fun, be with friends and family, and enjoy the outdoors. But regular exercise and physical activity can also have a direct impact on your everyday life. The benefits they provide can help you stay strong and fit enough to perform your daily activities, get around, and maintain your independence.

## Four Types of Exercises to Try

Older adults who are inactive lose ground in four areas that are important for staying healthy and independent:

- endurance
- strength
- balance
- flexibility

Research suggests that you can maintain or at least partially restore these four areas through exercise and physical activity and that doing so improves fitness.

For example, increasing your endurance will make it easier for you to walk farther, faster, and uphill. Strengthening your muscles will make you stronger. Improving your balance can help your sense of body control, and increasing flexibility helps keep your body limber and flexible.

The goal is to be creative and choose from each of the four types— endurance, strength, balance, and flexibility. Mixing it up will help you reap the benefits of each type of exercise, as well as reduce the risk for injury.

## How Increased Endurance Helps You

Endurance, or aerobic, activities like brisk walking or swimming increase your breathing and heart rate and improve the health of your heart, lungs and circulatory system. They can make it easier for you to

- push your grandchildren on the swings
- vacuum
- work in the garden
- rake leaves
- play a sport

## How Increased Muscle Strength Helps You

Strength exercises like lifting weights and using resistance bands can increase muscle strength. Lower-body strength exercises also will improve your balance. Increased muscle strength can maintain your ability to

- climb stairs
- carry groceries
- open jars
- carry a full laundry basket from the basement to the second floor
- carry your smaller grandchildren
- lift bags of mulch in the garden

## How Good Balance Helps You

Balance exercises like tai chi can improve your ability to control and maintain your body's position, whether you are moving or still. Good balance is important to help prevent falls and avoid the disability that may result from falling. Improving your balance can help you

- prevent falls

- stand on tiptoe to reach something on the top shelf

- walk up and down the stairs

- walk on an uneven sidewalk without falling

### How Being Flexible Helps You

Flexibility, or stretching, exercises can help your body stay flexible and limber, which gives you more freedom of movement for your regular physical activity as well as for your everyday activities. Stretching exercises can improve your flexibility but will not improve your endurance or strength.

Improving your flexibility makes it easier for you to

- look over your shoulder to see what's behind you as you back the car out of the driveway

- make the bed

- bend over to tie your shoes

- reach for a food item on a kitchen shelf

- pull a sweater on over your head

- swing a golf club

## It's Never Too Late to Start

Exercise and physical activity can have a positive effect on your everyday life. Even if you think you're too old or too out of shape to exercise, becoming active on a regular basis will give you more energy and the ability to do things more easily, faster, and for longer than before. If you're already active, keep up the good work. If you don't exercise now, it's never too late to start.

# Chapter 2

# Sprains and Strains

## What Are Sprain and Strain?

A sprain is a stretch and/or tear of a ligament (a band of fibrous tissue that connects two or more bones at a joint). One or more ligaments can be injured at the same time. The severity of the injury will depend on the extent of injury (whether a tear is partial or complete) and the number of ligaments involved.

A strain is an injury to either a muscle or a tendon (fibrous cords of tissue that connect muscle to bone). Depending on the severity of the injury, a strain may be a simple overstretch of the muscle or tendon, or it can result from a partial or complete tear.

## What Causes a Sprain?

A sprain can result from a fall, a sudden twist, or a blow to the body that forces a joint out of its normal position and stretches or tears the ligament supporting that joint. Typically, sprains occur when people fall and land on an outstretched arm, slide into a baseball base, land on the side of their foot, or twist a knee with the foot planted firmly on the ground.

This chapter includes text excerpted from "Sprains and Strains—Questions and Answers about Sprains and Strains," National Institute of Arthritis and Musculoskeletal and Skin Diseases (NIAMS), January 2015.

## *Where Do Sprains Usually Occur?*

Although sprains can occur in both the upper and lower parts of the body, the most common site is the ankle. It is estimated that more than 628,000 ankle sprains occur in the United States each year.

The ankle joint is supported by several lateral (outside) ligaments and medial (inside) ligaments (see figure 2.1). Most ankle sprains happen when the foot turns inward as a person runs, turns, falls, or lands on the ankle after a jump. This type of sprain is called an inversion injury. The knee is another common site for a sprain. A blow to the knee or a fall is often the cause; sudden twisting can also result in a sprain (see figure 2.2).

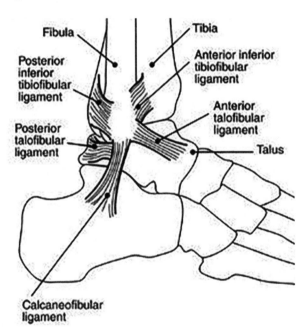

**Figure 2.1.** *Lateral View of the Ankle*

Sprains frequently occur at the wrist, typically when people fall and land on an outstretched hand. A sprain to the thumb is common in skiing and other sports. This injury often occurs when a ligament near the base of the thumb (the ulnar collateral ligament of the metacarpophalangeal joint) is torn (see figure 2.3).

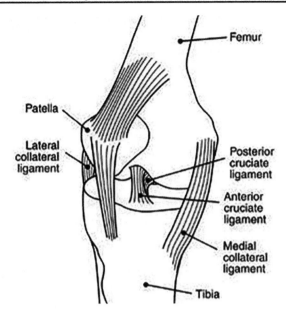

**Figure 2.2.** *Lateral View of the Knee*

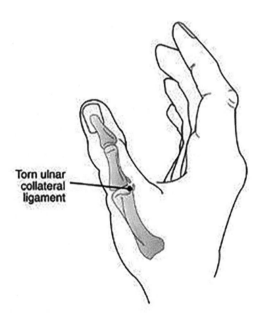

**Figure 2.3.** *Lateral View of the Thumb*

## What Are the Signs and Symptoms of a Sprain?

The usual signs and symptoms include pain, swelling, bruising, instability, and loss of the ability to move and use the joint (called functional ability). However, these signs and symptoms can vary in intensity, depending on the severity of the sprain. Sometimes people feel a pop or tear when the injury happens.

Doctors closely observe an injured site and ask questions to obtain information to diagnose the severity of a sprain. In general, a grade I or mild sprain is caused by overstretching or slight tearing of the ligaments with no joint instability. A person with a mild sprain usually experiences minimal pain, swelling, and little or no loss of functional ability. Bruising is absent or slight, and the person is usually able to put weight on the affected joint.

### When to See a Healthcare Provider for a Sprain

- You have severe pain and cannot put any weight on the injured joint.
- The injured area looks crooked or has lumps and bumps (other than swelling) that you do not see on the uninjured joint.
- You cannot move the injured joint.
- You cannot walk more than four steps without significant pain.
- Your limb buckles or gives way when you try to use the joint.
- You have numbness in any part of the injured area.
- You see redness or red streaks spreading out from the injury.
- You injure an area that has been injured several times before.
- You have pain, swelling, or redness over a bony part of your foot.
- You are in doubt about the seriousness of the injury or how to care for it.

A grade II or moderate sprain is caused by further, but still incomplete, tearing of the ligament and is characterized by bruising, moderate pain, and swelling. A person with a moderate sprain usually has more difficulty putting weight on the affected joint and experiences some loss of function. An X-ray may be needed to help the healthcare provider determine if a fracture is causing the pain and swelling. Magnetic resonance imaging is occasionally used to help differentiate between a significant partial injury and a complete tear in a ligament, or can be recommended to rule out other injuries.

People who sustain a grade III or severe sprain completely tear or rupture a ligament. Pain, swelling, and bruising are usually severe, and the patient is unable to put weight on the joint. An X-ray is usually taken to rule out a broken bone. When diagnosing any sprain, the healthcare provider will ask the patient to explain how the injury happened. He or she will examine the affected area and check its stability and its ability to move and bear weight.

## What Causes a Strain?

A strain is caused by twisting or pulling a muscle or tendon. Strains can be acute or chronic. An acute strain is associated with a recent trauma or injury; it also can occur after improperly lifting heavy objects or overstressing the muscles. Chronic strains are usually the result of overuse: prolonged, repetitive movement of the muscles and tendons.

## Where Do Strains Usually Occur?

Two common sites for a strain are the back and the hamstring muscle (located in the back of the thigh). Contact sports such as soccer, football, hockey, boxing, and wrestling put people at risk for strains. Gymnastics, tennis, rowing, golf, and other sports that require extensive gripping can increase the risk of hand and forearm strains. Elbow strains sometimes occur in people who participate in racquet sports, throwing, and contact sports.

## What Are the Signs and Symptoms of a Strain?

Typically, people with a strain experience pain, limited motion, muscle spasms, and possibly muscle weakness. They also can have localized swelling, cramping, or inflammation and, with a minor or moderate strain, usually some loss of muscle function. Patients typically have pain in the injured area and general weakness of the muscle when they attempt to move it. Severe strains that partially or completely tear the muscle or tendon are often very painful and disabling.

## How Are Sprains and Strains Treated?

### Reduce Swelling and Pain

Treatments for sprains and strains are similar and can be thought of as having two stages. The goal during the first stage is to reduce swelling and pain. At this stage, healthcare providers usually advise

21

patients to follow a formula of rest, ice, compression, and elevation (R.I.C.E) for the first 24 to 48 hours after the injury. The healthcare provider also may recommend an over-the-counter or prescription medication to help decrease pain and inflammation.[1]

[1] *All medicines can have side effects. Some side effects may be more severe than others. You should review the package insert that comes with your medicine and ask your healthcare provider or pharmacist if you have any questions about the possible side effects.*

For people with a moderate or severe sprain, particularly of the ankle, a hard cast may be applied. This often occurs after the initial swelling has subsided. Severe sprains and strains may require surgery to repair the torn ligaments, muscle, or tendons. Surgery is usually performed by an orthopaedic surgeon.

It is important that moderate and severe sprains and strains be evaluated by a healthcare provider to allow prompt, appropriate treatment to begin. This chapter lists some signs that should alert people to consult their healthcare provider. However, a person who has any concerns about the seriousness of a sprain or strain should always contact a healthcare provider for advice.

*RICE Therapy*

- **Rest**

   Reduce regular exercise or activities of daily living as needed. Your healthcare provider may advise you to put no weight on an injured area for 48 hours. If you cannot put weight on an ankle or knee, crutches may help. If you use a cane or one crutch for an ankle injury, use it on the uninjured side to help you lean away and relieve weight on the injured ankle.

- **Ice**

   Apply an ice pack to the injured area for 20 minutes at a time, four to eight times a day. A cold pack, ice bag, or plastic bag filled with crushed ice and wrapped in a towel can be used. To avoid cold injury and frostbite, do not apply the ice for more than 20 minutes.

- **Compression**

   Compression of an injured ankle, knee, or wrist may help reduce swelling. Examples of compression bandages are elastic wraps, special boots, air casts, and splints. Ask your healthcare provider for advice on which one to use and how tight to apply the bandage safely.

* **Elevation**

  If possible, keep the injured ankle, knee, elbow, or wrist elevated on a pillow, above the level of the heart, to help decrease swelling.

## Begin Rehabilitation

The second stage of treating a sprain or strain is rehabilitation, with the overall goal of improving the condition of the injured area and restoring its function. The healthcare provider will prescribe an exercise program designed to prevent stiffness, improve range of motion, and restore the joint's normal flexibility and strength. Some patients may need physical therapy during this stage. When the acute pain and swelling have diminished, the healthcare provider will instruct the patient to do a series of exercises several times a day. These are very important because they help reduce swelling, prevent stiffness, and restore normal, pain-free range of motion. The healthcare provider can recommend many different types of exercises, depending on the injury. A patient with an injured knee or foot will work on weight-bearing and balancing exercises. The duration of the program depends on the extent of the injury, but the regimen commonly lasts for several weeks.

Another goal of rehabilitation is to increase strength and regain flexibility. Depending on the patient's rate of recovery, this process begins about the second week after the injury. The healthcare provider will instruct the patient to do a series of exercises designed to meet these goals. During this phase of rehabilitation, patients progress to more demanding exercises as pain decreases and function improves.

The final goal is the return to full daily activities, including sports when appropriate. Patients must work closely with their healthcare provider or physical therapist to determine their readiness to return to full activity. Sometimes people are tempted to resume full activity or play sports despite pain or muscle soreness. Returning to full activity before regaining normal range of motion, flexibility, and strength increases the chance of reinjury and may lead to a chronic problem.

The amount of rehabilitation and the time needed for full recovery after a sprain or strain depend on the severity of the injury and individual rates of healing. For example, a mild ankle sprain may require 3 to 6 weeks of rehabilitation; a moderate sprain could require 2 to 3 months. With a severe sprain, it can take 8 to 12 months to return to full activities. Extra care should be taken to avoid reinjury.

## Can Sprains and Strains Be Prevented?

People can do many things to help lower their risk of sprains and strains:

- Avoid exercising or playing sports when tired or in pain.

- Maintain a healthy, well-balanced diet to keep muscles strong.

- Maintain a healthy weight.

- Practice safety measures to help prevent falls. For example, keep stairways, walkways, yards, and driveways free of clutter; anchor scatter rugs; and salt or sand icy sidewalks and driveways in the winter.

- Wear shoes that fit properly.

- Replace athletic shoes as soon as the tread wears out or the heel wears down on one side.

- Do stretching exercises daily.

- Be in proper physical condition to play a sport.

- Warm up and stretch before participating in any sport or exercise.

- Wear protective equipment when playing.

- Run on even surfaces.

# Chapter 3

# *Bursitis and Tendinitis*

## What Are Bursitis and Tendinitis?

Bursitis and tendinitis are both common conditions that cause swelling around muscles and bones. They occur most often in the shoulder, elbow, wrist, hip, knee, or ankle.

A bursa is a small, fluid-filled sac that acts as a cushion between a bone and other moving body parts such as muscles, tendons, or skin. Bursae are found throughout the body. Bursitis occurs when a bursa becomes swollen.

A tendon is a flexible band of tissue that connects muscles to bones. Tendons can be small, like those found in the hand or ankle, or large, like the Achilles tendon in the heel. Tendons help create movement by making the muscles push or pull the bones in different ways. Tendinitis is the severe swelling of a tendon.

## What Causes These Conditions?

People get bursitis by overusing a joint. It can also be caused by direct trauma. It usually occurs at the knee or elbow. Kneeling or leaning your elbows on a hard surface for a long time can make bursitis start. Tendinitis usually occurs after repeated injury to a certain area

This chapter includes text excerpted from "Fast Facts about Bursitis and Tendinitis," National Institute of Arthritis and Musculoskeletal and Skin Diseases (NIAMS), November 2014.

such as the wrist or ankle. Tendons become less flexible with age and become more prone to damage.

Doing the same kinds of movements every day or putting stress on joints increases the risk for both conditions. People like carpenters, gardeners, musicians, and athletes often get bursitis or tendinitis. Infection, arthritis, gout, thyroid disease, and diabetes can also cause swelling of a bursa or tendon. Both bursitis and tendinitis are more frequent the older you get.

## What Parts of the Body Are Affected?

Tendinitis causes pain and soreness around a joint. Some common forms of tendinitis are named after the sports that increase their risk. They include tennis elbow, golfer's elbow, pitcher's shoulder, swimmer's shoulder, and jumper's knee.

### Tennis Elbow and Golfer's Elbow

Tennis elbow is an injury to the tendon in the outer elbow. Golfer's elbow affects the inner tendon of the elbow. Any activity that involves a lot of wrist turning or hand gripping, such as using tools, shaking hands, or twisting, can bring on these conditions. Pain occurs near the elbow. It can also travel into the upper arm or forearm.

### Shoulder Tendinitis, Bursitis, and Impingement Syndrome

Two types of tendinitis can affect the shoulder. Biceps tendinitis causes pain in the front or side of the shoulder. Pain may also travel down to the elbow and forearm. Raising your arm over your head may also be painful. The biceps muscle in the front of the upper arm helps secure the arm bone in the shoulder socket. It also helps control the speed of the arm during overhead movement. For example, you may feel pain when swinging a racquet or pitching a ball.

Rotator cuff tendinitis causes shoulder pain at the top of the shoulder and the upper arm. Reaching, pushing, pulling, or lifting the arm above shoulder level can make the pain worse.

Even lying on the painful side can worsen the problem. The rotator cuff is a group of muscles that attach the arm to the shoulder blade. This "cuff" allows the arm to lift and twist. Repeated motion of the arms can damage and wear down the tendons, muscles, and bone. Impingement syndrome is a squeezing of the rotator cuff.

Jobs that require frequent overhead reaching and sports involving lots of use of the shoulder may damage the rotator cuff or bursa.

Rheumatoid arthritis also can inflame the rotator cuff and result in tendinitis and bursitis. Any of these can lead to severe swelling and impingement.

### Knee Tendinitis or Jumper's Knee

If you overuse a tendon during activities such as dancing, bicycling, or running, it may become stretched, torn, and swollen. Trying to break a fall can also damage tendons around the kneecap. This type of injury often happens to older people whose tendons may be weaker and less flexible. Pain in the tendons around the knee is sometimes called jumper's knee. This is because it often happens to young people who play sports like basketball. The overuse of the muscles and force of hitting the ground after a jump can strain the tendon. After repeated stress from jumping, the tendon may swell or tear.

People with tendinitis of the knee may feel pain while running, jumping, or walking quickly. Knee tendinitis can increase the risk for large tears to the tendon.

### Achilles Tendinitis

The Achilles tendon connects the calf muscle to the back of the heel. Achilles tendinitis is a common injury that makes the tendon swell, stretch, or tear. It's usually caused by overuse. It can also result from tight or weak calf muscles. Normal aging and arthritis can also stiffen the tendon.

Achilles tendon injuries can happen when climbing stairs or otherwise overworking the calf muscle. But these injuries are most common in "weekend warriors" who don't exercise regularly or don't take time to warm up before they do. Among athletes, most Achilles injuries seem to occur in sprinting or jumping sports. Athletes who play football, tennis, and basketball can all be affected by Achilles tendinitis. An injury almost always retires the athlete for the rest of the season.

Achilles tendinitis can be a long-term condition. It can also cause what appears to be a sudden injury. When a tendon is weakened by age or overuse, trauma can cause it to rupture. These injuries can be sudden and agonizing.

## How Are These Conditions Diagnosed?

Diagnosis of tendinitis and bursitis begins with a medical history and physical exam. You will describe the pain and when and where the pain occurs. The doctor may ask you whether it gets better or worse during the day. Another important clue is what makes the pain go away or come back. There are other tests a doctor may use including:

- Selective tissue tension test to find out which tendon is affected.

- Palpation or touching specific areas of the tendon to pinpoint the swelling.

- X-ray to rule out arthritis or bone problems.

- MRI (magnetic resonance imaging), which can show damage to both bone and soft tissue.

- Anesthetic injection test to see if the pain goes away.

- Taking fluid from the swollen area to rule out infection.

## What Kind of Healthcare Professional Treats These Conditions?

Your regular doctor or a physical therapist can treat most cases of tendinitis and bursitis. Cases that don't respond to normal treatment may be referred to a specialist.

## How Are Bursitis and Tendinitis Treated?

The focus of treatment is to heal the injured bursa or tendon. The first step is to reduce pain and swelling. This can be done with rest, tightly wrapping or elevating the affected area, or taking drugs that bring down the swelling. Aspirin, naproxen, and ibuprofen all serve that purpose. Ice may be helpful in recent, severe injuries, but is of little or no use in long-term cases. When ice is needed, an ice pack can be held on the affected area for 15 to 20 minutes every 4 to 6 hours for 3 to 5 days. A healthcare provider may suggest longer use of ice and a stretching program.

Your healthcare provider may also suggest limiting activities that involve the affected joint.

Support equipment may be suggested such as:

- An elbow band for tennis elbow

- A brace for the ankle or foot

- A splint for the knee or hand

Other treatments may include:

- Ultrasound, which are gentle sound-wave vibrations that warm deep tissues and improve blood flow

- An electrical current that pushes a corticosteroid drug through the skin directly over the swollen bursa or tendon

- Gentle stretching and strengthening exercises

- Massage of the soft tissue.

If there is no improvement, your doctor may inject a drug into the area around the swollen bursa or tendon. If the joint still does not improve after 6 to 12 months, the doctor may perform surgery to repair damage and relieve pressure on the tendons and bursae.

If the bursitis is caused by an infection, the doctor will prescribe antibiotics.

If a tendon is completely torn, surgery may be needed to repair the damage.

Repairing a tendon tear requires an exercise program to restore the ability to bend and straighten the joint and to strengthen the muscles around it to prevent repeat injury. An exercise program may last 6 months.

# Chapter 4

# *Repetitive Motion Disorders*

Repetitive motion disorders (RMDs) are a family of muscular conditions that result from repeated motions performed in the course of normal work or daily activities. RMDs include carpal tunnel syndrome, bursitis, tendonitis, epicondylitis, ganglion cyst, tenosynovitis, and trigger finger.

RMDs are caused by too many uninterrupted repetitions of an activity or motion, unnatural or awkward motions such as twisting the arm or wrist, overexertion, incorrect posture, or muscle fatigue. RMDs occur most commonly in the hands, wrists, elbows, and shoulders, but can also happen in the neck, back, hips, knees, feet, legs, and ankles. The disorders are characterized by pain, tingling, numbness, visible swelling or redness of the affected area, and the loss of flexibility and strength. For some individuals, there may be no visible sign of injury, although they may find it hard to perform easy tasks Over time, RMDs can cause temporary or permanent damage to the soft tissues in the body—such as the muscles, nerves, tendons, and ligaments—and compression of nerves or tissue.

Generally, RMDs affect individuals who perform repetitive tasks such as assembly line work, meatpacking, sewing, playing musical instruments, and computer work. The disorders may also affect individuals who engage in activities such as carpentry, gardening, and tennis.

---

This chapter includes text excerpted from "Repetitive Motion Disorders Information Page," National Institute of Neurological Disorders and Stroke (NINDS), September 21, 2016.

## Treatment

Treatment for RMDs usually includes reducing or stopping the motions that cause symptoms. Options include taking breaks to give the affected area time to rest, and adopting stretching and relaxation exercises. Applying ice to the affected area and using medications such as pain relievers, cortisone, and anti-inflammatory drugs can reduce pain and swelling. Splints may be able to relieve pressure on the muscles and nerves. Physical therapy may relieve the soreness and pain in the muscles and joints. In rare cases, surgery may be required to relieve symptoms and prevent permanent damage. Some employers have developed ergonomic programs to help workers adjust their pace of work and arrange office equipment to minimize problems.

## Prognosis

Most individuals with RMDs recover completely and can avoid re-injury by changing the way they perform repetitive movements, the frequency with which they perform them, and the amount of time they rest between movements. Without treatment, RMDs may result in permanent injury and complete loss of function in the affected area.

Chapter 5

# Sudden Cardiac
# Arrest (SCA) in Athletes

A few years back, with less than 30 seconds left in overtime in Fennville High School's final regular season men's basketball game, a winning layup was scored that brought Fennville's team an undefeated record. With district playoffs in Fennville's future, the gymnasium was full of celebration. Within moments, the crowd went silent as their star player collapsed to the ground. Wes Leonard, the player who had scored the winning basket moments before was now unconscious. Over 2,000 fans stood stunned, waiting for paramedics to arrive. Although an automated external defibrillator (AED) was present at the school,

This chapter contains text excerpted from the following sources: Text in this chapter begins with excerpts from "Can Sudden Cardiac Death of the Young Be Prevented?" Centers for Disease Control and Prevention (CDC), March 10, 2015; Text beginning with the heading "What Is Sudden Cardiac Arrest?" is excerpted from "What Is Sudden Cardiac Arrest?" National Heart, Lung, and Blood Institute (NHLBI), June 22, 2016; Text beginning with the heading "Screening for Sudden Cardiac Death before Participation in High School and Collegiate Sports" is excerpted from "Screening for Sudden Cardiac Death before Participation in High School and Collegiate Sports," Agency for Healthcare Research and Quality (AHRQ), U.S. Department of Health and Human Services (HHS), July 2013. Reviewed June 2017; Text beginning with the heading "Sudden Cardiac Arrest: Prevention" is excerpted from "National Athletic Trainers' Association Position Statement: Preventing Sudden Death in Sports," Agency for Healthcare Research and Quality (AHRQ), U.S. Department of Health and Human Services (HHS), January 2012. Reviewed June 2017.

it was not charged and cardiopulmonary resuscitation (CPR) was not performed because people did not think that cardiac arrest could be at fault in someone so young. Wes was later declared dead at a local hospital and the autopsy showed that he died of cardiac arrest due to an enlarged heart.

Sudden deaths of young athletes bring attention to an important public health problem known as sudden cardiac death of the young (SCDY), which occurs in nonathletes, too. On average, an estimated 66 athletes die suddenly of cardiac cause each year in the United States. Importantly, SCDY is known to have a strong hereditary component in many cases.

## What Is Sudden Cardiac Arrest?

Sudden cardiac arrest (SCA) is a condition in which the heart suddenly and unexpectedly stops beating. If this happens, blood stops flowing to the brain and other vital organs. SCA usually causes death if it's not treated within minutes.

To understand SCA, it helps to understand how the heart works. The heart has an electrical system that controls the rate and rhythm of the heartbeat. Problems with the heart's electrical system can cause irregular heartbeats called arrhythmias. There are many types of arrhythmias. During an arrhythmia, the heart can beat too fast, too slow, or with an irregular rhythm. Some arrhythmias can cause the heart to stop pumping blood to the body—these arrhythmias cause SCA.

SCA is not the same as a heart attack. A heart attack occurs if blood flow to part of the heart muscle is blocked. During a heart attack, the heart usually doesn't suddenly stop beating. SCA, however, may happen after or during recovery from a heart attack. People who have heart disease are at higher risk for SCA. However, SCA can happen in people who appear healthy and have no known heart disease or other risk factors for SCA.

Most people who have SCA die from it—often within minutes. Rapid treatment of SCA with a defibrillator can be lifesaving. A defibrillator is a device that sends an electric shock to the heart to try to restore its normal rhythm.

## What Causes Sudden Cardiac Arrest?

Ventricular fibrillation (v-fib) causes most sudden cardiac arrests (SCAs). V-fib is a type of arrhythmia. During v-fib, the ventricles (the heart's lower chambers) don't beat normally. Instead, they quiver very rapidly and irregularly. When this happens, the heart pumps little or no blood to the body. V-fib is fatal if not treated within a few minutes.

Other problems with the heart's electrical system also can cause SCA. For example, SCA can occur if the rate of the heart's electrical signals becomes very slow and stops. SCA also can occur if the heart muscle doesn't respond to the heart's electrical signals. Certain diseases and conditions can cause the electrical problems that lead to SCA. Examples include coronary heart disease (CHD), also called coronary artery disease; severe physical stress; certain inherited disorders; and structural changes in the heart.

Several research studies are underway to try to find the exact causes of SCA and how to prevent them.

### Coronary Heart Disease

CHD is a disease in which a waxy substance called plaque builds up in the coronary arteries. These arteries supply oxygen-rich blood to your heart muscle.

Plaque narrows the arteries and reduces blood flow to your heart muscle. Eventually, an area of plaque can rupture (break open). This may cause a blood clot to form on the plaque's surface.

A blood clot can partly or fully block the flow of oxygen-rich blood to the portion of heart muscle fed by the artery. This causes a heart attack.

During a heart attack, some heart muscle cells die and are replaced with scar tissue. The scar tissue damages the heart's electrical system. As a result, electrical signals may spread abnormally throughout the heart. These changes to the heart increase the risk of dangerous arrhythmias and SCA.

CHD seems to cause most cases of SCA in adults. Many of these adults, however, have no signs or symptoms of CHD before having SCA.

### Physical Stress

Certain types of physical stress can cause your heart's electrical system to fail. Examples include:

- Intense physical activity. The hormone adrenaline is released during intense physical activity. This hormone can trigger SCA in people who have heart problems.

- Very low blood levels of potassium or magnesium. These minerals play an important role in your heart's electrical signaling.

35

- Major blood loss.
- Severe lack of oxygen.

*Inherited Disorders*

A tendency to have arrhythmias runs in some families. This tendency is inherited, which means it's passed from parents to children through the genes. Members of these families may be at higher risk for SCA.

An example of an inherited disorder that makes you more likely to have arrhythmias is long QT syndrome (LQTS). LQTS is a disorder of the heart's electrical activity. Problems with tiny pores on the surface of heart muscle cells cause the disorder. LQTS can cause sudden, uncontrollable, dangerous heart rhythms.

People who inherit structural heart problems also may be at higher risk for SCA. These types of problems often are the cause of SCA in children.

*Structural Changes in the Heart*

Changes in the heart's normal size or structure may affect its electrical system. Examples of such changes include an enlarged heart due to high blood pressure or advanced heart disease. Heart infections also may cause structural changes in the heart.

## Who Is at Risk for Sudden Cardiac Arrest?

The risk of SCA increases:

- With age
- If you are a man. Men are more likely than women to have SCA.
- Some studies show that blacks—particularly those with underlying conditions such as diabetes, high blood pressure, heart failure, and chronic kidney disease or certain cardiac findings on tests such as an electrocardiogram—have a higher risk for SCA.

*Major Risk Factor*

The major risk factor for SCA is coronary heart disease. Most people who have SCA have some degree of coronary heart disease; however, many people may not know that they have coronary heart disease until SCA occurs. Usually their coronary heart disease is "silent"—that is, it has no signs or symptoms. Because of this, doctors and nurses have not detected it.

Many people who have SCA also have silent, or undiagnosed, heart attacks before sudden cardiac arrest happens. These people have no clear signs of heart attack, and they don't even realize that they've had one.

### Other Risk Factors

Other risk factors for SCA include:

- A personal history of arrhythmias

- A personal or family history of SCA or inherited disorders that make you prone to arrhythmias

- Drug or alcohol abuse

- Heart attack

- Heart failure

## What Are the Signs and Symptoms of Sudden Cardiac Arrest?

Usually, the first sign of sudden cardiac arrest (SCA) is loss of consciousness (fainting). At the same time, no heartbeat (or pulse) can be felt.

Some people may have a racing heartbeat or feel dizzy or light-headed just before they faint. Within an hour before SCA, some people have chest pain, shortness of breath, nausea (feeling sick to the stomach), or vomiting.

## How Is Sudden Cardiac Arrest Diagnosed?

Sudden cardiac arrest (SCA) happens without warning and requires emergency treatment. Doctors rarely diagnose SCA with medical tests as it's happening. Instead, SCA often is diagnosed after it happens. Doctors do this by ruling out other causes of a person's sudden collapse.

### Specialists Involved

If you're at high risk for SCA, your doctor may refer you to a cardiologist. This is a doctor who specializes in diagnosing and treating heart diseases and conditions. Your cardiologist will work with you to decide whether you need treatment to prevent SCA.

Some cardiologists specialize in problems with the heart's electrical system. These specialists are called cardiac electrophysiologists.

### Diagnostic Tests and Procedures

Doctors use several tests to help detect the factors that put people at risk for SCA.

- EKG (Electrocardiogram)
- Echocardiography
- MUGA Test or Cardiac MRI
- Cardiac Catheterization
- Electrophysiology Study
- Blood Tests

## How Is Sudden Cardiac Arrest Treated?

### Emergency Treatment

Sudden cardiac arrest (SCA) is an emergency. A person having SCA needs to be treated with a defibrillator right away. This device sends an electric shock to the heart. The electric shock can restore a normal rhythm to a heart that's stopped beating.

To work well, defibrillation must be done within minutes of SCA. With every minute that passes, the chances of surviving SCA drop rapidly.

Police, emergency medical technicians, and other first responders usually are trained and equipped to use a defibrillator. Call 9-1-1 right away if someone has signs or symptoms of SCA. The sooner you call for help, the sooner lifesaving treatment can begin.

### Automated External Defibrillators

AEDs are special defibrillators that untrained bystanders can use. These portable devices often are found in public places, such as shopping malls, golf courses, businesses, airports, airplanes, casinos, convention centers, hotels, sports venues, and schools.

AEDs are programmed to give an electric shock if they detect a dangerous arrhythmia, such as ventricular fibrillation. This prevents giving a shock to someone who may have fainted but isn't having SCA. You should give cardiopulmonary resuscitation (CPR) to a person having SCA until defibrillation can be done.

## Treatment in a Hospital

If you survive SCA, you'll likely be admitted to a hospital for ongoing care and treatment. In the hospital, your medical team will closely watch your heart. They may give you medicines to try to reduce the risk of another SCA.

While in the hospital, your medical team will try to find out what caused your SCA. If you're diagnosed with coronary heart disease, you may have percutaneous coronary intervention, also known as coronary angioplasty, or coronary artery bypass grafting. These procedures help restore blood flow through narrowed or blocked coronary arteries.

Often, people who have SCA get a device called an implantable cardioverter defibrillator (ICD). This small device is surgically placed under the skin in your chest or abdomen. An ICD uses electric pulses or shocks to help control dangerous arrhythmias.

## How Can Death Due to Sudden Cardiac Arrest Be Prevented?

Ways to prevent death due to sudden cardiac arrest (SCA) differ depending on whether:

- You've already had SCA
- You've never had SCA but are at high risk for the condition
- You've never had SCA and have no known risk factors for the condition

### For People Who Have Survived Sudden Cardiac Arrest

If you've already had SCA, you're at high risk of having it again. Research shows that an implantable cardioverter defibrillator (ICD) reduces the chances of dying from a second SCA. An ICD is surgically placed under the skin in your chest or abdomen. The device has wires with electrodes on the ends that connect to your heart's chambers. The ICD monitors your heartbeat.

If the ICD detects a dangerous heart rhythm, it gives an electric shock to restore the heart's normal rhythm. Your doctor may give you medicine to limit irregular heartbeats that can trigger the ICD.

### Implantable Cardioverter Defibrillator

An ICD isn't the same as a pacemaker. The devices are similar, but they have some differences. Pacemakers give off low-energy electrical

39

pulses. They're often used to treat less dangerous heart rhythms, such as those that occur in the upper chambers of the heart. Most new ICDs work as both pacemakers and ICDs.

### *For People at High Risk for a First Sudden Cardiac Arrest*

If you have severe coronary heart disease (CHD), you're at increased risk for SCA. This is especially true if you've recently had a heart attack.

Your doctor may prescribe a type of medicine called a beta blocker to help lower your risk for SCA. Your doctor also may discuss beginning statin treatment if you have an elevated risk for developing heart disease or having a stroke. Doctors usually prescribe statins for people who have:

- Diabetes

- Heart disease or had a prior stroke

- High LDL cholesterol levels

Your doctor also may prescribe other medications to:

- Decrease your chance of having a heart attack or dying suddenly.

- Lower blood pressure.

- Prevent blood clots, which can lead to heart attack or stroke.

- Prevent or delay the need for a procedure or surgery, such as angioplasty or coronary artery bypass grafting.

- Reduce your heart's workload and relieve coronary heart disease symptoms.

Take all medicines regularly, as your doctor prescribes. Don't change the amount of your medicine or skip a dose unless your doctor tells you to. You should still follow a heart-healthy lifestyle, even if you take medicines to treat your coronary heart disease.

Other treatments for coronary heart disease—such as percutaneous coronary intervention, also known as coronary angioplasty, or coronary artery bypass grafting—also may lower your risk for SCA. Your doctor also may recommend an ICD if you're at high risk for SCA.

### *For People Who Have No Known Risk Factors for Sudden Cardiac Arrest*

CHD seems to be the cause of most SCAs in adults. CHD also is a major risk factor for angina (chest pain or discomfort) and heart attack, and it contributes to other heart problems. Following a heart-healthy lifestyle can help you lower your risk for CHD, SCA, and other heart problems. A heart-healthy lifestyle includes:

- Heart-healthy eating
- Aiming for a healthy weight
- Managing stress
- Physical activity
- Quitting smoking

## Screening for Sudden Cardiac Death before Participation in High School and Collegiate Sports

The American College of Preventive Medicine (ACPM) supports an evaluation prior to participating in high school and collegiate sports using a standardized history and physical (H&P) (i.e., using standardized items as developed by the American Heart Association (AHA) to ensure uniformity and consistency in risk factor assessment). ACPM recommends against routine screening for potential SCD with electrocardiogram (ECG), echocardiography, and genetic testing in individuals without personal risk factors. The recommendations by ACPM address only mass screening approaches to detecting SCD and are not targeted toward individuals who may be identified by their healthcare provider as "above average" risk who may benefit from additional testing. ACPM supports the adoption of the National Heart, Lung, and Blood Institute (NHLBI) Working Group research agenda to evaluate the effectiveness of any screening program in reducing SCD, its cost–benefit ratio, and its impact on health outcomes.

## The 12-Element AHA Recommendations for Preparticipation Cardiovascular Screening of Competitive Athletes: Medical History

### Personal History

1. Exertional chest pain/discomfort
2. Unexplained syncope/near-syncope
3. Excessive exertional and unexplained dyspnea/fatigue, associated with exercise

41

4. Prior recognition of a heart murmur

5. Elevated systemic blood pressure

*Family History*

6. Premature death (sudden and unexpected, or otherwise) before age 50 years due to heart disease, in ≥1 relative

7. Disability from heart disease in a close relative aged <50 years

8. Specific knowledge of certain cardiac conditions in family members: hypertrophic or dilated cardiomyopathy, long-QT syndrome or other ion channelopathies, Marfan syndrome, or clinically important arrhythmias

*Physical Examination*

9. Heart murmur

10. Femoral pulses to exclude aortic coarctation

11. Physical stigmata of Marfan syndrome

12. Brachial artery blood pressure (sitting position)

## Sudden Cardiac Arrest: Prevention

Access to early defibrillation is essential. A goal of less than 3–5 minutes from the time of collapse to delivery of the first shock is strongly recommended. The preparticipation physical examination should include the completion of a standardized history form and attention to episodes of exertional syncope or presyncope, chest pain, a personal or family history of sudden cardiac arrest or a family history of sudden death, and exercise intolerance.

## Recognition

Sudden cardiac arrest should be suspected in any athlete who has collapsed and is unresponsive. A patient's airway, breathing, circulation, and heart rhythm (using the automated external defibrillator) should be assessed. An AED should be applied as soon as possible for rhythm analysis. Myoclonic jerking or seizure-like activity is often present after collapse from SCA and should not be mistaken for a seizure. Occasional or agonal gasping should not be mistaken for normal breathing.

## Management

CPR should be provided while the AED is being retrieved, and the AED should be applied as soon as possible. Interruptions in chest compressions should be minimized by stopping only for rhythm analysis and defibrillation. Treatment should proceed in accordance with the updated American Heart Association (AHA) guidelines, which recommend that healthcare professionals follow a sequence of chest compressions (C), airway (A), and breathing (B).

Chapter 6

# *Athletes and Skin Disorders*

## *Chapter Contents*

# Section 6.1

## *Preventing Skin Diseases in Athletes*

This section contains text excerpted from the following
sources: Text in this section begins with excerpts from
"Otes from the Field: Outbreak of Skin Lesions among
High School Wrestlers—Arizona, 2014," Centers for
Disease Control and Prevention (CDC), May 29, 2015;
Text beginning with the heading "General Information
about MRSA" is excerpted from "Methicillin-resistant
Staphylococcus aureus (MRSA)," Centers for Disease
Control and Prevention (CDC), February 9, 2016.

Skin infections are a common problem among athletes at all levels
of competition; among wrestlers, 8.5 percent of all adverse events
are caused by skin infections. Wrestlers are at risk because of the
constant skin-to-skin contact required during practice and competition. The most common infections transmitted among high school
wrestlers include fungal infections (e.g., ringworm), the viral infection herpes gladiatorum caused by herpes simplex virus–1 (HSV-1),
and bacterial infections (e.g., impetigo) caused by *Staphylococcus* or
*Streptococcus* species, including methicillin-resistant *Staphylococcal
aureus* (MRSA).

### *General Information about MRSA*

- MRSA is methicillin-resistant *Staphylococcus aureus*, a type
  of staph bacteria that is resistant to several antibiotics. In the
  general community, MRSA most often causes skin infections.
  In some cases, it causes pneumonia (lung infection) and other
  issues. If left untreated, MRSA infections can become severe and
  cause sepsis—a life-threatening reaction to severe infection in
  the body.

- In a healthcare setting, such as a hospital or nursing home,
  MRSA can cause severe problems such as bloodstream infections, pneumonia and surgical site infections.

46

## Who Is at Risk, and How Is MRSA Spread in the Community?

Anyone can get MRSA on their body from contact with an infected wound or by sharing personal items, such as towels or razors, that have touched infected skin. MRSA infection risk can be increased when a person is in activities or places that involve crowding, skin-to-skin contact, and shared equipment or supplies. People including athletes, daycare and school students, military personnel in barracks, and those who recently received inpatient medical care are at higher risk.

## How Common Is MRSA?

Studies show that about one in three people carry staph in their nose, usually without any illness. Two in 100 people carry MRSA. There are not data showing the total number of people who get MRSA skin infections in the community.

## Can I Prevent MRSA? How?

- There are the steps you can take to reduce your risk of MRSA infection:

  - Maintain good hand and body hygiene. Wash hands often, and clean your body regularly, especially after exercise.

  - Keep cuts, scrapes and wounds clean and covered until healed.

  - Avoid sharing personal items such as towels and razors.

  - Get care early if you think you might have an infection.

## What Are MRSA Symptoms?

Sometimes, people with MRSA skin infections first think they have a spider bite. However, unless a spider is actually seen, the irritation is likely not a spider bite. Most staph skin infections, including MRSA, appear as a bump or infected area on the skin that might be:

- Red
- Swollen
- Painful

- Warm to the touch
- Full of pus or other drainage
- Accompanied by a fever

## What Should I Do If I See These Symptoms?

If you or someone in your family experiences these signs and symptoms, cover the area with a bandage, wash your hands, and contact your doctor. It is especially important to contact your doctor if signs and symptoms of an MRSA skin infection are accompanied by a fever.

## What Should I Do If I Think I Have a Skin Infection?

- You can't tell by looking at the skin if it is a staph infection (including MRSA).
- Contact your doctor if you think you have an infection. Finding infections early and getting care make it less likely that the infection will become severe.
- Do not try to treat the infection yourself by picking or popping the sore.
- Cover possible infections with clean, dry bandages until you can be seen by a doctor, nurse, or other healthcare provider.

## How to Prevent Spreading MRSA

- Cover your wounds. Keep wounds covered with clean, dry bandages until healed. Follow your doctor's instructions about proper care of the wound. Pus from infected wounds can contain MRSA so keeping the infection covered will help prevent the spread to others. Bandages and tape can be thrown away with the regular trash. Do not try to treat the infection yourself by picking or popping the sore.
- Clean your hands often. You, your family, and others in close contact should wash their hands often with soap and water or use an alcohol-based hand rub, especially after changing the bandage or touching the infected wound.
- Do not share personal items. Personal items include towels, washcloths, razors and clothing, including uniforms.

- Wash used sheets, towels, and clothes with water and laundry detergent. Use a dryer to dry them completely.

- Wash clothes according to manufacturer's instructions on the label. Clean your hands after touching dirty clothes.

## Steps to Take If You Think an Athlete Might Have a Skin Infection

- Refer athletes with possible infections to a healthcare provider such as team physician, athletic trainer, school nurse, or primary care doctor.

- If the athlete is younger than 18 years old, notify parents/guardians about the possible infection.

- Instruct the athletes with a potential or confirmed infection or open wound to avoid using whirlpools or therapy pools not cleaned between athletes and other common-use water facilities like swimming pools until infections and wounds are healed.

- Review and implement cleaning and disinfecting guidance.

- Educate athletes about ways to prevent spreading the infection.

- Make sure supplies are available to comply with prevention measures (e.g., soap in shower and at sinks, bandages for covering wounds, hand hygiene such as alcohol-based hand rubs).

- Make sure athletes:
  - keep wounds covered and contained
  - shower immediately after participation
  - shower before using whirlpools
  - wash and dry uniforms after each use
  - report possible infections to coach, athletic trainer, school nurse, other healthcare providers, or parents.

Using the criteria above, consider excluding the athlete from participation until evaluated by a healthcare provider.

## Recommended Practices for Treating Athletes with Skin Infections

- Use Standard Precautions, including hand hygiene before and after contact and after removing gloves, when caring for nonintact skin or possible infections.

- If hands are not visibly dirty and no sinks are available for hand washing (for example, while on the field) alcohol-based hand rubs and sanitizers can be used to improve hand hygiene.

- Ensure infected wounds on athletes are properly covered.

- Encourage athletes to cover acute, noninfected wounds (e.g., abrasions, blisters, lacerations) until healed to prevent infection.

## Excluding Athletes with MRSA Infections from Participation

- If sport-specific rules do not exist, in general, athletes should be excluded if wounds cannot be properly covered during participation.

- The term "properly covered" means that the skin infection is covered by a securely attached bandage or dressing that will contain all drainage and will remain intact throughout the activity. If wounds can be properly covered, good hygiene measures should be stressed to the athlete such as performing hand hygiene before and after changing bandages and throwing used bandages in the trash.

- A healthcare provider might exclude an athlete if the activity poses a risk to the health of the infected athlete (such as injury to the infected area), even though the infection can be properly covered.

- Athletes with active infections or open wounds should not use whirlpools or therapy pools not cleaned between athletes and other common-use water facilities like swimming pools until infections and wounds are healed.

# Section 6.2

## *Athletes and Skin Cancer Risk*

This section includes text excerpted from "Skin Cancer—Basic Information," Centers for Disease Control and Prevention (CDC), January 22, 2014.

### *What Is Skin Cancer?*

Skin cancer is the most common form of cancer in the United States. The two most common types of skin cancer—basal cell and squamous cell carcinomas—are highly curable, but can be disfiguring and costly. Melanoma, the third most common skin cancer, is more dangerous and causes the most deaths. The majority of these three types of skin cancer are caused by exposure to ultraviolet (UV) light.

#### *Ultraviolet (UV) Light*

Ultraviolet (UV) rays are an invisible kind of radiation that comes from the sun, tanning beds, and sunlamps. UV rays can penetrate and change skin cells.

The three types of UV rays are ultraviolet A (UVA), ultraviolet B (UVB), and ultraviolet C (UVC):

- UVA is the most common kind of sunlight at the earth's surface, and reaches beyond the top layer of human skin. Scientists believe that UVA rays can damage connective tissue and increase a person's risk of skin cancer.

- Most UVB rays are absorbed by the ozone layer, so they are less common at the earth's surface than UVA rays. UVB rays, which help produce vitamin D in the skin, don't reach as far into the skin as UVA rays, but they still can be damaging.

- UVC rays are very dangerous, but they are absorbed by the ozone layer and do not reach the ground.

In addition to sunburn, too much exposure to UV rays can change skin texture, cause the skin to age prematurely, and can lead to

51

skin cancer. UV rays also have been linked to eye conditions such as cataracts.

The National Weather Service (NWS) and the Environmental Protection Agency (EPA) developed the UV Index (www.epa.gov/enviro/uv-index-search) to forecast the risk of overexposure to UV rays. It lets you know how much caution you should take when working, playing, or exercising outdoors.

The UV Index predicts exposure levels on a 1 to 15 scale; higher levels indicate a higher risk of overexposure. Calculated on a next-day basis for dozens of cities across the United States, the UV Index takes into account clouds and other local conditions that affect the amount of UV rays reaching the ground.

## What Are the Risk Factors for Skin Cancer?

People with certain risk factors are more likely than others to develop skin cancer. Risk factors vary for different types of skin cancer, but some general risk factors are having:

- Exposure to the sun through work and play.

- A lighter natural skin color.

- Family history of skin cancer.

- A personal history of skin cancer.

- A history of sunburns, especially early in life.

- A history of indoor tanning.

- Skin that burns, freckles, reddens easily, or becomes painful in the sun.

- Blue or green eyes.

- Blond or red hair.

- Certain types and a large number of moles.

## Tanning and Burning

Ultraviolet (UV) rays come from the sun or from indoor tanning (using a tanning bed, booth, or sunlamp to get tan). When UV rays reach the skin's inner layer, the skin makes more melanin. Melanin is the pigment that colors the skin. It moves toward the outer layers of the skin and becomes visible as a tan.

A tan does not indicate good health. A tan is a response to injury, because skin cells signal that they have been hurt by UV rays by producing more pigment.

People burn or tan depending on their skin type, the time of year, and how long they are exposed to UV rays. The six types of skin, based on how likely it is to tan or burn, are:

- Always burns, never tans, sensitive to UV exposure.
- Burns easily, tans minimally.
- Burns moderately, tans gradually to light brown.
- Burns minimally, always tans well to moderately brown.
- Rarely burns, tans profusely to dark.
- Never burns, deeply pigmented, least sensitive.

Although everyone's skin can be damaged by UV exposure, people with skin types I and II are at the highest risk.

## What Are the Symptoms of Skin Cancer?

A change in your skin is the most common sign of skin cancer. This could be a new growth, a sore that doesn't heal, or a change in a mole. Not all skin cancers look the same.

A simple way to remember the signs of melanoma is to remember the A-B-C-D-Es of melanoma:

- "A" stands for asymmetrical. Does the mole or spot have an irregular shape with two parts that look very different?
- "B" stands for border. Is the border irregular or jagged?
- "C" is for color. Is the color uneven?
- "D" is for diameter. Is the mole or spot larger than the size of a pea?
- "E" is for evolving. Has the mole or spot changed during the past few weeks or months?

Talk to your doctor if you notice changes in your skin such as a new growth, a sore that doesn't heal, a change in an old growth, or any of the A-B-C-D-Es of melanoma.

## What Can I Do to Reduce My Risk of Skin Cancer?

Protection from ultraviolet (UV) radiation is important all year round, not just during the summer or at the beach. UV rays from the sun can reach you on cloudy and hazy days, as well as bright and sunny days. UV rays also reflect off of surfaces like water, cement, sand, and snow. Indoor tanning (using a tanning bed, booth, or sunlamp to get tan) exposes users to UV radiation.

The hours between 10 a.m. and 4 p.m. Daylight Saving Time (9 a.m. to 3 p.m. standard time) are the most hazardous for UV exposure outdoors in the continental United States. UV rays from sunlight are the greatest during the late spring and early summer in North America.

Few easy options for protection from UV radiation:

- Stay in the shade, especially during midday hours.
- Wear clothing that covers your arms and legs.
- Wear a hat with a wide brim to shade your face, head, ears, and neck.
- Wear sunglasses that wrap around and block both UVA and UVB rays.
- Use sunscreen with sun protection factor (SPF) 15 or higher, and both UVA and UVB protection.
- Avoid indoor tanning.

## How Can I Protect My Children from the Sun?

Just a few serious sunburns can increase your child's risk of skin cancer later in life. Kids don't have to be at the pool, beach, or on vacation to get too much sun. Their skin needs protection from the sun's harmful ultraviolet (UV) rays whenever they're outdoors.

**Cover up.** When possible, long-sleeved shirts and long pants and skirts can provide protection from UV rays. Clothes made from tightly woven fabric offer the best protection. A wet T-shirt offers much less UV protection than a dry one, and darker colors may offer more protection than lighter colors. Some clothing certified under international standards comes with information on its ultraviolet protection factor.

**Get a hat.** Hats that shade the face, scalp, ears, and neck are easy to use and give great protection. Baseball caps are popular among kids, but they don't protect their ears and neck. If your child chooses a cap, be sure to protect exposed areas with sunscreen.

**Wear sunglasses.** They protect your child's eyes from UV rays, which can lead to cataracts later in life. Look for sunglasses that wrap around and block as close to 100 percent of both UVA and UVB rays as possible.

**Apply sunscreen.** Use sunscreen with at least SPF 15 and UVA and UVB protection every time your child goes outside. For the best protection, apply sunscreen generously 30 minutes before going outdoors. Don't forget to protect ears, noses, lips, and the tops of feet.

Take sunscreen with you to reapply during the day, especially after your child swims or exercises. This applies to waterproof and water-resistant products as well. Follow the directions on the package for using a sunscreen product on babies less than 6 months old. All products do not have the same ingredients; if your or your child's skin reacts badly to one product, try another one or call a doctor. Your baby's best defense against sunburn is avoiding the sun or staying in the shade. Keep in mind, sunscreen is not meant to allow kids to spend more time in the sun than they would otherwise. Try combining sunscreen with other options to prevent UV damage.

**Seek shade.** UV rays are strongest and most harmful during midday, so it's best to plan indoor activities then. If this is not possible, seek shade under a tree, an umbrella, or a pop-up tent. Use these options to prevent sunburn, not to seek relief after it's happened.

### Too Much Sun Hurts

**Turning pink?** Unprotected skin can be damaged by the sun's UV rays in as little as 15 minutes. Yet it can take up to 12 hours for skin to show the full effect of sun exposure. So, if your child's skin looks "a little pink" today, it may be burned tomorrow morning. To prevent further burning, get your child out of the sun.

**Tan?** There's no other way to say it—tanned skin is damaged skin. Any change in the color of your child's skin after time outside—whether sunburn or suntan—indicates damage from UV rays.

**Cool and cloudy?** Children still need protection. UV rays, not the temperature, do the damage. Clouds do not block UV rays, they filter them—and sometimes only slightly.

**Oops!** Kids often get sunburned when they are outdoors unprotected for longer than expected. Remember to plan ahead, and keep sun protection handy—in your car, bag, or child's backpack.

Chapter 7

# Exercise-Induced Asthma in Athletes

Exercise-induced asthma (also called exercise-induced broncho-spasm) is asthma that is triggered by physical activity. Vigorous exercise will cause symptoms for most students who have asthma if their asthma is not well-controlled. Some students experience asthma symptoms only when they exercise. Asthma varies from student to student and often from season to season or even hour by hour. At times, programs for students who have asthma may need to be temporarily modified, such as by varying the type, intensity, duration, and/or frequency of activity. At all times, students who have asthma should be included in activities as much as possible. Remaining behind in the gym or library or frequently sitting on the bench can set the stage for teasing, loss of self-esteem, unnecessary restriction of activity, and low levels of physical fitness.

## Exercise-Induced Bronchoconstriction and Asthma

Vigorous physical exercise can be followed by transient clinical signs and symptoms similar to an asthma attack and are due to

This chapter contains text excerpted from the following sources: Text in this chapter begins with excerpts from "Asthma and Physical Activity in the School," National Heart, Lung, and Blood Institute (NHLBI), April 2012. Reviewed June 2017; Text beginning with the heading "Exercise-Induced Bronchoconstriction and Asthma" is excerpted from "Exercise-Induced Bronchoconstriction and Chronic Asthma," Agency for Healthcare Research and Quality (AHRQ), March 2010. Reviewed June 2017.

postexercise bronchoconstriction (i.e., a narrowing of the airways). Clinical symptoms include coughing, wheezing, shortness of breath, excessive mucus production, chest tightness, chest pain, or an 'itching or scratching sensation' in the chest. Though it is more common in people with asthma, it also occurs in people without asthma.

Exercise-induced bronchoconstriction (EIB) is defines as "the airway obstruction that occurs in association with exercise without regard to the presence of chronic asthma" and Exercise-induced asthma (EIA) as "the condition in which exercise induces symptoms of asthma in patients who have asthma." Acute bronchoconstriction associated with EIB/EIA peaks rapidly, 3–15 minutes after exercise stops, then remits spontaneously within 20–60 minutes. It does not cause a persistent deterioration in lung function.

Following recovery, a refractory period of 40 minutes to 3 hours is present. During this time repeat exercise causes less bronchoconstriction. Two of the most common pulmonary function measures used to quantify the degree of bronchoconstriction are the forced expiratory volume in 1 second (FEV1) and the peak expiratory flow (PEF), with FEV1 considered the more reliable and valid. Both measures will decrease from baseline preexercise values in susceptible individuals. It is proposed that the increase in minute ventilation caused by vigorous exercise triggers the airway narrowing. Some episodes are severe enough that the person will require an inhaled bronchodilator agent to reverse the bronchoconstriction.

Approximately 20.5 million people in the United States (7 percent) have asthma. Between 60 and 90 percent of people with asthma experience EIA and consider exercise a major trigger of asthma symptoms. Prevalence of EIB is lower (6–13 percent) in populations with no history of asthma or allergy. Among elite athletes the prevalence is reported to range from 10–50 percent. The signs and symptoms of EIB/EIA often go unrecognized or are blamed on lack of conditioning. Some people will avoid exercise and some parents, teachers, and coaches of children with asthma may impose restrictions on which activities will be allowed. With a proper diagnosis and treatment, children and adults have successfully competed at all levels of physical activity.

## What Is Exercise-Induced Bronchoconstriction and Asthma?

Vigorous physical exercise can be followed by transient clinical signs and symptoms of asthma due to airway narrowing. The phenomenon was first recorded around 150 AD by Aretaeus of Cappodocia.

Airway obstruction following exercise was first observed among individuals with underlying asthma from which the term exercise-induced asthma (EIA) was derived. Asthma is a chronic inflammatory disorder of the airways in which many cells and cellular elements play a role, and it is associated with bronchial (or airway) hyperresponsiveness. Similar postexercise asthma-like symptoms have been observed in persons without the presence of coexisting asthma, particularly in athletes. In this population the phenomenon has been referred to as exercise-induced bronchoconstriction (EIB).

The underlying mechanisms of EIB and EIA are multifactorial and complex. Whether the two phenomena have the same pathogenesis is still unknown and continues to be explored. In the early 1970s, Chan-Yeung et al recognized that the severity of the airway constriction was associated with the level of ventilation. In normal nasal breathing, inspired air is heated to body temperature and is completely saturated with water in the first few generations of the airways. There is a marked increase in minute ventilation during and following strenuous exercise and, as a result, the nose is unable to condition the increased volume of air. The added burden on the lower airways, down to the tenth generation and beyond, to warm and humidify the large volume of air triggers osmotic and thermal changes. Loss of water in the periciliary fluid layer of the airway produces a hyperosmotic environment that may stimulate degranulation of pulmonary mucosa mast cells with subsequent release of several inflammatory mediators such as histamine, leukotrienes, prostaglandin, platelet activating factors, and neuropeptides from sensory nerves.

Theorists propose that the released mediators stimulate bronchial smooth muscle spasm and rapid rewarming leads to increased bronchial circulation and engorged capillary beds (or airway edema) that may intensify the obstruction.

## Magnitude and Importance of the Condition

According to National Center for Health Statistics (NCHS) estimates, approximately 20.5 million Americans (seven percent) have asthma. Between 60–90 percent of people with asthma experience EIA and consider exercise a major trigger of their asthma symptoms. Some claim that all asthmatics will experience EIA if ventilation is sufficiently high. Prevalence of EIB is lower (6–13 percent) in a population with no history of asthma or allergy. Several studies conducted among athletes have reported the prevalence of EIB/EIA to range from 11–50 percent. High level endurance training in sports such as cross-country skiing, swimming, and long distance running may increase bronchial hyper-responsiveness (BHR) and cause inflammation in the airways because these athletes are repeatedly exposed to cold air, inhaled irritants, and allergens.

Asthma is known to have a negative impact on health-related quality of life. The threat of an asthma attack may result in withdrawal from physical and social activities, which can lead to deconditioning, weight gain, and to an altered sense of self-esteem. Both recreational and elite athletes tend to minimize or deny symptoms due to embarrassment, fear of repercussions, or lack of understanding of what they are experiencing. EIB/EIA and asthma have an impact on quality of life. The fear of sudden breathlessness creates a sense of panic, which may prevent children and adults from participating in sports and cause parents of children with asthma to impose restrictions. Fear of failure and sub optimal performance in sports may lead many individuals suffering from EIB/EIA to opt for sedentary activities. Unrecognized EIB/EIA can result in serious public health consequences.

## Diagnosis of Exercise-Induced Bronchoconstriction and Asthma

Potential EIB/EIA can be detected by taking a thorough medical history. EIB/EIA is suspected when individuals, who otherwise have good lung function, complain of recurrent shortness of breath and symptoms of cough, wheeze, chest pain, or prolonged recovery time following exercise. These symptoms are independent of a person's conditioning level. If symptoms are relieved by inhaling a short-acting beta-agonist (SABA) or if symptoms are prevented by taking a SABA before exercise, a diagnosis of EIB/EIA is strongly supported. The degree of airway constriction can be measured objectively by a spectrum of pulmonary function tests; however, most clinicians and laboratories use the FEV1 or, very occasionally, the peak expiratory flow (PEF).

When a patient's history suggests EIB/EIA, measuring the change in FEV1 before and after a standardized exercise challenge test (ECT) on a treadmill or bicycle ergometer can assist in making the diagnosis. The American Thoracic Society (ATS) has published guidelines for conducting a standardized ECT, which include recommendations for environmental control, as well as the level and duration of intensity required to ensure a sufficiently vigorous challenge. Minute ventilation must reach the target level in the first 4 minutes of the challenge. The standardized laboratory ECT has not always demonstrated sufficient sensitivity to identify EIB/EIA in elite athletes who perform in many venues and with widely varying intensity and duration, therefore, other surrogate tests have been recommended. Some of the current options include sport specific challenges, the free running asthma screening test (FRAST), measures of direct bronchial responsiveness to methacholine (MCH) and indirect responsiveness to eucapnic voluntary hyperpnea (EVH) or mannitol.

In the general population, vigorous exercise should cause little to no prolonged decrease in airflow following exercise.

## Treatment of Exercise-Induced Bronchoconstriction and Asthma

The goal of treatment is to prevent or, at least, to reduce the severity of the bronchoconstriction and symptoms so that an individual can participate in any activity, regardless of its intensity and duration, without serious respiratory limitations. Through a combination of education, a commitment to fitness, pharmacologic intervention, and use of nonpharmacologic strategies, EIB/EIA can be successfully managed in the majority of cases. Different pharmaceutical agents that appear to operate on different phases of the response can provide at least partial relief from EIB/EIA. The most commonly used agents are inhaled SABA and long-acting beta-agonist (LABA) agents. Other agents include mast cell stabilizing agents (MCS), short-acting anticholinergics (SAAC), leukotriene receptor antagonists (LTRA), and inhaled corticosteroids (ICS). Theophyllines, antihistamines, calcium channel blockers, heparin, and furosemide have also been shown to have some degree of effectiveness.

There are many unresolved issues with respect to the treatment of EIB/EIA with pharmaceutical agents. There is concern that the continuous use of the SABA and LABA agents to control asthma over the long-term could lead to a decrease in efficacy when also used prophylactically to control EIA. A development of tolerance, or tachyphylaxis, to SABA or LABA agents may not only decrease their protective effect, but also shorten their duration of action. In the case of SABAs, a serious concern is that continuous use will decrease its impact as a rescue medication in the case of severe EIA.

Chapter 8

# Sports Nutrition, Weight Maintenance, and Hydration

## Chapter Contents

# Section 8.1

# *Basic Facts about Sports Nutrition*

This section includes text excerpted from "Healthy Foods and Beverages for Youth in Sports," President's Council on Fitness, Sports and Nutrition (PCFSN), May 13, 2016.

## Healthy Foods and Beverages for Youth in Sports

Nutritious eating habits promote healthy development and allow young people to perform their best in school and other activities. Parents, doctors, school officials, public health leaders, and youth themselves have recognized the importance of adopting better eating habits and creating opportunities to make healthy foods and beverages more easily available. Working together, these groups have made significant efforts to improve the foods and beverages available in many schools. Although much more can be accomplished in school settings, overall, these changes have led to better diets and healthier students. One setting that has received comparatively less attention for encouraging healthy eating is youth sports. Youth sports are terrific venues for promoting health because sports touch the lives of many youth.

Nowadays, youth sports are more popular than they have ever been. More than 44 million youth in the United States participate in sports each year, and two in three students in high school play on at least one sports team at their school or in their community. Sports, including soccer, basketball, tennis, and dance, among others, offer youth an opportunity to engage in vigorous physical activity while they learn how to work together, have fun, and compete toward a common goal. For these reasons and many more, participation in sport can promote healthy development for youth and adolescents.

## Unhealthy Eating Is an Accepted Part of Youth Sports

Unfortunately, youth sport activities are not currently living up to their potential as a setting for promoting healthy eating. According to the *Dietary Guidelines for Americans*, healthy eating emphasizes foods such as fruits, vegetables, whole grains, lean meats, and low-fat milk products. Healthy eating provides a balance of protein, carbohydrates, fat, water, vitamins, and minerals and a limited amount of calories. Unhealthy eating includes foods and beverages that are high in fat, sugar, sodium, and calories. It is possible for youth to find unhealthy food and beverage options most anywhere they go, including from vending machines, concessions, convenience stores, and fast food restaurants. This is especially true in youth sport settings.

Youth who participate in sports consume more fast food, more sugary drinks, and more calories overall than youth who are not involved in sport. The foods and beverages that are convenient and widely available to youth in sport settings are generally unhealthy. For example, concession stands are common in youth sport settings. Typical choices at concession stands include items such as chocolate and other candy, ice cream, salty snacks, sugary beverages, and high-fat, calorie-dense entrees such as hot dogs and pizza. Healthier alternatives are rare. Additionally, parents often organize schedules for providing treats after each game for their child's team. These treats often include candy, doughnuts, chips, and sugary drinks. Parents report that team members and other parents can have a negative reaction when offering healthy choices for postevent treats, such as fruit. Youth sport schedules often overlap with regular family mealtimes and encourage eating away from home. Eating meals outside the home at fast food restaurants is associated with excess body weight and indicators of poor cardiovascular health.

## Physical Activity and Eating Habits in Sport Are out of Balance

The widespread availability of unhealthy foods and beverages in sport settings helps contribute to a cultural norm of accepting, and even expecting, unhealthy eating as a part of youth sport. Parents and coaches view postgame snacks, concession stand items, and fast food meals in youth sport as an occasional indulgence that is permitted, even if it is inconsistent with the foods prepared at home. We have heard anecdotally, and when conducting systematic focus group research, that part of the reason that coaches and parents may relax their usual standards for healthy eating is that they see youth engaging in vigorous exercise during sport. Parents and coaches report that they believe this activity offsets the potential downside of any unhealthy foods or beverages they may have consumed. A common view of postgame treats is exemplified by the following statement from the parent of a child participating in sport: "These kids have been running around for an hour. They can have ice cream."

Despite this belief, research suggests that parents, coaches, and young athletes may overestimate the amount of physical activity sports provide. Studies that objectively measure the amount of physical activity youth gain during sports have found that only about one in four achieve recommended levels of daily activity. The U.S. Department of Health and Human Services (HHS) *Physical Activity Guidelines for Americans,* recommend that children and adolescents accumulate 60 minutes of moderate to vigorous physical activity each day. Examples of moderate intensity physical activity for adolescents include baseball, yard work, hiking, and brisk walking while examples of vigorous activity include jumping rope, bike riding, karate, basketball, and cross-country skiing. The objective evidence suggests that participating in sports provides an average of 30 minutes of the recommended 60 minutes of physical activity. While most sports involve vigorous physical activity, they also involve considerable time in light activity or no activity, such as waiting on the sidelines to enter the game and standing around between plays or while receiving instruction from coaches. The amount of energy expended in sport can vary by type of sport, age of the participant, coaching practices, and other factors, but the data suggest the amount of energy expended in sports is relatively modest. If youth consume the types of foods that are widely available in youth sport settings, they may be overcompensating for the amount of energy they expended in the sport's activity by taking in extra calories. They are also consuming foods and beverages that may fail to provide the appropriate balance of nutrients that comprise a healthy diet.

## Why Is Healthy Eating So Challenging for Young Athletes?

Recent research has started to identify some of the challenges to healthy eating for youth involved in sports. A significant contributor to the lack of healthy eating in youth sports is simply the busy schedules that many families with young children confront. Youth sport practices and competitions occur on several occasions each week at night, and on weekends. In some cases these events can entail considerable travel. Families with multiple children involved in sport and other activities can feel stretched thin simply from transporting them to various locations. Parents who participated in a research told that youth sport activities reduce the frequency of family meals at home. Parents and youth involved in activities want foods and beverages that are convenient and easy to consume while they are "on the go." The time pressures of their children's activities regularly lead them to pick up fast food and eat in the car on the way to or from youth sport events. Youth who attend sport competitions that involve several games or events over the course of a day often rely on foods and beverages from the concession stand.

Normative attitudes and behaviors also contribute to unhealthy eating in youth sport settings. Widespread availability of unhealthy foods and beverages makes them appear to be acceptable and expected.

In addition, teams will often have a postgame treat or meal at a fast food restaurant. Parents and coaches reported that the social benefits for the team (e.g., team bonding) often outweigh the importance of eating a more nutritious meal. Parents who are committed to good nutrition can find it difficult to voice their concerns in these situations. Finally, parents and coaches of teams reported that they did not feel they had adequate knowledge about nutrition and the best ways to properly feed young athletes. Participants in a research reported that they were sometimes confused by seemingly conflicting advice about nutrition in the media and they wanted clear guidance about what was best for youth involved in sports.

**Table 8.1.** Estimated Calorie Needs per Day by Age, Gender, and Physical Activity Level

| Age (Years) | Males | | | Females | | |
|---|---|---|---|---|---|---|
| | Sedentary | Moderately Active | Active | Sedentary | Moderately Active | Active |
| 6–8 | 1,400 | 1,600 | 1,800–2,000 | 1,200–1,400 | 1,400–1,600 | 1,600–1,800 |
| 9–13 | 1,600–2,000 | 1,800–2,200 | 2,000–2,600 | 1,400–1,600 | 1,600–2,000 | 1,800–2,200 |
| 14–16 | 2,000–2,400 | 2,400–2,800 | 2,800–3,200 | 1,800 | 2,000 | 2,400 |
| 17–18 | 2,400 | 2,800 | 3,200 | 1,800 | 2,000 | 2,400 |

# What Does a Developing Young Athlete Need to Eat Balanced Diet?

Despite the many challenges, youth who participate in sports can benefit from eating a well-balanced, nutritious diet. In general, the dietary needs of youth athletes do not significantly differ from their nonsport participating counterparts. *The Dietary Guidelines for Americans 2015–2020* recommend a balanced intake that consists of fruits and vegetables, grains (with at least half whole grains), fat-free or low-fat dairy, a variety of protein foods, and oils. Also recommended is limiting the amount of saturated fat, added sugars, and sodium (salt). Consuming a variety of these foods provides adequate macronutrients and micronutrients needed to support youth development and optimal sport performance. Macronutrients are nutrients the body needs in larger amounts (e.g., carbohydrate, protein, and fat) and micronutrients are nutrients the body needs in smaller amounts (e.g., vitamins and minerals). Each macro- and micronutrient plays an essential role in healthy youth development. The roles macronutrients play in the body and food sources of each are described below.

**Carbohydrate:** Carbohydrate is the main fuel source for the body. Once digested, the body converts carbohydrate to glucose that will be used for energy or stored for later use in the muscles and liver. There are two types of carbohydrate: simple and complex. Simple carbohydrates are digested more quickly and are found in fruit, vegetables, and dairy. Complex carbohydrates are digested more slowly and are found in a variety of foods including bread, pasta, and rice.

Sources: Whole grains (pasta, bread, rice), dairy, fruit, vegetables

**Protein:** Protein helps regulate the function of cells, tissues, and organs in the body. For athletes, protein is also important for muscle repair and recovery.

Sources: Lean meat and poultry, fish, beans, dairy, eggs, nuts/seeds

**Fat:** Fat provides energy when carbohydrate is not available, is essential for the absorption of some vitamins (A, D, E, and K), and aids in maintaining body temperature.

Sources: Oil, avocado, nuts/seeds

## How Many Daily Calories Does a Youth Athlete Need?

Nutritional needs for athletes depend on many factors including age, gender, sport, and activity/competition level. Depending on activity intensity (e.g., sedentary, moderate or vigorous intensity), different daily calorie needs are recommended for youth by the U.S. Department of Agriculture (USDA) and U.S. Department of Health and Human Services (HHS). Examples of moderate intensity activities include riding a bike and walking briskly. Vigorous (i.e., active) activities include running, jumping rope, and playing sports such as basketball, soccer, tennis, and hockey. These activities should make youth sweat and breathe hard. The calorie recommendations based on different activity levels for males and females are shown in Table 8.1. Finding the right balance between energy expenditure and energy intake will help an athlete avoid energy deficit or excess. Energy deficit can delay growth and puberty, as well as impact bone density, and energy excess can lead to overweight.

## Eating before an Activity/Sport

For youth involved in sport, eating before an activity is essential to provide the body with enough energy for best performance. For activities that are in the morning, eat breakfast at least one hour in advance. Finding a good combination of complex and simple carbohydrates with some protein and fat, such as a piece of whole wheat toast (complex carbohydrate) with peanut butter (protein and fat) and a small banana (simple carbohydrate), will provide a slow release of energy throughout the activity. For activities that occur after school, athletes could benefit from eating a snack about an hour before the activity to allow enough digestion time to prevent stomach discomfort during the activity. Some individuals may experience discomfort from meals/snacks that are higher in fat and fiber before activity. A combination of carbohydrates, lower fat, lower fiber, and plenty of plain water may be ideal.

Some small meal examples may include yogurt with fruit, an apple with peanut butter, or whole grain crackers and string cheese. There are a variety of nutritious food options for young athletes to eat before an activity. Parents and coaches can work with their athletes to ensure that a balanced preactivity meal is consumed by the athlete prior to sport participation.

## Eating during an Activity/Sport

Many youth athletes compete in all-day tournaments or have several games in one day. In this case, eating and hydrating between activities is important to fuel the body for the rest of the event. Eating five to six small meals throughout the day could be a good approach. These meals can consist of a variety of easy to digest, nutrient-dense ingredients that provide sustainable energy for the athletes to support their nutritional needs throughout the competition. When events are less than two hours apart, a nutrient-dense, high-carbohydrate snack like fruit with yogurt or a granola bar is ideal. A regular meal (e.g., whole wheat sandwich with lean meat and vegetables, a piece of fruit, and milk) can be eaten when games are longer than a few hours apart.

## Eating after an Activity/Sport

Consuming carbohydrate- and protein-containing foods within a couple of hours postactivity can help to replenish energy stores that were used to fuel the activity and repair muscles. Parents, coaches, and young athletes should aim for whole foods (i.e., less processed) and foods that are bright and colorful (e.g., fruits and vegetables), such as whole wheat spaghetti with tomato sauce, chicken breast, a salad with a variety of vegetables, and milk.

## Should Young Athletes Consume More of Some Nutrients?

Overall, a well-balanced diet with plenty of water is adequate for youth who participate in sport. However, assuring athletes consume adequate amounts of calcium, vitamin D, and iron should be considered. Calcium supports muscle contraction, bone growth, and strength. The Recommended Dietary Allowance for calcium is 1,000 mg/day for 6–8 year olds and 1,300 mg/day for 9–18 year olds. Calcium-rich foods include dairy products, dark leafy green vegetables, and fortified cereals. Vitamin D is also essential for bone health and aids in calcium absorption. The Recommended Dietary Allowance for vitamin D is 600 IU/day for 6–18 year olds. Vitamin D-rich foods include egg yolks, tuna, fortified milk, orange juice, and cereals. Iron helps with muscle repair and improves the body's ability to transfer oxygen to working muscles. The Recommended Dietary Allowance for iron is 10 mg/day for 6–8 year olds, 8 mg/day for 9–13 year olds, 11 mg/day for 14–18 year old males and 15 mg/day for 14–18 year old females. Iron-rich foods include meat, poultry, beans, dark green vegetables, and iron-fortified cereals.

## Is There Anything Athletes Should Limit?

The body's ability to perform will be enhanced if an athlete limits foods that are high in saturated fat, added sugars, and sodium. This includes fast food, processed foods, sweetened beverages (nondiet soft drinks/sodas, sweetened teas, flavored juice drinks, energy drinks, etc.), and snacks and beverages with added sugar. Unfortunately, these characteristics describe the foods and beverages that are typically available in youth sport settings. Not only could these foods and beverages inhibit athletic performance, but they can increase body weight and promote chronic disease. Youth involved in sports should choose foods that will fuel their body healthfully and provide sustainable nutrition for their needs as they compete.

## Finding the Right Balance

Many parents believe their child needs a lot of additional calories because they are being physically active in sport. As noted in Table 8.1, however, active youth do not require considerably more calories than their peers who are less active. Young athletes (less than 12 years old) rarely burn enough energy (calories) through sport to require a supplemental snack. The additional calories may leave them vulnerable to excess weight gain. In recent years, it has become common for parents to provide snacks after games and practices. These snack foods are often high in calories and low in nutrients. Parents have a unique and important role when it comes to providing foods for their young athlete because parents are the primary influencer at this age.

Providing water and nutrient-dense snacks should be the focus, not "treats." As young athletes turn into adolescents, the primary influencer often shifts from parents to coaches and peers. Educating coaches, parents, and young athletes about proper fuel for enhanced performance is essential to reduce the likelihood of calorie overcompensation; that is, consuming too many calories post-game/ -practice than expended (burned). Parents and coaches may need additional education about the amount of calories and the right balance of foods their young athletes need. Unless a child is an endurance athlete or participating in an all-day event, three well-balanced meals that meet their caloric and nutrient needs, and possibly light nutritious snacks between meals, should supply sufficient energy.

## Providing a Healthy Food Environment

A healthy food environment is one that provides nutritious foods and beverages that are affordable, convenient, and accessible in a way that makes them an easy choice. It also limits access to foods and beverages that have high levels of fat, sugar, sodium, and calories. The food environment at most youth sporting events is not very healthy. On game days, concession stands are stocked with high calorie, high sugar, and low nutrient foods such as hot dogs, pizza, "walking tacos," candy, and sodas/soft drink. The culture of concession stands has been to raise money for the hosting organization, as foods commonly served are high in demand and low in cost to prepare and/or offer. Parents also routinely provide postgame snacks that are sugary, salty, or fatty, rather than nutritious. Fast food restaurants are a convenient choice for busy families shuttling their children to various activities, including sport practices and events, but these venues tend to offer foods and beverages that are unhealthy.

Not only are these foods commonly available in youth sport settings undesirable for athletic performance, but some parents have expressed their concerns over the lack of available healthy options during sport events. Barriers to including healthful foods at sporting events include lack of sport nutrition knowledge and resistance to change because organizations rely on them for fund raising. Public health professionals are working with key stakeholders to improve the food environment in the home, in schools, at worksites, in child care centers, and in healthcare facilities. A similar focus is needed to improve the food environment in youth sport settings. Concerted effort is needed to improve the quality and offer more fresh, local, and healthy food and beverage options, provide appropriate portion sizes to meet the nutritional needs of young athletes, and support those settings by implementing and enforcing strong standards.

Sports are a fun and engaging opportunity for children and adolescents to develop healthy habits they can carry with them into adulthood. One of those skills can be healthy eating. However, the way youth sports are currently operating may be teaching youth and families unhealthy eating habits. Change is needed to support healthy, growing, youth athletes. More attention is needed to change the types of foods and beverages that are available and accepted in youth sport settings. Youth, parents, and coaches can become more aware of the unhealthy options that are available and speak out to make their preferences known. Parents can help organizations offer healthier options and figure out ways to make those options feasible and sustainable and align with fund raising goals. Organizations can commit to promoting health as a priority. Considerable change has occurred to improve the foods and beverages available in schools with the attention, commitment, and leadership of many different stakeholders. Similar change is needed, and is possible, for youth sport.

## Section 8.2

# *Female Athlete Triad*

This section contains text excerpted from the following sources: Text in this section begins with excerpts from "Do You Exercise a Lot?" girlshealth.gov, Office on Women's Health (OWH), March 27, 2015; Text under the heading "Amenorrheic Women and the Female Athlete Triad" is excerpted from "Calcium," Office of Dietary Supplements (ODS), National Institutes of Health (NIH), November 17, 2016.

Being active is great. In fact, girls should be active at least an hour each day. Sometimes, though, a girl will be very active (such as running every day or playing a competitive sport), but not eat enough to fuel her activity. This can lead to health problems. What happens when girls don't eat enough to fuel their activity:

- A problem called "low energy availability"
- Period (menstrual) problems
- Bone problems

These three sometimes are called the female athlete triad. ("Triad" means a group of three.) They sometimes also are called Athletic Performance and Energy Deficit. (This means you have a "deficit," or lack, of the energy your body needs to stay healthy.)

### *A Problem Called "Low Energy Availability"*

Your body needs healthy food to fuel the things it does, like fight infections, heal wounds, and grow. If you exercise, your body needs extra food for your workout. You can get learn how much food to eat based on your activity level using the SuperTracker tool (www.choosemyplate.gov/MyPlate-Daily-Checklist).

"Energy availability" means the fuel from food that is not burned up by exercise and so is available for growing, healing, and more. If you exercise a lot and don't get enough nutrition, you may have low energy availability. That means your body won't be as healthy and strong as it should be.

Some female athletes diet to lose weight. They may do this to qualify for their sport or because they think losing weight will help them perform better. But eating enough healthy food is key to having the strength you need to succeed. Also, your body needs good nutrition to make hormones that help with things like healthy periods and strong bones.

Sometimes, girls may exercise too much and eat too little because they have an eating disorder. Eating disorders are serious and can even lead to death, but they are treatable.

## Period (Menstrual) Problems

If you are very active, or if you just recently started getting your period (menstruating), you may skip a few periods. But if you work out really hard and do not eat enough, you may skip a lot of periods (or not get your period to begin with) because your body can't make enough of the hormone estrogen.

You may think you wouldn't mind missing your period, but not getting your period should be taken seriously. Not having your period can mean your body is not building enough bone, and the teenage years are the main time for building strong bones.

If you have been getting your period regularly and then miss three periods in a row, see your doctor. Not having your period could be a sign of a serious health problem or of being pregnant. Also see your doctor if you are 15 years old and still have not gotten your period.

## Bone Problems

Being physically active helps build strong bones. But you can hurt your bones if you don't eat enough healthy food to fuel all your activity. That's because your body won't be able to make the hormones needed to build strong bones.

One sign that your bones are weak is getting stress fractures, which are tiny cracks in bones. Some places you could get these cracks are your feet, legs, ribs, and spine.

Even if you don't have problems with your bones when you're young, not taking good care of them now can be a problem later in life. Your skeleton is almost completely formed by age 18, so it's important to build strong bones early in life. If you don't, then later on you could wind up with osteoporosis, which is a disease that makes it easier for bones to break.

## Signs of Not Eating Enough and Eating Disorders

Sometimes, girls exercise a lot and do not eat enough because they want to lose weight. Sometimes, exercising just lowers a person's appetite. And sometimes limiting food can be a sign that a girl may be developing an eating disorder. Here are some signs that you or a friend may have a problem:

- Worrying about gaining weight if you don't exercise enough
- Trying harder to find time to exercise than to eat
- Chewing gum or drinking water to cope with hunger
- Often wanting to exercise rather than be with friends
- Exercising instead of doing homework or other responsibilities
- Getting very upset if you miss a workout, but not if you miss a meal
- Having people tell you they are worried you are losing too much weight

If you think you or a friend has a problem, talk to a parent, guardian, or trusted adult.

**Sometimes girls exercise a lot because they feel pressure to look a certain way.** Soccer star Brandi Chastain knows how bad that can feel. It took a while, she says, for her to realize that only she was in charge of how she felt about her body. "Body image is tough, but it is something we have to take charge of," Brandi says. "Because inside, only we know who we are."

## Amenorrheic Women and the Female Athlete Triad

Amenorrhea, the condition in which menstrual periods stop or fail to initiate in women of childbearing age, results from reduced circulating estrogen levels that, in turn, have a negative effect on calcium balance. Amenorrheic women with anorexia nervosa have decreased calcium absorption and higher urinary calcium excretion rates, as well as a lower rate of bone formation than healthy women. The "female athlete triad" refers to the combination of disordered eating, amenorrhea, and osteoporosis. Exercise-induced amenorrhea generally results in decreased bone mass. In female athletes and active women in the military, low bone-mineral density, menstrual irregularities, certain dietary patterns, and a history of prior stress fractures are associated with an increased risk of future stress fractures. Such women should be advised to consume adequate amounts of calcium and vitamin D. Supplements of these nutrients have been shown to reduce the risk of stress fractures in female Navy recruits during basic training.

# Section 8.3

# Healthy Hydration for Athletes

This section includes text excerpted from documents published by two public domain sources. Text under headings marked 1 are excerpted from "Healthy Foods and Beverages for Youth in Sports," President's Council on Fitness, Sports and Nutrition (PCFSN), May 13, 2016; Text under heading marked 2 is excerpted from "Drinking Water—Water and Nutrition," Centers for Disease Control and Prevention (CDC), October 5, 2016.

## Hydration for Youth Sports[1]

### Water Is the Best Choice

Just like eating the right foods, athletes need to stay hydrated. Drinking fluids before, during, and after activity and sport will prevent dehydration and improve performance and recovery. Athletes should never be thirsty and plain, nonflavored water should always be the first choice. Drinking water is crucial to avoid dehydration in young athletes. A few signs of dehydration include thirst, decreased urine output, dark yellow-colored urine, dry mouth, headaches, irritability, dizziness, and weakness. In addition to preventing dehydration by replacing fluids that have been lost through sweat, water helps with digestion and regulates body temperature. The American Academy of Pediatrics (AAP) recommends athletes be adequately hydrated preactivity and continue to hydrate during and after activity.

## Water and Nutrition[2]

Getting enough water every day is important for your health. Healthy people meet their fluid needs by drinking when thirsty and drinking with meals. Most of your fluid needs are met through the water and beverages you drink. However, you can get some fluids through the foods that you eat. For example, broth soups and foods with high water content such as celery, tomatoes, or melons can contribute to fluid intake.

### Water Helps Your Body

* Keep your temperature normal
* Lubricate and cushion joints
* Protect your spinal cord and other sensitive tissues
* Get rid of wastes through urination, perspiration, and bowel movements

### Your Body Needs More Water When You Are

* In hot climates
* More physically active
* Running a fever
* Having diarrhea or vomiting

### If You Think You Are Not Getting Enough Water, These Tips May Help

* Carry a water bottle for easy access when you are at work of running errands.
* Freeze some freezer safe water bottles. Take one with you for ice-cold water all day long.
* Choose water instead of sugar-sweetened beverages. This can also help with weight management. Substituting water for one 20-ounce sugar sweetened soda will save you about 240 calories. For example, during the school day students should have access to drinking water, giving them a healthy alternative to sugar-sweetened beverages.
* Choose water when eating out. Generally, you will save money and reduce calories.
* Add a wedge of lime or lemon to your water. This can help improve the taste and help you drink more water than you usually do.

**Table 8.2.** Amount of Water Recommended before, during, and after Activity

| Amount of Water Recommended before, during, and after Activity | |
|---|---|
| **Before Activity** | Drink 2–3 cups (16–24 ounces) of water two to three hours before activity |
| **During Activity** | About ½–1 cup (~3–8 ounces) of water every 20 minutes for 9–12 year old athletes and up to 4–6 cups (~34–50 ounces) per hour of water for adolescent athletes and those who sweat excessively. |
| **After Activity** | Drink 2–3 cups (16–24 ounces) of water after activity for every pound of body weight lost. |

*(Source: "Healthy Foods and Beverages for Youth in Sports," President's Council on Fitness, Sports and Nutrition (PCFSN).)*

## What about Sports Drinks?[1]

Sports drinks are heavily targeted to youth as a performance enhancer. Sports drinks are designed to replace lost fluid and electrolytes and provide additional carbohydrates for energy. However, they contain extra calories, added sugars, and sodium that many young athletes do not need. If an athlete has been exercising for more than an hour and/or in hot and humid temperatures, sports drinks may be warranted. Otherwise, hydrating with plain water is the ideal choice.

Chapter 9

# Drug Use among Athletes

## Chapter Contents

# Section 9.1

# *Impact of Drugs on Athletes*

This section includes text excerpted from "The Coach's
Playbook against Drugs," U.S. Department of
Justice (DOJ), n.d. Reviewed June 2017.

## *On Why Players Use Drugs?*

Athletes can be overwhelmed by pressure:

• Pressure to win.

• Pressure to perform well.

• Pressure to maintain a "cool" image.

Some athletes turn to drugs, including alcohol, to relieve stress and
feel good. When athletes use alcohol or other drugs, they may achieve
this goal by feeling an initial "high." Other times, players turn to drugs
to sustain a good feeling. Coming off the field after a winning game, for
example, athletes may try to prolong that winning feeling by turning
to a mind-altering drug. On the other hand, if their team has lost the
game, they may want to replace depressed feelings with a "high" from
a mood-altering drug.

## *On How Drugs Really Affect Athletes?*

As you know, using drugs will not relieve stress or allow a game
high to last forever. By clearing up players' misconceptions about the
effects of drugs and explaining how drugs really affect our bodies, you
may be able to keep the team drug free. In particular, explain that:

• Drugs may make players feel good initially, but that the good
feelings are typically followed by unpleasant ones. Drugs don't
solve problems; they create problems and make coping with them
even harder. Drugs don't make stress go away; they create stress.

• Drugs will not enhance performance on the playing field. With
the possible exception of one type of drug—anabolic steroids—it

80

is simply not true that using drugs will enhance players' performance.

* Drugs actually interfere with an athlete's physical and mental ability. And, even though steroids may improve short-term performance, the physical side effects and emotional damage they cause far outweigh any gains.

## You Can Keep Your Team Drug Free

The "do's and don'ts" below are commonsense guidelines for handling situations that you are likely to encounter at one time or another.

**Don't—**

Pretend that you did not hear an athlete discussing plans for a party that will involve alcohol or drugs.

**Do—**

Immediately address the problem with the athlete and tell him or her that the plans are inappropriate and unacceptable for any member of the team. Tell the athlete that you are concerned and that you care. Ask if he or she needs any help. Tell him or her that drug use weakens an athlete's body and increases the risk of motor vehicle and other accidents.

**Don't—**

Choose to ignore the smell of marijuana.

**Do—**

Confront the athlete immediately. Make sure that he or she knows that you know. If you fail to act, the athlete may assume that this behavior is OK or that you don't care. Explain that marijuana is illegal and that the athlete can be arrested or suspended from school and sports for using it.

**Don't—**

Avoid enforcing rules—or enforce them selectively.

**Do—**

Be firm, set limits, and stick to them. Be sure that the rules you set are helpful in changing an athlete's behavior. Don't alienate or stigmatize athletes; engage them in the rulemaking.

**Don't—**

Ignore drug use because the team "needs" a particular athlete to play.

**Do—**

Set rules and enforce them consistently. Once you look away, team morale will suffer, as will your moral leadership. By opting to look the other way, you also fail in your responsibility to the athlete. If he or she gets hurt, how will you feel? Emphasize that the same rules apply to all team members and that you have a responsibility to enforce rules consistently.

**Don't—**

Ignore drug use by the coaching staff.

**Do—**

Ensure that everyone on your staff sets a good example. Your players will heed not just what you say, but what you do.

## Key Plays—How to Get Your Message Across

- Encourage participation in athletics by making your team an integral and exciting part of school or community life.

- Clearly express your expectation that players will not use drugs.

- Ensure that the players know the risks of drug use, especially those that affect athletic performance and their future.

- Emphasize the benefits of participating in sports, particularly benefits that young people care about, including:

  - Gaining the respect of peers.

  - Sharing new and exciting experiences with close friends.

  - Earning the respect and trust of parents and siblings.

  - Setting a good example for others (especially younger siblings).

  - Having a strong sense of self-worth and self-respect.

  - Increasing control over one's life and its direction.

  - Achieving personal growth and progress toward one's goals.

- Make sure the players know that drug use among preteens and early teens (ages 11 to 14) is a "fringe" behavior.

- Encourage athletes to set personal goals and assist them in making progress toward those goals.

- Have older players reinforce the idea that real "cool" kids don't use drugs—they disapprove of them.

- Help young people to develop appropriate decision making skills.

- Let players know that they can talk to you about their fears and concerns regarding drug use.

- Develop meaningful relationships with the young people.

## Effects of Using Drugs

### The Game Will Be Affected

Sports were designed to be a fun and competitive way to gain exercise. They were not designed to include drug use. Communicate the serious effect of drugs on the game by asking the players to guess how their foul shots, field goals, or home runs would be affected by drugs. To put it simply, they won't happen. Scientific studies show that drugs impair coordination and abilities. How does this translate on the athletic field?

- A basketball player using drugs is more likely to miss a game-winning free throw.

- A football receiver using marijuana is less likely to outrun a defender. Speed, lung capacity, muscle strength, and stamina all can drop with marijuana use.

- A skier using drugs likewise dramatically increases his or her chances of suffering a career-ending injury.

If a player's performance is weak because of drug use, the player will have to live knowing that he or she has disappointed the team, the coach, and others—all for a few minutes of a false high.

### Team Spirit Will Suffer

Drugs negatively affect not only a team's performance, but its sense of team spirit and cohesiveness as well. In particular, drug use can cause the following effects on the morale of the team:

- Lack of togetherness.

- Lack of concentration.
- Lack of commitment.
- Lack of energy.
- Lack of trust.

## Section 9.2

# *Steroids as Performance-Enhancing Substances*

This section includes text excerpted from "Anabolic Steroids,"
National Institute on Drug Abuse (NIDA), March 2016.

### *What Are Anabolic Steroids?*

Anabolic steroids are synthetic variations of the male sex hormone testosterone. The proper term for these compounds is anabolic-androgenic steroids. "Anabolic" refers to muscle building, and "androgenic" refers to increased male sex characteristics. Some common names for anabolic steroids are Gear, Juice, Roids, and Stackers.

Healthcare providers can prescribe steroids to treat hormonal issues, such as delayed puberty. Steroids can also treat diseases that cause muscle loss, such as cancer and Acquired Immunodeficiency Syndrome (AIDS). But some athletes and bodybuilders abuse these drugs to boost performance or improve their physical appearance.

### *How Do People Abuse Anabolic Steroids?*

People who abuse anabolic steroids usually take them orally or inject them into the muscles. These doses may be 10 to 100 times higher than doses prescribed to treat medical conditions. Steroids are also applied to the skin as a cream, gel, or patch.

Some athletes and others who abuse steroids believe that they can avoid unwanted side effects or maximize the drugs' effects by taking them in ways that include:

- cycling—taking doses for a period of time, stopping for a time, and then restarting

- stacking—combining two or more different types of steroids

- pyramiding—slowly increasing the dose or frequency of abuse, reaching a peak amount, and then gradually tapering off

There is no scientific evidence that any of these practices reduce the harmful medical consequences of these drugs.

## How Do Anabolic Steroids Affect the Brain?

Anabolic steroids work differently from other drugs of abuse; they do not have the same short-term effects on the brain. The most important difference is that steroids do not trigger rapid increases in the brain chemical dopamine, which causes the "high" that drives people to abuse other substances. However, long-term steroid abuse can act on some of the same brain pathways and chemicals—including dopamine, serotonin, and opioid systems—that are affected by other drugs. This may result in a significant effect on mood and behavior.

### Short-Term Effects

Abuse of anabolic steroids may lead to mental problems, such as:

- paranoid (extreme, unreasonable) jealousy

- extreme irritability

- delusions—false beliefs or ideas

- impaired judgment

Extreme mood swings can also occur, including "roid rage"—angry feelings and behavior that may lead to violence.

## What Are the Other Health Effects of Anabolic Steroids?

Aside from mental problems, steroid use commonly causes severe acne. It also causes the body to swell, especially in the hands and feet.

### Long-Term Effects

Anabolic steroid abuse may lead to serious, even permanent, health problems such as:

- kidney problems or failure

85

- liver damage
- enlarged heart, high blood pressure, and changes in blood cholesterol, all of which increase the risk of stroke and heart attack, even in young people

Several other effects are gender- and age-specific:

- In men:
  - shrinking testicles
  - decreased sperm count
  - baldness
  - development of breasts
  - increased risk for prostate cancer
- In women:
  - growth of facial hair or excess body hair
  - male-pattern baldness
  - changes in or stop in the menstrual cycle
  - enlarged clitoris
  - deepened voice
- In teens:
  - stunted growth (when high hormone levels from steroids signal to the body to stop bone growth too early)
  - stunted height (if teens use steroids before their growth spurt)

Some of these physical changes, such as shrinking sex organs in men, can add to mental side effects such as mood disorders.

## Are Anabolic Steroids Addictive?

Even though anabolic steroids do not cause the same high as other drugs, they can lead to addiction. Studies have shown that animals will self-administer steroids when they have the chance, just as they do with other addictive drugs. People may continue to abuse steroids despite physical problems, high costs to buy the drugs, and negative effects on their relationships. These behaviors reflect steroids' addictive potential. Research has further found that some steroid users turn to other drugs, such as opioids, to reduce sleep problems and irritability caused by steroids.

People who abuse steroids may experience withdrawal symptoms when they don't use, including:

- mood swings

- fatigue

- restlessness

- loss of appetite

- sleep problems

- decreased sex drive

- steroid cravings

One of the more serious withdrawal symptoms is depression, which can sometimes lead to suicide attempts.

## How Can People Get Treatment for Anabolic Steroid Addiction?

Some people seeking treatment for anabolic steroid addiction have found behavioral therapy to be helpful. More research is needed to identify the most effective treatment options. In certain cases of severe addiction, patients have taken medicines to help treat symptoms of withdrawal. For example, healthcare providers have prescribed antidepressants to treat depression and pain medicines for headaches and muscle and joint pain. Other medicines have been used to help restore the patient's hormonal system.

# Part Two

# Preventing Sports Injuries

Chapter 10

# Sports Injury Prevention and First Aid Treatment

## Prevention of Sports Injury

Individuals play sports for a variety of reasons: to stay fit, control weight, prevent disease, or to improve their mental wellbeing. However participating in a sport carries with it the chance of injury, with injuries to the muscles and bones being the most common. Therefore, it is important to understand how sports injuries can be prevented before they occur and how their impact can be minimized if they do happen.

Injury prevention in sports takes place on three levels:

- **Level 1:** Early prevention focused on strategies that educate athletes and prepare them to successfully participate in a sport. This includes suitable training and conditioning, appropriate equipment, a thorough understanding of the sport's rules, and the overall commitment of coaches, referees, and teammates to safe play.

- **Level 2:** If an injury does occur, early detection and treatment of that injury can prevent it from progressing to a more serious stage.

"Sports Injury Prevention and First Aid Treatment," © 2017 Omnigraphics. Reviewed June 2017.

- **Level 3:** Preventing an injury's recurrence by implementing a targeted rehabilitation program and specific preventive measures, such as a warm up regime or the use of a protective brace.

## Risk Factors in Sports Injuries

- Muscle tightness: The length of a muscle plays a major role in athletics. A tight muscle puts a significant load on the surrounding structures such as bones and ligaments. At the same time, a highly flexible muscle is not always desirable since it may not provide adequate support. A fine balance between flexibility and tightness is essential for the prevention of sports injuries.

- Muscle weakness: Muscle weakness is a risk factor in overuse injuries rather than acute sports injuries. Adequate strength training and conditioning are key to building muscle strength.

- Joint instability: When the tissues around a joint, such as a knee or a shoulder, are weak, the joint can be prone to slipping out of place. A traumatic injury, such as a hit or a fall, can then cause a dislocation. Chronic overuse can also aggravate joint instability.

- Physical fitness: An appropriate level of overall physical fitness for a particular sport is essential as a means of preventing injuries.

- Sport-specific skills and techniques: The athlete must develop specific skills and proper techniques required for the sport. Good technique will enhance the athlete in utilizing the ground reaction force and proper dissipation of that force. Poor skills and techniques are major predisposing factor for sports injuries as it increases stress on the muscles, tendons, ligaments, and bones.

- Level of competition: Players may get exposed to greater levels of injury as they progress to various levels of competition, putting higher demands on themselves and pushing their mind and body to their limits.

- Poor posture: Bad posture results in complex compensatory mechanisms causing structural malalignment and imbalance. This will put lot of undue stress on the soft tissues like muscles, ligaments, and bones.

- Overtraining: Overtraining causes muscle fatigue. When physical demands of sport are placed on the fatigued muscle, it may result in poor muscular response and injuries.

- Injury profile of the sport: Certain sport, because of its nature, involves certain risk of injuries when compared to other sports. For example, contact sports like boxing have high risk of injuries when compared to noncontact sports.

- Protective equipment: Poor quality and improper size of the protective equipment put the athlete at a greater risk for sports injuries.

## Strategies of Prevention

- Warm up: Taking the time to warm up before playing is an essential strategy for preventing sports injuries. Performing light aerobics, for example walking or jogging around the field, helps loosen muscles and increases blood flow. Stretching exercises and sport-specific drills will also help athletes be more flexible.

- Cool down: Cooling down allow athletes to transition and recover from intense exertion, preventing muscle cramps and dizziness. Like warming up, cooling down usually consists of light aerobics and gentle stretching.

- Sports massage: Massage therapy that is targeted to the needs of specific athletes and sports can increase flexibility and aid in recovery from some sports injuries.

- Preparation: The risk of injury can also be minimized if athletes commit to a training schedule that helps them to build and maintain their skill and strength. Sharpening sport-specific abilities can also be key to avoiding an injury.

- Playing by the rules: Athletes, coaches, referees, and umpires must adhere to and enforce the rules of the game to keep players safe. For children, making sure competition is realistic is important as well.

- Environment: Extremes of heat and cold as well as high altitude can result in a range of issues, including dehydration, frostbite, or altitude sickness. Proper preparation, such as staying hydrated throughout a game, and acclimatization can keep athletes out of danger. Sporting surfaces also should be considered.

- Equipment: Sports equipment should be of good quality, correctly fitted, comfortable, and appropriate.

## First Aid for Sports Injuries

Sporting emergencies can be divided into 3 categories:

1. Trauma to a previously well athlete. This may include a sprain, break, or concussion.

2. Aggravation of a previously recognized medical problem, such as heart disease, asthma, or diabetes.

3. Onset of a previously unrecognized medical problem (for example, heart attack).

## Emergency Preparedness

Adequate preparation and proper medical coverage of a sporting event are essential for handling any emergencies.

## Equipment

The following equipment should be a part of an available emergency kit:

- Ice packs/cold water
- Compression bandages
- Splints, collars, crutches, and slings
- Light, strong stretcher
- Basic supply of medicines
- Oxygen supply and mask
- Equipment for cardiopulmonary resuscitation (CPR)

## Treatment

Once responders reach the injured athlete on the field, a quick assessment of the circulation, airway and breathing has to be made.

A conscious athlete should be checked via his or her response to questions. If the athlete has collapsed and does not appear to be breathing, responders should first call 911 and then initiate cardiopulmonary resuscitation (CPR).

If the responder is untrained in CPR, they can administer 100–120 uninterrupted chest compressions a minute until paramedics arrive.

If the person is trained in CPR, after 30 chest compressions, a head-tilt, chin-lift maneuver can be done to clear and open the airway. Following the 30 chest compressions, 2 rescue breaths can be given mouth-to-mouth or mouth-to-nose if the mouth is seriously injured or can't be opened.

## Acute Soft Tissue Injuries

Once the cause of the injury is determined, the main objective of first aid treatment for any soft tissue injury is to prevent, stop, and reduce swelling. The swelling will cause pain and loss of motion, which will limit the use of the muscles.

To control swelling, the PRICE (Protection, Rest, Ice, Compression, and Elevation) method should be used as a part of the first aid treatment:

- Protection—The athlete should sit out any further action and the injury protected from further aggravation.

- Rest—The injured part like upper or lower limb should be immobilized using an external support (slings, splints or crutches), and any activities that worsen the injury should be suspended.

- Ice—Ice causes the blood vessels to constrict, thereby limiting swelling at the injury site. Ice can be applied every two hours for no more than 20 minutes at a time. The skin temperature should return to normal before icing again.

- Compression—Compression involves wrapping the injured body part with an elastic bandage or wrap. This is very important as it quickly helps keep swelling to a minimum. If possible, apply ice to the injured area over the compression wrap to limit the swelling.

- Elevation—Elevating the injured area helps in reducing the blood flow and swelling to the area, as gravity assists in draining the excess collection of fluid.

Depending on the extent of the injury, the athlete should be sent to a hospital or a doctor's office as early as possible to prevent further complications and damage.

## References

1. "Sports Injury First Aid Treatment," Verywell.com, 2016.

2. "Cardiopulmonary resuscitation (CPR): First aid," Mayo Clinic, 2006.

Chapter 11

# Protective Equipment
# for Athletes

## Chapter Contents

Section 11.1

*Athletic Shoes*

Text in this section is excerpted from "Selecting Running
Shoes," © 2014 American College of Sports Medicine.
Reprinted with permission.

Running shoes should be selected after careful consideration. With
so many brands and styles of shoes on the market today, it is important to find the best fit for your feet and your needs. There is no "right
shoe" that fits all runners. However, research and injury patterns
have shown that there are some general characteristics of a good, safe
running shoe.

A running shoe should protect the feet against injury, but
should not do the work of the foot by providing excessive cushioning and lots of extra support in the arch. A shoe should com-
plement a strong foot. With new companies and shoe options on
the market, you can do a bit of research online to find the types
of shoes that may interest you. Review the specifications on shoe
material, weight and heel to toe drop to find brands that follow
the general guidelines below.

### Characteristics of a Good, Safe Running Shoe Include

• Minimal heel-to-toe drop: This drop is the difference in the
  thickness of the heel cushion to the thickness in the forefoot
  cushion area. Shoes with no drop or a small drop 6mm or less
  are the best choice for allowing the foot to normally support
  loading during each gait cycle

• Neutral: This means the shoe does not contain motion control
  or stability components. These extra components interfere with
  normal foot motion during weight bearing.

• Light in weight: (10 ounces or less for a men's size 9; 8 ounces or
  less for women's size 8)

# Where Can You Look for Running Shoes?

Check in with a local running club and ask the leadership where their members commonly purchase shoes, or which merchants have knowledgeable staff who have expertise with running shoes.

## How to Buy a Running Shoe

- Every time you shop for running shoes, have your feet sized in the store. Be aware that you may have different sized right and left feet. For some runners, buying shoes of slightly different sizes may be best. Forcing a shoe that is too tight on one foot will cause foot pain over time.

- Foot shape or arch height are not good indicators of what kind of running shoe to buy.

- Avoid buying shoes based on advice given after someone in a store has watched you walk. Your gait and foot motion are very different when you walk and run.

- Be aware that all runners pronate, or drop the foot inward. Pronation is a normal foot motion during walking and running. Pronation alone should not be a reason to select a running shoe. Runners may be told while shopping that because pronation is occurring, a shoe with arch support is best. In fact, the opposite may be true. Pronation should occur and is a natural shock absorber. Stopping pronation with materials in the shoes may actually cause foot or knee problems to develop. Excessive pronation can occur, but in most cases can be corrected with therapy and exercises to strengthen the foot, leg and hip rather than by a shoe.

- Buy running shoes at the end of the day when your feet have 'swollen' as much as they will and the shoes will not feel tight.

- Be sure the shoe has a wide toe box. The toe box is the area where your forefoot and toes are. You should be able to wiggle your toes easily. Narrow toe boxes do not permit the normal splay, or spread of the foot bones during running. This will prevent your feet from being able to safely distribute the forces during the loading phase of gait.

- There should be at least ½ inch of room between the toes and front of shoe, about enough space to place your thumb between your big toe and the front of the shoe.

- Test the shoe to determine if it is too narrow: take the insert out of the shoes and step on them on the ground. Does your foot hang over the sides of the insert? If so, your shoe is too narrow.

- When you test running in the shoe, be sure that the heel does not slip.

## Shoe Qualities to Avoid

- High, thick cushioning: Soft cushioning may actually encourage runners to adopt worse biomechanics and land with greater impact than shoes with less cushioning.

- Shoes that have a high heel cushion and low forefoot cushion (a "high profile shoe", or a high heel to toe drop)

- Extra arch support inserts or store based orthotics. These items are often not necessary. Orthotics should be considered temporary fixes (<6-8 weeks) until foot strength is increased. A therapist can help you with exercises that can strengthen the foot so that you do not need arch supports on a daily basis.

## Transition from Old to New Shoe

Be aware that when you change from one shoe to another, there should be a transition period in which you may need to wear the new shoes for part of a run. Over a couple weeks, the time wearing the new shoe can increase until the entire run is performed with the new shoe.

Exercises to increase foot and hip strength should be done before and as you transition to the new shoe. When initially exercising in shoes with minimal drop, the lower extremities will need to adapt by activating muscles in the hip and gluteal (buttock) area. There may be some initial soreness in these muscle areas for the first couple of weeks.

If you are switching from a shoe with a high heel-to-toe drop to a shoe with a low or zero drop, consider using a transition shoe with a moderate heel-to-toe drop for a few months while you adapt; after this adaptation, then switch to the shoe with minimal or zero drop.

## When Should You Buy New Running Shoes?

- A general rule of thumb is to purchase new shoes for every 350 miles, but limited science has not identified the ideal time frame for all running shoes. Different shoes will vary in wear based on what materials they are made from, and whether the shoes are used for more than running. Faster wear may occur if the shoes are used for other activities on a daily basis than if they were used for running alone.

- If there are wear patterns on the shoe that reveal the sole layers underneath, discard the shoes. Uneven wear on the shoe sole causes changes in running mechanics that lead to injury.

# Section 11.2

# *Helmets*

This section contains text excerpted from the following sources: Text beginning with the heading "Why Are Helmets So Important?" is excerpted from "Which Helmet for Which Activity?" U.S. Consumer Product Safety Commission (CPSC), May 16, 2014; Text beginning with the heading "Your Child's or Teen's Helmet" is excerpted from "Heads up—Helmet Safety," Centers for Disease Control and Prevention (CDC), February 16, 2015.

## Why Are Helmets So Important?

For many recreational activities, wearing a helmet can reduce the risk of a severe head injury and even save your life.

## How Does a Helmet Protect My Head?

During a typical fall or collision, much of the impact energy is absorbed by the helmet, rather than your head and brain.

## Does This Mean That Helmets Prevent Concussions?

No. No helmet design has been proven to prevent concussions. The materials that are used in most of today's helmets are engineered to

101

absorb the high impact energies that can produce skull fractures and severe brain injuries. However, these materials have not been proven to counteract the energies believed to cause concussions. Beware of claims that a particular helmet can reduce or prevent concussions.

To protect against concussion injury, play smart. Learn the signs and symptoms of a concussion so that after a fall or collision, you can recognize the symptoms, get proper treatment, and prevent additional injury.

## Are All Helmets the Same?

No. There are different helmets for different activities. Each type of helmet is made to protect your head from the kind of impacts that typically are associated with a particular activity or sport. Be sure to wear a helmet that is appropriate for the particular activity you're involved in. Helmets designed for other activities may not protect your head as effectively.

## How Can I Tell Which Helmet Is the Right One to Use?

There are safety standards for most types of helmets. Bicycle and motorcycle helmets must comply with mandatory federal safety standards. Helmets for many other recreational activities are subject to voluntary safety standards.

Helmets that meet the requirements of a mandatory or voluntary safety standard are designed and tested to protect the user from receiving a skull fracture or severe brain injury while wearing the helmet. For example, all bicycle helmets manufactured after 1999 must meet the U.S. Consumer Product Safety Commission (CPSC) bicycle helmet standard (16 C.F.R. part 1203); helmets meeting this standard provide protection against skull fractures and severe brain injuries when the helmet is used properly.

The protection that the appropriate helmet can provide is dependent upon achieving a proper fit and wearing it correctly; for many activities, chin straps are specified in the standard, and they are essential for the helmet to function properly. For example, the bicycle standard requires that chin straps be strong enough to keep the helmet on the head and in the proper position during a fall or collision.

Helmets that meet a particular standard will contain a special label or marking that indicates compliance with that standard (usually found on the liner inside of the helmet, on the exterior surface, or attached to the chin strap). Don't rely solely on the helmet's name or appearance, or claims made on the packaging, to determine whether the helmet meets the appropriate requirements for your activity.

Don't choose style over safety. When choosing a helmet, avoid helmets that contain nonessential elements that protrude from the helmet (e.g., horns, Mohawks)—these may look interesting, but they may prevent the helmet's smooth surface from sliding after a fall, which could lead to injury.

Don't add anything to the helmet, such as stickers, coverings, or other attachments that aren't provided with the helmet, as such items can negatively affect the helmet's performance.

Avoid novelty and toy helmets that are made only to look like the real thing; such helmets are not made to comply with any standard and can be expected to offer little or no protection.

## Are There Helmets That I Can Wear for More than One Activity?

Yes, but only a few. For example, you can wear a United States Consumer Product Safety Commission (CPSC)-compliant bicycle helmet while bicycling, recreational in-line skating or roller skating, or riding a kick scooter.

## Are There Any Activities for Which One Should Not Wear a Helmet?

Yes. Children should not wear a helmet when playing on playgrounds or climbing trees. If a child wears a helmet during these activities, the helmet's chin strap can get caught on the equipment or tree branches and pose a risk of strangulation. The helmet may also prevent a child's head from moving through an opening that the body can fit through, and entrap the child by his/her head.

## How Can I Tell If My Helmet Fits Properly?

A helmet should be both comfortable and snug. Be sure that the helmet is worn so that it is level on your head—not tilted back on the top of your head or pulled too low over your forehead. Once on your head, the helmet should not move in any direction, back-to-front or side-to-side. For helmets with a chin strap, be sure the chin strap is securely fastened so that the helmet doesn't move or fall off during a fall or collision.

103

If you buy a helmet for a child, bring the child with you so that the helmet can be tested for a good fit. Carefully examine the helmet and the accompanying instructions and safety literature.

## What Can I Do If I Have Trouble Fitting the Helmet?

Depending on the type of helmet, you may have to apply the foam padding that comes with the helmet, adjust the straps, adjust the air bladders, or make other adjustments specified by the manufacturer. If these adjustments do not work, consult with the store where you bought the helmet or with the helmet manufacturer. Do not add extra padding or parts, or make any adjustments that are not specifically outlined in the manufacturer's instructions. Do not wear a helmet that does not fit correctly.

## Will I Need to Replace a Helmet after an Impact?

That depends on the severity of the impact and whether the helmet was designed to withstand one impact (a single-impact helmet) or more than one impact (a multiple-impact helmet). For example, bicycle helmets are designed to protect against the impact from just a single fall, such as a bicyclist's fall onto the pavement. The foam material in the helmet will crush to absorb the impact energy during a fall or collision. The materials will not protect you again from an additional impact. Even if there are no visible signs of damage to the helmet, you must replace it after such an event.

Other helmets are designed to protect against multiple impacts. Two examples are football and ice hockey helmets. These helmets are designed to withstand multiple impacts of the type associated with the respective activities. However, you may still have to replace the helmet after one severe impact if the helmet has visible signs of damage, such as a cracked shell or permanent dent in the shell or liner. Consult the manufacturer's instructions or certification stickers on the helmet for guidance on when the helmet should be replaced.

## How Long Are Helmets Supposed to Last?

Follow the guidance provided by the manufacturer. In the absence of such guidance, it may be prudent to replace your helmet within 5–10 years of purchase, a decision that can be based, at least in part, on how much the helmet was used, how it was cared for, and where it was stored. Cracks in the shell or liner, a loose shell, marks on the liner, fading of the shell, evidence of crushed foam in the liner, worn straps, and missing pads or other parts, are all reasons to replace a helmet. Regular replacement may minimize any reduced effectiveness that could result from degradation of materials over time, and allow you to take advantage of recent advances in helmet protection.

### Child's or Teen's Helmet Safety

A child's helmet should fit properly and be:

- Well maintained

- Age appropriate

- Worn consistently and correctly

- Appropriately certified for use

While there is no concussion-proof helmet, a helmet can help protect the child or teen from a serious brain or head injury. Even with a helmet, it is important for the child or teen to avoid hits to the head.

# Section 11.3

# Eye Protection

This section contains text excerpted from the following sources:
Text beginning with the heading "Sports and Protective Eyewear" is excerpted from "About Sports Eye Injury and Protective Eyewear," National Eye Institute (NEI), March 26, 2008. Reviewed June 2017; Text under the heading "Sports-Specific Risk" is excerpted from "Sport-Specific Risk," National Eye Institute (NEI), June 2, 2008. Reviewed June 2017; Text under the heading "Protective Eyewear" is excerpted from "Protective Eyewear," National Eye Institute (NEI), June 16, 2016.

### Sports and Protective Eyewear

Parents and coaches play an important role in making sure young athletes protect their eyes and properly gear up for the game. Protective eyewear should be part of any uniform because it plays such an important role in reducing sports-related eye injury.

Eye injuries are the leading cause of blindness in children in the United States and most injuries occurring in school-aged children are sports-related.

Ninety percent of sports-related eye injuries can be avoided with the use of protective eyewear. Protective eyewear includes safety glasses and goggles, safety shields, and eye guards designed for a particular sport. Ordinary prescription glasses, contact lenses, and sunglasses do not protect against eye injuries. Safety goggles should be worn over them.

Most youth sports leagues do not require the use of eye protection. Parents and coaches must insist that children wear safety glasses or goggles whenever they play.

Protective eyewear, which is made of ultra-strong polycarbonate, is 10 times more impact resistant than other plastics, and does not reduce vision. All children who play sports should use protective eyewear—not just those who wear eyeglasses or contact lenses. For children who do wear glasses or contact lenses, most protective eyewear can be made to match their prescriptions. It is especially important for student athletes who have vision in only one eye or a history of eye injury or eye surgery to use protective eyewear.

Whether you are a parent, teacher, or coach, you can encourage schools to adopt a policy on protective eyewear. Meanwhile, parents and coaches should insist that children wear protective eyewear whenever they play sports and be good role models and wear it themselves.

## Sports-Specific Risk

Some sports carry a greater risk than others. For example, baseball is the leading cause of sports-related eye injury in children 14 and under and is considered high risk. Football carries a moderate risk.

High Risk:

- Baseball
- Basketball
- Boxing
- Hockey

- Paintball
- Racquetball
- Softball
- Squash

Moderate Risk:

- Badminton

- Fishing

- Football
- Golf

- Soccer
- Tennis

Low Risk:

- Bicycling
- Diving
- Skiing

- Swimming
- Wrestling

## Protective Eyewear

Whether you're on the basketball court, in chemistry class, or sitting by the pool, wearing protective eyewear is the best way to keep your eyes healthy and injury-free. In fact, the majority of eye injuries can be prevented by wearing the right protective eyewear. Check out the list of activities below to see what you need to protect your eyes.

**Play BasketBall or Soccer:** Wear sports goggles with polycarbonate lenses.

**Going for a bike ride:** Always wear a helmet. You'll also want sunglasses or glasses with clear lenses to protect your eyes from the wind and any bugs.

**Play baseball:** If you're up to bat, wear a helmet with an attached faceguard. If you're fielding, wear sports goggles.

**Swimming or playing water sports:** Wear swim goggles to protect your eyes from dirt, germs and bacteria, and pool chemicals.

**Spending time in the sun:** Wear your sunglasses. They protect your eyes from the sun's ultraviolet (UV) rays, which can damage your eyes. Pick sunglasses that block 99% or 100% of both UVA and UVB radiation.

**Are you a paintball pro:** Always wear your paintball goggles or mask.

**Play ice hockey:** You need a face mask or polycarbonate guard that's attached to a helmet.

**Are you a football player:** Always wear your helmet with an attached face shield.

**Play lacrosse:** Girls need protective goggles but have the option to wear headgear with full face protection. Boys are required to wear a helmet with a full face mask. So are goalies, regardless of whether you're a boy or a girl.

**Into field hockey:** Goalies need helmets with a full face mask. All other players should wear sports goggles. Girls' lacrosse goggles also work for field hockey.

**Into a racquet sport like squash or racquetball:** Wear sports goggles with polycarbonate lenses.

Chapter 12

# Sports Safety Tips

## Chapter Contents

# Section 12.1

# *Baseball*

Text in this section is © 1995-2017. The Nemours
Foundation/KidsHealth®. Reprinted with permission.

There's a reason why baseball has been called our national pastime for decades. It's as American as hot dogs and apple pie. It's been a summer tradition in big cities and little towns across the U.S.A. for generations. It's a great team sport, and it's fun.

## Why Baseball Safety Is Important

Baseball is by no means a dangerous sport. But it can present a very real risk of injuries from things like wild pitches, batted balls, and collisions in the field.

At the high-school level, some pitchers can throw fastballs that reach 80-plus miles per hour, speedy enough to cause painful welts, broken bones, even concussions. Excessive pitching and improper throwing mechanics can lead to major league arm problems, and base runners and fielders frequently collide while running at top speed.

## Gear Guidelines

As with all sports, wearing and using the right gear can go a long way toward preventing injuries. The amount of equipment required for baseball isn't on par with football or hockey, but it is every bit as important. Players need to be sure they always have all the gear required by their league.

Most leagues will insist on the following:

- Batting helmets must be worn whenever a player is at bat, waiting to bat, or running the bases. Some leagues may even require pitchers to wear them. Helmets should always fit properly and be worn correctly. If the helmet has a chin strap, it should be fastened, and if the helmet has an eye shield or other faceguard, this should be in good condition, securely attached to the helmet.

- A catcher should always wear a helmet, facemask, throat guard, full-length chest protector, athletic supporter with a cup, shin guards and a catcher's mitt whenever they are catching pitches, whether it's in the game, in the bullpen or during warm-ups.

- Baseball spikes should have molded plastic cleats rather than metal ones. Most youth leagues don't allow spikes with metal cleats.

- Some leagues have guidelines dictating what kind of bat a player can use. Some aluminum bats may be banned for hitting batted balls too hard. Be sure to check the league's policy before choosing a bat.

- All players should wear athletic supporters; most, particularly pitchers and infielders, should wear protective cups. Rules regarding which players must wear cups vary from league to league.

- Additional gear that some players like includes sliding pants, which are meant to go under baseball pants to protect against scrapes and cuts; batting gloves, which can keep hands from getting sore while hitting; shin and foot guards, which are designed to protect against balls fouled straight down; and mouthguards.

## Breakaway Bases

Base paths are one of the most common places injuries happen. This is especially true when players slide into a traditional stationary base, which puts a rigid obstacle in their path as they slide. Sliding into a fixed base can result in foot, ankle, and lower-leg injuries.

As a result, doctors have started recommending that leagues install breakaway bases in all of their playing fields. These bases, which snap onto grommets on an anchored rubber mat, can be dislodged when a runner slides into one, lessening the chances that a base runner will get injured. During the course of normal base-running, the base is stable and does not detach.

## Before Starting the Game

Ideally, kids should get plenty of exercise before the season begins and be in the best shape possible before swinging a bat for the first time. This will not only lower the risk of injury, but it will also make them better ballplayers.

Just as with any other sport, warming up and stretching before a baseball game is very important. However, remember that in baseball, kids should pay particular attention to their throwing arm. Most will require plenty of warm-up before they can safely attempt a long, hard throw.

Different players have different preferences when it comes to warming up their arms. Some like to make short throws, while others prefer to start with long, easy tosses. Regardless of how a player chooses to warm up, the idea is to start with soft throws meant to stretch muscles and loosen up joints. As the arm warms up, the intensity of throws should be gradually increased until the player is throwing as he or she would during a game situation. Make sure that all bats, balls, and other equipment used during warm-ups are safely put away before play begins, and always inspect the playing field for holes and debris, especially broken glass.

## During Game Play

Painful collisions can and do occur in baseball. With attention focused on the ball, it's easy to lose track of where people are. If there's any doubt as to who should field a ball, one player should call for it as loudly as he or she can to let the others know to back away. Players should practice doing this with teammates to get used to listening for each other's voices.

While batting, it's important for kids to stand confidently in the batter's box and not be afraid of the ball. That being said, baseballs are hard objects. Getting hit with a pitch hurts. Kids should know how to safely get out of the way if a pitch is headed toward them. The best way to do this is to duck and turn away from the pitcher, exposing the back and rear end to the pitch instead of the face and midsection.

On the base paths, players should practice running the bases with their heads up, looking out for other players and batted balls. They should also know how to slide correctly. Many leagues make it illegal for kids to slide headfirst, as this can lead to head injuries and facial cuts.

## Excessive Pitching

Pitching, particularly for adolescent arms that are still growing, puts an enormous amount of strain on joints and tendons. Injuries to wrists, elbows, rotator cuffs, ligaments, and tendons can result from excessive pitching but can be largely avoided if players and coaches follow a few simple guidelines:

- Make sure pitchers adhere to league rules regarding the maximum number of innings they're allowed to throw. This will generally range from four to 10 innings per week. If a kid plays for more than one team, include all innings pitched each week, not just the ones for each team.

- Most leagues follow rules regarding the number of pitches kids can throw in a game. Keep in mind that even major league pitchers have strict pitch counts to keep their arms healthy. Here are the pitch count limits recommended by U.S.A. Little League and the American Sports Medicine Institute:

  - 7–8 years old: 50 pitches a day or 75 pitches a week

  - 9–10 years old: 75 pitches a day or 100 pitches a week

  - 11–12 years old: 85 pitches a day or 115 pitches a week

  - 13–16 years old: 95 pitches a day

  - 17–18 years old: 105 pitches a day

- Pitchers under 14 should limit total pitches to less than 1,000 per season and 3,000 per year.

- All players should take at least 3 months off per year from overhead sports (i.e., sports that involve a lot of overhead arm movements like baseball or volleyball).

- If pitchers feel persistent pain in their throwing arm, they should not be allowed to pitch again until the pain goes away.

## *A Few Other Reminders*

- Make sure a responsible adult is on hand any time a baseball game is played, whether it's a parent, coach, or umpire. In the event someone gets seriously hurt, an adult should be around to take an injured player to the emergency room.

- Make sure first aid is readily available.

- Steroids or human growth hormones aren't just illegal—they're dangerous.

# Section 12.2

# *Hockey*

Text in this section is © 1995-2017. The Nemours
Foundation/KidsHealth®. Reprinted with permission.

With nonstop action and high-speed team play, hockey is a great sport for kids. Sometimes called "the fastest game on ice," it's a great way to get exercise, and with youth and adult programs throughout the country, chances are no matter what your child's age or skill level, there is a league near you to play in.

As fun as it is, though, hockey carries a very real risk of injury. To keep your kids as safe as possible, follow these tips.

## *Why Hockey Safety Is Important*

At its highest levels, from high school to college to the NHL, hockey allows "checking," an action that involves a player colliding with an opposing player to stop his forward momentum. This can lead to numerous injuries from players hitting one another or colliding with the ice surface or the boards that line the rink. Even in so-called "no-check" leagues, there will always be a lot of contact. Falls are very common, and ice is just as hard as concrete to land on.

In addition, with every player carrying a stick and wearing sharpened skates, accidents are bound to occur. There's also a good chance that sooner or later kids will get hit by the puck, which is made of hard rubber and can leave a nasty bruise if it catches them in the wrong spot. And, since hockey involves strenuous physical activity, pulled muscles and sprains are a hazard for players who don't warm up and stretch properly.

## *Getting in Gear*

Before kids start playing hockey, it's very important to get them all the right equipment and make sure they know how to put it on and use it correctly. Skates and a helmet are a good place to start, but there is a lot more they'll need to wear to keep themselves safe.

Never let your child play a game of hockey without:

- **Helmet**—When it comes to preventing serious injuries, this is the most important piece of equipment. Helmets should be certified by the Hockey Equipment Certification Council (HECC) and should include a full facemask with a protective chin cup and a chin strap. Make sure to get your kids a helmet that fits properly, and insist that they always keep the chin strap fastened and tightened to ensure that the helmet stays in place.

- **Skates**—As with helmets, be sure to get your kids skates that fit well. They're going to lace them up tight, so the wrong size skates can really hurt their feet. Skates should offer plenty of ankle support and have a steel or hard plastic toe cup. It's also important to keep skates sharp so they perform better and are less likely to get caught in ruts in the ice.

- **Shoulder pads, elbow pads, knee and shin pads**—These are all specific to hockey. Soccer or lacrosse equipment won't give the protection needed. Lower leg (knee and shin) pads should have a hard plastic exterior and reach the top of your child's skates.

- **Hockey pants**—Also called breezers, these should reach to the knee and offer padding in the front, rear, and sides of the upper legs and midsection.

- **Gloves**—Another sport-specific item, hockey gloves should allow for mobility while protecting well past the wrist.

- **Athletic supporter and cup**—These are incorporated into most hockey undershorts these days but can also come from other sports.

- **Neck protector**—Although some leagues don't require them, neck protectors are helpful at guarding against wayward hockey sticks and skate blades.

- **Mouthguard**—These not only protect the teeth, but also the lips, cheeks, and tongue, and can help prevent jaw injuries.

## Goalie Gear

Charged with putting their bodies between flying pucks and the goal, hockey goalies need a whole different set of equipment to keep themselves safe. Helmets, skates, neck guards and athletic protectors and cups are all different for goalies than they are for other positions.

In addition, goalies should always wear:

- **Leg pads**—These should always be the correct length and be thick enough to protect against even the hardest slapshot.

- **Arm pads and chest protector**—Arm pads should reach all the way to the wrist. Chest protectors should wrap slightly around the sides to keep a child's entire front well armored.

- **Blocker glove**—This glove should allow your child's fingers to grip the stick easily but be very thick and cover most of the forearm.

- **Catcher glove**—Similar to a first baseman's glove in baseball, catcher gloves should have thick padding over the wrist and palm and should also come well up the forearm.

## Before the Puck Is Dropped

Everything kids do during a hockey game will be done while they are skating, so be sure they know how to skate well before they play a game. Most rinks offer learn-to-skate classes and open skating sessions when they can practice. Kids should know how to stop, turn, and get up when they fall. It's also helpful for them to know how to skate, stop, and turn while skating backwards.

Once you feel they're good enough skaters and they've got the proper equipment and know how to use it, they'll be ready to hit the ice. Before games, hockey players generally skate around the rink a few times to warm up. Kids should use this time to loosen their joints and stretch their muscles. Some skaters warm up and stretch before getting on the ice.

Important muscle groups to stretch before a game include:

- **Hip and groin**—Kids can stretch out the groin area while skating by bending knees and extending one leg out to the side. The front of the hip can be stretched by dragging one foot behind and getting low to the ice.

- **Back and torso**—Shooting the puck, which your child will hopefully be doing a lot of, subjects midsections to a strenuous twisting motion that most people aren't used to doing. Trunk twists while holding the stick in front, and toe touches can also be done while skating around the rink.

- **Hamstrings**—Have kids use the side boards of the rink to swing legs forward and back to help stretch hamstrings and hip flexors.

## *Keeping It Safe during a Game*

There's a reason why tripping, hooking, slashing, high-sticking and cross-checking bring penalties. Hockey sticks can easily go from being a piece of equipment to being a dangerous weapon. Be sure that your kids know all the rules governing the use of sticks and follow them to the letter. You wouldn't want them to get hit by someone else's stick, and no one wants to get hit by theirs.

Other penalties designed to keep the game safe involve roughing, boarding, and checking from behind. These all have to do with players colliding with one another. If your kids' league allows checking, make sure they know the difference between a legal check and an illegal one, and be adamant that they never hit anyone from behind. If they play in a "no-check" league, it means just that: *no* checking.

As far as fighting is concerned, players in the NHL may throw off their gloves and start punching one another, but if your child does it, he or she can expect to pay a harsh penalty. Almost every youth league will kick players out of the game and suspend them for at least one more game for their first fighting penalty. They won't just be hurting themselves; they'll be letting their team down. Don't allow fighting of any kind.

Also, never let your kids play a game of hockey without adult supervision. Even if they follow every safety tip, accidents can still happen. There should always be a stocked first-aid kit and a responsible adult on hand in the event of an injury or other emergency. Likewise, be sure to have their games officiated by certified referees who are familiar with the specific rules of the league.

## *Pond Hockey*

Playing a game of hockey with friends on a frozen pond can be lots of fun, but ponds present their own unique set of safety problems. An adult should always check the ice to make sure it's thick enough to support the weight of kids before they're allowed play, and they should stay away from any parts of the pond or lake where it looks like the ice may be thin. Tell your kids that if a puck goes in a suspect area, they should just let it go. They can always get another puck. It's not worth the risk of hypothermia or drowning for them to go after it.

Frozen ponds also go hand in hand with very cold temperatures. Be sure your kids wear plenty of warm clothing in addition to all their hockey gear anytime they play outdoors, and if they're playing on a sunny day, be sure they use sunscreen on their faces. The sun's rays reflecting off ice and snow can be very intense.

117

Now that you know the best ways to keep your kids safe, encourage them to get out there and hit the ice. Hockey is a great game that they'll want to play for as long as they can. Just remember that accidents and injuries can still occur no matter how prepared they are. Make sure your kids follow these tips, though, and you can minimize their risk significantly.

# Section 12.3

# *Football*

This section contains text excerpted from the following sources: Text beginning with the heading "Gear up" is excerpted from "BAM! Body and Mind—Football Activity Card," Centers for Disease Control and Prevention (CDC), June 9, 2015; Text beginning with the heading "Football Helmet Safety: Start with the Right Size" is excerpted from "Get a Heads up on Football Helmet Safety," Centers for Disease Control and Prevention (CDC), July 14, 2013. Reviewed June 2017.

## *Gear up*

Always wear a helmet with a face mask and jaw pads, and a mouthpiece to protect against those hard hits. Because football is a contact sport, there are many different pieces of gear you should wear to protect different areas of your body. For upper body protection, you should wear a neck roll to prevent whiplash, shoulder pads, rib pads, arm pads and elbow pads. For leg protection, you should wear hip pads, tailbone pads, thigh pads, and knee pads. Most leagues require all this, but it's a good idea to protect yourself even in backyard games.

## *Play It Safe*

Be sure to stretch and warm up before every practice and game and always wear your protective gear. To avoid getting hurt, learn from your coaches how to block and tackle correctly. Don't tackle with the top of your head or helmet—not only is it illegal, but it can cause injury to both players. If you play in an organized league, there are lots of rules—and they are there for a reason—to keep you safe. If you break these rules, you risk not only getting hurt, or hurting someone else, but your team will be penalized. If you're playing in the backyard with your friends, stay safe by sticking to touch or flag football, and only play with kids who are around your age and size.

## How to Play

There are lots of skills needed to play football from throwing and catching the ball to blocking and tackling the other players. There's even a national Punt, Pass, and Kick contest devoted just to the main skills you need. League teams are a great way to learn all the rules and strategies of football. Pop Warner is the most popular youth football league, but there are many others nationwide.

**Throwing the ball.** Grip the ball by placing each of your fingers between each lace of the ball. Bring your throwing arm back with your elbow bent. Extend your free arm (the one without the ball) in front of you and point to your target. Snap your throwing arm forward, releasing the ball, and follow through with your shoulders and hips. When you are finished, your throwing arm should be pointing toward your target with your palm facing the ground.

**Catching the ball.** Hold your arms out with your elbows slightly bent in front of your chest. Bring your hands together, touching the thumbs and index fingers to make a triangle with your fingers. Catch the nose of the ball in the triangle, and use your chest to help trap the ball. Bring your arms in around the ball and hold it tight against you.

**Punting the ball.** Place your feet shoulder-width apart with your kicking foot slightly in front. Slightly bend your knees and bend your body forward a little. Hold the ball out in front of you with the laces facing upward. Take two steps forward, beginning with your kicking foot and drop the ball toward your kicking foot. Kick the ball hard with the top of your foot and follow through with your leg as high as you can.

## Football Helmet Safety: Start with the Right Size

### Bring the Athlete

Bring the athlete with you when buying a new helmet to make sure that you can check for a good fit.

### Head Size

To find out the size of the athlete's head, wrap a soft tape measure around the athlete's head, just above their eyebrows and ears. Make sure the tape measure stays level from front to back. (If you don't have a soft tape measure, you can use a string and then measure it against a ruler.)

### *Sizes Will Vary*

Helmet sizes often will vary from brand-to-brand and with different models. Each helmet will fit differently, so it is important to check out the manufacturer's website for the helmet brand's fit instructions and sizing charts, as well as to find out what helmet size fits the athlete's head size.

## Get a Good Fit

### *General Fit*

A football helmet should feel snug with no spaces between the pads and the athlete's head. The helmet should not slide on the head with the chin strap in place. If the helmet can be removed while the chin strap is in place, then the fit is too loose. Some helmets have a unique fitting system or use an air bladder system that requires inflation with a special needle to avoid puncturing the air bladders.

### *Ask*

Ask the athlete how the helmet feels on their head. While it needs to have a snug fit, a helmet that is too tight can cause headaches.

### *Hairstyle*

The athlete should try on the helmet with the hairstyle he will wear while at practices and games. Helmet fit can change if the athlete's hairstyle changes. For example, a long-haired athlete who gets a very short haircut may need to adjust the fit of the helmet.

### *Coverage*

A football helmet should not sit too high or low on their head. To check, make sure ear holes line up with athlete's ears, and helmet pad covers athlete's head from middle of his forehead to back of his head.

## Vision

Make sure you can see the athlete's eyes and that he can see straight forward and side-to-side.

## Chin straps

The chin strap should be centered under the athlete's chin and fit snugly. Tell the athlete to open their mouth wide...big yawn! The helmet should pull down on their head. If not, the chin strap needs to be tighter. Once the chin strap is fastened, the helmet should not move in any direction, back-to-front or side-to-side.

# Take Care of the Helmet

## Check for Damage

DO NOT allow the athlete to use a cracked or broken helmet or a helmet that is missing any padding or parts. For air bladder-equipped helmets, make sure to check for proper inflation. DO NOT alter, remove or replace padding or internal parts unless supervised by a trained equipment manager. Check for missing or loose parts and padding before the season and regularly during the season.

## Cleaning

Clean the helmet often inside and out with warm water and mild detergent. DO NOT soak any part of the helmet, put it close to high heat, or use strong cleaners.

## Protect

DO NOT let anyone sit or lean on the helmet.

## Storage

Do not store a football helmet in a car. The helmet should be stored in a room that does not get too hot or too cold and where the helmet is away from direct sunlight.

## Decoration

DO NOT decorate (paint or put stickers on) the helmet without checking with the helmet manufacturer, as this may affect the safety of the helmet. This information may also be found on the instructions label or on the manufacturer's website.

## *Look for a Football Helmet with Labels That*

- Have the date of manufacture. This information will be helpful in case the helmet is recalled; and

- Say National Operating Committee on Standards for Athletic Equipment (NOCSAE®) certified. That label means that the helmet has been tested for safety and meets safety standards.

If the helmet is not new, you should also look for a label that includes the date the helmet was expertly repaired and approved for use (reconditioned/recertified). Helmets that have been properly reconditioned and recertified will have a label with the date of recertification and the name of the reconditioning company.

## *Know When to Replace a Football Helmet*

### *Reconditioning*

Reconditioning involves having an expert inspect and repair a used helmet by: fixing cracks or damage, replacing missing parts, testing it for safety, and recertifying it for use. Helmets should be reconditioned regularly by a licensed National Athletic Equipment Reconditioner Association (NAERA) member. DO NOT allow the athlete to use a used helmet that is not approved/recertified for use by a NAERA reconditioner.

### *10 and Out*

Football helmets should be replaced no later than 10 years from the date of manufacture. Many helmets will need to be replaced sooner, depending upon wear and tear.

# Section 12.4

# *Soccer*

This section includes text excerpted from "Brain Injury
Safety Tips and Prevention," Centers for Disease
Control and Prevention (CDC), March 14, 2017.

## *Prevention Tips*

- Follow U.S. Soccer recommendations:

  - No heading for any athletes age 10 and under.

  - Limit heading only to practices for athletes ages 11 to 13.

- Teach athletes ways to lower the chances of getting a concussion, including ways to avoid collisions with other athletes.

- Enforce the rules of the sport for fair play, safety, and sportsmanship.

- Ensure athletes avoid unsafe actions such as:

  - Hitting another athlete in the head;

  - Using their head to contact another athlete;

  - Making illegal contacts or colliding with another athlete; and/or

  - Trying to injure or put another athlete at risk for injury.

- Work with the game or event administrator to remove tripping hazards and ensure that equipment, such as goalposts, have padding that is in good condition.

## *Why This Is Important*

- Girls have higher rates of concussion than boys in high school soccer.

- Concussions in high school soccer most commonly occur when an athlete is heading the ball.

- About 1 in 3 concussions among girls happens during heading (31%).

- About 1 in 4 concussions among boys happens during heading (28%).

- Concussions sustained while heading the ball most commonly result from:

- Player-to-player contact (74% for boys and 58% for girls)

- Player-to-equipment contact (such as contact with the ball or goalpost) (13% for boys and 35% for girls)

# Section 12.5

# *Skateboarding*

This section includes text excerpted from "Skateboarding Safety," U.S. Consumer Product Safety Commission (CPSC), December 2, 2011. Reviewed June 2017.

## *Skateboarding Safety*

Like other sports activities, skateboarding has risks. Vehicle traffic, trick riding, and excessive speed can lead to collisions, loss of control, and falls. Even experienced riders have been injured and killed.

*Take knowledge to the extreme, and follow these important tips for safer riding:*

- **Wear protective gear when riding**—especially a helmet. Wearing a helmet can mean the difference between life and death. Don't become another statistic.

- **Stay clear of moving vehicles.** Some of the most common and severe skateboarding accidents involve collisions with moving vehicles. Don't ride where you are likely to encounter traffic. Never hitch a ride ("skitch") onto a moving vehicle.

- **Inspect/adjust your board before you ride.** Always check for excessive play (looseness) and any broken or cracked parts. Serious defects should be fixed by a qualified repair shop.

- **Ride during the day.** Avoid riding at dusk and dawn or in other low-light conditions where you cannot see or be seen easily by vehicles.

- **Inspect your riding terrain.** Skateboarders should inspect the area where they will be riding for holes, bumps, rocks, and debris.

- **Never ride alone.** Accidents happen. Ride with friends and bring a phone. Children under 8 years old should be supervised closely.

- **Ride wisely.** Don't ride faster than you can handle. You can lose control of your skateboard at any speed. Never lie down on a skateboard in motion.

- **Don't drink and ride.** Alcohol and drugs reduce your ability to control your skateboard and react to unexpected circumstances, greatly increasing your chances of injury and death.

## What Is Speed Wobble?

Speed wobble happens when a skateboard begins to shimmy from side to side unexpectedly. Within seconds, this can lead to a board rocking so violently that the rider is thrown to the ground before having a chance to react.

### *Ways to Reduce the Risk of Speed Wobble*

- Ride forward and crouch on your board.
- Longer boards increase stability.
- Boards with wider hangers (wheels that are farther apart) give riders greater control.
- Keep trucks, wheels, nuts, and mounting screws tightened properly to improve stability at higher speeds.

## Always Wear a Helmet

- A helmet should fit snugly with the chin strap fastened because it can come off upon impact if it is too loose.
- The helmet should be level with the head, not tilted back.
- Wear a helmet designed for skateboarding (hard shell with foam interior).

## Other Suggested Protective Gear

• Wrist guards are especially important for reducing the risk of fractures.

• Use knee and elbow pads.

• Wear flat-soled shoes.

# Section 12.6

# *Bicycle Safety*

This section contains text excerpted from the following sources:
Text in this section begins with excerpts from "Bicycle Safety,"
Centers for Disease Control and Prevention (CDC), April 11, 2016;
Text under the heading "Bike Helmets Safety" is excerpted from
"Helmet Safety—Bike Helmet Fact Sheet," Centers for Disease
Control and Prevention (CDC), February 16, 2015.

While only 1 percent of all trips taken in the United States are by bicycle, bicyclists face a higher risk of crash-related injury and deaths than occupants of motor vehicles do.

## How Big Is the Problem?

*Deaths and Injuries*

In 2013 in the United States, over 900 bicyclists were killed and there were an estimated 494,000 emergency department visits due to bicycle-related injuries.

*Cost*

Data from 2010 show fatal and nonfatal crash-related injuries to bicyclists resulted in lifetime medical costs and productivity losses of $10 billion.

# What Are the Major Risk Factors?

- Adolescents and young adults (15–19 years) and adults aged 40 years and older have the highest bicycle death rates.

- Children (5–14 years), adolescents, and young adults (15–24 years) have the highest rates of nonfatal bicycle-related injuries, accounting for more than one-third of all bicycle-related injuries seen in U.S. emergency departments.

- Males are much more likely to be killed or injured on bicycles than are females.

- Most bicyclist deaths occur in urban areas and at nonintersection locations.

# How Can Bicycle-Related Injuries and Deaths Be Prevented?

*Effective Interventions*

Effective interventions to reduce injuries and fatalities to bicyclists include the following:

*Bicycle Helmets*

Bicycle helmets reduce the risk of head and brain injuries in the event of a crash. All bicyclists, regardless of age, can help protect themselves by wearing properly fitted bicycle helmets every time they ride.

*Promising Interventions*

Interventions that have shown promise for reducing injuries and fatalities to bicyclists include the following:

*Active Lighting and Rider Visibility*

- Fluorescent clothing can make bicyclists visible from further away than regular clothing during the daytime.

- Retro-reflective clothing can make bicyclists more visible at night.

- Active lighting can include front white lights, rear red lights, or other lighting on the bicycle or bicyclist. This lighting may improve the visibility of bicyclists.

# *Bike Helmets Safety*

## *Start with the Right Size*

### *Bring the Bike Rider*

Bring your child or teen with you when buying a new helmet to make sure that you can check for a good fit.

### *Head Size*

To find out the size of your child's or teen's head, wrap a soft tape measure around his or her head, just above their eyebrows and ears. Make sure the tape measure stays level from front to back. (If you don't have a soft tape measure, you can use a string and then measure it against a ruler.)

### *Sizes Will Vary*

Helmet sizes often will vary from brand-to-brand and with different models. Each helmet will fit differently, so it is important to check out the manufacturer's website for the helmet brand's fit instructions and sizing charts, as well as to find out what helmet size fits your child's or teen's head size.

## *Get a Good Fit*

### *General Fit*

The helmet should fit snugly all around, with no spaces between the foam and bike rider's head.

### *Ask*

Ask your child or teen how the helmet feels on their head. While it needs to have a snug fit, a helmet that is too tight can cause headaches.

### *Hairstyle*

Bike helmets are available for riders with long hair. Your child or teen should try on the helmet with the hairstyle he or she will wear while bike riding. Helmet fit can change if your child's or teen's hairstyle changes. For example, a long-haired bike rider who gets a very short haircut may need to adjust the fit of the helmet.

*Adjustments*

Some bike helmets have removable padding or a universal fit ring that can be adjusted to get a good fit.

*Coverage*

A bike helmet should not sit too high or low on the rider's head. To check, make sure the bottom of the pad inside the front of the helmet is one or two finger widths above the bike rider's eyebrows. The back of the helmet should not touch the top of the bike rider's neck.

*Vision*

Make sure you can see your child's or teen's eyes and that he or she can see straight forward and side-to-side.

*Side Straps*

The side straps should make a "V" shape under, and slightly in front of, the bike rider's ears.

*Chin Straps*

The chin strap should be centered under the bike rider's chin and fit snugly, so that no more than one or two fingers fit between the chin and the strap. Tell your child or teen to open their mouth wide... big yawn! The helmet should pull down on their head. If not, the chin strap needs to be tighter. If needed, you can pull the straps from the back of the helmet to adjust the chin straps. Once the chin strap is fastened, the helmet should not move in any direction, back-to-front or side-to-side.

**Take Care of the Helmet**

*Check for Damage*

DO NOT allow your bike rider to use a cracked or broken helmet or a helmet that is missing any padding or parts.

*Cleaning*

Clean the helmet often inside and out with warm water and mild detergent. DO NOT soak any part of the helmet, put it close to high heat, or use strong cleaners.

*Protect*

DO NOT let anyone sit or lean on the helmet.

*Storage*

Do not store a bike helmet in a car. The helmet should be stored in a room that does not get too hot or too cold and where the helmet is away from direct sunlight.

*Decoration*

DO NOT decorate (paint or put stickers on) the helmet without checking with the helmet manufacturer, as this may affect the safety of the helmet. This information may also be found on the instructions label or on the manufacturer's website.

## Look for a Bike Helmet with Labels That

• Have the date of manufacture. This information will be helpful in case the helmet is recalled; and

• Say U.S. Consumer Product Safety Commission (CPSC) certified. That label means that the helmet has been tested for safety and meets the federal safety standard.

Some bike helmets may also have a label stating that they are American Society for Testing and Materials (ASTM), Snell, or American National Standards Institute (ANSI) certified. These labels let you know that the helmet has also passed the safety tests of these organizations.

## When to Replace a Bike Helmet

*One Impact*

Replace any bicycle helmet that is damaged or has been involved in a crash. Bicycle helmets are designed to help protect the rider's brain and head from one serious impact, such as a fall onto the pavement. You may not be able to see the damage to the foam, but the foam materials in the helmet will crush after an impact. That means that the foam in the helmet won't be able to help protect the rider's brain and head from another impact.

*Multi-Use Helmets*

Some helmet companies have created multi-use helmets for biking, skateboarding, and other activities. Multi-use helmets are designed to withstand multiple very minor hits; however, a multi-use helmet MUST be replaced if it has been involved in a serious crash or is damaged. Before your child or teen uses a multi-use helmet for biking, make sure the helmet has a CPSC label certifying it for biking.

## Section 12.7

# *Golf*

Text in this section is © 1995-2017. The Nemours
Foundation/KidsHealth®. Reprinted with permission.

Golf is an excellent challenge, physically as well as mentally, and it's also a great social activity.

It might seem silly to put golf and danger in the same sentence, but injuries can and do happen. Golf balls and golf clubs are very hard objects that can cause considerable damage if they strike you, and golfers need to be aware of the dangers posed by everything from lightning to repetitive stress injuries.

To learn how to stay safe on the golf course, follow these tips.

## *Why Is Golf Safety Important?*

As sports go, golf is pretty safe, but there's always potential for injury. The golf swing puts a tremendous amount of pressure on your back and your joints, particularly if you are prone to swinging too hard or your technique isn't the best. Back pain, elbow tendonitis, and pain in the shoulders, hands, and wrists are all common golf injuries.

Less common but more serious injuries can happen if someone gets hit by a golf ball or club. Though it's extremely rare, people have actually died from being hit by golf balls. And then there are golf-cart mishaps: Golfers have been known to get seriously injured when golf carts are driven in a hazardous manner or if they dangle their feet or hands out of a cart while it's moving.

Fortunately, most traumatic injuries can be avoided by using common sense and following the rules.

## Before You Tee Up

Always warm up by taking a light walk, jogging, or doing jumping jacks before you play golf. Do trunk twists and other stretches to help loosen up your back, and be sure to stretch your shoulders, arms, elbows, and wrists. Take a few easy practice swings, gradually increasing your range of motion.

When practicing your swing at the driving range, start with wedges and short irons that call for a shorter swing. Gradually work up to long irons and woods that require a full swing. This not only will help your golf game, it will also go a long way toward preventing injuries.

If you will be playing on a sunny day, use plenty of sunscreen on any exposed skin, and wear a wide-brimmed hat to shade your eyes and protect your face. A typical round of golf takes more than 4 hours to complete. You will be out in the sun the entire time, especially if you walk the course instead of riding in a cart. Sunburns are no fun, and neither is dehydration, another problem you might encounter on hot days. Be sure to drink plenty of fluids before, during, and after your round.

## On the Course

Be aware of your surroundings at all times, and keep track of the people around you. It should be easy to know the locations of the players in your group, which will generally number four or less. But you need to also take note of where other groups are located.

Any time you have a golf club in your hands and are preparing to swing, make sure everyone else is a safe distance away. Never swing a club if someone else is near you, whether you're taking a practice swing or hitting the ball.

When other players in your group are swinging clubs, don't assume that they are watching out for you. Be proactive and give them a wide berth so that you don't run the risk of being struck by a club. And never stand in a place where you could be hit by a ball when another golfer in your group is playing.

When the time comes to hit the ball, be sure there are no golfers ahead of you who might be in range of your shot. This includes golfers to the right and left who might be in danger if you slice or hook the ball onto an adjacent hole. Wait until you're sure other golfers are out of the way before you hit.

## What's "Fore"?

Sometimes, despite all your precautions, you will hit a ball in the direction of other golfers. It's possible a golfer was hidden by trees or a hill and you didn't see them until after you've hit the ball. In cases like this, yell out "Fore!" as loudly as you can. This will let other golfers know that a ball is headed their way and they should take cover.

If, while you are playing, you hear someone yell "Fore!" don't turn your head to look for the ball. Instead, seek cover behind a tree or a golf cart. If that's not possible, cover your head and face with your arms.

## Lightning Precautions

Lightning can be a big hazard on the golf course. Because you're exposed and carrying metal clubs, your risk of getting struck is greater than normal. Check the weather before you head out to the course, and never try to play during a thunderstorm.

Most golf courses these days will sound an alarm if lightning is spotted in the area. If you hear an alarm or see lightning yourself, head for the clubhouse right away. If you can't get to the clubhouse, don't seek cover under trees, which attract lightning. Instead, seek out a designated lightning shelter or bathroom. Be sure the structure you choose has walls, as open-walled structures will not protect you from a lightning strike.

If no shelter is available, drop your clubs and move away from them and your cart. Stay away from trees and water, seek out a low-lying area, and keep a safe distance from other members of your group to make yourselves smaller targets.

## Golf-Cart Safety

Golf carts should only be driven by licensed drivers or if an adult is present. If you are going to drive a cart, read the directions and safety rules posted on the cart. It's not difficult, but carts can be dangerous if they aren't driven properly.

As much as possible, stay on cart paths, and never try to go off-roading across bumpy terrain. Drive straight up and down hills, and take it slow while going downhill or around turns. Look out for other carts where cart paths intersect, and never hang your feet, legs, arms, or hands out of a cart while it is in motion.

## A Few Other Reminders

- **Practice good golf etiquette.** Wait for your turn to play, allow other golfers to get out of range before hitting, and keep quiet while others are playing.

- **Don't move ahead into other groups.** If a group ahead of you is playing slowly, it can be frustrating having to wait. Don't give in to the temptation to hit into their group. It could result in a very serious injury. Instead take a deep breath and a few more practice swings, or politely ask to "play through." If you see a course marshall, ask him if he can say something to the slow golfers to help speed up play.

- **Use the right equipment.** Swinging a golf club can often cause you to get blisters on your hands, and on hot days sweaty palms can make clubs hard to grip. If either of these is the case, use a golf glove or two. Typically, right-handed golfers will want a glove for their left hand, and vice versa.

Golf shoes will give you much better traction than sneakers and help you avoid slipping while you swing. Get a pair of shoes with plastic spikes, as most courses will not allow metal spikes.

Common sense and a little forethought can go a long way toward keeping you injury-free on the golf course. Just use your head, and chances are you'll golf for years to come without having to worry about getting hurt.

# Section 12.8

# *Tennis*

Text in this section is © 1995–2017. The Nemours Foundation/KidsHealth®. Reprinted with permission.

Looking for a good way to stay in shape and have fun? Try tennis. Whether you're a member of a club with an organized league or just like to head out to the public courts once in a while, tennis is an easy game to get started playing. Just get yourself some tennis shoes, a racquet, and a friend, and you're ready to go.

Serious injuries in tennis are rare, but there are some injuries you need to be aware of before you start playing. We've all heard of "tennis elbow," which is one of a number of overuse injuries that can result from playing tennis. Traumatic injuries are also a possibility, from sprained ankles to torn ligaments and even concussions.

## Why Is Tennis Safety Important?

Tennis injuries fall into two categories: cumulative injuries that result from overuse (called overuse injuries), and acute or traumatic injuries caused by sudden force or impact. Most injuries in tennis are overuse injuries.

Overuse injuries include tennis elbow (lateral epicondylitis), tendonitis of the shoulder, wrist, and Achilles, growth plate injuries, and stress fractures.

Acute injuries include ankle sprains, muscle strains, knee injuries (including ACL tears), and back injuries.

## Gear Guidelines

Tennis gear may seem pretty straightforward, but putting some thought into the racquet, socks, and shoes you use can go a long way toward preventing injuries.

Here are a few basic guidelines to follow when choosing equipment:

- **Racquet.** Using a racquet that is too light or too heavy can increase your risk of shoulder and elbow injuries. Likewise, a racquet with the wrong grip size or the wrong amount of tension in the strings can be hard on your wrists and arms. Consult a trained professional at a tennis specialty store to make sure you get a racquet that is appropriate for your size and skill level.

- **Sneakers.** Be sure to get shoes that are specifically designed for tennis and the court surface. Tennis shoes should support your heel and help keep your ankle from rolling, and decrease side-to-side sliding, which can take a toll on your ankles and feet. Additionally, if you plan to play on courts made of asphalt, concrete, or other hard surfaces, heel inserts may minimize the stress on your lower back.

- **Socks.** Choose socks made from synthetic fabrics rather than cotton, as these will help keep your feet dry and prevent blisters. For added support, you might want to consider wearing two pairs of socks or specially padded tennis socks.

## Before You Play

As with any sport, staying in shape will help your game and help you prevent injuries. This means getting plenty of exercise and eating right year round. Also, as with all sports, you should warm up and stretch before playing tennis. Do some jumping jacks or run in place for a minute or two to warm up your muscles, and then stretch your arms, wrists, shoulders, and legs. Dynamic stretching uses many muscle groups in a sport specific manner and can be incorporated into your warm-up.

Inspect the court where you will be playing before you start. If it's a hard court, be sure there are no cracks or holes that might trip you up. Be sure there are no loose tennis balls or other objects on or near the court. If you plan to play at night, be sure the court is well lit. And never play on a wet court, regardless of whether it's a hard court, soft court, or grass court. Even the slightest amount of moisture on a court will make it slippery—and that can lead to injury.

Make sure there is first aid available wherever you play, as well as someone who knows how to administer it. Be sure to note the location of a nearby phone in the event of an emergency. Lastly, drink plenty of water before, during, and after you play. If it's a sunny day, apply sunscreen to any exposed skin, and wear a hat and light-colored clothing to help keep yourself cool.

## While Playing

Using proper technique will not only make you a better tennis player, it will also help to prevent injuries. For instance, when serving or hitting an overhand, try not to arch your back too much, and instead focus on bending your knees and raising your heels. If you have questions about your technique, consider taking a lesson from a trained instructor.

Have water on hand to drink during breaks in play, and try to take some time to rest in the shade between games and sets. If the handle of your racquet becomes wet from perspiration, dry it frequently to avoid getting blisters on your hands.

If you feel any pain or discomfort in your joints or muscles, stop playing immediately. Don't resume playing until you have completely recovered. Playing through pain will only make injuries worse.

If you get an acute or traumatic injury, seek immediate medical attention. If you've had a previous injury, get expert advice on taping or bracing your injured body part.

## A Few Other Reminders

- Proper stretching, strengthening, and warm-up help prevent common overuse injuries.

- Give yourself plenty of time off to rest between matches and training sessions. Overtraining is one of the most common causes of tennis injuries. Your body needs time to recover. This will not only help prevent injuries, it will also help you get the most out of your abilities.

- Avoid playing in adverse weather conditions. Hot weather presents a real risk of heat-related illness and cold weather can lead to muscle injury if you don't warm up enough.

Before you play a match, practice hitting with a friend or consider taking lessons from a professional instructor. This will allow you to learn proper technique. Practicing playing the right way and remembering to warm up and cool down can help you avoid most common injuries. Next thing you know, that might be you serving for the championship at Wimbledon.

# Section 12.9

# *Running*

Text in this section is © 1995-2017. The Nemours Foundation/KidsHealth®. Reprinted with permission.

Whether it's as part of a high school track program or cross-country team or just a way of getting in shape, running is a wonderful sport. It's great exercise, virtually anyone can do it, and all you really need to get started is a good pair of sneakers.

But running is not without its risks. Injuries—from sprained ankles and blisters to stress fractures and tendonitis—are common. And runners need to be aware of some hazards (from vehicles to wild animals) when choosing a place to run.

To keep things safe while running, follow these tips:

## Avoiding Running Injuries

Up to half of all runners are injured every year, so the odds are good that at some point in your running career you will get injured.

Running, especially on asphalt or other hard surfaces, puts a lot of stress on the legs and back. This can lead to lots of different problems. The most common running injuries include sprained ankles, blisters, tendonitis, chondromalacia (runner's knee), iliotibial band (ITB) syndrome, heel pain, and shin splints. Teen runners are also at risk of growth plate injuries.

Two steps can help you avoid serious injuries from running:

1.   **Try to prevent injuries from happening in the first place.** Use the right gear, warm up your muscles before you start, and take precautions to deal with weather conditions— like staying well hydrated in hot weather and keeping muscles warm in the cold.

2.   **Stop running as soon as you notice signs of trouble.** Ignoring the warning signs of an injury will only lead to bigger problems down the road.

## Gear Guidelines

Running might require less gear than other sports, but it is still vitally important to get the right equipment to minimize the stresses it puts on your body. Anyone who has ever run in the wrong shoes can tell you what a painful experience it can be, and anyone who has run in the wrong socks probably has blisters to prove it.

Here are a few tips to make sure you get the right footwear before you start running:

### Shoes

Before you buy a pair of running sneakers, know what sort of foot you have. Are your feet wide or narrow? Do you have flat feet? High arches? Different feet need different sneakers to provide maximum support and comfort. If you don't know what sort of foot you have or what kind of sneaker will work best for you, consult a trained professional at a running specialty store.

Minimalist shoes are becoming popular, but there's no evidence that they reduce injuries. Look for running shoes that provide good support, starting with a thick, shock-absorbing sole. Runners with flat feet should choose shoes that advertise "motion control" or "stability." Runners with high-arched feet should look for shoes that describe themselves as "flexible" or "cushioned."

Wearing shoes that fit correctly is more important in running than in virtually any other sport. As you rack up the miles, any hot spots or discomfort will become magnified and lead to blisters, toenail problems, and may contribute to leg problems.

If you plan on running on trails or in bad weather, you'll need trail-running shoes with extra traction, stability, and durability. Whichever type of shoes you end up purchasing, make sure they are laced up snugly so they're comfortable but not so tight that they cause discomfort.

### Socks

Running socks come in a variety of materials, thicknesses, and sizes. The most important factor is material. Stay away from socks made from 100 percent cotton. When cotton gets wet, it stays wet, leading to blisters in the summer and cold feet in the winter. Instead, choose socks made from wool or synthetic materials such as polyester and acrylic.

Some runners like thicker socks for extra cushioning while others prefer thin socks, particularly in warm weather. Make sure you wear the socks you plan to wear when running while you try on sneakers to ensure a proper fit.

## Choose Where to Run

One of the nice things about running is that you can do it almost anywhere. Running on a track or indoors on a treadmill are options, but lots of runners prefer the variety and challenge of running on roads or trails.

In most cases, it will be possible to simply step out your front door and begin. That being said, there are definitely safer places to run and places that you might want to avoid.

## Road Runners

Look for streets that have sidewalks or wide shoulders. If there are no sidewalks or shoulders, and you find yourself having to run in the street, try to find an area with minimal automobile traffic. Always run toward oncoming cars so you can see any potential problems before they reach you.

Avoid running routes that take you through bad neighborhoods. If you're running in an unfamiliar area, be prepared to change your route or turn around if you sense that the area you're headed toward may not be safe. Trust your intuition.

Find someone to run with if you can—there's safety in numbers. Can't find a running partner? Consider joining a running club through your school or the local parks and recreation department. When running in a group, be sure to run single file and keep to the side of the road. Always yield the right-of-way to vehicles at intersections. Don't assume that cars will stop or alter their paths for you. Obey all traffic rules and signals.

## Trail Runners

Choose well-maintained trails. Steer clear of trails that are overgrown or covered with fallen branches—you don't want to trip or encounter ticks or poison ivy! Also, you should avoid trails that travel through deserted areas or take you far away from homes and businesses. Know the location of public phones and the fastest way back to civilization in the event of an emergency.

Watch for dogs or wild animals. If you encounter a mountain lion, bear, or other dangerous animal stop running and face it. Running may trigger the animal's instinct to attack. Make yourself look larger by raising your hands over your head. Give the animal plenty of room to escape. If the animal appears to be acting aggressively, throw rocks, sticks, or whatever is readily available at it. Stay facing the animal.

If you run into an aggressive dog, don't make eye contact—the dog might see this as a threat. The dog may be trying to defend its territory, so stop running and walk to the other side of the street. If the dog approaches, stand still. In a firm, calm voice, say "No" or "Go home." If you keep running into the same dog, choose a new route or file a report with animal control.

## Plan for Weather

### Rain and Snow

If you intend to run in rain or snow, make sure you dress for the conditions (windproof jacket, hat, gloves, etc.). Wear synthetic fabrics that will help wick away moisture from your body. Consider putting Vaseline or Band-aids on your nipples to keep them from being chafed by a wet shirt.

## Wind

If it's windy, run more slowly than you normally would when facing into the wind. This will help you keep from overexerting yourself while still giving you the same amount of exercise. Try to start your run by heading into the wind so that you will have the wind at your back later in the run when you are tired.

## Heat

On hot days, drink plenty of water before your run and bring extra water with you. Heat prostration can be a very serious problem for runners. Wear white clothing to reflect the sun's rays and a hat to shade your head from the sun, and stop running if you feel faint or uncomfortable in any way.

## Before You Start

Before you begin, warm up. Start with a brisk walk or light jog, or do some jumping jacks to get the blood flowing. Then be sure to stretch well, with a particular focus on your calves, hamstrings, quadriceps, and ankles. Dynamic stretching, where you do slow, controlled movements to improve range of motion is thought to be more effective than static stretching before a run or workout.

Carry a few essentials with you. These include some form of identification, a cell phone or change for a pay phone, and a whistle. Don't wear headphones or earbuds or anything else that might make you less aware of your surroundings while you run.

Tell a friend or family member your running route and when you plan to return. If no one is available, write down your plans so you can be located in the event of an emergency.

## While Running

Try to run only during daylight hours, if possible. If you must run at night, avoid dimly lit areas and wear bright and/or reflective clothes so that others can see you clearly.

When you begin, have a definite idea of how far you intend to go. Less experienced runners should start by running short distances until they buildup their stamina and get a better idea of how far they can run safely.

Younger teens are still developing and may be at more risk for injury from overtraining and running long distances. As a general guideline, a 10K race is the upper limit of what a 13-year-old should attempt, and no one under 18 should try to run a marathon. (Most marathons limit their entries to people 18 and older.)

Stay alert. The more aware you are of your surroundings and the other people around you, the less vulnerable you will be. Staying safe while running involves the same common sense you use to stay safe anywhere else, like avoiding parked cars and dark areas, and taking note of who is directly behind you and ahead of you.

If a car passes you more than once or seems suspicious, try to note or take a photo of the license plate number. Make it clear that you are aware of the vehicle. Most runners don't get attacked, especially if they take precautions like running in populated areas. You just need to use common sense.

Chapter 13

# Winter Sports Safety

## Concussion in Winter Sports

Each winter, hundreds of thousands of young athletes head out to ice and ski slopes to enjoy, practice, and compete in various winter sports. There's no doubt that these sports are a great way for kids and teens to stay healthy, as well as learn important leadership and team-building skills. But there are risks to pushing the limits of speed, strength, and endurance. And athletes who push the limits sometimes don't recognize their own limitations—especially when they've had a concussion.

A concussion is a type of traumatic brain injury—or TBI—caused by a bump, blow, or jolt to the head or by a hit to the body that causes the head and brain to move rapidly back and forth. This sudden movement can cause the brain to bounce around or twist in the skull, stretching

This chapter contains text excerpted from the following sources: Text under the heading "Concussion in Winter Sports" is excerpted from "Concussion in Winter Sports," Centers for Disease Control and Prevention (CDC), December 24, 2012. Reviewed June 2017; Text under the heading "Head and Neck Injuries in Winter Sports" is excerpted from "Head and Neck Injuries in Winter Sports," Office of Disease Prevention and Health Promotion (ODPHP), U.S. Department of Health and Human Services (HHS), January 20, 2016; Text under the heading "Snowboard Helmet Safety" is excerpted from "Get a Heads up on Snowboard Helmet Safety," Centers for Disease Control and Prevention (CDC), July 14, 2013. Reviewed June 2017; Text under the heading "Tips for Winter Sports Safety" is excerpted from "Winter Sports Safety," U.S. Department of Agriculture (USDA), November 27, 2007. Reviewed June 2017.

and damaging the brain cells and creating chemical changes in the brain.

While most athletes with a concussion recover quickly and fully, some will have symptoms that last for days or even weeks. A more serious concussion can last for months or longer.

That's why Centers for Disease Control and Prevention (CDC) and the National Football League (NFL) teamed up with USA Hockey, the U.S. Ski and Snowboarding Association (USSA), and 12 other national governing bodies for sports to develop a poster for young athletes. This poster lets athletes know that all concussions are serious and emphasizes the importance of reporting their injury. It also provides athletes with a list of concussion signs, symptoms, and steps they should take if they think they have a concussion.

The poster was created through CDC's "Heads Up" educational campaign that includes resources for high school and youth sports coaches, school professionals, and healthcare professionals. These initiatives include materials and information to help identify concussions and immediate steps to take when one is suspected.

## Prevention and Preparation: On and Off the Ice and Ski Slopes

**Insist that safety comes first.** No one technique or safety equipment is 100 percent effective in preventing concussion, but there are things you can do to help minimize the risks for concussion and other injuries.

For example, to help prevent injuries:

- Make sure to wear approved and properly-fitted protective equipment. Such equipment should be well-maintained and be worn consistently and correctly.

- Enforce no hits to the head or other types of dangerous play in hockey and other sports.

- Practice safe playing techniques and encourage athletes to follow the rules of play.

**Learn about concussion.** Before strapping on your skates, skis or snowboard, learn concussion symptoms and dangers signs, and their potential long-term consequences.

**Order and display the concussion poster.** CDC and the NFL encourage parents, coaches, and school professionals to display this poster in team locker rooms, competition and tournament sites, gymnasiums, ice rinks, and schools nationwide.

## Head and Neck Injuries in Winter Sports

With the growth of the X Games, winter "extreme" sports like freestyle skiing and snowboarding are as popular as ever. These sports send athletes far into the air and down the slopes and ramps at tremendous speeds. Injuries, especially concussions and other traumatic brain injuries (TBI), unfortunately can occur.

Knowing just how common these injuries are in winter sports can help us take steps to prevent some of these brain injuries.

### Extreme Sports Injuries to the Head and Neck

A study published in the *Orthopaedic Journal of Sports Medicine* looked at the incidence of head and neck injuries in seven extreme sports—snowboarding, snow skiing, snowmobiling, surfing, skateboarding, mountain biking, and motocross. The study is helpful to provide injury data, as these sports often lack the ability for organizing bodies to track participants. Plus this study allows us to compare rates of concussions in winter sports like skiing and snowboarding to the risks in warm-weather activities.

The study's findings are summarized below:

- Skateboarding, snowboarding, skiing and motocross had the highest number of head and neck injuries. Mountain biking, snowmobiling, and surfing had the lowest numbers.

- Snowboarding had the most concussions. In fact, about 30 percent of concussions in extreme sports occurred in snowboarding. Snow skiing was associated with about 25 percent of concussions.

- Skateboarding and motocross had the most severe head and neck injuries, like skull fractures and cervical spine fractures.

### Tips to Prevent Head Injuries in Winter Sports

While the data might seem frightening, there are some steps that might decrease your chance of suffering traumatic brain injuries in winter sports:

- Wear a helmet. Helmets are critical in extreme winter sports like skiing and snowboarding, which account for a significant number of concussions.

145

- Do everything possible to optimize the conditions where you are performing these activities. Stay within the marked boundaries on the slopes and watch out for obstacles and hazardous conditions.

- Try to participate in these activities in places where medical care is not far away. Professional competitions have doctors and emergency medical services, but many people perform these activities in remote locations. Seek medical attention if there is any question that you might have suffered a traumatic brain injury, no matter how minor it might seem.

## Snowboard Helmet Safety

### Start with the Right Size

*Bring the Snowboarder*

Bring your child or teen with you when buying a new helmet to make sure that you can check for a good fit.

*Head Size*

To find out the size of your child's or teen's head, wrap a soft tape measure around his or her head, just above their eyebrows and ears. Make sure the tape measure stays level from front to back. (If you don't have a soft tape measure, you can use a string and then measure it against a ruler.)

*Sizes Will Vary*

Helmet sizes often will vary from brand-to-brand and with different models. Each helmet will fit differently, so it is important to check out the manufacturer's website for the helmet brand's fit instructions and sizing charts, as well as to find out what helmet size fits your child's or teen's head size.

### Get a Good Fit

*General Fit*

A snowboard helmet should fit snugly all around, with no spaces between the foam or padding and the snowboarder's head.

*Ask*

Ask your child or teen how the helmet feels on their head. While it needs to have a snug fit, a helmet that is too tight can cause headaches.

*Hairstyle*

Your child or teen should try on the helmet with the hairstyle he or she will wear while snowboarding. Helmet fit can change if your child's or teen's hairstyle changes. For example, a long-haired snowboarder who gets a very short haircut may need to adjust the fit of the helmet.

*Coverage*

A snowboard helmet should not sit too high or low on their head. To check, make sure the helmet sits low enough in the front to protect the snowboarder's forehead, about 1 inch above the eyebrows, and the back of the helmet does not touch the top of the snowboarder's neck.

*Adjustments*

Some snowboard helmets have removable padding that can be adjusted to get a good fit.

*Goggles*

Have your child or teen try on the helmet with the goggles they will wear on the slopes. The helmet should fit snugly on top of the goggles, with no space between the helmet and the top of the goggles. However, the helmet should not sit so low on the snowboarder's head that it pushes down on the goggles.

*Vision*

Make sure that the snowboarder can see straight forward and side-to-side.

*Chin Straps*

The chin strap should be centered under the snowboarder's chin and fit snugly, so that no more than one or two fingers fit between the chin and the strap. Tell your child or teen to open their mouth wide...big yawn! The helmet should pull down on their head. If not, the chin strap needs to be tighter. Once the chin strap is fastened, the helmet should not move in any direction, back-to-front or side-to-side.

## Take Care of the Helmet

### Check for Damage

DO NOT allow your snowboarder to use a cracked or broken helmet or a helmet that is missing any padding or parts.

### Cleaning

Clean the helmet often inside and out with warm water and mild detergent. DO NOT soak any part of the helmet, put it close to high heat, or use strong cleaners.

### Protect

DO NOT let anyone sit or lean on the helmet.

### Storage

Do not store a snowboard helmet in a car. The helmet should be stored in a room that does not get too hot or too cold and where the helmet is away from direct sunlight.

### Decoration

DO NOT decorate (paint or put stickers on) the helmet without checking with the helmet manufacturer, as this may affect the safety of the helmet. This information may also be found on the instructions label or on the manufacturer's website.

## Look for the Labels

### Look for a Snowboard Helmet with Labels That

- Have the date of manufacture. This information will be helpful in case the helmet is recalled; and

- Say ASTM certified. That label means that the helmet has been tested for safety and meets safety standards.

## When to Replace a Snowboarder's Helmet

Snowboard helmets are designed to withstand more than one very minor hit. However, a snowboard helmet MUST be replaced if it has been involved in a serious crash or is damaged.

## Multi-Use Helmets

Some helmet companies have created multi-use helmets for biking, skateboarding, and other activities. Multi-use helmets are designed to withstand multiple very minor hits; however, a multi-use helmet MUST be replaced if it has been involved in a serious crash or is damaged. Before your child or teen uses a multi-use helmet for snowboarding, make sure the helmet has an ASTM label certifying it for snowboarding.

## Tips for Winter Sports Safety

Be responsible when skiing, snowmobiling, and snowboarding with these quick tips:

- Low snow, don't go. Avoid areas with inadequate snow cover. Traveling in these conditions can damage plants and soils just below the snow's surface.

- Travel only in areas designated for your type of winter travel.

- Avoid traveling in potential avalanche areas. use terrain to your advantage, avoiding steep slopes, cornices, and gullies or depressions, periodically check for clues to an unstable snow-pack. Remember, one person at a time on slopes. An avalanche transceiver, shovel, and probe should be worn on your body at all times in an avalanche terrain.

- Respect established ski tracks. If traveling by foot or snowshoe don't damage existing ski tracks.

- If a person develops hypothermia, warm the person up by rubbing them vigorously and getting them into dry clothes. Give them warm nonalcoholic liquids.

- If you must have a fire, use a fire pan.

- Dispose of all sanitary waste properly by backing it out or bury it in a shallow hole in the snow.

Chapter 14

# Resistance Training Safety

Resistance training—also known as strength or weight training—is an exercise method used to increase muscle size and strength, improve sports performance and overall health, and reduce the risk of injuries. It involves pushing, pulling, or lifting against a counterforce—such as a resistance band, dumbbell, or weight machine—in order to challenge muscles and break down tissues. The body responds to such physical stress by rebuilding itself in a stronger and more resilient form.

Both competitive and casual athletes use resistance training to increase strength and power in order to improve their performance. Ordinary people can benefit from resistance training, as well, by gaining the strength they need to climb stairs, lift children, or carry packages. The physical adaptations the body makes in response to resistance training can also help reduce the risk of injuries. Studies have shown that strength training and other forms of physical activity build bone density, which decreases the risk of osteoporosis and related fractures. Weight training also increases the size and strength of connective tissue—such as ligaments and tendons—that supports joints. By maintaining muscle mass and strength, resistance training also protects against some of the common injuries related to aging, such as falls, fractures, and lower back injuries.

## Developing a Training Program

Although resistance training can help reduce the risk of injuries, it can also cause injuries if done improperly. Before starting any exercise

"Resistance Training Safety," © 2017 Omnigraphics. Reviewed June 2017.

program, it is important to check with a doctor and receive medical clearance. The next step is to consult with a professional trainer or sports physiologist to develop a safe program aimed at meeting personal or sport-specific goals. A qualified trainer will typically perform the following services:

- evaluate the athlete's current level of strength, fitness, and willingness to commit to the program;

- analyze the demands of the sport or activity, including typical movement patterns and the participant's relative need for speed, endurance, strength, and power;

- select exercises designed to develop sport-specific muscle groups and movements, strengthen the core, and create muscular balance to prevent injury;

- determine the optimal routine, including the order of exercises, number of repetitions and sets, load, and length of rest intervals;

- establish the ideal frequency of resistance training.

## Working out Safely

Even after developing a resistance training program with the help of a professional, it is important to keep the following safety measures in mind to prevent injury:

- warm up before and cool down after each session;

- use proper form, focusing on smooth, controlled movements;

- breathe throughout a workout—exhaling while working against resistance, and inhaling while releasing tension or lowering a weight—in order to avoid straining;

- begin with light weights and increase the load gradually, by no more than 10 percent per week;

- work all major muscle groups in order to promote balanced development;

- incorporate rest days to allow muscles to recover and rebuild.

## Overuse Injuries

Resistance training works by placing physical stress on muscles, bones, ligaments, and tendons. When it is done properly, the body responds to the stress by rebuilding itself and growing stronger in the process. Other forms of exercise and activity have a similar effect. But sometimes the body's repair mechanisms cannot keep up with the repetitive micro-trauma caused by resistance training or participation in sports. When the breakdown of muscles, bones, and connective tissue occurs more rapidly than they can be rebuilt, the result is overuse injuries.

Overuse injuries—also known as repetitive strain or cumulative trauma injuries—are very common among athletes. Some well-known examples include shin splints, tendonitis, tennis elbow, jumper's knee, and swimmer's shoulder. Overuse injuries tend to appear gradually, with the symptoms subtly getting worse over time. If left untreated, however, they can cause chronic pain or turn into a debilitating injury. Overuse injuries differ from acute injuries, which are also common in sports. Acute injuries typically occur suddenly due to a traumatic impact or event. Some well-known types of acute injuries include fractures, sprains, and dislocations.

Although overuse injuries can happen to anyone, the following factors increase the risk:

- using poorly designed training plans;

- increasing the frequency, duration, or intensity of exercise too quickly;

- attempting to return from an injury before it is completely healed;

- using poor form or making changes in technique;

- using worn-out or improper equipment;

- developing physical imbalances in muscles or joints;

- overtraining for a single sport;

- failing to warm up or cool down properly.

## Treating Overuse Injuries

Since overuse injuries occur so gradually, they can be difficult to diagnose and treat. Some of the most common treatment and prevention methods include:

- taking time off or cutting back on an exercise program;

- applying ice to minor aches and pains following workouts;

- taking anti-inflammatory medications;
- elevating or applying compression to the affected area;
- cross-training to develop new muscle groups and add variety to a workout regimen;
- working with a trainer or physical therapist to improve form and technique;
- using high-quality, well-maintained gear;
- increasing activity level gradually;
- avoiding exercising to the point of pain or exhaustion;
- incorporating resistance training to improve strength, stability, and resilience.

## References

1. Davies, Phil. "How to Design a Resistance Training Program for Your Sport," Sports Fitness Advisor, 2016.

2. Hoffman, Jay. "Resistance Training and Injury Prevention," American College of Sports Medicine, n.d.

3. Matava, Matthew J. "Overuse Injury," Stop Sports Injuries, 2017.

4. "Overuse Injury: How to Prevent Training Injuries," Mayo Clinic, 2017.

5. "Seven Tips for a Safe and Successful Strength Training Program," Harvard Health Publications, 2017.

Chapter 15

# Outdoor Sports Safety in Weather Conditions

## Chapter Contents

# Section 15.1

# *Safety in the Heat*

This section contains text excerpted from the following sources:
Text in this section begins with excerpts from "Exercising in
Hot Weather," U.S. Public Health Service Commissioned Corps
(PHSCC), U.S. Department of Health and Human Services (HHS),
December 25, 2016; Text under the heading "Tips for Practicing and
Competing in Hot and Humid Conditions for Athletes" is
excerpted from "Tips for Practicing and Competing in Hot and Humid
Conditions for Athletes," Office of Disease Prevention and Health
Promotion (ODPHP), U.S. Department of Health and
Human Services (HHS), August 26, 2015.

Summer is the season when much of the United States is under
an excessive heat warning. It is also the time that many amateur,
recreational, and elite athletes transition from indoor programs to
outdoor warm or hot weather exercise regimens. As the temperature
and humidity rise, so does the incidence of environmental heat-related
exertional illnesses. Understanding warm and/or hot weather definitions is very important for an athlete or just an exerciser for fitness so
that they may better comprehend heat illness, preventative measures,
and treatment options if necessary. Of the many relevant heat-related
definitions, the heat index is one of the most important.

**Steadman or Heat Index:** The combination of air temperature
and humidity that gives a description of how the temperature feels.
This is not the actual air temperature. When the heat index is at or
over 90 degrees Fahrenheit, extreme caution should be considered
before exercising outdoors.

## *Heat Illness: What Is It and How Do You Manage It?*

Heat illness or exertional heat illness progresses along a continuum
from the mild (heat rash and/or heat cramps and/or heat syncope)
through the moderate (heat exhaustion) to the life-threatening (heat-
stroke). Anyone is susceptible to a heat-related exertional illness. It
is very important that the athlete or exerciser understand that the

presentation of signs and symptoms associated with heat exertional illness does not necessarily follow this continuum. A dehydrated, non-acclimated or deconditioned individual may right away present with signs and symptoms consistent with heat stroke and not the milder symptoms first.

**Heat Cramps** are associated with excessive sweating during exercise and are usually caused by dehydration, electrolyte (primarily salt) loss, and inadequate blood flow to the peripheral muscles. They usually occur in the quadriceps, hamstrings, and calves.

Treatment for heat cramps is rehydration with an electrolyte (salt) solution and muscle stretch.

**Heat Syncope** results from physical exertion in a hot environment. In an effort to increase heat loss, the skin blood vessels dilate to such an extent that blood flow to the brain is reduced causing symptoms of headache, dizziness, faintness, increased heart rate, nausea, vomiting, restlessness, and possibly even a brief loss of consciousness.

Treatment for heat syncope is to sit or lie down in a cool environment with elevation of the feet. Hydration is very important so there is not a possible progression to heat exhaustion or heat stroke.

**Heat Exhaustion** is a shock-like condition that occurs when excessive sweating causes dehydration and electrolyte loss. A person with heat exhaustion may have headache, nausea, dizziness, chills, fatigue, and extreme thirst. Signs of heat exhaustion are pale and clammy skin, rapid and weak pulse, loss of coordination, decreased performance, dilated pupils, and profuse sweating.

Treatment for heat exhaustion is to immediately stop the activity and properly hydrate with chilled water and/or an electrolyte replacement sport beverage. The exerciser should be cleared by his/her physician before resuming sport or other strenuous outdoor activities.

**Exertional Heat Stroke (Hyperthermia)** is a life-threatening condition in which the body's thermal regulatory mechanism is overwhelmed. There are two types heat stroke—fluid depleted (slow onset) and fluid intact (fast onset). Fluid depleted means that the individual is not hydrating at a rate sufficient to function in a heat challenge situation. Fluid intact means that the extreme heat overwhelms the individual even though the fluid level is sufficient. Key signs of heat stroke are hot skin (not necessarily dry skin), peripheral vasoconstriction (pale or ashen colored skin), high pulse rate, high respiratory rate, decreased urine output, and a core temperature (taken rectally)

157

over 104 or 105 degrees Fahrenheit, and pupils may be dilated and unresponsive to light.

Treatment for heat stroke is to move the person to a cool shaded area and reduce the body temperature immediately. If immediate medical attention is not available, immerse the person in a cool bath while covering the extremities with cool wet cloths and massaging the extremities to propel the cooled blood back into the core.

**Exercise-Induced Hyponatremia (water intoxication)** is most commonly associated with prolonged exertion during sustained, high-intensity endurance activities such as marathons or triathlons. In most cases, it is attributable to excess free water intake, which fails to replenish the sometimes massive sodium losses that result from sweating. Symptoms of hyponatremia can vary from lightheadedness, malaise, nausea, to altered mental status. Risk factors include hot weather, female athletes/exercisers, poor performance, and possibly the use of nonsteroidal anti-inflammatory medications.

As a treatment for hyponatremia, new guidelines advise runners to drink only as much fluid as they lose due to sweating during a race. The International Marathon Medical Directors Association (IMMDA) recommends that, during extended exercise, athletes drink no more than 31 ounces (or about 800 milliliters) of water per hour. Individuals involved in strenuous exercise in warm or hot weather should consider the sodium (salt) concentration of the beverage being consumed.

## How Can You Prevent Exertional Heat-Related Illnesses?

Some recommendations on how to prevent exertional heat-related illness include:

- When exercising in high heat and humidity, rest 10 minutes for every hour and change wet clothing frequently.

- Avoid the midday sun by exercising before 10 a.m. or after 6 p.m., if possible.

- Use a sunscreen with a rating of SPF-15 or lower dependent upon skin type. Ratings above SPF-15 can interfere with the skin's thermal regulation.

- Wear light-weight and breathable clothing.

- Weigh yourself pre- and post-exercise. If there is a less than a 2 percent weight loss after exercise, you are considered mildly dehydrated. With a 2 percent and greater weight loss, you are considered dehydrated.

* During hot weather training, dehydration occurs more frequently and has more severe consequences. Drink early and at regular intervals according to the American College of Sports Medicine (ACSM). The perception of thirst is a poor index of the magnitude of fluid deficit. Monitoring your weight loss and ingesting chilled volumes of fluid during exercise at a rate equal to that lost from sweating is a better method to preventing dehydration.

* Rapid fluid replacement is not recommended for rehydration. Rapid replacement of fluid stimulates increased urine production, which reduces the body water retention.

* Individuals involved in a short bout of exercise are generally fine with water fluid replacement of an extra 8–16 ounces. A sports drink (with salt and potassium) is suggested for exercise lasting longer than an hour, such as a marathon, and at a rate of about 16 to 24 ounces an hour depending upon the amount you sweat and the heat index.

* Replace fluids after long bouts of exercise (greater than an hour) at a rate of 16 ounces of fluid per pound of body weight lost during exercise.

* Avoid caffeinated, protein, and alcoholic drinks, e.g., colored soda, coffee, tea.

* Acclimate to exercising outdoors, altitude, and physical condition. General rule of thumb is 10–14 days for adults and 14–21 days for children (prepubescent) and older adults (> 60 years). Children and older adults are less heat tolerant and have a less effective thermoregulatory system.

* Educate and prepare yourself for outdoor activities. Many websites offer heat index calculations for your local weather conditions. Two websites that will calculate the heat index for you are www.erh.noaa.gov/box/calculate2.html and www.compuweather. com/shared/weather_calculator.htm.

Summer weather does not have to sideline your outdoor exercise regimen. The above suggestions can help you plan and find ways to modify your routine to exercise safely in warm, hot, and humid weather.

# Tips for Practicing and Competing in Hot and Humid Conditions for Athletes

The hot and humid summer conditions can place tremendous stress on the bodies of young athletes. They also pose a risk for serious heat-related medical illness. One option for dealing with the heat would be to avoid it altogether. However, many sports activities, like summer football practices, take place outside during the day. Athletes are left pondering ways to train and compete safely in these conditions. Here are some ideas that might help prepare for sports and exercise in the heat.

## Acclimatization

It can take elite athletes anywhere from a few days to two weeks for their cardiovascular systems to adjust to the hot temperatures. Those of us in less-than-optimal shape might take even longer.

Rather than training at full speed right away, it is probably safer, and better for your athletic performance, to gradually increase your exposure. Slowly increase the volume, duration, and intensity of your training in the heat. Add protective equipment and uniforms throughout the adjustment period.

Many states have acclimatization guidelines that mandate the length of practices and the equipment worn during the first days of practice. These guidelines aim to help the athletes' bodies get used to the conditions.

## Hydration

Ideally you want to stay hydrated while training. You must take in roughly the same amount of fluid you lose in sweat to maintain hydration. It is a good idea to drink fluids throughout the day, including before, during and after sports and exercise.

Water is probably the best beverage for most people. For intense heat or longer training sessions, drinks with sodium and electrolytes can help restore fluids.

For athletes training or competing over many days, weighing yourself daily can help you determine if you are adequately replacing lost fluids.

## Breaks during Training

While you might not be able to take breaks during a competition, you can add them to your training sessions. Experiment with breaking up physical activity into shorter blocks of time. If possible, try to go in the shade or indoors for a few minutes.

### Rest and Recovery Periods between Competitions

If you must play several games or matches in a single day, as in weekend tournaments, coaches can work with event organizers to schedule at least two hours of rest and recovery between contests.

### Cooling Measures

Many options to cool your body before and during activity exist. Precooling your body with ice towels before you train or compete is one option. Fans, ice vests, and even cold baths can help athletes in extreme conditions.

Finally, it is critical that you stop and seek medical attention if you develop any signs or symptoms of heat illness, such as dizziness, weakness, or nausea. Pay attention to your teammates and watch for signs that they might be struggling.

Exertional heat stroke is rare, but it can occur even in highly trained athletes. Fortunately you can prevent most of these events by preparing ahead of time and taking some simple steps while we train and compete in the heat.

# Section 15.2

# *Cold Weather Safety*

"Cold Weather Safety," © 2017 Omnigraphics.
Reviewed June 2017.

Winter activities like alpine skiing, snowboarding, cross-country skiing, snowshoeing, sledding, and ice skating are enjoyed by millions of people each year. Yet exercising outdoors in cold weather involves certain health risks, including potentially serious conditions like frostbite and hypothermia. Understanding the potential hazards and taking appropriate precautions allows people to stay safe and healthy while participating in winter sports.

# Health Risks of Cold-Weather Activities

Although cold-weather activities can be safe and enjoyable for most people, those with health conditions like asthma, circulatory problems, or heart disease should get approval from a doctor before starting a winter exercise program. In addition, everyone should take simple precautions like leaving information about their intended exercise route and return time with a friend or family member in case a problem should arise. Some of the common health risks associated with cold-weather activities include frostbite, hypothermia, dehydration, and slip-and-fall injuries.

## Frostbite

Frostbite occurs when skin and body tissue freezes through exposure to extreme cold. Frostbite is a serious injury, as damaged tissue typically cannot regenerate and must be surgically removed. Frostbite usually affects bare skin on the face—such as the nose, cheeks, or ears—or the extremities furthest from the heart—such as the fingers and toes. In the early stages of frostbite, common symptoms include tingling, aching, burning, or stinging sensations in the affected area, followed by a loss of sensation or numbness. The skin may also appear bright red or mottled grey, and the body part may become swollen. If these signs of frostbite appear, it is important to seek shelter immediately, warm the area slowly, and seek medical treatment if feelings of numbness continue.

## Hypothermia

Hypothermia occurs when the core temperature decreases to the point where the body is unable to maintain normal functions. Shivering is usually the first sign of a decrease in core temperature, as the body initiates involuntary muscle movement in an effort to generate heat. If the core temperature continues to fall, the body directs blood flow away from the extremities to protect the vital organs. At this point, motor functions begin to slow down and muscles may become rigid, causing problems with dexterity and coordination. As hypothermia reaches a severe stage, brain function is affected as well, producing such symptoms as slurred speech, confusion, irritability, and fatigue. Hypothermia becomes life-threatening if the core temperature drops from its normal 98.6°F (37°C) to around 92°F (33°C). Although hypothermia is most common in temperatures below freezing, it can occur even in 50°F (10°C) weather. Children and elderly people are more vulnerable to hypothermia than healthy adults. Other factors that increase the risk of hypothermia include inappropriate attire, wet clothing, and dehydration.

## Dehydration

Although most people only worry about dehydration in hot weather, it is a serious health concern in cold weather as well. Breathing cold, dry winter air and perspiring through exercise leads to fluid loss through evaporation. In addition, the body's tendency to concentrate blood flow in the core when exposed to cold temperatures causes the kidneys to produce more urine than usual. Since these factors can increase the risk of dehydration, it is important to consume extra fluids before, during, and after winter workouts. Covering the nose and mouth with a scarf can also help reduce fluid loss.

## Slips and Falls

Many cold-weather injuries occur due to issues related to poor visibility or unsafe terrain. Shortened daylight hours during the winter months forces many people to exercise at night, when temperatures are colder and they are less able to see obstacles like potholes or patches of ice. Falling and blowing snow can also limit visibility. Meanwhile, icy or snow-covered streets, sidewalks, and jogging paths can create slippery surfaces that may cause people to fall down or twist an ankle. In extreme conditions, the safest approach may be to stick to areas that are familiar and are regularly cleared of snow, or to work out indoors at a gym.

## Staying Safe Outdoors in Winter

With proper precautions, outdoor exercise can be safe and enjoyable even at the peak of winter. Key features of preparing for cold-weather fitness activities include paying attention to the forecast, dressing in layers of clothing to preserve body heat, protecting the extremities from frostbite, and wearing proper safety equipment.

## Check the Forecast

The first step in planning for outdoor activities in winter is being aware of the weather forecast. Snow, ice, and wind can develop quickly and create dangerous conditions for people who are unprepared. The outdoor air temperature is an important consideration, since the risk of frostbite is very low when the thermometer reads 5° Fahrenheit (-15° Celsius) or higher. In temperatures of -18°F (-28°C) or lower, however, frostbite can affect exposed skin within minutes. Exposure to moisture from rain, snow, or sweat also increases the risk of hypothermia by making it more difficult for the body to maintain its core temperature.

## Watch the Wind Chill

Wind is another important thing to consider when preparing for outdoor exercise. The U.S. National Weather Service (NWS) has established the wind-chill factor as a tool to inform people about the added cooling effect of wind velocity. High wind speeds multiply the impact of cold temperatures on exposed skin, increasing the risk of frostbite and hypothermia. Exercisers who move at high speeds, like bicyclists or alpine skiers, must also consider the effect of their own velocity on cold exposure. Riding at 15 miles per hour into a 10 mph headwind, for instance, creates a wind-chill equivalent of 25 mph.

## Dress in Layers

The key to preventing hypothermia is conserving body heat by wearing appropriate clothing. Studies have shown that wearing several layers of lightweight clothing provides better insulation than wearing a single layer of heavy clothing, because the air trapped between the layers provides a barrier to heat loss. An ideal system of cold-weather exercise clothing includes a lightweight, quick-drying synthetic fabric next to the skin, an insulating layer of fleece or wool in the middle, and a waterproof, breathable outer layer with a zipper for easy removal. It is best to avoid wearing cotton or other natural fibers that retain moisture, because wet clothing loses most of its insulating properties. It is also important to avoid overdressing because the body naturally generates heat during exercise. Since up to 40 percent of body heat escapes through the head, wearing a hat is another great way to protect against hypothermia.

## Protect the Extremities

The hands, feet, and face are particularly vulnerable to frostbite because the body diverts blood flow away from the extremities to protect the core in response to cold. Layering works well for protecting the hands and feet from the effects of cold while exercising. A thin pair of synthetic socks worn under thermal socks, or thin glove liners worn beneath a heavier pair of wool or fleece-lined mittens, provides insulation as well as options for removal if one layer becomes wet or sweaty. Chemical heat packs or battery-powered socks and gloves are also available to help keep hands and feet warm in extreme temperatures. It is also important to cover the face and ears with a scarf, ski mask, headband, or balaclava.

## Wear Safety Gear

To stay safe while exercising outdoors in the winter, it is important to choose the right equipment. Walking, running, or biking in low-light or snowy conditions, for instance, is significantly safer for people who wear reflective clothing and use a head lamp. Boots or shoes should provide sufficient traction on snowy or icy terrain. Experts also suggest wearing a protective helmet while participating in high-speed winter sports like alpine skiing or snowboarding. Finally, exercising in the snow amplifies the risk of sun damage to the skin and eyes, so it is important to wear sunscreen, lip balm, and sunglasses or goggles that feature protection from ultraviolet radiation.

## References

1. Gestl, Jon. "Winter Weather Workouts," Topend Sports, 2004.

2. Niemann, Andrew, and Susan Yeargin. "Cold Weather Sports: Recognizing and Preventing Dehydration, Hypothermia, and Frostbite," MomsTeam, 2017.

3. "Winter Fitness: Safety Tips for Exercising Outdoors," Mayo Clinic, 2017.

# Section 15.3

# *Lightning Safety*

This section contains text excerpted from the following sources: Text in this section begins with excerpts from "Lightning: Information for Organized Sporting Events," Centers for Disease Control and Prevention (CDC), December 23, 2013. Reviewed June 2017; Text beginning with the heading "Lightning Kills Play It Safe" is excerpted from "Lightning Kills Play It Safe," National Oceanic and Atmospheric Administration (NOAA), U.S. Department of Commerce (DOC), September 21, 2015.

Lightning is the most frequent weather hazard affecting athletic events, such as baseball, football, swimming, skiing, track and field, soccer, and lacrosse. Lightning can strike and injure both players and spectators in outdoor stadiums during an organized sporting event.

## Action Plans

Large outdoor stadiums should have action plans and procedures for lightning safety. These plans should include the following:

- An evacuation plan for both players and spectators
- A person monitoring all weather forecasts and reports
- A safe shelter

### *Evacuation Plan Specifics*

Evacuation plans should include specific evacuation directions for stadium personnel to communicate to fans to avoid or reduce confusion. Also, evacuation procedures should be posted on tickets, flyers, large screens, and posters to increase awareness.

## Precautions

If you are attending an organized sporting event at an outdoor stadium during a lightning storm, you can minimize your risk of being struck by taking precautions:

- Remain calm.

- Listen for instructions from stadium personnel.

- Move to the designated safe shelters, away from metal poles and the open field. These shelters should be determined before the event if a chance of a storm exists.

- Wait for an all-clear signal, which should occur approximately 30 minutes after you hear the last clap of thunder.

## Lightning Kills Play It Safe

Each year in the United States, more than four hundred people are struck by lightning. On average, about 70 people are killed and many others suffer permanent neurological disabilities. Most of these tragedies can be avoided if proper precautions are taken. When thunderstorms threaten, coaches and sports officials must not let the desire to start or complete an athletic activity hinder their judgment when the safety of participants and spectators is in jeopardy.

## It Is Important for Coaches and Officials to Know Some Basic Facts about Lightning and Its Dangers

- **All thunderstorms produce lightning and are dangerous.** In an average year, lightning kills more people in the United States than either tornadoes or hurricanes.

- **Lightning often strikes outside the area of heavy rain and may strike as far as 10 miles from any rainfall.** Many deaths from lightning occur ahead of storms because people wait too long before seeking shelter, or after storms because people return outside too soon.

- **If you hear thunder, you are in danger.** Anytime thunder is heard, the thunderstorm is close enough to pose an immediate lightning threat to your location.

- **Lightning leaves many victims with permanent disabilities.** While only a small percentage of lightning strike victims die, many survivors must learn to live with very serious, lifelong disabilities.

# *To Avoid Exposing Athletes and Spectators to the Risk of Lightning Take the Following Precautions*

• **Postpone activities if thunderstorms are imminent.** Prior to an event, check the latest forecast and, when necessary, postpone activities early to avoid being caught in a dangerous situation. Stormy weather can endanger the lives of participants, staff, and spectators.

• **Plan ahead.** Have a lightning safety plan. Know where people will go for safety, and know how much time it will take for them to get there. Have specific guidelines for suspending the event or activity so that everyone has time to reach safety before the threat becomes significant. Follow the plan without exception.

• **Keep an eye on the sky.** Pay attention to weather clues that may warn of imminent danger. Look for darkening skies, flashes of lightning, or increasing wind, which may be signs of an approaching thunderstorm.

• **Listen for thunder.** If you hear thunder, immediately suspend your event and instruct everyone to get to a safe place. Substantial buildings provide the best protection. Once inside, stay off corded phones, and stay away from any wiring or plumbing. Avoid sheds, small or open shelters, dugouts, bleachers, or grandstands. If a sturdy building is not nearby, a hard-topped metal vehicle with the windows closed will offer good protection, but avoid touching any metal.

• **Avoid open areas.** Stay away from trees, towers, and utility poles. Lightning tends to strike the taller objects.

• **Stay away from metal bleachers, backstops and fences.** Lightning can travel long distances through metal.

• **Do not resume activities until 30 minutes after the last thunder was heard.**

• **As a further safety measure, officials at outdoor events may want to have a tone-alert NOAA Weather Radio.** The radio will allow you to monitor any short-term forecasts for changing weather conditions, and the tone-alert feature can automatically alert you in case a severe thunderstorm watch or warning is issued.

## *If You Feel Your Hair Stand on End (Indicating Lightning Is about to Strike)*

- **Crouch down on the balls of your feet, put your hands over your ears, and bend your head down.** Make yourself as small a target as possible and minimize your contact with the ground.

- **Do not lie flat on the ground.**

## *What to Do If Someone Is Struck by Lightning*

- **Lightning victims do not carry an electrical charge, are safe to handle, and need immediate medical attention.**

- **Call for help.** Have someone call 9-1-1 or your local ambulance service. Medical attention is needed as quickly as possible.

- **Give first aid.** Cardiac arrest is the immediate cause of death in lightning fatalities. However, some deaths can be prevented if the victim receives the proper first aid immediately. Check the victim to see that they are breathing and have a pulse and continue to monitor the victim until help arrives. Begin CPR if necessary.

- **If possible, move the victim to a safer place.** An active thunderstorm is still dangerous. Don't let the rescuers become victims. Lightning CAN strike the same place twice.

# Part Three


# Head and Facial Injuries

Chapter 16

# Sports-Related Head Injuries

## Chapter Contents

# Section 16.1

# *Traumatic Brain Injuries (TBI)*

This section includes text excerpted from "Traumatic Brain Injury: Hope through Research," National Institute of Neurological Disorders and Stroke (NINDS), September 2015.

Traumatic brain injury (TBI) is the leading cause of death and disability in children and young adults in the United States. TBI is also a major concern for elderly individuals, with a high rate of death and hospitalization due to falls among people age 75 and older. Depending on the severity of injury, TBI can have a lasting impact on quality of life for survivors of all ages—impairing thinking, decision making and reasoning, concentration, memory, movement, and/or sensation (e.g., vision or hearing), and causing emotional problems (personality changes, impulsivity, anxiety, and depression) and epilepsy.

## *What Is a Traumatic Brain Injury (TBI)?*

A TBI occurs when physical, external forces impact the brain either from a penetrating object or a bump, blow, or jolt to the head. Not all blows or jolts to the head result in a TBI. For the ones that do, TBIs can range from mild (a brief change in mental status or consciousness) to severe (an extended period of unconsciousness or amnesia after the injury). There are two broad types of head injuries: penetrating and nonpenetrating.

1. *Penetrating TBI* (also known as open TBI) occurs when the skull is pierced by an object (for example, a bullet, shrapnel, bone fragment, or by a weapon such as hammer, knife, or baseball bat). With this injury, the object enters the brain tissue.

2. *Nonpenetrating TBI* (also known as closed head injury or blunt TBI) is caused by an external force that produces movement of the brain within the skull. Causes include falls, motor vehicle crashes, sports injuries, or being struck by an object. Blast injury due to explosions is a focus of intense study but how it causes brain injury is not fully known.

Some accidents such as explosions, natural disasters, or other extreme events can cause both penetrating and nonpenetrating TBI in the same person.

## How Does TBI Affect the Brain?

TBI-related damage can be confined to one area of the brain, known as a focal injury, or it can occur over a more widespread area, known as a diffuse injury. The type of injury is another determinant of the effect on the brain. Some injuries are considered primary, meaning the damage is immediate. Other consequences of TBI can be secondary, meaning they can occur gradually over the course of hours, days, or weeks. These secondary brain injuries are the result of reactive processes that occur after the initial head trauma.

There are a variety of immediate effects on the brain, including various types of bleeding and tearing forces that injure nerve fibers and cause inflammation, metabolic changes, and brain swelling.

- *Diffuse axonal injury (DAI)* is one of the most common types of brain injuries. DAI refers to widespread damage to the brain's white matter. White matter is composed of bundles of axons (projections of nerve cells that carry electrical impulses). Like the wires in a computer, axons connect various areas of the brain to one another. DAI is the result of shearing forces, which stretch or tear these axon bundles. This damage commonly occurs in auto accidents, falls, or sports injuries. It usually results from rotational forces (twisting) or sudden deceleration. It can result in a disruption of neural circuits and a breakdown of overall communication among nerve cells, or neurons, in the brain. It also leads to the release of brain chemicals that can cause further damage. These injuries can cause temporary or permanent damage to the brain, and recovery can be prolonged.

- *Concussion*—a type of mild TBI that may be considered a temporary injury to the brain but could take minutes to several months to heal. Concussion can be caused by a number of things including a bump, blow, or jolt to the head, sports injury or fall, motor vehicle accident, weapons blast, or a rapid acceleration or deceleration of the brain within the skull (such as the person having been violently shaken). The individual either suddenly loses consciousness or has sudden altered state of consciousness or awareness, and is often called "dazed" or said to have his/her "bell rung." A second concussion closely following the first one

175

causes further damage to the brain—the so-called "second hit" phenomenon—and can lead to permanent damage or even death in some instances.

• *Hematomas*—a pooling of blood in the tissues outside of the blood vessels. Hematomas can develop when major blood vessels in the head become damaged, causing severe bleeding in and around the brain. Different types of hematomas form depending on where the blood collects relative to the meninges. The meninges are the protective membranes surrounding the brain, which consist of three layers: dura mater (outermost), arachnoid mater (middle), and pia mater (innermost).

  • *Epidural hematomas* involve bleeding into the area between the skull and the dura mater. These can occur with a delay of minutes to hours after a skull fracture damages an artery under the skull, and are particularly dangerous.

  • *Subdural hematomas* involve bleeding between the dura and the arachnoid mater, and like epidural hematomas expert pressure on the outside of the brain. Their effects vary depending on their size and extent to which they compress the brain. They are very common in the elderly after a fall.

  • *Subarachnoid hemorrhage* is bleeding that occurs between the arachnoid mater and the pia mater and their effects vary depending on the amount of bleeding.

  • Bleeding into the brain itself is called an *intracerebral hematoma* and damages the surrounding tissue.

• *Contusions*—a bruising or swelling of the brain that occurs when very small blood vessels bleed into brain tissue. Contusions can occur directly under the impact site (i.e., a coup injury) or, more often, on the complete opposite side of the brain from the impact (i.e., a contrecoup injury). They can appear after a delay of hours to a day.

• *Coup/Contrecoup lesions*—contusions or subdural hematomas that occur at the site of head impact as well as directly opposite the coup lesion. Generally they occur when the head abruptly decelerates, which causes the brain to bounce back and forth within the skull (such as in a high-speed car crash). This type of injury also occurs in shaken baby syndrome, a severe head injury that results when an infant or toddler is shaken forcibly enough to cause the brain to bounce back and forth against the skull.

*Skull fractures*—breaks or cracks in one or more of the bones that form the skull. They are a result of blunt force trauma and can cause damage to the underlying areas of the skull such as the membranes, blood vessels, and brain. One main benefit of helmets is to prevent skull fracture.

The first 24 hours after mild TBI are particularly important because subdural hematoma, epidural hematoma, contusion, or excessive brain swelling (edema) are possible and can cause further damage. For this reason doctors suggest watching a person for changes for 24 hours after a concussion.

- *Hemorrhagic progression of a contusion (HPC)* contributes to secondary injuries. HPCs occur when an initial contusion from the primary injury continues to bleed and expand over time. This creates a new or larger lesion—an area of tissue that has been damaged through injury or disease. This increased exposure to blood, which is toxic to brain cells, leads to swelling and further brain cell loss.

- Secondary damage may also be caused by a breakdown in the *blood-brain barrier*. The blood-brain barrier preserves the separation between the brain fluid and the very small capillaries that bring the brain nutrients and oxygen through the blood. Once disrupted, blood, plasma proteins, and other foreign substances leak into the space between neurons in the brain and trigger a chain reaction that causes the brain to swell. It also causes multiple biological systems to go into overdrive, including inflammatory responses which can be harmful to the body if they continue for an extended period of time. It also permits the release of neurotransmitters, chemicals used by brain cells to communicate, which can damage or kill nerve cells when depleted or overexpressed.

- Poor blood flow to the brain can also cause secondary damage. When the brain sustains a powerful blow, swelling occurs just as it would in other parts of the body. Because the skull cannot expand, the brain tissue swells and the pressure inside the skull rises; this is known as *intracranial pressure (ICP)*. When the intracranial pressure becomes too high it prevents blood from flowing to the brain, which deprives it of the oxygen it needs to function. This can permanently damage brain function.

## What Are the Leading Causes of TBI?

Transportation accidents involving automobiles, motorcycles, bicycles, and pedestrians account for half of all TBIs and are the major cause of TBIs in people under age 75.

According to data from the Centers for Disease Control and Prevention (CDC), falls are the most common cause of TBIs and occur most frequently among the youngest and oldest age groups.

The second and third most common causes of TBI are unintentional blunt trauma (accidents that involved being struck by or against an object), followed closely by motor vehicle accidents. Blunt trauma is especially common in children younger than 15 years old, causing nearly a quarter of all TBIs. Assaults account for an additional 10 percent of TBIs, and include abuse-related TBIs, such as head injuries that result from shaken baby syndrome.

Unintentional blunt trauma includes sports-related injuries, which are also a major cause of TBI. Overall, bicycling, football, playground activities, basketball, and soccer result in the most TBI-related emergency room visits. The cause of these injuries does vary slightly by gender. According to the CDC, among children age 10–19, boys are most often injured while playing football or bicycling. Among girls, TBI occur most often while playing soccer or basketball or while bicycling. Anywhere from 1.6 million to 3.8 million sports- and recreation-related TBIs are estimated to occur in the United States annually.

TBIs caused by blast trauma from roadside bombs became a common injury to service members in military conflicts. From 2000–2014 more than 320,000 military service personnel sustained TBIs, though these injuries were not all conflict related. The majority of these TBIs were classified as mild head injuries and due to similar causes as those that occur in civilians.

Adults age 65 and older are at greatest risk for being hospitalized and dying from a TBI, most likely from a fall. TBI-related deaths in children aged 4 years and younger are most likely the result of assault. In young adults aged 15–24 years, motor vehicle accidents are the most likely cause. In every age group, serious TBI rates are higher for men than for women. Men are more likely to be hospitalized and are nearly three times more likely to die from a TBI than women.

## What Are the Signs and Symptoms of TBI?

The effects of TBI can range from severe and permanent disability to more subtle functional and cognitive difficulties that often go undetected during initial evaluation. These problems may emerge days later. Headache, dizziness, confusion, and fatigue tend to start immediately after an injury, but resolve over time. Emotional symptoms such as frustration and irritability tend to develop later on during the recovery period. Many of the signs and symptoms can be easily missed as people may appear healthy even though they act or feel different. Many of the symptoms overlap with other conditions, such as depression or sleep disorders. If any of the following symptoms appear suddenly or worsen over time following a TBI, especially within the first 24 hours after the injury, people should see a medical professional on an emergency basis.

People should seek immediate medical attention if they experience any of the following symptoms:

- loss of or change in consciousness anywhere from a few seconds to a few hours

- decreased level of consciousness, i.e., hard to awaken

- convulsions or seizures

- unequal dilation in the pupils of the eyes or double vision

- clear fluids draining from the nose or ears

- nausea and vomiting

- new neurologic deficit, i.e., slurred speech; weakness of arms, legs, or face; loss of balance

Other common symptoms that should be monitored include:

- mild to profound confusion or disorientation

- problems remembering, concentrating, or making decisions

- headache

- light-headedness, dizziness, vertigo, or loss of balance or coordination

- sensory problems, such as blurred vision, seeing stars, ringing in the ears, bad taste in the mouth

- sensitivity to light or sound

- mood changes or swings, agitation (feeling sad or angry for no reason), combativeness, or other unusual behavior

- feelings of depression or anxiety

- fatigue or drowsiness; a lack of energy or motivation

- changes in sleep patterns (e.g., sleeping a lot more or having difficulty falling or staying asleep); inability to wake up from sleep

Diagnosing TBI in children can be challenging because they may be unable to let others know that they feel different. A child with a TBI may display the following signs or symptoms:

- changes in eating or nursing habits

- persistent crying, irritability, or crankiness; inability to be consoled

- changes in ability to pay attention; lack of interest in a favorite toy or activity

- changes in the way the child plays

- changes in sleep patterns

- sadness or depression

- loss of a skill, such as toilet training

- loss of balance or unsteady walking

- vomiting

In some cases, repeated blows to the head can cause *chronic traumatic encephalopathy (CTE)* — a progressive neurological disorder associated with a variety of symptoms, including cognition and communication problems, motor disorders, problems with impulse control and depression, confusion, and irritability. CTE occurs in those with extraordinary exposure to multiple blows to the head and as a delayed consequence after many years. Studies of retired boxers have shown that repeated blows to the head can cause a number of issues, including memory problems, tremors, and lack of coordination and dementia. Studies have demonstrated rare cases of CTE in other sports with repetitive mild head impacts (e.g., soccer, wrestling, football, and rugby). A single, severe TBI also may lead to a disorder called *posttraumatic dementia (PTD)*, which may be progressive and share some features with CTE. Studies assessing patterns among large populations of people with TBI indicate that moderate or severe TBI in early or mid-life may be associated with increased risk of dementia later in life.

*Effects on Consciousness*

A TBI can cause problems with arousal, consciousness, awareness, alertness, and responsiveness. Generally, there are four abnormal states that can result from a severe TBI:

1. *Brain death*—The lack of measurable brain function and activity after an extended period of time is called brain death and may be confirmed by studies that show no blood flow to the brain.

2. *Coma*—A person in a coma is totally unconscious, unaware, and unable to respond to external stimuli such as pain or light. Coma generally lasts a few days or weeks after which an individual may regain consciousness, die, or move into a vegetative state.

3. *Vegetative state*—A result of widespread damage to the brain, people in a vegetative state are unconscious and unaware of their surroundings. However, they can have periods of unresponsive alertness and may groan, move, or show reflex responses. If this state lasts longer than a few weeks it is referred to as a persistent vegetative state.

4. *Minimally conscious state*—People with severely altered consciousness who still display some evidence of self-awareness or awareness of one's environment (such as following simple commands, yes/no responses).

## How Is TBI Diagnosed?

Although the majority of TBIs are mild they can still have serious health implications. Of greatest concern are injuries that can quickly grow worse. All TBIs require immediate assessment by a professional who has experience evaluating head injuries. A neurological exam will assess motor and sensory skills and the functioning of one or more cranial nerves. It will also test hearing and speech, coordination and balance, mental status, and changes in mood or behavior, among other abilities. Screening tools for coaches and athletic trainers can identify the most concerning concussions for medical evaluation.

Initial assessments may rely on standardized instruments such as the **Acute Concussion Evaluation (ACE)** form from the Centers for Disease Control and Prevention (CDC) or the **Sport Concussion Assessment Tool 2**, which provide a systematic way to assess a person who has suffered a mild TBI. Reviewers collect information about the characteristics of the injury, the presence of amnesia (loss of memory) and/or seizures, as well as the presence of physical, cognitive, emotional, and sleep-related symptoms. The ACE is also used to track symptom recovery over time. It also takes into account risk factors (including concussion, headache, and psychiatric history) that can impact how long it takes to recover from a TBI.

When necessary, medical providers will use brain scans to evaluate the extent of the primary brain injuries and determine if surgery will be needed to help repair any damage to the brain. The need for imaging is based on a physical examination by a doctor and a person's symptoms.

Computed tomography (CT) is the most common imaging technology used to assess people with suspected moderate to severe TBI. CT scans create a series of cross-sectional X-ray images of the skull and brain and can show fractures, hemorrhage, hematomas, hydrocephalus, contusions, and brain tissue swelling. CT scans are often used to assess the damage of a TBI in emergency room settings.

Magnetic resonance imaging (MRI) may be used after the initial assessment and treatment as it is a more sensitive test and picks up subtle changes in the brain that the CT scan might have missed.

Unlike moderate or severe TBI, milder TBI may not involve obvious signs of damage (hematomas, skull fracture, or contusion) that can be identified with current neuroimaging. Instead, much of what is believed to occur to the brain following mild TBI happens at the cellular level. Significant advances have been made in the last decade to image milder TBI damage. For example, diffusion tensor imaging (DTI) can image white matter tracts, more sensitive tests like fluid-attenuated inversion recovery (FLAIR) can detect small areas of damage, and susceptibility-weighted imaging very sensitively identifies bleeding. Despite these improvements, currently available imaging technologies, blood tests, and other measures remain inadequate for detecting these changes in a way that is helpful for diagnosing the mild concussive injuries.

Neuropsychological tests to gauge brain functioning are often used in conjunction with imaging in people who have suffered mild TBI. Such tests involve performing specific cognitive tasks that help assess memory, concentration, information processing, executive functioning, reaction time, and problem solving. The Glasgow Coma Scale (GCS) is the most widely used tool for assessing the level of consciousness after TBI. The standardized 15-point test measures a person's ability to open his or her eyes and respond to spoken questions or physical prompts for movement.

182

Many athletic organizations recommend establishing a baseline picture of an athlete's brain function at the beginning of each season, ideally before any head injuries have occurred. Baseline testing should begin as soon as a child begins a competitive sport. Brain function tests yield information about an individual's memory, attention, and ability to concentrate and solve problems. Brain function tests can be repeated at regular intervals (every 1–2 years) and also after a suspected concussion. The results may help healthcare providers identify any effects from an injury and allow them make more informed decisions about whether a person is ready to return to their normal activities.

## How Is TBI Treated?

Many factors, including the size, severity, and location of the brain injury, influence how a TBI is treated and how quickly a person might recover. One of the critical elements to a person's prognosis is the severity of the injury. Although brain injury often occurs at the moment of head impact, much of the damage related to severe TBI develops from secondary injuries which happen days or weeks after the initial trauma. For this reason, people who receive immediate medical attention at a certified trauma center tend to have the best health outcomes.

### Treating Mild TBI

Individuals with mild TBI, such as concussion, should focus on symptom relief and "brain rest." In these cases, headaches can often be treated with over-the-counter pain relievers. People with mild TBI are also encouraged to wait to resume normal activities until given permission by a doctor. People with a mild TBI should:

- Make an appointment for a follow-up visit with their healthcare provider to confirm the progress of their recovery.

- Inquire about new or persistent symptoms and how to treat them.

- Pay attention to any new signs or symptoms even if they seem unrelated to the injury (for example, mood swings, unusual feelings of irritability). These symptoms may be related even if they occurred several weeks after the injury.

Even after symptoms resolve entirely, people should return to their daily activities gradually. Brain functionality may still be limited despite an absence of outward symptoms. Very little is known about the long-term effects of concussions on brain function. There is no clear timeline for a safe return to normal activities although there are guidelines such as those from the American Academy of Neurology (AAN) and the American Medical Society for Sports Medicine (AMSSM) to help determine when athletes can return to practice or competition. Further research is needed to better understand the effects of mild TBI on the brain and to determine when it is safe to resume normal activities.

Preventing future concussions is critical. While most people recover fully from a first concussion within a few weeks, the rate of recovery from a second or third concussion is generally slower.

In the days or weeks after a concussion, a minority of individuals may develop postconcussion syndrome (PCS). People can develop this syndrome even if they never lost consciousness. The symptoms include headache, fatigue, cognitive impairment, depression, irritability, dizziness and balance trouble, and apathy. These symptoms usually improve without medical treatment within one to a few weeks but some people can have longer lasting symptoms.

In some cases of moderate to severe TBI, persistent symptoms may be related to conditions triggered by imbalances in the production of hormones required for the brain to function normally. Hormone imbalances can occur when certain glands in the body, such as the pituitary gland, are damaged over time as result of the brain injury. Symptoms of these hormonal imbalances include weight loss or gain, fatigue, dry skin, impotence, menstrual cycle changes, depression, difficulty concentrating, hair loss, or cold intolerance. When these symptoms persist 3 months after their initial injury or when they occur up to 3 years after the initial TBI, people should speak with a healthcare provider about their condition.

## Treating Severe TBI

Immediate treatment for the person who has suffered a severe TBI focuses on preventing death; stabilizing the person's spinal cord, heart, lung, and other vital organ functions; and preventing further brain damage. Persons with severe TBI generally require a breathing machine to ensure proper oxygen delivery and breathing.

During the acute management period, healthcare providers monitor the person's blood pressure, flow of blood to the brain, brain temperature, pressure inside the skull, and the brain's oxygen supply. A common practice called intracranial pressure ICP monitoring involves inserting a special catheter through a hole drilled into the skull. Doctors frequently rely on ICP monitoring as a way to determine if and when medications or surgery are needed in order to prevent secondary brain injury from swelling. People with severe head injury may require surgery to relieve pressure inside the skull, get rid of damaged or dead brain tissue (especially for penetrating TBI), or remove hematomas.

In-hospital strategies for managing people with severe TBI aim to prevent conditions including:

• infection, particularly pneumonia

• deep vein thrombosis (blood clots that occur deep within a vein; risk increases during long periods of inactivity)

People with TBIs may need nutritional supplements to minimize the effects that vitamin, mineral, and other dietary deficiencies may cause over time. Some individuals may even require tube feeding to maintain the proper balance of nutrients.

Following the acute care period, people with severe TBI are often transferred to a rehabilitation center where a multidisciplinary team of healthcare providers help with recovery. The rehabilitation team includes neurologists, nurses, psychologists, nutritionists, as well as physical, occupational, vocational, speech, and respiratory therapists.

*Cognitive rehabilitation therapy (CRT)* is a strategy aimed at helping individuals regain their normal brain function through an individualized training program. Using this strategy, people may also learn compensatory strategies for coping with persistent deficiencies involving memory, problem solving, and the thinking skills to get things done. CRT programs tend to be highly individualized and their success varies. A 2011 Institute of Medicine (IOM) report concluded that cognitive rehabilitation interventions need to be developed and assessed more thoroughly.

## Other Factors That Influence Recovery

*Genes*

Evidence suggests that genetics play a role in how quickly and completely a person recovers from a TBI. For example, researchers have found that apolipoprotein E ε4 (ApoE4)—a genetic variant associated with higher risks for Alzheimer disease—is associated with worse health outcomes following a TBI. Much work remains to be done to understand how genetic factors, as well as how specific types of head injuries in particular locations, affect recovery processes. It is hoped that this research will lead to new treatment strategies and improved outcomes for people with TBI.

*Age*

Studies suggest that age and the number of head injuries a person has suffered over his or her lifetime are two critical factors that impact recovery. For example, TBI-related brain swelling in children can be very different from the same condition in adults, even when the primary injuries are similar. Brain swelling in newborns, young infants, and teenagers often occurs much more quickly than it does in older individuals. Evidence from very limited CTE studies suggest that younger people (ages 20 to 40) tend to have behavioral and mood changes associated with CTE, while those who are older (ages 50+) have more cognitive difficulties.

Compared with younger adults with the same TBI severity, older adults are likely to have less complete recovery. Older people also have more medical issues and are often taking multiple medications that may complicate treatment (e.g., blood-thinning agents when there is a risk of bleeding into the head). Further research is needed to determine if and how treatment strategies may need to be adjusted based on a person's age.

## Can TBI Be Prevented?

The best treatment for TBI is prevention. Unlike most neurological disorders, head injuries can be prevented. According to the CDC, doing the following can help prevent TBIs:

- Wear the correct helmet and make sure it fits properly when riding a bicycle, skateboarding, and playing sports like hockey and football.

- Wear a seatbelt when you drive or ride in a motor vehicle.

- Install window guards and stair safety gates at home for young children.

- Never drive under the influence of drugs or alcohol.

- Improve lighting and remove rugs, clutter, and other trip hazards in the hallway.

- Use nonslip mats and install grab bars next to the toilet and in the tub or shower for older adults.

- Install handrails on stairways.

- Improve balance and strength with a regular physical activity program.

- Ensure children's playgrounds are made of shock-absorbing material, such as hardwood mulch or sand.

## Section 16.2

# *Concussions*

This section includes text excerpted from "Concussion at Play—Opportunities to Reshape the Culture around Concussion," Centers for Disease Control and Prevention (CDC), July 30, 2015.

Each day, hundreds of thousands of young athletes practice and compete in a wide variety of sports. Physical activity, sports participation, and play in general are great ways for children and teens to build and maintain healthy bones and muscles, lower their chances for depression and chronic diseases (such as diabetes), learn leadership and teamwork skills, and do well in school. However, research shows that when it comes to concussion, young athletes are at risk.

A concussion is a type of traumatic brain injury—or TBI—caused by a bump, blow, or jolt to the head or body that causes the head and brain to move rapidly back and forth. This sudden movement can cause the brain to bounce around or twist in the skull, creating chemical changes in the brain and sometimes stretching and damaging the brain cells.

Most children and teens with a concussion feel better within a couple of weeks. However, for some, symptoms may last for months or longer and can lead to short- and long-term problems affecting how a young person thinks, acts, learns, and feels. Parents, coaches, healthcare providers, and school professionals all play an important role in supporting young athletes so that they can thrive on the playing field, at school, and in all parts of their lives.

# Concussion Knowledge and Awareness

*On the Rise*

Along with the rise in the number of educational efforts on concussion, research over the last 5 years shows that the level of awareness and knowledge about concussion among these groups has grown. For example:

• The majority of youth (ages 13–18) have heard about concussion and understand the dangers of this injury.

• Most parents view concussions as a serious injury and know that continuing to play with a concussion could cause further injury or even death.

• Many coaches are aware of general concussion symptoms and understand that an athlete does not need to lose consciousness to have a concussion.

• Healthcare providers in many areas are aware of and have access to referral networks for patients with concussion.

*Gaps Still Remain*

Even though knowledge and awareness of concussion is growing, research shows that there are still important gaps to be filled.

• Some parents are not familiar with state concussion laws or school or league protocols on children returning to learn and play.

• Coaches may not be able to identify subtle concussion symptoms and may not be aware of the importance of managing cognitive activities following a concussion.

• Some healthcare providers do not feel they have adequate training on concussion, and the use of evidence-based and standardized assessment tools and guidelines is limited.

• While similar research about school professionals' knowledge and awareness of concussion is not currently available, the important role that school professionals play in concussion identification and management is clear.

## Concussion Attitudes and Behaviors

### Too Many Young Athletes Do Not Report Concussion Symptoms

Reporting a possible concussion is the most important action young athletes can take to bring their injury to light. Reporting symptoms will facilitate an athlete being properly assessed, monitored, and treated and taking needed time to heal. Yet, research shows that too many young athletes do not take this critical first step.

In one study, researchers interviewed a group of almost 800 high school athletes during the course of a season and found that:

- Sixty-nine percent of athletes with a possible concussion played with concussion symptoms.

- Forty percent of those athletes said that their coaches were not aware that they had a possible concussion.

In a different study, 50 female and male high school athletes were asked what they would do if they thought they had a concussion:

- They most commonly answered, "I would keep playing and see how I felt" or "I would take a little break and return to play."

- None said that they would stop playing entirely if they experienced concussion symptoms.

### After a Concussion, Young Athletes Are Returning to Play Too Soon

Young athletes should never return to play the same day of the injury. In addition, they should not return to play until an appropriate healthcare provider says it is okay. However, many young athletes are returning to play too soon following a concussion.

In a study of 150 young patients seen in an emergency department for concussion, many did not take time to heal fully before returning to their usual activities:

- Thirty-nine percent reported returning to play on the same day of their concussion.

- More than half (58 percent) returned to play without medical clearance.

# Opportunities to Reshape the Culture around Concussion

## The Way Coaches Talk about Concussion Influences Young Athletes' Decisions to Report Concussion Symptoms

Young athletes depend on their coaches for guidance and need to feel comfortable in order to report their symptoms to their coaches, athletic trainers, teammates, and parents. In fact, young athletes' beliefs about their coaches' expectations on reporting may trump their own knowledge or intention to report a possible concussion.

The way coaches talk about concussion affects young athletes' behaviors around reporting symptoms:

- Young athletes who receive negative messages from their coaches, or who are insulted by their coaches for reporting an injury, may feel pressured to keep playing with concussion symptoms.

- On the other hand, young athletes who receive positive messages from their coach and are praised for symptom reporting are more likely to report their concussion symptoms.

**ACTION STEP:** Coaches should foster an environment where young athletes feel comfortable reporting a concussion. Before and during the season, coaches should talk about concussion and ask young athletes to share and discuss their concerns about reporting a concussion.

**WHY THIS IS IMPORTANT:** Young athletes are more likely to report concussion symptoms accurately when they receive positive messages about reporting from their coach.

## Young Athletes May Feel Pressure to Hide Their Concussion Symptoms

Research shows that despite the importance of reporting their concussion symptoms, many young athletes are unaware that they have a concussion or may not report a possible concussion because they:

- Do not think a concussion is serious.

- Are worried about losing their position on the team or do not want to stop playing.

- Do not want to let their coach or teammates down.

190

• Are concerned about jeopardizing their future sports career or about what their coach or teammates might think of them.

**ACTION STEP:** Coaches should keep a list of concussion signs and symptoms and a concussion action plan on hand and visibly posted where young athletes play games and practice. Coaches should review this list frequently with their athletes.

**WHY THIS IS IMPORTANT:** Most young athletes understand the potentially dangerous consequences of a concussion, such as long-term disability and death. Yet young athletes may be unable to identify some symptoms, like a ringing in the ears or fatigue caused by a concussion.

Coaches also may have difficulty identifying some subtle concussion signs and symptoms, such as vision problems, sensitivity to light and noise, and problems with sleep.

## Young Athletes Are More Likely to Play with a Concussion during a Big Game

Young athletes may be more reluctant to tell a coach or athletic trainer about a possible concussion in a championship game compared to a regular game. Researchers presented the following situation to 58 young athletes: "During a championship game, you develop an injury that does not significantly hinder your ability to play, but could result in severe or permanent injury if you continue to play. Do you tell your coach or athletic trainer, or do you say nothing and continue to play?"

• Fifty-two percent of young athletes said they would always report an injury during a championship game or event.

• Thirty-six percent of young athletes said that they would sometimes tell their coach or athletic trainer, while 7 percent said they would never tell their coach or athletic trainer about the injury.

Similarly, the same researchers asked a group of 314 coaches if they would remove a young athlete from play with concussion symptoms in different scenarios:

• Ninety-two percent of coaches reported they would remove the young athlete from play when the importance of the game or event was not included in the scenario.

- When the scenario included a championship game, 17–20 percent of coaches indicated that they would allow a concussed athlete to keep playing.

**ACTION STEP:** Parents and coaches need to communicate to athletes that a concussion should be reported no matter how important the game or event seems. Athletes should know that health and safety always come first.

**WHY THIS IS IMPORTANT:** Parents and coaches greatly influence how athletes think about sports, such as their motivation to play, enjoyment of the sport, goals, and decision-making. Young athletes may not report their symptoms because they feel pressure from or worry about letting down their coach, parent(s), or teammates.

## *Healthcare Providers and School Professionals Can Help Young Athletes Successfully Return to Learn and Play*

As many as a third of young athletes do not receive clear discharge instructions after going to an emergency department with concussion symptoms. When discharge instructions are provided, healthcare providers often give instructions on return to play but not on return to learn.

There is limited research about school professionals' knowledge of concussion, yet the most important action that school professionals can take is to support young athletes during their recovery process as they return to learn. A student's quality of care is improved when school professionals across the school setting work in collaboration to achieve positive school outcomes. Healthcare providers and school professionals can guide young athletes and their parents as they return to activity in the classroom and on the playing field.

**ACTION STEP:** Parents should receive written instructions from healthcare providers on return to learn and return to play strategies. This information needs to be given to an athlete's coach and school.

**WHY THIS IS IMPORTANT:** Youth athletes and their parents need guidance to support them as they return to learn and play. Coaches and school professionals will benefit from these written instructions as well. Young athletes also need to take time to heal before returning to school since thinking and learning can be difficult when the brain is still healing. In one study, 30 percent of students reported a decline in school performance or attendance after a concussion.

## Creating a Safe Sport Culture

Athletes thrive when they:

- Have fun playing their sport.

- Receive positive messages and praise from their coaches for concussion symptom reporting.

- Have parents who talk with them about concussion and model and expect safe play.

- Feel comfortable reporting symptoms of a possible concussion to coaches.

- Support their teammates sitting out of play if they have concussion.

- Get written instructions from a healthcare provider on when to return to school and play.

## Education Efforts Help Play a Role in Concussion Safety

Participation in concussion education may support increased symptom reporting by athletes. A survey of almost 170 high school athletes in six sports found that young athletes who were more knowledgeable about concussion were more likely to report a concussion during practice.

Another study of high school athletes who received concussion education from any source were more likely to report concussion symptoms to a coach or athletic trainer compared to athletes with no education. Specifically:

- Seventy-two percent of athletes who had received concussion education indicated that they would always notify their coach of concussion symptoms.

- Only 12 percent of athletes who had no history of concussion education stated they would always report their concussion symptoms to their coach.

Similarly, coaches who receive coaching education are more likely to correctly recognize concussion signs and symptoms and feel comfortable deciding whether an athlete needs to be evaluated for a possible concussion.

**ACTION STEP:** Educate young athletes and coaches on the importance of concussion throughout the season using materials that have been evaluated and shown to be effective. Education efforts should be coupled with programmatic and league policy activities.

**WHY THIS IS IMPORTANT:** Educational efforts should be tailored to meet the needs of and address the main concerns reported by athletes. Improving coaches' and young athletes' knowledge alone may not always result in increased concussion reporting by athletes. A pilot study implemented in 40 high schools that included standardized protocols for schools and medical providers, education and training, and coordination among the key stakeholders led to an increase in the number of concussions identified, reported, and treated.

## Young Athletes Look to Parents and Coaches to Understand the Culture of Safety

A young athlete's views and actions on the sports field are influenced by those of their parents, coaches, teammates, and even spectators. Together, these groups shape a "sports culture."

**Action Steps: Expect Safe Play. Model Safe Play. Reinforce Safe Play.**

### Expect Safe Play

Why this is important: While not risk-free, sports are a great way for children and teens to stay healthy and can help them do well in school. Young athletes look to their coaches and parents to learn which actions are okay in the "team's culture" and how to follow safe play and the rules of the sport.

### Model Safe Play

Why this is important: Children and teens learn from what they see their parents doing. In a study of parents and their children who ski and snowboard:

- Ninety-six percent of children who wore a helmet said that their parents also wore a ski or snowboard helmet.

- Among parents who did not wear a helmet, only 17 percent of their children wore one.

*Reinforce Safe Play*

Why this is important: As many as 25 percent of the concussions reported among high school athletes result from aggressive or illegal play activity. A culture that supports aggressive or unsportsmanlike behavior among young athletes can increase their chances of getting a concussion or other serious injury. Such an atmosphere also encourages athletes to hide concussion symptoms and keep playing when they are hurt.

Chapter 17

# Sports Injuries to the Face

## Chapter Contents

# Section 17.1

## *Jaw Injuries*

"Jaw Injuries," © 2017 Omnigraphics.
Reviewed June 2017.

The jawbone, or mandible, is a U-shaped structure that extends from the chin to the ears. It connects to the skull at the temporomandibular joints (TMJ), which allow the jaw to open and close and move from side to side. Jaw injuries, such as a dislocated jaw or broken jaw (mandibular fracture), are fairly common in sports. The jawbone itself is vulnerable to fracture from impact with a ball or stick, while the TMJ can be damaged or unhinged from a blow to the mouth or a fall. Even athletes who take precautions like wearing a mouth guard and helmet can still experience jaw injuries because of the exposed location of the jawbone. Since jaw injuries can affect eating and breathing, they are considered serious conditions that require immediate medical attention.

### *Causes of Jaw Injuries*

Most jaw injuries occur due to facial trauma, such as a blow to the chin, mouth, or face. Although broken and dislocated jaws may occur due to motor vehicle accidents, industrial accidents, slip-and-fall accidents, or physical assaults, they are also common in sports. Sports that involve sticks—such as hockey, field hockey, and lacrosse—pose a particular risk of jaw injuries because of the additional force of swinging equipment. Fighting sports—such as boxing and mixed martial arts—also have a high incidence of jaw injuries. Yet broken and dislocated jaws can occur in many other types of sports and activities as well, including football, soccer, basketball, baseball, volleyball, skiing, and mountain biking.

### *Symptoms of Jaw Injuries*

When the mandible sustains a fracture, the bone typically breaks in multiple places on opposite sides of the jaw. A broken jawbone may remain in alignment, or it may be displaced or separated at the point of the fracture. In either case, the symptoms may include pain, swelling, bruising, bleeding from the mouth, loose teeth, and difficulty moving the jaw, speaking, or chewing. A displaced jaw fracture may involve additional symptoms, such as abnormality in the shape or appearance of the face, misalignment (malocclusion) of the teeth, and numbness in the chin and mouth. Symptoms of a dislocated jaw are likely to include pain, difficulty speaking and chewing, misalignment of the teeth, and drooling.

## Diagnosis and Treatment of Jaw Injuries

Jaw injuries should be considered medical emergencies. The immediate treatment—particularly if the athlete is unconscious—is to clear the airway of any broken teeth and blood. The athlete should then be positioned sitting up or lying on one side with their head tilted to allow any blood to run out of the mouth rather than into the throat. The jaw can be stabilized for transport to a hospital by gently wrapping gauze or an ace bandage under the chin and around the top of the head. An icepack can also be applied to help relieve pain and reduce swelling.

Diagnosis of a broken or dislocated jaw typically involves a physical examination and X-rays. Magnetic resonance imaging (MRI) or other tools may be used to determine whether muscles or ligaments in the face may be torn or damaged. Since jaw injuries most often result from a blow to the head, the athlete should also be evaluated for a possible concussion. Signs of concussion include headache, dizziness, confusion, nausea, ringing in the ears, sensitivity to light, and memory loss.

Treatment for a dislocated jaw involves returning it to the proper position through manual manipulation or surgery. A clean, minor, nondisplaced jaw fracture can often be immobilized and allowed to heal on its own. Severe, displaced, or multiple fractures of the jawbone, however, usually require surgical repair. In most cases, fractured or dislocated jaws must be wired together for four to six weeks to promote healing. A combination of wires and elastic bands are used to immobilize the jaw and align the teeth. Since the wires prevent the patient from opening their mouth, they cannot chew solid food and must obtain nutrition from a liquid diet. It is important to keep a wire-cutting tool on hand throughout the healing process in case the jaw must be opened due to choking or vomiting.

## Recovery from Jaw Injuries

Athletes who have an injury that requires their jaw to be wired shut must follow a liquid diet. Since they are unable to open their mouth or chew solid food, the available sources of nutrition are pureed fruits and vegetables, well-cooked meats, and soft grains taken through a straw. Experts recommend eating small, frequent meals and supplementing with whole milk, fruit juices, nutritional drinks, and even baby food to get enough calories and maintain weight. Even after the wires are removed, athletes should continue to follow a soft diet to protect the jaw during recovery. Pasta, rice, soup, canned meats, yogurt, and soft fruits are good choices, while raw produce, crunchy snacks, and chewy foods should be avoided.

Doctors usually approve light exercise—such as walking, resistance training, and stationery cycling—to maintain fitness and muscle tone while recovering from a jaw injury. If the jaw is wired, it is important to avoid strenuous exercise that requires breathing through the mouth. Most athletes can return to normal activities within a few months after the wires are removed. They may need to wear a mouth guard, face mask, or other protective device. Although broken and dislocated jaws heal successfully in most cases, some athletes experience recurring pain and stiffness in the jaw afterward—a condition known as temporomandibular joint disorder.

## References

1. "Be Smart about Jaw Injuries in Sports," MedCenter TMJ, February 16, 2016.

2. Roth, Erika. "Broken or Dislocated Jaw," Healthline, 2015.

3. Ziegler, Terry. "Broken Jaw (Mandibular Fracture)," SportsMD, 2016.

# Section 17.2

## *Eye Injuries*

This section contains text excerpted from the following sources: Text under the heading "Sports That May Put You at Risk for Eye Injuries" is excerpted from "Sports and Your Eyes," National Eye Institute (NEI), June 16, 2016; Text under the heading "Simple Steps to Prevent Eye Injuries in Sports" is excerpted from "Simple Steps to Prevent Eye Injuries in Sports," Office of Disease Prevention and Health Promotion (ODPHP), U.S. Department of Health and Human Services (HHS), October 1, 2014; Text under the heading "Protect Your Eyes When You Exercise" is excerpted from "Protect Your Eyes When You Exercise," *Go4Life*, National Institutes of Health (NIH), January 25, 2017.

### Sports That May Put You at Risk for Eye Injuries

#### *Gear Up!*

If you play sports, you know they can be a lot of fun. The last thing you want to do is miss a game, especially if it's because you're hurt. That's why you should always follow the rules and wear the right safety gear.

Think about your favorite sport. Do you wear anything to protect your eyes, like goggles or a face mask? You might think you don't need protective eyewear, but sports-related eye injuries are serious. Eye injuries are a leading cause of blindness among children in the United States. The good news is that most eye injuries can be prevented with the right protective eyewear.

#### *Protective Eyewear Fast Facts*

• Everyone should wear protective eyewear.

• Ordinary prescription glasses, contact lenses, and sunglasses won't protect you from injuries. Most protective eyewear can be made to match your prescription.

• For the best protection, use eyewear made of ultra-strong polycarbonate.

• Choose eyewear specifically made for your sport and make sure it fits comfortably on your face.

## Simple Steps to Prevent Eye Injuries in Sports

Most athletes think of knee and shoulder problems when we talk about sports-related injuries. With fall sports in full swing, it is important to remember that eye injuries in sports are not only common, but they are potentially very serious.

According to the American Academy of Ophthalmology (AAO), sports account for approximately 100,000 eye injuries each year. Roughly 42,000 of those injuries require evaluation in emergency departments. In fact, a patient with a sports-related eye injury presents to a United States emergency room every 13 minutes. It is estimated that sports-related eye injuries cost between $175 million and $200 million per year.

Generally baseball, basketball and racquet sports cause the highest numbers of eye injuries. One of every three of these eye injuries in sports occurs in children. In kids between the ages of five and 14, baseball is the leading cause. Basketball is a common culprit in athletes aged 15 and older. And boxing and martial arts present a high risk for serious eye injuries.

These eye injuries can be mild ones, but serious injuries like orbital fractures, corneal abrasions and detached retina can occur. Approximately 13,500 people become legally blind from sports-related eye injuries every year.

Fortunately the American Academy of Ophthalmology (AAO) estimates that 90 percent of eye injuries are preventable. October is Eye Injury Prevention Month, so athletes should remember these simple tips to avoid serious eye damage in sports:

• Wear appropriate eye protection, especially in basketball, racket sports, field hockey and soccer. In baseball, ice hockey and men's lacrosse, an athlete should wear a helmet with a polycarbonate shield. Polycarbonate lenses are believed to be 10 times more resistant to impact than other materials. All protective eyewear should comply with American Society of Testing Materials (ASTM) standards.

• Wear additional protective eyewear, if you wear contact lenses or glasses. Contacts offer no protection against impacts to the eye. Glasses and sunglasses do not provide adequate protection and could shatter upon impact, increasing the danger to the eye.

202

- Wear eye protection for all sports if you are functionally one-eyed, meaning one eye has normal vision and the other is less than 20/40 vision

- Inspect protective eyewear regularly and replace when it appears worn or damaged.

Last, if an eye injury does occur, every athlete should consider going to an emergency department or consulting an ophthalmologist. Even a seemingly minor injury can actually be potentially serious and lead to loss of vision. Remember, 90 percent of sports-related eye injuries can be prevented.

## Protect Your Eyes When You Exercise

Emergency room doctors treat an estimated 42,000 sports-related eye injuries each year in the United States. Nearly all of them could be prevented with protective eyewear.

Sports at moderate to high risk for eye injuries include: basketball, baseball, softball, ice hockey, tennis, soccer, volleyball, football, fishing, and golf. Studies show that protective eyewear does not hinder the player's sight while participating in athletics. In fact, some athletes can even play better because they're less afraid of getting hit in the eye.

Play it safe! Protect your eyes:

- Protective eyewear includes safety glasses and goggles, safety shields, and eye guards that are specially designed to provide the right protection for a certain activity.

- You still need protective eyewear that's approved for your sport even if you don't wear glasses or contacts.

- Ordinary prescription glasses, contact lenses, and sunglasses do not protect you from sports-related eye injury. You need to wear safety goggles over them.

- Experts recommend ultra-strong polycarbonate lenses for eye protection. Make sure they are in sport-appropriate frames or goggles.

- Many eye care providers sell protective eyewear, as do some sporting goods stores. Protective eyewear is sport-specific with the proper ASTM standards written on the packaging. This makes it easy to decide which pair is best for each activity.

# Section 17.3

# *Cauliflower Ear*

Text in this section is from "What Is Cauliflower Ear?" © 2017
Osborne Head & Neck Institute. Reprinted with permission.

Around the mid-1800s, speculations arose regarding the condition
of "cauliflower ear." Some thought it was a symptom of insanity, while
others argued that it resulted from the insane hitting themselves, or
being struck around the ear by psychiatric staff. The idea that cauliflower ear is related to mental illness has gradually dissipated. We
now have proven causes and effective treatments for this condition.

## *What Is Cauliflower Ear?*

- Cauliflower ear is medically known as an **auricular hematoma**. The external ear is made of cartilage and it is the shape
  of the cartilage that gives the ear its distinctive shell-like shape.
  The cartilage is lined by perichondrium, a tight layer of connective tissue.

- Auricular hematoma/cauliflower ear occurs when the ear cartilage is injured (from a blow or other form of trauma). Trauma
  results in fluid or blood collecting between the perichondrium
  and the cartilage. This blood or fluid can become permanent and
  scarred, resulting in the appearance of cauliflower ear.

## *What Causes Cauliflower Ear Formation?*

The most common cause of cauliflower ear is a direct hit to the ear.
When the cartilage of the ear is injured, it is separated from the perichondrium by blood or fluid from the injury. The collection of blood is
called a hematoma. The perichondrium supplies blood and nutrients
to the cartilage so when they are separated, the supply of nutrients is
disrupted. Because the blood supply is lost, the cartilage is not able
to heal easily and instead forms scar tissue. This scar tissue contributes to the swollen and misshapen appearance, thought to resemble
a cauliflower.

## Who Is Susceptible to Developing Cauliflower Ear?

- Athletes involved in close-contact sports are the likeliest to develop cauliflower ear. This condition is most common among:

  - boxers

  - wrestlers

  - martial artists

  - However, auricular hematoma may develop in anyone, after a single blow to the ear.

## What Are the Symptoms of Cauliflower Ear?

- pain, swelling, or bruising in the affected area

- deformity of the curvature of the ear

- loss of hearing

- ringing in the ear (tinnitus)

- pain/tenderness of the ear cartilage

## How Can Cauliflower Ear Be Treated?

As soon as the injury is noted, consultation with a facial plastic surgeon should be undertaken so that the blood may be drained via a small incision in the ear. After drainage, it is important that the perichondrium lie flat on the cartilage again, so that more fluid does not reaccumulate. To reapproximate the skin and the cartilage, a pressure bandage is applied. Antibiotics are often prescribed to prevent or treat infections of the outer ear, or to reduce any inflammation. Cosmetic procedures are also available to improve and refine the ear's appearance.

## How Can Cauliflower Ear Be Prevented?

To prevent injuries that can cause cauliflower ear, headgear should be worn during close-contact sports. This protective gear will protect the ears, decreasing the risk for injury or trauma. It is crucial that the headgear is of proper fit; a loose helmet can easily slip out of place, and a helmet that is too tight may damage the ears. If one should sustain an injury to the ear, medical evaluation should be sought immediately. Prompt attention by an able physician will decrease the chances of developing cauliflower ear.

# Part Four

# Back, Neck, and Spine Injuries

Chapter 18

# Lower Back Pain

If you have lower back pain, you are not alone. About 80 percent of adults experience low back pain at some point in their lifetimes. It is the most common cause of job-related disability and a leading contributor to missed work days. In a large survey, more than a quarter of adults reported experiencing low back pain during the past 3 months.

Men and women are equally affected by low back pain, which can range in intensity from a dull, constant ache to a sudden, sharp sensation that leaves the person incapacitated. Pain can begin abruptly as a result of an accident or by lifting something heavy, or it can develop over time due to age-related changes of the spine. Sedentary lifestyles also can set the stage for low back pain, especially when a weekday routine of getting too little exercise is punctuated by strenuous weekend workout.

Most low back pain is acute, or short-term, and lasts a few days to a few weeks. It tends to resolve on its own with self-care and there is no residual loss of function. The majority of acute low back pain is mechanical in nature, meaning that there is a disruption in the way the components of the back (the spine, muscle, intervertebral discs, and nerves) fit together and move.

*Subacute low back pain* is defined as pain that lasts between 4 and 12 weeks.

*Chronic back pain* is defined as pain that persists for 12 weeks or longer, even after an initial injury or underlying cause of acute low

This chapter includes text excerpted from "Low Back Pain Fact Sheet," National Institute of Neurological Disorders and Stroke (NINDS), December 2014.

back pain has been treated. About 20 percent of people affected by acute low back pain develop chronic low back pain with persistent symptoms at one year. In some cases, treatment successfully relieves chronic low back pain, but in other cases pain persists despite medical and surgical treatment.

The magnitude of the burden from low back pain has grown worse in recent years. In 1990, a study ranking the most burdensome conditions in the United States in terms of mortality or poor health as a result of disease put low back pain in sixth place; in 2010, low back pain jumped to third place, with only ischemic heart disease and chronic obstructive pulmonary disease ranking higher.

## What Structures Make up the Back?

The lower back where most back pain occurs includes the five vertebrae (referred to as L1-L5) in the lumbar region, which supports much of the weight of the upper body. The spaces between the vertebrae are maintained by round, rubbery pads called intervertebral discs that act like shock absorbers throughout the spinal column to cushion the bones as the body moves. Bands of tissue known as ligaments hold the vertebrae in place, and tendons attach the muscles to the spinal column. Thirty-one pairs of nerves are rooted to the spinal cord and they control body movements and transmit signals from the body to the brain.

## What Causes Lower Back Pain?

The vast majority of low back pain is mechanical in nature. In many cases, low back pain is associated with spondylosis, a term that refers to the general degeneration of the spine associated with normal wear and tear that occurs in the joints, discs, and bones of the spine as people get older. Some examples of mechanical causes of low back pain include:

- **Sprains and strains** account for most acute back pain. Sprains are caused by overstretching or tearing ligaments, and strains are tears in tendon or muscle. Both can occur from twisting or lifting something improperly, lifting something too heavy, or overstretching. Such movements may also trigger spasms in back muscles, which can also be painful.

- **Intervertebral disc degeneration** is one of the most common mechanical causes of low back pain, and it occurs when the

210

usually rubbery discs lose integrity as a normal process of aging. In a healthy back, intervertebral discs provide height and allow bending, flexion, and torsion of the lower back. As the discs deteriorate, they lose their cushioning ability.

* **Herniated or ruptured discs** can occur when the intervertebral discs become compressed and bulge outward (herniation) or rupture, causing low back pain.

* **Radiculopathy** is a condition caused by compression, inflammation and/or injury to a spinal nerve root. Pressure on the nerve root results in pain, numbness, or a tingling sensation that travels or radiates to other areas of the body that are served by that nerve. Radiculopathy may occur when spinal stenosis or a herniated or ruptured disc compresses the nerve root.

* **Sciatica** is a form of radiculopathy caused by compression of the sciatic nerve, the large nerve that travels through the buttocks and extends down the back of the leg. This compression causes shock-like or burning low back pain combined with pain through the buttocks and down one leg, occasionally reaching the foot. In the most extreme cases, when the nerve is pinched between the disc and the adjacent bone, the symptoms may involve not only pain, but numbness and muscle weakness in the leg because of interrupted nerve signaling. The condition may also be caused by a tumor or cyst that presses on the sciatic nerve or its roots.

* **Spondylolisthesis** is a condition in which a vertebra of the lower spine slips out of place, pinching the nerves exiting the spinal column.

* **A traumatic injury**, such as from playing sports, car accidents, or a fall can injure tendons, ligaments or muscle resulting in low back pain. Traumatic injury may also cause the spine to become overly compressed, which in turn can cause an intervertebral disc to rupture or herniate, exerting pressure on any of the nerves rooted to the spinal cord. When spinal nerves become compressed and irritated, back pain and sciatica may result.

* **Spinal stenosis** is a narrowing of the spinal column that puts pressure on the spinal cord and nerves that can cause pain or numbness with walking and over time leads to leg weakness and sensory loss.

- **Skeletal irregularities** include scoliosis, a curvature of the spine that does not usually cause pain until middle age; lordosis, an abnormally accentuated arch in the lower back; and other congenital anomalies of the spine.

Low back pain is rarely related to serious underlying conditions, but when these conditions do occur, they require immediate medical attention. Serious underlying conditions include:

- **Infections** are not a common cause of back pain. However, infections can cause pain when they involve the vertebrae, a condition called osteomyelitis; the intervertebral discs, called discitis; or the sacroiliac joints connecting the lower spine to the pelvis, called sacroiliitis.

- **Tumors** are a relatively rare cause of back pain. Occasionally, tumors begin in the back, but more often they appear in the back as a result of cancer that has spread from elsewhere in the body.

- **Cauda equina syndrome** is a serious but rare complication of a ruptured disc. It occurs when disc material is pushed into the spinal canal and compresses the bundle of lumbar and sacral nerve roots, causing loss of bladder and bowel control. Permanent neurological damage may result if this syndrome is left untreated.

- **Abdominal aortic aneurysms** occur when the large blood vessel that supplies blood to the abdomen, pelvis, and legs becomes abnormally enlarged. Back pain can be a sign that the aneurysm is becoming larger and that the risk of rupture should be assessed.

- **Kidney stones** can cause sharp pain in the lower back, usually on one side.

Other underlying conditions that predispose people to low back pain include:

- **Inflammatory diseases of the joints** such as arthritis, including osteoarthritis and rheumatoid arthritis as well as spondylitis, an inflammation of the vertebrae, can also cause low back pain. Spondylitis is also called spondyloarthritis or spondyloarthropathy.

- **Osteoporosis** is a metabolic bone disease marked by a progressive decrease in bone density and strength, which can lead to painful fractures of the vertebrae.

- **Endometriosis** is the buildup of uterine tissue in places outside the uterus.

- **Fibromyalgia**, a chronic pain syndrome involving widespread muscle pain and fatigue.

## How Is Low Back Pain Diagnosed?

A complete medical history and physical exam can usually identify any serious conditions that may be causing the pain. During the exam, a healthcare provider will ask about the onset, site, and severity of the pain; duration of symptoms and any limitations in movement; and history of previous episodes or any health conditions that might be related to the pain. Along with a thorough back examination, neurologic tests are conducted to determine the cause of pain and appropriate treatment. The cause of chronic lower back pain is often difficult to determine even after a thorough examination.

Imaging tests are not warranted in most cases. Under certain circumstances, however, imaging may be ordered to rule out specific causes of pain, including tumors and spinal stenosis. Imaging and other types of tests include:

- X-ray
- Computerized tomography (CT)
- Myelograms
- Discography
- Magnetic resonance imaging (MRI)
- Electrodiagnostics
- Bone scans
- Ultrasound imaging
- Blood tests

## How Is Back Pain Treated?

Treatment for low back pain generally depends on whether the pain is acute or chronic. In general, surgery is recommended only if there is evidence of worsening nerve damage and when diagnostic tests indicate structural changes for which corrective surgical procedures have been developed.

Conventionally used treatments and their level of supportive evidence include:

- Hot or cold packs

- Activity

- Strengthening exercises

- Physical therapy

- Medications

  - Analgesic medications

  - Nonsteroidal anti-inflammatory drugs (NSAIDs)

  - Anticonvulsants

  - Antidepressants

  - Counter-irritants

- Spinal manipulation and spinal mobilization

- Traction

- Acupuncture

- Biofeedback

- Nerve block therapies

- Epidural steroid injections

- Transcutaneous electrical nerve stimulation (TENS)

- Surgery

  - Vertebroplasty and kyphoplasty

  - Spinal laminectomy

  - Discectomy or microdiscectomy

  - Foraminotomy

  - Intradiscal electrothermal therapy (IDET)

  - Nucleoplasty, also called plasma disc decompression (PDD)

  - Radiofrequency denervation

  - Spinal fusion

  - Artificial disc replacement

## Can Back Pain Be Prevented?

Recurring back pain resulting from improper body mechanics is often preventable by avoiding movements that jolt or strain the back, maintaining correct posture, and lifting objects properly. Many work-related injuries are caused or aggravated by stressors such as heavy lifting, contact stress (repeated or constant contact between soft body tissue and a hard or sharp object), vibration, repetitive motion, and awkward posture. Using ergonomically designed furniture and equipment to protect the body from injury at home and in the workplace may reduce the risk of back injury.

The use of lumbar supports in the form of wide elastic bands that can be tightened to provide support to the lower back and abdominal muscles to prevent low back pain remains controversial. Such supports are widely used despite a lack of evidence showing that they actually prevent pain. Multiple studies have determined that the use of lumbar supports provides no benefit in terms of the prevention and treatment of back pain. Although there have been anecdotal case reports of injury reduction among workers using lumbar support belts, many companies that have back belt programs also have training and ergonomic awareness programs. The reported injury reduction may be related to a combination of these or other factors. Furthermore, some caution is advised given that wearing supportive belts may actually lead to or aggravate back pain by causing back muscles to weaken from lack of use.

Chapter 19

# Spondylolysis and Spondylolisthesis

Spondylolysis (spon-dee-low-lye-sis) and spondylolisthesis (spon-dee-low-lis-thee-sis) are common causes of low back pain in young athletes.

Spondylolysis is a crack or stress fracture in one of the vertebrae, the small bones that make up the spinal column. The injury most often occurs in children and adolescents who participate in sports that involve repeated stress on the lower back, such as gymnastics, football, and weight lifting.

In some cases, the stress fracture weakens the bone so much that it is unable to maintain its proper position in the spine—and the vertebra starts to shift or slip out of place. This condition is called spondylolisthesis.

For most patients with spondylolysis and spondylolisthesis, back pain and other symptoms will improve with conservative treatment. This always begins with a period of rest from sports and other strenuous activities.

Patients who have persistent back pain or severe slippage of a vertebra, however, may need surgery to relieve their symptoms and allow a return to sports and activities.

---

Text in this chapter is from "Spondylolysis and Spondylolisthesis," © 1995-2017 American Academy of Orthopaedic Surgeons. Reprinted with permission.

## Anatomy

Your spine is made up of 24 small rectangular-shaped bones, called
vertebrae, which are stacked on top of one another. These bones connect to create a canal that protects the spinal cord.

The five vertebrae in the lower back comprise the lumbar spine.
Other parts of your spine include:

**Spinal cord and nerves.** These "electrical cables" travel through
the spinal canal carrying messages between your brain and muscles.
Nerve roots branch out from the spinal cord through openings in the
vertebrae.

**Facet joints.** Between the back of the vertebrae are small joints
that provide stability and help to control the movement of the spine.
The facet joints work like hinges and run in pairs down the length of
the spine on each side.

**Intervertebral disks.** In between the vertebrae are flexible intervertebral disks. These disks are flat and round and about a half inch
thick. Intervertebral disks cushion the vertebrae and act as shock
absorbers when you walk or run.

## Description

Spondylolysis and spondylolisthesis are different spinal conditions—but they are often related to each other.

### Spondylolysis

In spondylolysis, a crack or stress fracture develops through the
*pars interarticularis*, which is a small, thin portion of the vertebra that
connects the upper and lower facet joints.

Most commonly, this fracture occurs in the fifth vertebra of the
lumbar (lower) spine, although it sometimes occurs in the fourth lumbar vertebra. Fracture can occur on one side or both sides of the bone.

The pars interarticularis is the weakest portion of the vertebra. For
this reason, it is the area most vulnerable to injury from the repetitive
stress and overuse that characterize many sports.

Spondylolysis can occur in people of all ages but, because their spines
are still developing, children and adolescents are most susceptible.

Many times, patients with spondylolysis will also have some degree
of spondylolisthesis.

*Spondylolisthesis*

If left untreated, spondylolysis can weaken the vertebra so much that it is unable to maintain its proper position in the spine. This condition is called spondylolisthesis.

In spondylolisthesis, the fractured pars interarticularis separates, allowing the injured vertebra to shift or slip forward on the vertebra directly below it. In children and adolescents, this slippage most often occurs during periods of rapid growth—such as an adolescent growth spurt.

Doctors commonly describe spondylolisthesis as either low grade or high grade, depending upon the amount of slippage. A high-grade slip occurs when more than 50 percent of the width of the fractured vertebra slips forward on the vertebra below it. Patients with high-grade slips are more likely to experience significant pain and nerve injury and to need surgery to relieve their symptoms.

## Cause

*Overuse*

Both spondylolysis and spondylolisthesis are more likely to occur in young people who participate in sports that require frequent overstretching (hyperextension) of the lumbar spine—such as gymnastics, football, and weight lifting. Over time, this type of overuse can weaken the pars interarticularis, leading to fracture and/or slippage of a vertebra.

*Genetics*

Doctors believe that some people may be born with vertebral bone that is thinner than normal—and this may make them more vulnerable to fractures.

## Symptoms

In many cases, patients with spondylolysis and spondylolisthesis do not have any obvious symptoms. The conditions may not even be discovered until an X-ray is taken for an unrelated injury or condition.

When symptoms do occur, the most common symptom is lower back pain. This pain may:

• Feel similar to a muscle strain

• Radiate to the buttocks and back of the thighs

• Worsen with activity and improve with rest

In patients with spondylolisthesis, muscle spasms may lead to additional signs and symptoms, including:

- Back stiffness
- Tight hamstrings (the muscles in the back of the thigh)
- Difficulty standing and walking

Spondylolisthesis patients who have severe or high-grade slips may have tingling, numbness, or weakness in one or both legs. These symptoms result from pressure on the spinal nerve root as it exits the spinal canal near the fracture.

## Doctor Examination

### Physical Examination

Your doctor will begin by taking a medical history and asking about your child's general health and symptoms. He or she will want to know if your child participates in sports. Children who participate in sports that place excessive stress on the lower back are more likely to have a diagnosis of spondylolysis or spondylolisthesis.

Your doctor will carefully examine your child's back and spine, looking for:

- Areas of tenderness
- Limited range of motion
- Muscle spasms
- Muscle weakness

Your doctor will also observe your child's posture and gait (the way he or she walks). In some cases, tight hamstrings may cause a patient to stand awkwardly or walk with a stiff-legged gait.

Imaging tests will help confirm the diagnosis of spondylolysis or spondylolisthesis.

### Imaging Tests

**X-rays.** These studies provide images of dense structures, such as bone. Your doctor may order X-rays of your child's lower back from a number of different angles to look for a stress fracture and to view the alignment of the vertebrae.

If X-rays show a "crack" or stress fracture in the pars interarticularis portion of the fourth or fifth lumbar vertebra, it is an indication of spondylolysis.

If the fracture gap at the pars interarticularis has widened and the vertebra has shifted forward, it is an indication of spondylolisthesis. An X-ray taken from the side will help your doctor determine the amount of forward slippage.

**Computerized tomography (CT) scans.** More detailed than plain X-rays, CT scans can help your doctor learn more about the fracture or slippage and can be helpful in planning treatment.

**Magnetic resonance imaging (MRI) scans.** These studies provide better images of the body's soft tissues. An MRI can help your doctor determine if there is damage to the intervertebral disks between the vertebrae or if a slipped vertebra is pressing on spinal nerve roots. It can also help your doctor determine if there is injury to the pars before it can be seen on X-ray.

## Treatment

The goals of treatment for spondylolysis and spondylolisthesis are to:

- Reduce pain
- Allow a recent pars fracture to heal
- Return the patient to sports and other daily activities

### Nonsurgical Treatment

Initial treatment is almost always nonsurgical in nature. Most patients with spondylolysis and low-grade spondylolisthesis will improve with nonsurgical treatment.

Nonsurgical treatment may include:

**Rest.** Avoiding sports and other activities that place excessive stress on the lower back for a period of time can often help improve back pain and other symptoms.

**Nonsteroidal anti-inflammatory drugs (NSAIDs).** NSAIDs such as ibuprofen and naproxen can help reduce swelling and relieve back pain.

**Physical therapy.** Specific exercises can help improve flexibility, stretch tight hamstring muscles, and strengthen muscles in the back and abdomen.

**Bracing.** Some patients may need to wear a back brace for a period of time to limit movement in the spine and provide an opportunity for a recent pars fracture to heal.

Over the course of treatment, your doctor will take periodic X-rays to determine whether the vertebra is changing position.

## Surgical Treatment

Surgery may be recommended for spondylolisthesis patients who have:

• Severe or high-grade slippage

• Slippage that is progressively worsening

• Back pain that has not improved after a period of nonsurgical treatment

Spinal fusion between the fifth lumbar vertebra and the sacrum is the surgical procedure most often used to treat patients with spondylolisthesis.

The goals of spinal fusion are to:

• Prevent further progression of the slip

• Stabilize the spine

• Alleviate significant back pain

### Surgical Procedure

Spinal fusion is essentially a "welding" process. The basic idea is to fuse together the affected vertebrae so that they heal into a single, solid bone. Fusion eliminates motion between the damaged vertebrae and takes away some spinal flexibility. The theory is that, if the painful spine segment does not move, it should not hurt.

During the procedure, the doctor will first realign the vertebrae in the lumbar spine. Small pieces of bone—called bone graft—are then placed into the spaces between the vertebrae to be fused. Over time, the bones grow together—similar to how a broken bone heals.

Prior to placing the bone graft, your doctor may use metal screws and rods to further stabilize the spine and improve the chances of successful fusion.

In some cases, patients with high-grade slippage will also have compression of the spinal nerve roots. If this is the case, your doctor may first perform a procedure to open up the spinal canal and relieve pressure on the nerves before performing the spinal fusion.

## Outcomes

The majority of patients with spondylolysis and spondylolisthesis are free from pain and other symptoms after treatment. In most cases, sports and other activities can be resumed gradually with few complications or recurrences.

To help prevent future injury, your doctor may recommend that your child do specific exercises to stretch and strengthen the back and abdominal muscles. In addition, regular check-ups are needed to ensure that problems do not develop.

Chapter 20

# Cervical Fractures (Broken Neck)

The seven bones in the neck are the cervical vertebrae. They support the head and connect it to the shoulders and body. A fracture, or break, in one of the cervical vertebrae is commonly called a broken neck.

Cervical fractures usually result from high-energy trauma, such as automobile crashes or falls. Athletes are also at risk. A cervical fracture can occur if:

- A football player "spears" an opponent with his head.

- An ice hockey player is struck from behind and rams into the boards.

- A gymnast misses the high bar during a release move and falls.

- A diver strikes the bottom of a shallow pool.

Any injury to the vertebrae can have serious consequences because the spinal cord, the central nervous system's connection between the brain and the body, runs through the center of the vertebrae. Damage to the spinal cord can result in paralysis or death. Injury to the spinal cord at the level of the cervical spine can lead to temporary or permanent paralysis of the entire body from the neck down.

---

Text in this chapter is from "Cervical Fractures (Broken Neck)," © 1995-2017 American Academy of Orthopaedic Surgeons. Reprinted with permission.

## Emergency Response

In a trauma situation, the neck should be immobilized until x-rays are taken and reviewed by a physician. Emergency medical personnel will assume that an unconscious individual has a neck injury and respond accordingly. The victim may experience shock and either temporary or permanent paralysis.

Conscious patients with an acute neck injury may or may not have severe neck pain. They may also have pain spreading from the neck to the shoulders or arms, resulting from the vertebra compressing a nerve. There may be some bruising and swelling at the back of the neck. The physician will perform a complete neurological examination to assess nerve function and may request additional radiographic studies, such as MRI or computed tomography (CT), to determine the extent of the injuries.

## Treatment

Treatment will depend on which of the seven cervical vertebrae are damaged and the kind of fracture sustained. A minor compression fracture can be treated with a cervical brace worn for 6 to 8 weeks until the bone heals. A more complex or extensive fracture may require traction, surgery, 2 to 3 months in a rigid cast, or a combination of these treatments.

## Prevention

Improvements in athletic equipment and rule changes have reduced the number of sports-related cervical fractures over the past 20 years. You can help protect yourself and your family if you:

- Always wear a seat belt when you are driving or a passenger in a car.

- Never dive in a shallow pool area, and be sure that young people are properly supervised when swimming and diving.

- Wear the proper protective equipment for your sport and follow all safety regulations, such as having a spotter and appropriate cushioning mats.

Chapter 21

# Spinal Cord Injuries

Until World War II, a serious spinal cord injury (SCI) usually meant certain death. Anyone who survived such injury relied on a wheelchair for mobility in a world with few accommodations and faced an ongoing struggle to survive secondary complications such as breathing problems, blood clots, kidney failure, and pressure sores. By the middle of the twentieth century, new antibiotics and novel approaches to preventing and treating bedsores and urinary tract infections revolutionized care after spinal cord injury. This greatly expanded life expectancy and required new strategies to maintain the health of people living with chronic paralysis. New standards of care for treating spinal cord injuries were established: reposition the spine, fix the bones in place to prevent further damage, and rehabilitate disabilities with exercise.

Nowadays, improved emergency care for people with spinal cord injuries, antibiotics to treat infections, and aggressive rehabilitation can minimize damage to the nervous system and restore function to varying degrees. Advances in research are giving doctors and people living with SCI hope that spinal cord injuries will eventually be repairable. With new surgical techniques and developments in spinal nerve regeneration, cell replacement, neuroprotection, and neurorehabilitation, the future for spinal cord injury survivors looks brighter than ever.

This chapter includes text excerpted from "Spinal Cord Injury: Hope through Research," National Institute of Neurological Disorders and Stroke (NINDS), July 2013. Reviewed June 2017.

# How Does the Spinal Cord Work?

To understand what can happen as the result of a spinal cord injury, it is important to understand the anatomy of the spinal cord and its normal functions.

The spinal cord is a tight bundle of neural cells (*neurons* and *glia*) and nerve pathways (*axons*) that extend from the base of the brain to the lower back. It is the primary information highway that receives sensory information from the skin, joints, internal organs, and muscles of the trunk, arms, and legs, which is then relayed upward to the brain. It also carries messages downward from the brain to other body systems. Millions of nerve cells situated in the spinal cord itself also coordinate complex patterns of movements such as rhythmic breathing and walking. Together, the spinal cord and brain make up the central nervous system (CNS), which controls most functions of the body.

The spinal cord is made up of neurons, glia, and blood vessels. The neurons and their dendrites (branching projections that receive input from axons of other neurons) reside in an H-shaped or butterfly-shaped region called gray matter. The gray matter of the cord contains *lower motor neurons*, which branch out from the cord to muscles, internal organs, and tissue in other parts of the body and transmit information commands to start and stop muscle movement that is under voluntary control. *Upper motor neurons* are located in the brain and send their long processes (axons) to the spinal cord neurons. Other types of nerve cells found in dense clumps of cells that sit just outside the spinal cord (called sensory ganglia) relay information such as temperature, touch, pain, vibration, and joint position back to the brain.

The axons carry signals up and down the spinal cord and to the rest of the body. Thousands of axons are bundled into pairs of spinal nerves that link the spinal cord to the muscles and the rest of the body. The function of these nerves reflects their location along the spinal cord.

- *Cervical* spinal nerves (C1 to C8) emerge from the spinal cord in the neck and control signals to the back of the head, the neck and shoulders, the arms and hands, and the diaphragm.

- *Thoracic* spinal nerves (T1 to T12) emerge from the spinal cord in the upper mid-back and control signals to the chest muscles, some muscles of the back, and many organ systems, including parts of the abdomen.

- *Lumbar* spinal nerves (L1 to L5) emerge from the spinal cord in the low back and control signals to the lower parts of the abdomen and the back, the buttocks, some parts of the external genital organs, and parts of the leg.

- *Sacral* spinal nerves (S1 to S5) emerge from the spinal cord in the low back and control signals to the thighs and lower parts of the legs, the feet, most of the external genital organs, and the area around the anus.

The outcome of any injury to the spinal cord depends upon the level at which the injury occurs in the neck or back and how many and which axons and cells are damaged; the more axons and cells that survive in the injured region, the greater the amount of function recovery. Loss of neurologic function occurs below the level of the injury, so the higher the spinal injury, the greater the loss of function.

A whitish mixture of proteins and fat-like substances called *myelin* covers the axons and allows electrical signals to flow quickly and freely. Myelin is much like the insulation around electrical wires. It is formed by axon-insulating cells called *oligodendrocytes*. Because of its whitish color, the outer section of the spinal cord—which is formed by bundles of myelinated axons—is called white matter.

The spinal cord, like the brain, is enclosed in three membrane layers called meninges: the dura mater (the tougher, most protective, outermost layer); the arachnoid (middle layer); and the pia mater (innermost and very delicate). The soft, gel-like spinal cord is protected by 33 rings of bone called *vertebrae*, which form the spinal column. Each vertebra has a circular hole, so when the rung-like bones are stacked one on top of the other there is a long hollow channel, with the spinal cord inside that channel. The vertebrae are named and numbered from top to bottom according to their location along the backbone: seven cervical vertebrae (C1-C7) are in the neck; twelve thoracic vertebrae (T1-T12) attach to the ribs; five lumbar vertebrae (L1-L5) are in the lower back; and, below them, five sacral vertebrae (S1-S5) that connect to the pelvis. The adult spinal cord is shorter than the spinal column and generally ends at the L1-L2 vertebral body level. A thick set of nerves from the lumbar and sacral cord form the "cauda equina" in the spinal canal below the cord.

The spinal column is not all bone. Between the vertebrae are discs of semirigid cartilage and narrow spaces called foramen that act as passages through which the spinal nerves travel to and from the rest of the body. These are places where the spinal cord is particularly vulnerable to direct injury.

## What Is a Spinal Cord Injury?

The vertebrae normally protect the soft tissues of the spinal cord, but they can be broken or dislocated in a variety of ways that puts harmful pressure on the spinal cord. Injuries can occur at any level of the spinal cord. The segment of the cord that is injured, and the severity of the damage to the nervous tissue, will determine which body functions are compromised or lost. An injury to a part of the spinal cord causes physiological consequences to parts of the body controlled by nerves at and below the level of the injury.

Motor vehicle accidents and catastrophic falls are the most common causes of physical trauma that breaks, crushes, or presses on the vertebrae and can cause irreversible damage at the corresponding level of the spinal cord and below. Severe trauma to the cervical cord results in paralysis of most of the body, including the arms and legs, and is called *tetraplegia* (though the older term, *quadriplegia*, is still in common use). Trauma to the thoracic nerves in the upper, middle, or lower back results in paralysis of the trunk and lower extremities, called *paraplegia*.

Penetrating injuries, such as gunshot or knife wounds, damage the spinal cord; however, most traumatic injuries do not completely sever the spinal cord. Instead, an injury is more likely to cause fractures and compression of the vertebrae, which then crush and destroy the axons that carry signals up and down the spinal cord. A spinal cord injury can damage a few, many, or almost all of the axons that cross the site of injury. A variety of cells located in and around the injury site may also die. Some injuries in which there is little or no nerve cell death but only pressure-induced blockage of nerve signaling or only demyelination without axonal damage will allow almost complete recovery. Others in which there is complete cell death across even a thin horizontal level of the spinal cord will result in complete paralysis.

## What Happens When the Spinal Cord Is Injured?

Traumatic spinal cord injury usually begins with a sudden, mechanical blow or rupture to the spine that fractures or dislocates vertebrae. The damage begins at the moment of **primary injury**, when the cord is stretched or displaced by bone fragments or disc material. Nerve signaling stops immediately but may not return rapidly even if there is no structural damage to the cord. In severe injury, axons are cut or damaged beyond repair, and neural cell membranes are broken. Blood vessels may rupture and cause bleeding into the spinal cord's central tissue, or bleeding can occur outside the cord, causing pressure by the blood clot on the cord.

Within minutes, the spinal cord near the site of severe injury swells within the spinal canal. This may increase pressure on the cord and cut blood flow to spinal cord tissue. Blood pressure can drop, sometimes dramatically, as the body loses its ability to self-regulate. All these changes can cause a condition known as *spinal shock* that can last from several hours to several days.

There is some controversy among neurologists about the extent and impact of spinal shock, and even its definition in terms of physiological characteristics. It appears to occur in approximately half of the cases of spinal cord injury and is usually directly related to the size and severity of the injury. During spinal shock, the entire spinal cord below the lesion becomes temporarily disabled, causing complete paralysis, loss of all reflexes, and loss of sensation below the affected cord level.

The primary injury initiates processes that continue for days or weeks. It sets off a cascade of biochemical and cellular events that kills neurons, strips axons of their protective myelin covering, and triggers an inflammatory immune system response. This is the beginning of the **secondary injury** process. Days, or sometimes even weeks later, after this second wave of damage has passed, the area of destruction has increased—sometimes to several segments above and below the original injury.

- **Changes in blood flow cause ongoing damage.** The major reduction in blood flow to the site following the initial injury can last for as long as 24 hours and become progressively worse if there is continued compression of the cord due to swelling or bleeding. Because of the greater blood flow needs of gray matter, the impact is greater on the central cord than on the outlying white matter. Blood vessels in the gray matter also become leaky, sometimes as early as 5 minutes after injury, which initiates spinal cord swelling. Cells that line the still-intact blood vessels in the spinal cord also begin to swell, and this further reduces blood flow to the injured area. The combination of leaking, swelling, and sluggish blood flow prevents the normal delivery of oxygen and nutrients to neurons, causing many of them to die.

- **Excessive release of neurotransmitters kills nerve cells.** After the injury, an excessive release of *neurotransmitters* (chemicals that allow neurons to signal each other) can cause additional damage by overstimulating nerve cells.

231

The neurotransmitter glutamate is commonly used by axons in the spinal cord to stimulate activity in other neurons. But when spinal cells are injured, their axons flood the area with glutamate and trigger additional nerve cell damage. This process kills neurons near the injury site and the myelin-forming oligodendrocytes at and beyond the injured area.

- **An invasion of immune system cells creates inflammation.** Under normal conditions, the blood-brain barrier keeps potentially destructive immune system cells from entering the brain or spinal cord. This barrier is a naturally-occurring result of closely spaced cells along the blood vessels that prevent many substances from leaving the blood and entering brain tissues. But when the blood-brain barrier breaks down, immune system cells—primarily white blood cells—can invade the spinal cord tissue and trigger an inflammatory response. This inflammatory response can cause additional damage to some neurons and may kill others.

- **Free radicals attack nerve cells.** Another consequence of inflammation is the increased production of highly reactive forms of oxygen molecules called free radicals—chemicals that modify the chemical structure of other molecules in damaging ways, for example, damaging cell membranes. Free radicals are produced naturally as a by-product of normal oxygen metabolism in small enough amounts that they cause no harm. But injury to the spinal cord causes cells to overproduce free radicals, which destroy critical molecules of the cell.

- **Nerve cells self-destruct.** For reasons that are still unclear, spinal cord injury sets off apoptosis—a normal process of cell death that helps the body get rid of old and unhealthy cells. Apoptosis kills oligodendrocytes in damaged areas of the spinal cord days to weeks after the injury. Apoptosis can strip myelin from intact axons in adjacent ascending and descending pathways, causing the axons to become dysfunctional and disrupting the spinal cord's ability to communicate with the brain.

- **Scarring occurs.** Following a spinal cord injury, astrocytes (star-shaped glial cells that support the brain and spinal cord) wall off the injury site by forming a scar, which creates a physical and chemical barrier to any axons which could potentially regenerate and reconnect. Even if some intact myelinated axons remain, there may not be enough to convey any meaningful information to or from the brain.

Researchers are especially interested in studying the mechanisms of this wave of secondary damage because finding ways to stop it could save spinal cord tissue and thereby enable greater functional recovery.

## What Immediate Treatments Are Available?

Injury to the spine isn't always obvious. Any injury that involves the head and neck, pelvic fractures, penetrating injuries in the area of the spine, or injuries that result from falling from heights should raise concerns regarding an unstable spinal column. Until imaging of the spine is done at an emergency or trauma center, people who might have spine injury should be cared for as if any significant movement of the neck or back could cause further damage.

At the accident scene, emergency personnel will immobilize the head and neck to prevent movement, put a rigid collar around the neck, and carefully place the person on a rigid backboard to prevent further damage to the spinal cord. Sedation may be given to relax the person and prevent movement. A breathing tube may be inserted if the injury is to the high cervical cord and the individual is at risk of respiratory arrest.

At the hospital or trauma center, realigning the spine using a rigid brace or axial traction (using a mechanical force to stretch the spine and relieve pressure on the spinal cord) is usually done as soon as possible to stabilize the spine and prevent additional damage. Fractured vertebrae, bone fragments, herniated discs, or other objects compressing the spinal column may need to be surgically removed. Spinal decompression surgery to relieve pressure within the spinal column also may be necessary in the days after injury. Results of a neurosurgical study show that, in some cases, earlier surgery is associated with better functional recovery.

## How Are Spinal Cord Injuries Diagnosed?

The emergency room physician will test the individual to see if there is any movement or sensation at or below the level of injury. Methods to assess autonomic function also have been established (American Spinal Injury Association, or ASIA, Autonomic Standards Classification, or ASC). Emergency medical tests for a spinal cord injury include:

- Magnetic resonance imaging (MRI)
- Computerized tomography (CT)
- Plane X-rays

# How Are Spinal Cord Injuries Classified?

Once the swelling from within and around the spinal cord has eased a bit—usually within a week to 10 days—physicians will conduct a complete neurological exam to classify the injury as complete or incomplete. An **incomplete injury** means that the ability of the spinal cord to convey messages to or from the brain is not completely lost. People with incomplete injuries retain some sensory function and may have voluntary motor activity below the injury site. A **complete injury** prevents nerve communications from the brain and spinal cord to parts of the body below the injury site. There is a total lack of sensory and motor function below the level of injury, even if the spinal cord was not completely severed. Studies have shown that people with incomplete injuries have a greater chance of recovering some function in the affected limbs than those with a complete injury.

Physicians use the International Standards of Neurologic Classification of Spinal Cord Injury (ISNCSCI) to measure the extent of neurologic injury following a spinal cord injury. The ASIA Impairment Scale (AIS) is used to categorize the degrees of injury into different groups.

# How Does a Spinal Cord Injury Affect the Rest of the Body and How Is It Treated?

People who survive a spinal cord injury often have medical complications resulting in bladder, bowel, and sexual dysfunction. They may also develop chronic pain, autonomic dysfunction, and spasticity (increased tone in and contractions of muscles of the arms and legs), but this is highly variable and poorly understood. Higher levels of injury may have an increased susceptibility to respiratory and heart problems.

- **Breathing.** A spinal cord injury high in the neck can affect the nerves and muscles in the neck and chest that are involved with breathing. Respiratory complications are often an indication of the severity of spinal cord injury. About one-third of those with injury to the neck area will need help with breathing and require respiratory support via intubation, which involves inserting a tube connected to a machine that pushes oxygen into the lungs and removes carbon dioxide) through the nose or throat and into the airway. This may be temporary or permanent depending upon the severity and location of injury. Any injury to the spinal cord between the C1-C4 segments, which supply the phrenic nerves leading to the diaphragm, can stop

breathing. (The phrenic nerves cause the diaphragm to move
and the lungs to expand.) People with these injuries need immediate ventilatory support. People with high cervical cord injury
may have trouble coughing and clearing secretions from their
lungs. Special training regarding breathing and swallowing may
be needed.

- **Pneumonia.** Respiratory complications are the leading cause
  of death in people with spinal cord injury, commonly as a result
  of pneumonia. Intubation increases the risk of developing venti-
  lator-associated pneumonia; individuals with spinal cord injury
  who are intubated have to be carefully monitored and treated
  with antibiotics if symptoms of pneumonia appear. Attention to
  clearing secretions and preventing aspiration of mouth contents
  into the lungs can prevent pneumonia.

- **Circulatory problems.** Spinal cord injuries can cause a variety
  of changes in circulation, including blood pressure instability,
  abnormal heart rhythms (arrhythmias) that may appear days
  after the injury, and blood clots. Because the brain's control of
  the cardiac nerves is cut off, the heart can beat at a dangerously
  slow pace, or it can pound rapidly and irregularly. Arrhythmias
  are more common and severe in the most serious injuries. Low
  blood pressure also often occurs due to changes in nervous system control of blood vessels, which then widen, causing blood
  to pool in the small arteries far away from the heart. Blood
  pressure needs to be closely monitored to keep blood and oxygen
  flowing through the spinal cord tissue, with the understanding
  that baseline blood pressure can be significantly lower than
  usual in people living with spinal cord injuries. Since muscle
  movement contributes to moving blood back to the heart, people
  with spinal cord injuries are at triple the usual risk for blood
  clots due to stagnation of blood flow in the large veins in the
  legs. Treatment includes anticoagulant drugs and compression
  stockings to increase blood flow in the lower legs and feet.

- **Spasticity and muscle tone.** When the spinal cord is damaged, information from the brain can no longer regulate reflex
  activity. Reflexes may become exaggerated over time, causing
  muscle spasticity. Muscles may waste away or diminish due to
  underuse. If spasms become severe enough, they may require
  medical treatment. For some, spasms can be as much of a help
  as they are a hindrance, since spasms can tone muscles that
  would otherwise waste away. Some people can even learn to use

the increased tone in their legs to help them turn over in bed, propel them into and out of a wheelchair, or stand.

- **Autonomic dysreflexia.** The autonomic nervous system controls involuntary actions such as blood pressure, heartbeat, and bladder and bowel function. Autonomic dysreflexia is a life-threatening reflex action that primarily affects those with injuries to the neck or upper back. It happens when there is an irritation, pain, or stimulus to the nervous system below the level of injury. The irritated area tries to send a sensory signal to the brain, but the signal may be misdirected, causing a runaway reflex action in the spinal cord that has been disconnected from the brain's regulation. Unlike spasms that affect muscles, autonomic dysreflexia affects blood vessels and organ systems controlled by the sympathetic nervous system. Anything that causes pain or irritation can set off autonomic dysreflexia, including a full bladder, constipation, cuts, burns, bruises, sunburn, pressure of any kind on the body, or tight clothing. Symptoms of its onset may include flushing or sweating, a pounding headache, anxiety, sudden increase in blood pressure, vision changes, or goose bumps on the arms and legs. Emptying the bladder or bowels and removing or loosening tight clothing are just a few of the possibilities that should be tried to relieve whatever is causing the irritation. If possible, the person should be kept in a sitting position, rather than lying flat, to keep blood flowing to the lower extremities and help reduce blood pressure.

- **Pressure sores (or pressure ulcers).** Pressure sores are areas of skin tissue that have broken down because of continuous pressure on the skin and reduced blood flow to the area. People with paraplegia and tetraplegia are susceptible to pressure sores because they may lose all or part of skin sensations and cannot shift their weight. As a result, individuals must be shifted periodically by a caregiver if they cannot shift positions themselves. Good nutrition and hygiene can also help prevent pressure sores by encouraging healthy skin. Special motorized rotating beds may be used to prevent and treat sores.

- **Pain.** Some people who have spinal cord nerve are paralyzed often develop neurogenic pain—pain or an intense burning or stinging sensation may be unremitting due to hypersensitivity in some parts of the body. It can either be spontaneous or triggered by a variety of factors and can occur even in parts of the body that have lost normal sensation. Almost all people with spinal cord injury are prone to normal musculoskeletal pain as well, such as shoulder pain due to overuse of the shoulder joint from using a wheelchair. Treatments for chronic pain include medications, acupuncture, spinal or brain electrical stimulation, and surgery. However, none of these treatments are completely effective at relieving neurogenic pain.

- **Bladder and bowel problems.** Most spinal cord injuries affect bladder and bowel functions because the nerves that control the involved organs originate in the segments near the lower end of the spinal cord and lose normal brain input. Although the kidneys continue to produce urine, bladder control may be lost and the risk of bladder and urinary tract infections increases. Some people may need to use a catheter to empty their bladders. The digestive system may be unaffected, but people recovering from a spinal cord injury may need to learn ways to empty their bowels. A change in diet may be needed to help with control.

- **Sexual function.** Depending on the level of injury and recovery from the trauma, sexual function and fertility may be affected. A urologist and other specialists can suggest different options for sexual functioning and health.

- **Depression.** Many people living with a spinal cord injury may develop depression as a result of lifestyle changes. Therapy and medicines may help treat depression.

Once someone has survived the injury and begins to cope psychologically and emotionally, the next concern is how to live with disabilities. Doctors are now able to predict with reasonable accuracy the likely long-term outcome of spinal cord injuries. This helps people experiencing SCI set achievable goals for themselves, and gives families and loved ones a realistic set of expectations for the future.

## How Does Rehabilitation Help People Recover from Spinal Cord Injuries?

No two people will experience the same emotions after surviving a spinal cord injury, but almost everyone will feel frightened, anxious, or confused about what has happened. It's common for people to have very mixed feelings: relief that they are still alive, but disbelief at the nature of their disabilities.

Rehabilitation programs combine physical therapies with skill-building activities and counseling to provide social and emotional support. The education and active involvement of the newly injured person and his or her family and friends is crucial.

A rehabilitation team is usually led by a doctor specializing in physical medicine and rehabilitation (called a physiatrist), and often includes social workers, physical and occupational therapists, recreational therapists, rehabilitation nurses, rehabilitation psychologists, vocational counselors, nutritionists, a caseworker, and other specialists.

In the initial phase of rehabilitation, therapists emphasize regaining communication skills and leg and arm strength. For some individuals, mobility will only be possible with the assistance of devices such as a walker, leg braces, or a wheelchair. Communication skills such as writing, typing, and using the telephone may also require adaptive devices for some people with tetraplegia.

Physical therapy includes exercise programs geared toward muscle strengthening. Occupational therapy helps redevelop fine motor skills, particularly those needed to perform activities of daily living such as getting in and out of a bed, self-grooming, and eating. Bladder and bowel management programs teach basic toileting routines. People acquire coping strategies for recurring episodes of spasticity, autonomic dysreflexia, and neurogenic pain.

Vocational rehabilitation includes identifying the person's basic work skills and physical and cognitive capabilities to determine the likelihood for employment; identifying potential workplaces and any assistive equipment that will be needed; and arranging for a user-friendly workplace. If necessary, educational training is provided to develop skills for a new line of work that may be less dependent upon physical abilities and more dependent upon computer or communication skills. Individuals with disabilities that prevent them from returning to the workforce are encouraged to maintain productivity by participating in activities that provide a sense of satisfaction and self-esteem, such as educational classes, hobbies, memberships in special interest groups, and participation in family and community events.

Recreation therapy encourages people with SCI to participate in recreational sports or activities at their level of mobility, as well as achieve a more balanced and normal lifestyle that provides opportunities for socialization and self-expression.

Adaptive devices also may help people with spinal cord injury to regain independence and improve mobility and quality of life. Such devices may include a wheelchair, electronic stimulators, assisted gait training, *neural prostheses*, computer adaptations, and other computer-assisted technology.

Chapter 22

# Disc Disorders

Your backbone, or spine, is made up of 26 bones called vertebrae. In between them are soft discs filled with a jelly-like substance. These disc cushion the vertebrae and keep them in place. As you age, the discs break down or degenerate. As they do, they lose their cushioning ability. This can lead to pain if the back is stressed.

A herniated disc is a disc that ruptures. This allows the jelly-like center of the disc to leak, irritating the nearby nerves. This can cause sciatica or back pain.

Your doctor will diagnose a herniated disc with a physical exam and, sometimes, imaging tests. With treatment, most people recover. Treatments include rest, pain and anti-inflammatory medicines, physical therapy, and sometimes surgery.

Also called: Bulging disc, Compressed disc, Herniated intervertebral disc, Herniated nucleus pulposus, Prolapsed disc, Ruptured disc, Slipped disc.

## Intervertebral Disc Disease

Intervertebral disc disease is a common condition characterized by the breakdown (degeneration) of one or more of the discs that separate

This chapter contains text excerpted from the following sources: Text in this chapter begins with excerpts from "Herniated Disk," National Library of Medicine (NLM), National Institutes of Health (NIH), October 18, 2016; Text beginning with the heading "Intervertebral Disc Disease" is excerpted from "Intervertebral Disc Disease," Genetics Home Reference (GHR), National Institutes of Health (NIH), October 2016.

241

the bones of the spine (vertebrae), causing pain in the back or neck and frequently in the legs and arms. The intervertebral discs provide cushioning between vertebrae and absorb pressure put on the spine.

While the discs in the lower (lumbar) region of the spine are most often affected in intervertebral disc disease, any part of the spine can have disc degeneration. Depending on the location of the affected disc or discs, intervertebral disc disease can cause periodic or chronic pain in the back or neck. Pain is often worse when sitting, bending, twisting, or lifting objects.

Degenerated discs are prone to out-pouching (herniation); the protruding disc can press against one of the spinal nerves that run from the spinal cord to the rest of the body. This pressure causes pain, weakness, and numbness in the back and legs. Herniated discs often cause nerve pain called sciatica that travels along the sciatic nerve, which runs from the lower back down the length of each leg.

As a disc degenerates, small bony outgrowths (bone spurs) may form at the edges of the affected vertebrae. These bone spurs may pinch (compress) the spinal nerves, leading to weakness or numbness in the arms or legs. If the bone spurs compress the spinal cord, affected individuals can develop problems with walking and bladder and bowel control. Over time, a degenerating disc may break down completely and leave no space between vertebrae, which can result in impaired movement, pain, and nerve damage.

## Frequency

Intervertebral disc disease is estimated to affect about 5 percent of the population in developed countries each year. Most individuals experience disc degeneration as they age; however, the severity of the degeneration and the pain associated with it varies.

## Genetic Changes

Intervertebral disc disease results from a combination of genetic and environmental factors. Some of these factors have been identified, but many remain unknown. Researchers have identified variations in several genes that may influence the risk of developing intervertebral disc disease. The most commonly associated genes provide instructions for producing proteins called collagens. Collagens are a family of proteins that strengthen and support connective tissues, such as skin, bone, cartilage, tendons, and ligaments. Collagens form a network of fibers that create structure and stability within the intervertebral discs. Specific variations in several collagen genes seem to affect the risk of developing intervertebral disc disease by impairing the ability of collagens to interact with each other, decreasing the stability of the disc and leading to its degeneration.

Normal variations in genes related to the body's immune function are also associated with an increased risk of developing intervertebral disc disease. These genes play a role in triggering an immune response when the body detects a foreign invader such as a virus. It is thought that these gene variants can lead to an immune response that results in inflammation and water loss (dehydration) of the discs, which causes their degeneration.

Variants in genes that play roles in the development and mainte-nance of the intervertebral discs and vertebrae have also been found to be associated with intervertebral disc disease. The associated variants can lead to disc degeneration and herniation. Researchers are work-ing to identify and confirm other genetic changes associated with an increased risk of intervertebral disc disease.

Nongenetic factors that contribute to the risk of intervertebral disc disease are also being studied. These factors include aging, smoking, obesity, chronic inflammation, and driving for long periods of time (for example, as a long-haul trucker or taxi driver).

Intervertebral disc disease can run in families, but the inheri-tance pattern is usually unknown. People with a first-degree relative (such as a parent or sibling) with intervertebral disc disease have an increased risk of developing the disorder themselves. Individuals may inherit a gene variation that increases the risk of intervertebral disc disease, but do not inherit the condition itself. Not all people with intervertebral disc disease have an identified gene variation that increases the risk, and not all people with such a gene variation will develop the disorder.

Chapter 23

# Spinal Nerve Injuries

## Chapter Contents

Section 23.1

# *Stingers*

This section contains text excerpted from the following sources: Text in this section begins with excerpts from "Brachial Plexus Injuries Information Page," National Institute of Neurological Disorders and Stroke (NINDS), October 18, 2007. Reviewed June 2017; Text beginning with the heading "Causes of Brachial Plexus Injuries (BPIs)" is excerpted from "Information about Brachial Plexus Injuries (BPI)," U.S. Social Security Administration (SSA), November 21, 2016.

The brachial plexus is a network of nerves that conducts signals from the spine to the shoulder, arm, and hand. Brachial plexus injuries are caused by damage to those nerves. Symptoms may include a limp or paralyzed arm; lack of muscle control in the arm, hand, or wrist; and a lack of feeling or sensation in the arm or hand. Brachial plexus injuries can occur as a result of shoulder trauma, tumors, or inflammation. There is a rare syndrome called Parsonage-Turner Syndrome, or brachial plexitis, which causes inflammation of the brachial plexus without any obvious shoulder injury. This syndrome can begin with severe shoulder or arm pain followed by weakness and numbness.

The severity of a brachial plexus injury is determined by the type of damage done to the nerves. The most severe type, avulsion, is caused when the nerve root is severed or cut from the spinal cord. There is also an incomplete form of avulsion in which part of the nerve is damaged and which leaves some opportunity for the nerve to slowly recover function. Neuropraxia, or stretch injury, is the mildest type of injury. Neuropraxia damages the protective covering of the nerve, which causes problems with nerve signal conduction, but does not always damage the nerve underneath.

## *Causes of Brachial Plexus Injuries (BPIs)*

Injuries can occur at any age. Stretching without the tearing of nerve fibers may result in a temporary loss of motor and/or sensory function (neurapraxia). When nerve fibers are torn, or avulsed (usually at the site of exit from the spinal canal), permanent motor and sensory loss may result. Sometimes torn nerve root fibers will begin to grow in an abnormal pattern and produce a benign tumor (neuroma). A neuroma can be painful and may block the proper reconnection of nerve root fibers.

Brachial plexus injuries (BPIs) can also occur during motor vehicle accidents, sport mishaps, and falls. On occasion, penetrating injuries to the brachial plexus occur during acts of violence. The extent of the initial functional loss depends on both the number of nerve fibers injured and the severity of the injury to the fibers.

## BPI and Pain

Brachial plexus injuries may result in a chronic pain syndrome despite the fact that there is reduced sensation in the affected area. Areas with diminished sensation are at risk for further injury, such as burns and/or pressure sores.

## Most Common Types of BPIs

1. Injuries to the upper brachial plexus affect the shoulder and upper arm (Erb palsy) and spare the hand. These injuries are the most common and have the best prognosis because most of these injuries are related to nerve fiber stretching (neurapraxis) rather than tearing (avulsion or rupture).

2. Injuries to the lower brachial plexus affect the forearm and hand (Klumpke Palsy). These injuries have a worse prognosis.

3. Extensive injuries that involve the entire plexus result in anesthesia and total paralysis of the hand, arm, shoulder and the diaphragm and chest wall musculature on the side of the injury. Such injuries have the poorest prognosis.

Most of the recovery from a BPI occurs during the first three months postinjury. BPI may occur in combination with other injuries or impairments. Other medical terms that might be found in medical reports describing BPI include: Erb Palsy (upper plexus injury), Klumpke Palsy (lower plexus injury), Brachial Plexus Palsy (BPP), Erb-Duchenne Palsy, Horner Syndrome (when sympathetic fibers are affected), and "Burners" or "Stingers" (usually associated with sports-related injuries).

## Treatment Options

The evaluation and treatment of BPI varies with the cause of the injury. When spontaneous recovery is not noted within the first few weeks following an injury, it is essential that a medical professional who specializes in treating BPI be consulted. When spontaneous improvement does not result during the first three months postinjury, significant functional recovery usually is not expected despite aggressive physical therapy and surgery. Early treatment most likely will include occupational and/or physical therapy to help maximize use of the affected arm while preventing contractures. If there is no evidence of improvement in function, further evaluation to address the potential for a surgical repair may be indicated. The clinical recovery noted following the initial surgery determines the need for other surgical procedures. The evaluation and treatment of other types of traumatic BPI usually proceed at a more rapid pace because such injuries are more commonly associated with the severance of nerve fibers. Maximizing functional use of the injured area is generally the overall goal of affected individuals, families and medical professionals.

# Section 23.2

# *Sciatica*

This section contains text excerpted from the following sources: Text in this section begins with excerpts from "Herniated Disk," National Library of Medicine (NLM) National Institutes of Health (NIH), October 18, 2016; Text under the heading "Causes of Sciatica" is excerpted from "Sciatica," National Library of Medicine (NLM), National Institutes of Health (NIH), March 25, 2016; Text beginning with the heading "Sports Injury and Sciatica" is excerpted from "Low Back Pain Fact Sheet," National Institute of Neurological Disorders and Stroke (NINDS), December 19, 2014.

Your backbone, or spine, is made up of 26 bones called vertebrae. In between them are soft disks filled with a jelly-like substance. These discs cushion the vertebrae and keep them in place. As you age, the disks break down or degenerate. As they do, they lose their cushioning ability. This can lead to pain if the back is stressed. A herniated disk is a disk that ruptures. This allows the jelly-like center of the disk to leak, irritating the nearby nerves. This can cause sciatica or back pain. Your doctor will diagnose a herniated disk with a physical exam and, sometimes, imaging tests. With treatment, most people recover. Treatments include rest, pain and anti-inflammatory medicines, physical therapy, and sometimes surgery.

## *Causes of Sciatica*

Sciatica is a symptom of a problem with the sciatic nerve, the largest nerve in the body. It controls muscles in the back of your knee and lower leg and provides feeling to the back of your thigh, part of your lower leg, and the sole of your foot. When you have sciatica, you have pain, weakness, numbness, or tingling. It can start in the lower back and extend down your leg to your calf, foot, or even your toes. It's usually on only one side of your body.

Causes of sciatica include:

• A ruptured intervertebral disk

• Narrowing of the spinal canal that puts pressure on the nerve, called spinal stenosis

- An injury such as a pelvic fracture.

In many cases no cause can be found. Sometimes sciatica goes away on its own. Treatment, if needed, depends on the cause of the problem. It may include exercises, medicines, and surgery.

## Sports Injury and Sciatica

**A traumatic injury**, such as from playing sports, car accidents, or a fall can injure tendons, ligaments or muscle resulting in low back pain. Traumatic injury may also cause the spine to become overly compressed, which in turn can cause an intervertebral disc to rupture or herniate, exerting pressure on any of the nerves rooted to the spinal cord. When spinal nerves become compressed and irritated, back pain and sciatica may result.

## Symptoms

**Sciatica** is a form of radiculopathy caused by compression of the sciatic nerve, the large nerve that travels through the buttocks and extends down the back of the leg. This compression causes shock-like or burning low back pain combined with pain through the buttocks and down one leg, occasionally reaching the foot. In the most extreme cases, when the nerve is pinched between the disc and the adjacent bone, the symptoms may involve not only pain, but numbness and muscle weakness in the leg because of interrupted nerve signaling. The condition may also be caused by a tumor or cyst that presses on the sciatic nerve or its roots.

## Treatment

Treatment for sciatic pain generally depends on whether the pain is acute or chronic. In general, surgery is recommended only if there is evidence of worsening nerve damage and when diagnostic tests indicate structural changes for which corrective surgical procedures have been developed. Conventionally used treatments and their level of supportive evidence include:

*Hot or cold packs* have never been proven to quickly resolve sciatica; however, they may help ease pain and reduce inflammation for people with acute, subacute, or chronic pain, allowing for greater mobility among some individuals.

*Activity*: Bed rest should be limited. Individuals should begin stretching exercises and resume normal daily activities as soon as possible, while avoiding movements that aggravate pain. Strong evidence shows that persons who continue their activities without bed rest following onset of low back pain appeared to have better back flexibility than those who rested in bed for a week. Other studies suggest that bed rest alone may make back pain worse and can lead to secondary complications such as depression, decreased muscle tone, and blood clots in the legs.

*Strengthening exercises*, beyond general daily activities, are not advised for acute sciatic pain. Maintaining and building muscle strength is particularly important for persons with skeletal irregularities. Healthcare providers can provide a list of beneficial exercises that will help improve coordination and develop proper posture and muscle balance.

*Physical therapy* programs to strengthen core muscle groups that support the low back, improve mobility and flexibility, and promote proper positioning and posture are often used in combinations with other interventions.

*Medications*: A wide range of medications are used to treat sciatica and low back pain. Some are available over-the-counter (OTC); others require a physician's prescription. Certain drugs, even those available OTC, may be unsafe during pregnancy, may interact with other medications, cause side effects, or lead to serious adverse effects such as liver damage or gastrointestinal ulcers and bleeding. Consultation with a healthcare provider is advised before use. The following are the main types of medications used for sciatic pain.

- **Analgesic medications** are those specifically designed to relieve pain. They include OTC acetaminophen and aspirin, as well as prescription opioids such as codeine, oxycodone, hydrocodone, and morphine. Opioids should be used only for a short period of time and under a physician's supervision. People can develop a tolerance to opioids and require increasingly higher dosages to achieve the same effect. Opioids can also be addictive. Their side effects can include drowsiness, constipation, decreased reaction time, and impaired judgment. Some specialists are concerned that chronic use of opioids is detrimental to people with back pain because they can aggravate depression, leading to a worsening of the pain.

- **Nonsteroidal anti-inflammatory drugs (NSAIDS)** relieve pain and inflammation and include OTC formulations (ibuprofen, ketoprofen, and naproxen sodium). Several others, including a type of NSAID called COX-2 inhibitors, are available only by

251

prescription. Long-term use of NSAIDs has been associated with stomach irritation, ulcers, heartburn, diarrhea, fluid retention, and in rare cases, kidney dysfunction and cardiovascular disease. The longer a person uses NSAIDs the more likely they are to develop side effects. Many other drugs cannot be taken at the same time a person is treated with NSAIDs because they alter the way the body processes or eliminates other medications.

- **Anticonvulsants**—drugs primarily used to treat seizures—may be useful in treating people with radiculopathy and radicular pain.

- **Antidepressants** such as tricyclics and serotonin and norepinephrine reuptake inhibitors have been commonly prescribed for chronic low back pain and sciatica.

- **Counter-irritants** such as creams or sprays applied topically stimulate the nerves in the skin to provide feelings of warmth or cold in order to dull the sensation of pain. Topical analgesics reduce inflammation and stimulate blood flow.

*Traction* involves the use of weights and pulleys to apply constant or intermittent force to gradually "pull" the skeletal structure into better alignment. Some people experience pain relief while in traction, but that relief is usually temporary. Once traction is released the pain tends to return. There is no evidence that traction provides any long-term benefits for people with low back pain.

*Acupuncture* is moderately effective for chronic sciatica and back pain. It involves the insertion of thin needles into precise points throughout the body. Some practitioners believe this process helps clear away blockages in the body's life force known as Qi. Others who may not believe in the concept of Qi theorize that when the needles are inserted and then stimulated (by twisting or passing a low-voltage electrical current through them) naturally occurring painkilling chemicals such as endorphins, serotonin, and acetylcholine are released. Evidence of acupuncture's benefit for back pain is conflicting and clinical studies continue to investigate its benefits.

*Biofeedback* is used to treat many acute pain problems. The therapy involves the attachment of electrodes to the skin and the use of an electromyography machine that allows people to become aware of and self-regulate their breathing, muscle tension, heart rate, and skin temperature. People regulate their response to pain by using relaxation techniques. Biofeedback is often used in combination with other treatment methods, generally without side effects.

252

Evidence is lacking that biofeedback provides a clear benefit for low back pain.

*Nerve block therapies* aim to relieve chronic pain by blocking nerve conduction from specific areas of the body. Nerve block approaches range from injections of local anesthetics, botulinum toxin, or steroids into affected soft tissues or joints to more complex nerve root blocks and spinal cord stimulation. When extreme pain is involved, low doses of drugs may be administered by catheter directly into the spinal cord. The success of a nerve block approach depends on the ability of a practitioner to locate and inject precisely the correct nerve. Chronic use of steroid injections may lead to increased functional impairment.

*Epidural steroid injections* are a commonly used short-term option for treating low back pain and sciatica associated with inflammation. Pain relief associated with the injections, however, tends to be temporary and the injections are not advised for long-term use. An NIH-funded randomized controlled trial assessing the benefit of epidural steroid injections for the treatment of chronic low back pain associated with spinal stenosis showed that long-term outcomes were worse among those people who received the injections compared with those who did not.

*Transcutaneous electrical nerve stimulation* (TENS) involves wearing a battery-powered device consisting of electrodes placed on the skin over the painful area that generate electrical impulses designed to block incoming pain signals from the peripheral nerves. The theory is that stimulating the nervous system can modify the perception of pain. Early studies of TENS suggested that it elevated levels of endorphins, the body's natural pain-numbing chemicals. More recent studies, however, have produced mixed results on its effectiveness for providing relief from low back pain.

## Surgery

When other therapies fail, surgery may be considered an option to relieve pain caused by serious musculoskeletal injuries or nerve compression. It may be months following surgery before the patient is fully healed, and he or she may suffer permanent loss of flexibility.

Surgical procedures are not always successful, and there is little evidence to show which procedures work best for their particular indications. Patients considering surgical approaches should be fully informed of all related risks. Surgical options include:

- **Spinal laminectomy** (also known as spinal decompression) is performed when spinal stenosis causes a narrowing of the

253

spinal canal that causes pain, numbness, or weakness. During the procedure, the lamina or bony walls of the vertebrae, along with any bone spurs, are removed. The aim of the procedure is to open up the spinal column to remove pressure on the nerves.

- **Discectomy or microdiscectomy** may be recommended to remove a disc, in cases where it has herniated and presses on a nerve root or the spinal cord, which may cause intense and enduring pain. Microdiscectomy is similar to a conventional discectomy; however, this procedure involves removing the herniated disc through a much smaller incision in the back and a more rapid recovery. Laminectomy and discectomy are frequently performed together and the combination is one of the more common ways to remove pressure on a nerve root from a herniated disc or bone spur.

# Part Five

# Shoulder and Upper Arm Injuries

Chapter 24

# Common Shoulder Problems

## What Are the Most Common Shoulder Problems?

The most movable joint in the body, the shoulder is also one of the most potentially unstable joints. As a result, it is the site of many common problems. They include sprains, strains, dislocations, separations, tendinitis, bursitis, torn rotator cuffs, frozen shoulder, fractures, and arthritis.

## What Are the Structures of the Shoulder and How Does It Function?

To better understand shoulder problems and how they occur, it helps to begin with an explanation of the shoulder's structure and how it functions.

The shoulder joint is composed of three bones: the clavicle (collarbone), the scapula (shoulder blade), and the humerus (upper arm bone) (see Figure 24.1). Two joints facilitate shoulder movement. The acromioclavicular (AC) joint is located between the acromion (the part of the scapula that forms the highest point of the shoulder) and the clavicle. The glenohumeral joint, commonly called the shoulder joint, is a ball-and-socket-type joint that helps move the shoulder forward and backward and allows the arm to rotate in a circular fashion or

This chapter includes text excerpted from "Shoulder Problems—Questions and Answers about Shoulder Problems," National Institute of Arthritis and Musculoskeletal and Skin Diseases (NIAMS), April 2014.

hinge out and up away from the body. (The "ball," or humerus, is the top, rounded portion of the upper arm bone; the "socket," or glenoid, is a dish-shaped part of the outer edge of the scapula into which the ball fits.) The capsule is a soft tissue envelope that encircles the glenohumeral joint. It is lined by a thin, smooth synovial membrane.

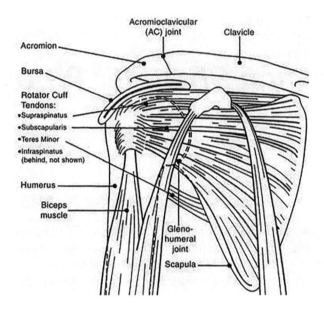

**Figure 24.1.** *Structure of the Shoulder*

In contrast to the hip joint, which more closely approximates a true ball-and-socket joint, the shoulder joint can be compared to a golf ball and tee, in which the ball can easily slip off the flat tee. Because the bones provide little inherent stability to the shoulder joint, it is highly dependent on surrounding soft tissues such as capsule ligaments and the muscles surrounding the rotator cuff to hold the ball in place. Whereas the hip joint is inherently quite stable because of the encircling bony anatomy, it also is relatively immobile. The shoulder, on the other hand, is relatively unstable but highly mobile, allowing an individual to place the hand in numerous positions. It is, in fact, one of the most mobile joints in the human body.

The bones of the shoulder are held in place by muscles, tendons, and ligaments. Tendons are tough cords of tissue that attach the shoulder muscles to bone and assist the muscles in moving the shoulder. Ligaments attach shoulder bones to each other, providing stability. For example, the front of the joint capsule is anchored by three glenohumeral ligaments. The rotator cuff is a structure composed of tendons

258

that work along with associated muscles to hold the ball at the top of the humerus in the glenoid socket and provide mobility and strength to the shoulder joint. Two filmy sac-like structures called bursae permit smooth gliding between bones, muscles, and tendons. They cushion and protect the rotator cuff from the bony arch of the acromion.

## What Are the Origins and Causes of Shoulder Problems?

The shoulder is easily injured because the ball of the upper arm is larger than the shoulder socket that holds it. To remain stable, the shoulder must be anchored by its muscles, tendons, and ligaments.

Although the shoulder is easily injured during sporting activities and manual labor, the primary source of shoulder problems appears to be the natural age-related degeneration of the surrounding soft tissues such as those found in the rotator cuff. The incidence of rotator cuff problems rises dramatically as a function of age and is generally seen among individuals who are more than 60 years old. Often, the dominant and nondominant arm will be affected to a similar degree. Overuse of the shoulder can lead to more rapid age-related deterioration.

Shoulder pain may be localized or may be felt in areas around the shoulder or down the arm. Disease within the body (such as gallbladder, liver, or heart disease, or disease of the cervical spine of the neck) also may generate pain that travels along nerves to the shoulder. However, these other causes of shoulder pain are beyond the scope of this chapter, which will focus on problems within the shoulder itself.

## How Are Shoulder Problems Diagnosed?

As with any medical issue, a shoulder problem is generally diagnosed using a three-part process.

- Medical history

- Physical examination

- Tests

- Standard X-ray

- Arthrogram

- Ultrasound

- MRI (magnetic resonance imaging)

# What Should I Know about Specific Shoulder Problems?

## Dislocation

The shoulder joint is the most frequently dislocated major joint of the body. In a typical case of a dislocated shoulder, either a strong force pulls the shoulder outward (abduction) or extreme rotation of the joint pops the ball of the humerus out of the shoulder socket. Dislocation commonly occurs when there is a backward pull on the arm that either catches the muscles unprepared to resist or overwhelms the muscles. When a shoulder dislocates frequently, the condition is referred to as shoulder instability. A partial dislocation in which the upper arm bone is partially in and partially out of the socket is called a subluxation.

## Separation

A shoulder separation occurs where the collarbone (clavicle) meets the shoulder blade (scapula). When ligaments that hold the joint together are partially or completely torn, the outer end of the clavicle may slip out of place, preventing it from properly meeting the scapula. Most often, the injury is caused by a blow to the shoulder or by falling on an outstretched hand.

## Rotator Cuff Disease: Tendinitis and Bursitis

These conditions are closely related and may occur alone or in combination.

Tendinitis is inflammation (redness, soreness, and swelling) of a tendon. In tendinitis of the shoulder, the rotator cuff and/or biceps tendon become inflamed, usually as result of being pinched by surrounding structures. The injury may vary from mild inflammation to involvement of most of the rotator cuff. When the rotator cuff tendon becomes inflamed and thickened, it may get trapped under the acromion. Squeezing of the rotator cuff is called impingement syndrome.

Bursitis, or inflammation of the bursa sacs that protect the shoulder, may accompany tendinitis and impingement syndrome. Inflammation caused by a disease such as rheumatoid arthritis may cause rotator cuff tendinitis and bursitis. Sports involving overuse of the shoulder and occupations requiring frequent overhead reaching are other potential causes of irritation to the rotator cuff or bursa and may lead to inflammation and impingement.

If the rotator cuff and bursa are irritated, inflamed, and swollen, they may become squeezed between the head of the humerus and the acromion. Repeated motion involving the arms, or the effects of the aging process on shoulder movement over many years, may also irritate and wear down the tendons, muscles, and surrounding structures.

## Torn Rotator Cuff

Rotator cuff tendons often become inflamed from overuse, aging, or a fall on an outstretched hand or another traumatic cause. Sports or occupations requiring repetitive overhead motion or heavy lifting can also place a significant strain on rotator cuff muscles and tendons. Over time, as a function of aging, tendons become weaker and degenerate. Eventually, this degeneration can lead to complete tears of both muscles and tendons. These tears are surprisingly common. In fact, a tear of the rotator cuff is not necessarily an abnormal situation in older individuals if there is no significant pain or disability. Fortunately, these tears do not lead to any pain or disability in most people. However, some individuals can develop very significant pain as a result of these tears and they may require treatment.

## Frozen Shoulder (Adhesive Capsulitis)

As the name implies, movement of the shoulder is severely restricted in people with a "frozen shoulder." This condition, which doctors call adhesive capsulitis, is frequently caused by injury that leads to lack of use due to pain. Rheumatic disease progression and recent shoulder surgery can also cause frozen shoulder. Intermittent periods of use may cause inflammation. Adhesions (abnormal bands of tissue) grow between the joint surfaces, restricting motion. There is also a lack of synovial fluid, which normally lubricates the gap between the arm bone and socket to help the shoulder joint move. It is this restricted space between the capsule and ball of the humerus that distinguishes adhesive capsulitis from a less complicated painful, stiff shoulder. People with diabetes, stroke, lung disease, rheumatoid arthritis, and heart disease, or those who have been in an accident, are at a higher risk for frozen shoulder. People between the ages of 40 and 70 are most likely to experience it.

## Fracture

A fracture involves a partial or total crack through a bone. The break in a bone usually occurs as a result of an impact injury, such as a fall or blow to the shoulder. A fracture usually involves the clavicle or the neck (area below the ball) of the humerus.

### Arthritis of the Shoulder

Arthritis is a degenerative disease caused by either wear and tear of the cartilage (osteoarthritis) or an inflammation (rheumatoid arthritis) of one or more joints. Arthritis not only affects joints, but may also affect supporting structures such as muscles, tendons, and ligaments.

## Treat Shoulder Injuries with RICE (Rest, Ice, Compression, and Elevation)

If you injure a shoulder, try the following:

**Rest.** Reduce or stop using the injured area for 48 hours.

**Ice.** Put an ice pack on the injured area for 20 minutes at a time, 4–8 times per day. Use a cold pack, ice bag, or a plastic bag filled with crushed ice that has been wrapped in a towel.

**Compression.** Compress the area with bandages, such as an elastic wrap, to help stabilize the shoulder. This may help reduce the swelling.

**Elevation.** Keep the injured area elevated above the level of the heart. Use a pillow to help elevate the injury.

If pain and stiffness persist, see a doctor.

Chapter 25

# *Frozen Shoulder*

As the name implies, movement of the shoulder is severely restricted in people with a "frozen shoulder." This condition, which doctors call adhesive capsulitis, is frequently caused by injury that leads to lack of use due to pain. Rheumatic disease progression and recent shoulder surgery can also cause frozen shoulder. Intermittent periods of use may cause inflammation. Adhesions (abnormal bands of tissue) grow between the joint surfaces, restricting motion. There is also a lack of synovial fluid, which normally lubricates the gap between the arm bone and socket to help the shoulder joint move. It is this restricted space between the capsule and ball of the humerus that distinguishes adhesive capsulitis from a less complicated painful, stiff shoulder. People with diabetes, stroke, lung disease, rheumatoid arthritis, and heart disease, or those who have been in an accident, are at a higher risk for frozen shoulder. People between the ages of 40 and 70 are most likely to experience it.

## *Signs and Symptoms*

With a frozen shoulder, the joint becomes so tight and stiff that it is nearly impossible to carry out simple movements, such as raising the arm. Stiffness and discomfort may worsen at night.

---

This chapter includes text excerpted from "Shoulder Problems—Questions and Answers about Shoulder Problems," National Institute of Arthritis and Musculoskeletal and Skin Diseases (NIAMS), April 2014.

# Diagnosis

A doctor may suspect a frozen shoulder if a physical examination reveals limited shoulder movement. X-rays usually appear normal.

# Treatment

Treatment of this disorder focuses on restoring joint movement and reducing shoulder pain. Usually, treatment begins with nonsteroidal anti-inflammatory drugs and the application of heat, followed by gentle stretching exercises. These stretching exercises, which may be performed in the home with the help of a physical therapist, are the treatment of choice. In some cases, transcutaneous electrical nerve stimulation (TENS) with a small battery-operated unit may be used to reduce pain by blocking nerve impulses. If these measures are unsuccessful, an intra-articular injection of steroids into the glenoid humeral joint can result in marked improvement of the frozen shoulder in a large percentage of cases. In those rare people who do not improve from nonoperative measures, manipulation of the shoulder under general anesthesia and an arthroscopic procedure to cut the remaining adhesions can be highly effective in most cases.

Chapter 26

# Rotator Cuff Disease

Tendinitis is inflammation (redness, soreness, and swelling) of a tendon. In tendinitis of the shoulder, the rotator cuff and/or biceps tendon become inflamed, usually as a result of being pinched by surrounding structures. The injury may vary from mild inflammation to involvement of most of the rotator cuff. When the rotator cuff tendon becomes inflamed and thickened, it may get trapped under the acromion. Squeezing of the rotator cuff is called impingement syndrome.

Bursitis, or inflammation of the bursa sacs that protect the shoulder, may accompany tendinitis and impingement syndrome. Inflammation caused by a disease such as rheumatoid arthritis may cause rotator cuff tendinitis and bursitis. Sports involving overuse of the shoulder and occupations requiring frequent overhead reaching are other potential causes of irritation to the rotator cuff or bursa and may lead to inflammation and impingement.

If the rotator cuff and bursa are irritated, inflamed, and swollen, they may become squeezed between the head of the humerus and the acromion. Repeated motion involving the arms, or the effects of the aging process on shoulder movement over many years, may also irritate and wear down the tendons, muscles, and surrounding structures.

This chapter includes text excerpted from "Shoulder Problems—Questions and Answers about Shoulder Problems," National Institute of Arthritis and Musculoskeletal and Skin Diseases (NIAMS), April 2014.

## Signs and Symptoms

Signs of these conditions include the slow onset of discomfort and pain in the upper shoulder or upper third of the arm and/or difficulty sleeping on the shoulder. Tendinitis and bursitis also cause pain when the arm is lifted away from the body or overhead. If tendinitis involves the biceps tendon (the tendon located in front of the shoulder that helps bend the elbow and turn the forearm), pain will occur in the front or side of the shoulder and may travel down to the elbow and forearm. Pain may also occur when the arm is forcefully pushed upward overhead.

## Diagnosis

Diagnosis of tendinitis and bursitis begins with a medical history and physical examination. X-rays do not show tendons or the bursae, but may be helpful in ruling out bony abnormalities or arthritis. The doctor may remove and test fluid from the inflamed area to rule out infection. Impingement syndrome may be confirmed when injection of a small amount of anesthetic (lidocaine hydrochloride) into the space under the acromion relieves pain.

## Treatment

The first step in treating these conditions is to reduce pain and inflammation with rest, ice, and anti-inflammatory medicines such as aspirin and ibuprofen (Advil,* Motrin†). In some cases, the doctor or therapist will use ultrasound (gentle sound-wave vibrations) to warm deep tissues and improve blood flow. Gentle stretching and strengthening exercises are added gradually. These may be preceded or followed by use of an ice pack. If there is no improvement, the doctor may inject

---

*Brand names included in this chapter are provided as examples only, and their inclusion does not mean that these products are endorsed by the National Institutes of Health (NIH) or any other Government agency. Also, if a particular brand name is not mentioned, this does not mean or imply that the product is unsatisfactory.*

†All medicines can have side effects. Some side effects may be more severe than others. You should review the package insert that comes with your medicine and ask your healthcare provider or pharmacist if you have any questions about the possible side effects.

a corticosteroid medicine into the space under the acromion. Although steroid injections are a common treatment, they must be used with caution because they may lead to tendon rupture. If there is still no improvement after 6–12 months, the doctor may recommend either arthroscopic or open surgery to repair damage and relieve pressure on the tendons and bursae.

Chapter 27

# *Shoulder Impingement*

Squeezing of the rotator cuff is called impingement syndrome. Bursitis, or inflammation of the bursa sacs that protect the shoulder, may accompany tendinitis and impingement syndrome. Inflammation caused by a disease such as rheumatoid arthritis may cause rotator cuff tendinitis and bursitis. Sports involving overuse of the shoulder and occupations requiring frequent overhead reaching are other potential causes of irritation to the rotator cuff or bursa and may lead to inflammation and impingement. If the rotator cuff and bursa are irritated, inflamed, and swollen, they may become squeezed between the head of the humerus and the acromion. Repeated motion involving the arms, or the effects of the aging process on shoulder movement over many years, may also irritate and wear down the tendons, muscles, and surrounding structures.

## *Diagnosis*

Diagnosis of tendinitis and bursitis begins with a medical history and physical examination. X-rays do not show tendons or the bursae,

This chapter contains text excerpted from the following sources: Text in this chapter begins with excerpts from "Shoulder Problems—Questions and Answers about Shoulder Problems," National Institute of Arthritis and Musculoskeletal and Skin Diseases (NIAMS), April 2014; Text beginning with the heading "Subacromial Impingement Syndrome without a Rotator Cuff Tear" is excerpted from "Shoulder Conditions Diagnosis and Treatment Guideline," Industrial Insurance Medical Advisory Committee (IIMAC), Department of Labor (DOL), September 2016.

269

but may be helpful in ruling out bony abnormalities or arthritis. The doctor may remove and test fluid from the inflamed area to rule out infection. Impingement syndrome may be confirmed when injection of a small amount of anesthetic (lidocaine hydrochloride) into the space under the acromion relieves pain.

## Treatment

The first step in treating these conditions is to reduce pain and inflammation with rest, ice, and anti-inflammatory medicines such as aspirin and ibuprofen (Advil, Motrin). In some cases, the doctor or therapist will use ultrasound (gentle sound-wave vibrations) to warm deep tissues and improve blood flow. Gentle stretching and strengthening exercises are added gradually. These may be preceded or followed by use of an ice pack. If there is no improvement, the doctor may inject a corticosteroid medicine into the space under the acromion. Although steroid injections are a common treatment, they must be used with caution because they may lead to tendon rupture. If there is still no improvement after 6 to 12 months, the doctor may recommend either arthroscopic or open surgery to repair damage and relieve pressure on the tendons and bursae.

## Subacromial Impingement Syndrome without a Rotator Cuff Tear

Subacromial impingement syndrome (SIS) results when the soft tissues of the glenohumeral joint, between the coracoacromial arch and the humeral tuberosity, are compressed, disturbing the normal sliding mechanism of the shoulder when the arm is elevated. SIS can be an occupational disease. Occurrence has been associated with heavy overhead work, high force and repetition.

### Diagnosis and Treatment

Patients may report generalized shoulder pain. An objective clinical finding is pain with active elevation. To confirm the diagnosis of SIS, an MRI should reveal evidence of tendinopathy/tendinitis or a rotator cuff tear.

Nonoperative treatments of SIS have been shown to be as effective as subacromial decompression. For decompression to be allowed for SIS, the diagnosis must be verified by pain relief from a subacromial injection of local anesthetic, and the patient must have failed to improve function and decrease pain after twelve weeks of conservative care.

Subacromial decompression is also a reasonable treatment option for massive, irreparable rotator cuff tears that are not amenable to repair.

Chapter 28

# Shoulder Dislocation

The shoulder joint is the most frequently dislocated major joint of the body. In a typical case of a dislocated shoulder, either a strong force pulls the shoulder outward (abduction) or extreme rotation of the joint pops the ball of the humerus out of the shoulder socket. Dislocation commonly occurs when there is a backward pull on the arm that either catches the muscles unprepared to resist or overwhelms the muscles. When a shoulder dislocates frequently, the condition is referred to as shoulder instability. A partial dislocation in which the upper arm bone is partially in and partially out of the socket is called a subluxation.

## Signs and Symptoms

The shoulder can dislocate either forward, backward, or downward. When the shoulder dislocates, the arm appears out of position. Other symptoms include pain, which may be worsened by muscle spasms, swelling, numbness, weakness, and bruising. Problems seen with a dislocated shoulder are tearing of the ligaments or tendons reinforcing the joint capsule and, less commonly, bone and/or nerve damage.

---

This chapter includes text excerpted from "Shoulder Problems—Questions and Answers about Shoulder Problems," National Institute of Arthritis and Musculoskeletal and Skin Diseases (NIAMS), April 2014.

## Diagnosis

Doctors usually diagnose a dislocation by a physical examination; X-rays may be taken to confirm the diagnosis and to rule out a related fracture.

## Treatment

Doctors treat a dislocation by putting the ball of the humerus back into the joint socket, a procedure called a closed reduction. The arm is then stabilized for several weeks in a sling or a device called a shoulder immobilizer. Usually the doctor recommends resting the shoulder and applying ice three or four times a day. After pain and swelling have been controlled, the patient enters a rehabilitation program that includes exercises. The goal is to restore the range of motion of the shoulder, strengthen the muscles, and prevent future dislocations. These exercises may progress from simple motion to the use of weights.

After treatment and recovery, a previously dislocated shoulder may remain more susceptible to reinjury, especially in young, active individuals. Ligaments may have been stretched or torn, and the shoulder may tend to dislocate again. A shoulder that dislocates severely or often, injuring surrounding tissues or nerves, usually requires surgical repair to tighten stretched ligaments or reattach torn ones.

Sometimes the doctor performs surgery through a tiny incision into which a small scope (arthroscope) is inserted to observe the inside of the joint. After this procedure, called arthroscopic surgery, the shoulder is generally stabilized for about 6 weeks. Full recovery takes several months. In other cases, the doctor may repair the dislocation using a traditional open surgery approach.

Chapter 29

# Muscle Tears and Tendon Injuries

## Chapter Contents

Section 29.1

# *Rotator Cuff Tears*

This section includes text excerpted from "Shoulder
Problems—Questions and Answers about Shoulder Problems,"
National Institute of Arthritis and Musculoskeletal and Skin
Diseases (NIAMS), April 2014.

Rotator cuff tendons often become inflamed from overuse, aging,
or a fall on an outstretched hand or another traumatic cause. Sports
or occupations requiring repetitive overhead motion or heavy lifting
can also place a significant strain on rotator cuff muscles and tendons. Over time, as a function of aging, tendons become weaker and
degenerate. Eventually, this degeneration can lead to complete tears
of both muscles and tendons. These tears are surprisingly common.
In fact, a tear of the rotator cuff is not necessarily an abnormal situation in older individuals if there is no significant pain or disability.
Fortunately, these tears do not lead to any pain or disability in most
people. However, some individuals can develop very significant pain
as a result of these tears and they may require treatment.

## *Signs and Symptoms*

Typically, a person with a rotator cuff injury feels pain over the deltoid muscle at the top and outer side of the shoulder, especially when
the arm is raised or extended out from the side of the body. Motions
like those involved in getting dressed can be painful. The shoulder
may feel weak, especially when trying to lift the arm into a horizontal position. A person may also feel or hear a click or pop when the
shoulder is moved. Pain or weakness on outward or inward rotation
of the arm may indicate a tear in a rotator cuff tendon. The patient
also feels pain when lowering the arm to the side after the shoulder
is moved backward and the arm is raised.

## *Diagnosis*

A doctor may detect weakness but may not be able to determine
from a physical examination where the tear is located. X-rays, if taken,

may appear normal. An MRI (magnetic resonance imaging) or ultrasound can help detect a full tendon tear or a partial tendon tear.

## Treatment

Doctors usually recommend that patients with a rotator cuff injury rest the shoulder, apply heat or cold to the sore area, and take medicine to relieve pain and inflammation. Other treatments might be added, such as electrical stimulation of muscles and nerves, ultrasound, or a cortisone injection near the inflamed area of the rotator cuff. If surgery is not an immediate consideration, exercises are added to the treatment program to build flexibility and strength and restore the shoulder's function. If there is no improvement with these conservative treatments and functional impairment persists, the doctor may perform arthroscopic or open surgical repair of the torn rotator cuff.

Treatment for a torn rotator cuff usually depends on the severity of the injury, the age and health status of the patient, and the length of time a given patient may have had the condition. Patients with rotator cuff tendinitis or bursitis that does not include a complete tear of the tendon can usually be treated without surgery. Nonsurgical treatments include the use of anti-inflammatory medication and occasional steroid injections into the area of the inflamed rotator cuff, followed by rehabilitative rotator cuff-strengthening exercises. These treatments are best undertaken with the guidance of a healthcare professional such as a physical therapist, who works in conjunction with the treating physician.

Surgical repair of rotator cuff tears is best for the following individuals.

- Younger patients, especially those with small tears. Surgery leads to a high degree of successful healing and reduces concerns about the tear getting worse over time.

- Individuals whose rotator cuff tears are caused by an acute, severe injury. These people should seek immediate treatment that includes surgical repair of the tendon.

Generally speaking, individuals who are older and have had shoulder pain for a longer period of time can be treated with nonoperative measures even in the presence of a complete rotator cuff tear. These people are often treated similarly to those who have pain but do not have a rotator cuff tear. Again, anti-inflammatory medication, use of steroid injections, and rehabilitative exercises can be very effective. When treated surgically, rotator cuff tears can be repaired by either arthroscopic or traditional open surgical techniques.

Section 29.2

# *Biceps Tendon Injuries*

Text in this section is from "Biceps Tendon Tear at the Shoulder,"
© 1995-2017 American Academy of Orthopaedic Surgeons.
Reprinted with permission.

Tendons attach muscles to bones. Your biceps tendons attach the biceps muscle to bones in the shoulder and in the elbow. If you tear the biceps tendon at the shoulder, you may lose some strength in your arm and have pain when you forcefully turn your arm from palm down to palm up.

Many people can still function with a biceps tendon tear, and only need simple treatments to relieve symptoms. If symptoms cannot be relieved by nonsurgical treatments, or if a patient requires complete recovery of strength, surgery to repair the torn tendon may be required.

## *Anatomy*

Your shoulder is a ball-and-socket joint made up of three bones: your upper arm bone (humerus), your shoulder blade (scapula), and your collarbone (clavicle).

The head of your upper arm bone fits into a rounded socket in your shoulder blade. This socket is called the glenoid. A combination of muscles and tendons keeps your arm bone centered in your shoulder socket. These tissues are called the rotator cuff. They cover the head of your upper arm bone and attach it to your shoulder blade.

The upper end of the biceps muscle has two tendons that attach it to bones in the shoulder. The long head attaches to the top of the shoulder socket (glenoid). The short head attaches to a bump on the shoulder blade called the coracoid process.

## *Description*

Biceps tendon tears can be either partial or complete.

* **Partial tears.** Many tears do not completely sever the tendon.

- **Complete tears.** A complete tear will split the tendon into two pieces.

In many cases, torn tendons begin by fraying. As the damage progresses, the tendon can completely tear, sometimes when lifting a heavy object.

The long head of the biceps tendon is more likely to be injured. This is because it is vulnerable as it travels through the shoulder joint to its attachment point in the socket. Fortunately, the biceps has two attachments at the shoulder. The short head of the biceps rarely tears. Because of this second attachment, many people can still use their biceps even after a complete tear of the long head.

When you tear your biceps tendon, you can also damage other parts of your shoulder, such as the rotator cuff tendons.

## Cause

There are two main causes of biceps tendon tears: injury and overuse.

### Injury

If you fall hard on an outstretched arm or lift something too heavy, you can tear your biceps tendon.

### Overuse

Many tears are the result of a wearing down and fraying of the tendon that occurs slowly over time. This naturally occurs as we age. It can be worsened by overuse—repeating the same shoulder motions again and again.

Overuse can cause a range of shoulder problems, including tendinitis, shoulder impingement, and rotator cuff injuries. Having any of these conditions puts more stress on the biceps tendon, making it more likely to weaken or tear.

### Risk Factors

Your risk for a tendon tear increases with:

- **Age.** Older people have put more years of wear and tear on their tendons than younger people.

- **Heavy overhead activities.** Too much load during weight-lifting is a prime example of this risk, but many jobs require heavy overhead lifting and put excess wear and tear on the tendons.

- **Shoulder overuse.** Repetitive overhead sports, such as swimming or tennis, can cause more tendon wear and tear.

- **Smoking.** Nicotine use can affect nutrition in the tendon.

- **Corticosteroid medications.** Using corticosteroids has been linked to increased muscle and tendon weakness.

## Symptoms

- Sudden, sharp pain in the upper arm

- Sometimes an audible pop or snap

- Cramping of the biceps muscle with strenuous use of the arm

- Bruising from the middle of the upper arm down toward the elbow

- Pain or tenderness at the shoulder and the elbow

- Weakness in the shoulder and the elbow

- Difficulty turning the arm palm up or palm down

- Because a torn tendon can no longer keep the biceps muscle tight, a bulge in the upper arm above the elbow ("Popeye Muscle") may appear, with a dent closer to the shoulder.

## Doctor Examination

### Medical History and Physical Examination

After discussing your symptoms and medical history, your doctor will examine your shoulder. The diagnosis is often obvious for complete ruptures because of the deformity of the arm muscle ("Popeye Muscle").

Partial ruptures are less obvious. To diagnose a partial tear, your doctor may ask you to bend your arm and tighten the biceps muscle. Pain when you use your biceps muscle may mean there is a partial tear.

It is also very important that your doctor identify any other shoulder problems when planning your treatment. The biceps can also tear near the elbow, although this is less common. A tear near the elbow will cause a "gap" in the front of the elbow. Your doctor will check your arm for damage to this area.

In addition, rotator cuff injuries, impingement, and tendinitis are some conditions that may accompany a biceps tendon tear. Your doctor may order additional tests to help identify other problems in your shoulder.

## *Imaging Tests*

X-rays. Although X-rays cannot show soft tissues like the biceps tendon, they can be useful in ruling out other problems that can cause shoulder and elbow pain.

Magnetic resonance imaging (MRI). These scans create better images of soft tissues. They can show both partial and complete tears.

## Treatment

### *Nonsurgical Treatment*

For many people, pain from a long head of biceps tendon tear resolves over time. Mild arm weakness or arm deformity may not bother some patients, such as older and less active people.

In addition, if you have not damaged a more critical structure, such as the rotator cuff, nonsurgical treatment is a reasonable option. This can include:

• **Ice.** Apply cold packs for 20 minutes at a time, several times a day to keep down swelling. Do not apply ice directly to the skin.

• **Nonsteroidal anti-inflammatory medications.** Drugs like ibuprofen, aspirin, or naproxen reduce pain and swelling.

• **Rest.** Avoid heavy lifting and overhead activities to relieve pain and limit swelling. Your doctor may recommend using a sling for a brief time.

• **Physical therapy.** Flexibility and strengthening exercises will restore movement and strengthen your shoulder.

### *Surgical Treatment*

Surgical treatment for a long head of the biceps tendon tear is rarely needed. However, some patients who develop cramping of the muscle or pain, or who require complete recovery of strength, such as athletes or manual laborers, may require surgery. Surgery may also be the right option for those with partial tears whose symptoms are not relieved with nonsurgical treatment.

**Procedure.** Several new procedures have been developed that repair the tendon with minimal incisions. The goal of the surgery is to re-anchor the torn tendon back to the bone. Your doctor will discuss with you the options that are best for your specific case.

**Complications.** Complications with this surgery are rare. Re-rupture of the repaired tendon is uncommon.

**Rehabilitation.** After surgery, your shoulder may be immobilized temporarily with a sling.

Your doctor will soon start you on therapeutic exercises. Flexibility exercises will improve range of motion in your shoulder. Exercises to strengthen your shoulder will gradually be added to your rehabilitation plan.

Be sure to follow your doctor's treatment plan. Although it is a slow process, your commitment to physical therapy is the most important factor in returning to all the activities you enjoy.

**Surgical Outcome.** Successful surgery can correct muscle deformity and return your arm's strength and function to nearly normal.

# Chapter 30

# *Collarbone Injuries*

The collarbone, also known as the clavicle, is an S-shaped bone that connects the breastbone (sternum) to the shoulder. It is clearly visible in most people as a horizontal ridge beneath the skin of the upper torso on both sides of the chest, running from the throat area outward to the shoulder joint. The clavicle plays an important role in the strength and stability of the shoulder and in the upward movement of the arm. It also provides protection for the brachial plexus, a network of nerves and blood vessels that run from the neck down the arm and into the hand. The collarbone attaches to shoulder blade (scapula) and the upper arm at the acromioclavicular (AC) joint, as well as to the upper chest at the sternoclavicular (SC) joint. Because of its prominent position and role in connecting the arm to the body, the collarbone is one of the most frequently broken bones in sports.

## *Causes*

About 85 percent of clavicle fractures occur due to falls or direct impacts to the point of the shoulder, while the remaining 15 percent occur due to falls onto an outstretched arm. Most fractures affect the middle third of the clavicle bone, which is structurally weaker and has less muscular reinforcement than the outer and inner thirds. Contact sports like football and hockey have a high incidence of clavicle fractures, as do sports with the potential for high-speed falls, such as

"Collarbone Injuries," © 2017 Omnigraphics. Reviewed June 2017.

mountain biking and snowboarding. Young men between the ages of 13 and 20 are statistically most likely to break their collarbones. On rare occasions, clavicle fractures occur in newborns during the birthing process or in older adults with brittle bones due to underlying medical conditions like osteoporosis or cancer.

## Symptoms

Athletes who fall or are hit on their shoulder and experience the following symptoms may have a broken collarbone:

- a pop, snap, or click sound at impact;

- immediate, sharp pain in the shoulder or upper chest;

- a painful, tent-like bump or bulge beneath the skin at the fracture site;

- swelling and bruising at the fracture site;

- weakness and restricted movement in the affected arm;

- a grinding or crunching sound upon trying to raise the affected arm;

- a downward or forward slumping appearance in the affected shoulder;

- numbness, tingling, and pale skin on the affected arm if the fracture pinches a nerve or compresses blood vessels.

## Diagnosis

Many athletes with a broken collarbone show up at the emergency room or a doctor's office with their affected arm held tightly against their body or supported in a makeshift sling. Moving—and especially raising—the affected arm is likely to be extremely painful. To diagnose a clavicle fracture, the doctor will typically inquire about how the injury occurred and then conduct a physical examination. The doctor will look for any asymmetry or abnormal appearance of the shoulders, as well as for a lump or bruise at the fracture site. An X-ray is usually ordered to confirm the location and severity of the fracture, including the extent to which the broken bone has displaced, shortened, or shattered.

The doctor will also check carefully to determine whether surrounding nerves, blood vessels, bones, tissues, and organs have sustained injuries. The type of collision that results in a broken collarbone can sometimes cause head, neck, and chest injuries. Broken ribs commonly occur in the same sort of trauma, for instance, and displaced clavicle or rib fractures can sometimes injure or puncture a lung. The doctor will also evaluate the blood flow and nerve sensation in the affected arm to see if any underlying structures have been damaged.

## Treatment

Around 90 percent of all broken collarbones heal on their own without surgery. The treatment for minimally displaced fractures generally involves immobilizing the affected arm in a sling or splint for a few weeks until the bone begins to repair itself. Prescription or over-the-counter medicines may be needed to relieve pain and inflammation. The athlete must avoid falls, collisions, and heavy lifting during the recovery process, although light exercise is usually permitted. A follow-up X-ray is typically performed around two weeks after the initial injury to ensure that the bone is aligned properly and that new growth has appeared at the fracture ends.

Severe or multiple clavicle fractures may require surgical intervention. Surgery is typically recommended in cases where the broken bone penetrates the skin, or where the ends of the bone shatter into fragments or are poorly aligned. Surgery is also recommended when there is injury to the nerves or blood vessels in the arm, or when there are additional fractures in the arm or ribs. The surgical procedure entails repositioning the bone and using a plate and screws to hold it in place. Following surgery, the athlete will use a sling or brace to immobilize the shoulder for approximately six weeks.

## Prognosis and Complications

Most people are able to return to normal activities within three months of a clavicle fracture, provided the bone has healed completely. Physical therapy or rehabilitation exercises may be needed to regain strength and range of motion in the shoulder joint. The physical demands of the sport should be taken into consideration, however, with a longer waiting time recommended before resuming contact sports and sports that require lifting the arms over the head. Wearing shoulder pads or other protective equipment can help prevent further injury.

Athletes who do not undergo surgery may notice a bump beneath the skin due to new bone formation at the fracture site, but it usually does not cause any discomfort. In rare cases, nonoperative treatment of a collarbone fracture involves complications such as malunion (imperfect healing) or nonunion (failure to heal), which can lead to pain, instability, and limited range of motion. Although these cases may require surgery, the prognosis for full recovery from surgery is good.

Up to 50 percent of athletes who have surgery may experience discomfort from the plate used to stabilize the clavicle fracture. In these cases, the plate can be removed six to nine months after the surgery. However, the holes from the screws create a slightly increased risk of a later fracture in that location. Delayed or incomplete healing also affects a small percentage of clavicle fractures that are surgically repaired. The risk is greatest in cases where the bone is aligned or fixed improperly, the surgical site becomes infected, or the athlete attempts to return to strenuous, full-contact activity before the bone is fully healed.

### References

1.  Bedi, Asheesh. "Broken Collarbone (Clavicle Fracture)," SportsMD, 2016.

2.  Davis, Charles Patrick, and John P. Cunha. "Broken Collarbone (Broken Clavicle)," EMedicineHealth, October 14, 2016.

3.  "Shoulder: Clavicle Fracture," Department of Orthopaedic Surgery, University of California-San Francisco, n.d.

# Part Six

# Injuries to the Elbows, Wrists, and Hands

Chapter 31

# Arm and Wrist Injuries

## Chapter Contents

Section 31.1

# Arm Fractures

"Arm Fractures," © 2017 Omnigraphics.
Reviewed June 2017.

The human arm contains three long bones: the humerus, or upper arm bone, which extends from the shoulder to the elbow; and the radius and ulna, or forearm bones, which extend from the elbow to the wrist. The radius is located on the same side of the forearm as the thumb, while the ulna is located on the same side as the little finger. These two bones work together to rotate the forearm and turn the palm of the hand up or down. All three arm bones can be broken, or fractured, in the falls, collisions, and impacts that frequently occur in sports. The severity of arm fractures varies from minor cracks in the bone to open fractures in which displaced bone fragments penetrate through the skin. Less severe, nondisplaced arm fractures are usually treated conservatively, with immobilization in a cast, splint, or brace, while more severe fractures may require surgical repair.

## Causes

The most common type of arm fracture affects the forearm bones near the distal end, which is closest to the wrist. Forearm fractures also occur in the middle segment of the bones and near the proximal end, which is closest to the elbow. Fractures usually occur in both the radius and the ulna simultaneously, although either bone can also be broken independently. Forearm fractures are fairly common among young children who climb trees or jump off swings or other playground equipment. The injuries also occur frequently among active teens and adults who participate in sports, especially sports that involve physical contact or a risk of high-speed falls onto hard surfaces, such as skateboarding. Falling on an outstretched arm can break the radius or ulna, as can a direct blow to the forearm.

Humerus fractures are less common than forearm fractures. They are typically caused by a direct impact to the upper arm in a high-speed collision or fall. A broken humerus can also result from falling on an outstretched arm or extreme twisting of the upper arm. A rare type of humerus fracture, known as a ball-thrower's fracture, happens when the upper arm muscles contract violently and create a spiral fracture around the bone. Outside of traumatic injuries, arm fractures sometimes occur in people whose bones are weakened by underlying medical conditions, such as osteoporosis or cancer.

## Symptoms

The symptoms of an arm fracture are similar regardless of which bone or bones have been broken. Depending on the severity of the fracture, the symptoms may include:

- pain

- swelling

- bruising

- limited range of motion

- visible deformity or shortening of the arm if the fracture is displaced

- numbness or weakness in the hand or wrist if nerves or blood vessels are injured

- bone fragments penetrating the skin in an open fracture.

## Diagnosis and Treatment

To diagnose an arm fracture, the doctor will review the athlete's medical history, including the circumstances under which the injury occurred and any previous history of injuries to the arm. Next, the doctor will evaluate the athlete's symptoms and conduct a medical examination of the arm, checking for areas of tenderness or deformity and testing range of motion, blood flow, and sensation. Finally, the doctor will order X-rays to confirm the diagnosis. X-rays can pinpoint the location of the fracture and show whether the bone is displaced or fragmented.

Humerus fractures can usually be treated without surgery. If there is mild displacement, the doctor may use a process called reduction to realign the parts of the bone. Then the athlete's arm will be immobilized in a cast, splint, or brace to protect it while the bone heals. Ice and anti-inflammatory medications can be used to relieve pain and reduce swelling. Once the fracture has healed, the athlete will need physical therapy or rehabilitation to restore strength and range of motion in the arm.

Since forearm fractures usually involve both the ulna and the radius, they are more likely to require surgery to maintain the proper rotating motion of the arm. Open fractures are almost always treated surgically due to the risk of infection from the bone puncturing the skin. Surgical treatment of an arm fracture involves aligning the pieces of the broken bone and stabilizing them to prevent movement while they heal. The surgeon will most likely use an internal fixation technique, which involves inserting metal plates and screws or a metal rod inside the arm to hold the bones together. Then the arm will be placed in a cast until the fractures heal. In the case of severe or multiple fractures, the surgeon may use an external fixation technique, which involves inserting metal pins or screws into the bone to hold a metal frame on the outside of the arm to stabilize the bone until it heals.

## Recovery and Complications

The recovery time for arm fractures depends on the severity of injury and type of treatment, as well as the patient's overall health. Minor fractures treated with a cast may only require four to eight weeks to heal, while severe fractures treated surgically may require twelve weeks or more. Although the prognosis for full recovery is very good for most arm fractures, it can take up to six months to regain full strength and range of motion in the arm.

Like all surgical procedures, surgery to repair arm fractures entails some risk of complications, including:

- infection

- damage to the surrounding nerves and blood vessels

- nonunion or malunion of the fracture, which may require additional surgery

- synostosis, a rare condition in which a bridge of bone forms between the radius and ulna during the healing process and limits its range of motion in the forearm.

### References

1. "Adult Forearm Fractures," OrthoInfo, 2017.

2. "Arm Fracture," Drugs.com, 2017.

3. Imm, Nick. "Forearm Injuries and Fractures," Patient, 2014.

# Section 31.2

# *Carpal Tunnel Syndrome*

This section includes text excerpted from "Carpal Tunnel
Syndrome Fact Sheet," National Institute of Neurological
Disorders and Stroke (NINDS), January 2017.

## What Is Carpal Tunnel Syndrome?

Carpal tunnel syndrome (CTS) occurs when the median nerve,
which runs from the forearm into the palm of the hand, becomes
pressed or squeezed at the wrist. The carpal tunnel—a narrow, rigid
passageway of ligament and bones at the base of the hand—houses
the median nerve and the tendons that bend the fingers. The median
nerve provides feeling to the palm side of the thumb and to the index,
middle, and part of the ring fingers (although not the little finger). It
also controls some small muscles at the base of the thumb.

Sometimes, thickening from the lining of irritated tendons or other
swelling narrows the tunnel and causes the median nerve to be compressed. The result may be numbness, weakness, or sometimes pain
in the hand and wrist, or occasionally in the forearm and arm. CTS is
the most common and widely known of the entrapment neuropathies,
in which one of the body's peripheral nerves is pressed upon.

## What Are the Symptoms of Carpal Tunnel Syndrome?

Symptoms usually start gradually, with frequent burning, tingling,
or itching numbness in the palm of the hand and the fingers, especially
the thumb and the index and middle fingers. Some carpal tunnel suf-
ferers say their fingers feel useless and swollen, even though little or
no swelling is apparent. The symptoms often first appear in one or both
hands during the night, since many people sleep with flexed wrists.
A person with carpal tunnel syndrome may wake up feeling the need
to "shake out" the hand or wrist. As symptoms worsen, people might
feel tingling during the day. Decreased grip strength may make it
difficult to form a fist, grasp small objects, or perform other manual
tasks. In chronic and/or untreated cases, the muscles at the base of

the thumb may waste away. Some people are unable to tell between hot and cold by touch.

## What Are the Causes of Carpal Tunnel Syndrome?

Carpal tunnel syndrome is often the result of a combination of factors that reduce the available space for the median nerve within the carpal tunnel, rather than a problem with the nerve itself. Contributing factors include trauma or injury to the wrist that cause swelling, such as sprain or fracture; an overactive pituitary gland; an underactive thyroid gland; and rheumatoid arthritis. Mechanical problems in the wrist joint, work stress, repeated use of vibrating hand tools, fluid retention during pregnancy or menopause, or the development of a cyst or tumor in the canal also may contribute to the compression. Often, no single cause can be identified.

## Who Is at Risk of Developing Carpal Tunnel Syndrome?

Women are three times more likely than men to develop carpal tunnel syndrome, perhaps because the carpal tunnel itself may be smaller in women than in men. The dominant hand is usually affected first and produces the most severe pain. Persons with diabetes or other metabolic disorders that directly affect the body's nerves and make them more susceptible to compression are also at high risk. Carpal tunnel syndrome usually occurs only in adults.

The risk of developing carpal tunnel syndrome is not confined to people in a single industry or job, but is especially common in those performing assembly line work—manufacturing, sewing, finishing, cleaning, and meat, poultry, or fish packing. In fact, carpal tunnel syndrome is three times more common among assemblers than among data-entry personnel.

## How Is Carpal Tunnel Syndrome Diagnosed?

Early diagnosis and treatment are important to avoid permanent damage to the median nerve.

- A medical history and physical examination of the hands, arms, shoulders, and neck can help determine if the person's discomfort is related to daily activities or to an underlying disorder, and can rule out other conditions that cause similar symptoms. The wrist is examined for tenderness, swelling, warmth, and discoloration. Each finger should be tested for sensation and the muscles at the base of the hand should be examined for strength and signs of atrophy.

- Routine laboratory tests and X-rays can reveal fractures, arthritis, and detect diseases that can damage the nerves, such as diabetes.

- Specific tests may reproduce the symptoms of CTS. In the Tinel test, the doctor taps on or presses over the median nerve in the person's wrist. The test is positive when tingling occurs in the affected fingers. Phalen maneuver (or wrist-flexion test) involves the person pressing the backs of the hands and fingers together with their wrists flexed as far as possible. This test is positive if tingling or numbness occur in the affected fingers within 1–2 minutes. Doctors may also ask individuals to try to make a movement that brings on symptoms.

- Electrodiagnostic tests may help confirm the diagnosis of CTS. A nerve conduction study measures electrical activity of the nerves and muscles by assessing the nerve's ability to send a signal along the nerve or to the muscle. Electromyography is a special recording technique that detects electrical activity of muscle fibers and can determine the severity of damage to the median nerve.

- Ultrasound imaging can show abnormal size of the median nerve. Magnetic resonance imaging (MRI) can show the anatomy of the wrist but to date has not been especially useful in diagnosing carpal tunnel syndrome.

## How Is Carpal Tunnel Syndrome Treated?

Treatments for carpal tunnel syndrome should begin as early as possible, under a doctor's direction. Underlying causes such as diabetes or arthritis should be treated first.

### Nonsurgical Treatments

- Splinting
- Avoiding daytime activities that may provoke symptoms
- Over-the-counter drugs
- Prescription medicines
- Alternative therapies

*Surgery*

- Carpal tunnel release
- Open release surgery
- Endoscopic surgery

## How Can Carpal Tunnel Syndrome Be Prevented?

At the workplace, workers can do on-the-job conditioning, perform stretching exercises, take frequent rest breaks, and ensure correct posture and wrist position. Wearing fingerless gloves can help keep hands warm and flexible. Workstations, tools and tool handles, and tasks can be redesigned to enable the worker's wrist to maintain a natural position during work. Jobs can be rotated among workers. Employers can develop programs in ergonomics, the process of adapting workplace conditions and job demands to the capabilities of workers. However, research has not conclusively shown that these workplace changes prevent the occurrence of carpal tunnel syndrome.

## Section 31.3

# *Scaphoid Fractures*

"Scaphoid Fractures," © 2017 Omnigraphics.
Reviewed June 2017.

The scaphoid is a small, curved bone in the wrist at the base of the thumb. It is one of eight small bones, known as the carpal bones, that make up the wrist joint. The scaphoid bone plays an important role in movement of the wrist and stability of the wrist joint. Due to its shape and position, it is also the most frequently broken bone in the wrist. Scaphoid fractures are usually caused by a sharp impact on an outstretched hand. Many people who sustain this type of injury are not aware of it, though, because the fracture may not appear on initial X-rays. Yet failure to diagnose and treat scaphoid fractures promptly can lead to complications, such as arthritis of the wrist.

## Causes and Symptoms

Most scaphoid fractures occur when athletes who are falling forward instinctively reach forward with their arms to absorb the impact. When their weight lands on an outstretched hand with the wrist bent backward, it can cause the scaphoid bone to break. This type of high-energy fall is common in sports such as skateboarding, snowboarding, and mountain biking. Some scaphoid fractures result from a blow to the palm of the hand, such as from holding a steering wheel during a front-end collision. In rare cases, scaphoid fractures are caused by repetitive stress on the wrist in activities like gymnastics.

Following a fall or impact, common symptoms that may indicate a scaphoid fracture include pain, swelling, and bruising in the wrist—especially on the thumb side. The pain may worsen upon moving the wrist or using the thumb to grasp objects. Pressing the area known as the anatomical snuffbox may also be painful. For some people, however, the symptoms of a scaphoid fracture are mild enough that they do not seek medical attention. They simply assume that the wrist is sprained and the symptoms will fade within a few days. It is vital to see a doctor if the pain persists, though, because of the potential complications of failing to treat a scaphoid fracture.

## Diagnosis

To diagnose a scaphoid fracture, a doctor will inquire about the circumstances of the injury and conduct a medical examination. The doctor will look for swelling or bruising in the wrist and check for pain when the patient moves the wrist in certain directions. Tenderness in an area known as the anatomical snuffbox is also considered an indication of a possible scaphoid fracture. When the thumb is held in a "thumbs up" position, the anatomical snuffbox appears as a hollow or depression on the back of the wrist between the tendons at the base of the thumb. This is the location of the scaphoid bone.

Following the physical examination, the doctor will perform tests to help determine whether the scaphoid has been broken. Although a standard X-ray is usually the first test ordered, around 20 percent of scaphoid fractures do not appear on X-rays because of the small size and overlapping arrangement of the carpal bones. In some cases, a scaphoid fracture will show up on an X-ray taken one to two weeks after the initial injury, once the bone has started to heal. For this reason, a repeat X-ray is often recommended if the initial results are negative. Magnetic resonance imaging (MRI) or computed tomography

(CT) scans may also be used to determine whether a scaphoid fracture exists.

## Treatment

The treatment for a scaphoid fracture depends on its severity, its location in the bone, and the amount of time that has elapsed since the injury occurred. There are two main classifications of severity: nondisplaced, in which the segments of bone remain in alignment; and displaced, in which the segments of bone have moved out of their correct position. Nondisplaced scaphoid fractures are usually treated conservatively by placing the wrist and forearm in a protective cast for six to twelve weeks to allow the bone to heal. Fractures of the distal pole of the scaphoid bone, closest to the thumb, usually heal successfully with conservative treatment because the distal end has a good blood supply. Recent fractures that are diagnosed promptly are also good candidates for casting.

The treatment is likely to include surgery, however, if the scaphoid fracture is displaced, affects the middle section (waist) or proximal pole (closest to the forearm) of the bone, and has existed for some time without being diagnosed. Fractures with these characteristics are less likely to heal properly without surgical intervention. The surgical procedure involves realigning the displaced segments of the bone and inserting a small screw or pin to hold them in the correct position until the bone is fully healed. For older fractures or segments of bone that do not receive an adequate blood supply, the surgeon may perform a bone graft. This procedure involves taking bone tissue from the forearm or hip and placing it around the scaphoid fracture to stimulate bone growth and speed healing. The doctor may also prescribe the use of a bone stimulator—a device that emits low-energy ultrasound waves—to promote bone growth.

## Recovery and Complications

Scaphoid fractures tend to heal more slowly than other types of broken bones. Most patients must wear a cast or splint for two to three months, during which time they are likely to be restricted from lifting, throwing, and participating in activities that involve a risk of falling. Once the cast is removed, most patients must undergo physical therapy with a certified hand therapist to alleviate stiffness and regain strength and range of motion in the wrist. Occupational therapy may also be recommended to help the patient regain the wrist functions needed to perform activities of daily living, such as tying shoes, fastening buttons, or cutting food.

Although the prognosis for full recovery is good for most scaphoid fractures—especially those that are diagnosed and treated promptly—this type of injury carries a risk of complications. Some of the complications that may occur include the following:

- Nonunion

  Nonunion occurs when a broken bone fails to heal within a reasonable amount of time, so the segments of the bone remain separate. Nonunion is a particular risk in scaphoid fractures because poor blood supply to certain sections of the bone limits the oxygen and nutrients available to support bone growth. Treatment for scaphoid nonunion usually involves surgery to insert a vascularized bone graft—a piece of bone tissue from another part of the body along with its blood supply—to increase blood flow and promote healing.

- Malunion

  Malunion occurs when a broken bone heals improperly, so the segments of the bone are not aligned correctly. Scaphoid malunion usually results in pain and restricted movement of the wrist. Treatment usually involves surgery to rebreak and realign the bone, along with a bone graft to promote healing.

- Avascular necrosis

  When a fracture disrupts the blood supply to part of a bone, the lack of oxygen and nutrients may cause that bone segment to collapse and die. This serious complication is known as avascular (meaning without blood) necrosis (death). The blood supply enters the scaphoid bone in its narrow middle section, known as the waist, which is also the point where fractures are most likely to occur. Avascular necrosis poses a risk for scaphoid fractures that are displaced or that go undiagnosed and untreated. Some cases can be treated effectively with a vascularized bone graft.

- Arthritis

  People who experience complications following a scaphoid fracture may eventually develop osteoarthritis of the wrist. This condition occurs when structural problems in the joint wear down the cartilage, causing pain, stiffness, weakness, and decreased range of motion. Anti-inflammatory medications, steroid injections, special splints, and surgery are the main options available to treat the symptoms of wrist arthritis.

*References*

1. Jones, Bertrand, and Tamara D. Rozental. "Scaphoid Fracture of the Wrist," Ortho Info, March 2016.

2. Laker, Scott R. "Scaphoid Injury Treatment and Management," EMedicine, April 6, 2015.

3. Payne, Jacqueline. "Scaphoid Wrist Fracture," Patient, September 23, 2016.

## Section 31.4

# *Wrist Fractures*

"Wrist Fractures," © 2017 Omnigraphics.
Reviewed June 2017.

The wrist is made up of ten separate bones: the two bones of forearm (called radius and ulna) and eight small bones at the base of the hand. A wrist fracture can happen in any of these ten bones. However, the most common fracture is the distal radius fracture, or Colles fracture, that occurs at the lower end of the radius. The Irish surgeon and anatomist, Abraham Colles, described this fracture in 1814 and hence the name "Colles" fracture.

Studies show that 1 out of every 10 broken bones is a broken wrist in the United States. This type of fracture commonly occur in contact sports, skiing, skating, and biking and the usual cause of injury is the athlete throwing out his or her hand to break a fall, known as a Fall on an Outstretched Hand (FOOSH) injury.

The break in the distal radius fracture can be of various types, such as:

• Non-displaced stable fracture, meaning that the bone has broken but the pieces have remained in place.

• A break in lower end of the radius that can extend into the wrist joint.

- A piece of broken bone that breaks through the skin (an open fracture).

- The bone may shatter into many pieces, known as a comminuted fracture.

- Unstable fractures with larger broken fragments that are not in place.

The above classification of a fracture is important because the course of treatment and the outcome is based on the nature of the fracture. Open and comminuted fractures are difficult to treat and residual problems like stiffness and deformity can result.

## Causes

FOOSH is the most common cause for wrist fractures. Osteoporosis, a condition in which bone become weak and porous, is another common cause, where even minor falls can result in a broken wrist. Severe trauma such as road traffic accidents and contact sports injuries can also cause bad fractures of the wrist.

## Signs and Symptoms

- Pain and swelling around the wrist.

- Difficulty moving and using the wrist and hand.

- Deformity—the wrist hangs or bends unnaturally.

- Tingling sensation or numbness in the fingers.

## Diagnosis

The surgeon will perform a physical examination of the wrist and hand. A set of X-rays will be ordered to ascertain the nature and location of the fracture. If the fracture is complicated, a computed tomography (CT) or magnetic resonance imaging (MRI) scan would be needed to get better details of the fracture fragments and soft tissue (ligaments) damages around the fracture.

## Treatment

Fractures are treated either by surgical or nonsurgical methods depending on the nature of the fracture.

If the fractured segments are stable and in good position nonsurgical treatment methods can be used.

If there is a displacement, realignment of the fractured segments are done by a surgeon and plaster cast will be applied. This is usually done under sedation by applying traction force on the fractured segments. This method is called closed reduction. There will be a repeat plaster casting 2 to 3 days later after the swelling subsides. Check X-rays will be taken during this period to make sure the fractured segments are in position.

A fracture with multiple displaced fragments and punctured skin makes it an unstable open fracture. This will require surgery for proper fracture reduction and immobilization. This surgical method is called open reduction and internal fixation (ORIF) where metal pins, wires, plates and screws are used to fix the fractures.

One basic rule common to both surgical and nonsurgical methods is putting the fractured segments back in position with proper alignment and preventing it from moving out of place. This is to prevent deformity and ensure full range of movements in the joints and return to normal functional activities.

The treatment method also depends on various other factors of the person such as their age, nature of sport, level of activity, and their overall health.

## Recovery

**Pain:** After a wrist fracture, a patient will experience a considerable amount of pain for a few days or weeks. Ice, elevation of the hand, and nonsteroidal anti-inflammatory drugs (NSAIDs) will help in coping with pain.

**Cast care:** Make sure you keep the cast dry. If it loosens as the swelling comes down, it has to be reapplied. If you have unrelenting pain, it is a warning sign for you to contact your surgeon.

It is important to keep moving your fingers, elbow and shoulder to prevent them from getting stiff.

## Return to play

Once the cast is removed, your physical therapist will work on your wrist and hand to get back the range of movement and functional ability. You will be able to resume lighter activities like swimming or exercising the lower body by 1 or 2 months after removing of the cast. Vigorous sports activities can be resumed after 3 to 6 months.

## References

1. "Wrist Fractures," American Society for Surgery of the Hand (ASSH), 2015.

2. "Distal Radius Fractures (Broken Wrist)," American Academy of Orthopaedic Surgeons (AAOS), 2013.

3. "Colles' Fracture (Distal Radius Fracture or Broken Wrist)," WebMD, 2017.

4. "Wrist Fractures," Patient Platform Limited, 2016.

Chapter 32

# Elbow Injuries

## Chapter Contents

# Section 32.1

# *Tennis Elbow*

This section includes text excerpted from "Tennis Elbow: Affecting More than Just Tennis Players," National Aeronautics and Space Administration (NASA), July 19, 2007. Reviewed June 2017.

Tennis Elbow, or Lateral Epicondylitis, is an inflammation of the tendons that cause pain in the elbow and arm. The tendons involved are responsible for attaching the muscles that extend the wrist and hand. Tennis elbow produces pain on the outer part of the arm, unlike the similar condition called golfer's elbow, which affects the tendons on the inside of the elbow. Despite the name Tennis elbow, patients can have symptoms without ever stepping foot on a tennis court. Tennis elbow is the primary reason people see their doctor for elbow pain, and it is most commonly seen in the dominant arm. Although it can occur at any age, the most common age range is 30 to 50 years old, and affects an equal number of women and men.

## *What Causes Tennis Elbow?*

Tennis elbow is considered a chronic condition because it occurs over time. Repetitive motions, such as using a screwdriver or swinging a racket, can put a strain on muscles and add stress to the tendons. The constant repetitive motion can eventually cause microscopic tears in the tissue surrounding the elbow. Tennis elbow can result from playing sports, but can also affect people with jobs or hobbies that require a recurring movement. A range of activities that involve repetitive motions include:

- **Sports:** Tennis, racquetball, fencing, golf

- **Work and Hobbies:** Typing, using a computer mouse, knitting, gardening, raking, using scissors, playing a musical instrument

- **Manual Occupations:** Painting, carpentry, plumbing, brick laying, using a screwdriver or hammer

## What Are Common Symptoms of Tennis Elbow?

Tennis elbow produces pain and tenderness on the lateral epicondyle, the bony knob on the outside of the elbow. The lateral epicondyle is where the inflamed tendons connect to the bone. In most cases the pain starts out mild and gradually becomes worse over weeks or months. Although the damage is in the elbow, there may be radiating or burning pain in the upper or lower arm, or outer part of the elbow. Pain may also occur when doing things with your hands. Tennis elbow may cause the most pain when:

- Lifting an object

- Gripping an object or making a fist

- Extending the forearm or straightening the wrist

- Shaking hands or opening a door

- Pressing on the outer surface of the elbow

To properly diagnose tennis elbow, your athletic trainer or doctor will do a thorough examination. The athletic trainer or doctor may have you flex your arm, wrist, and elbow to see where it hurts, and may press on the lateral epicondyle to reproduce symptoms. In more severe cases you may also need an X-ray or MRI (magnetic resonance imaging) to detect tennis elbow or rule out other problems.

## What Are Treatment Options for Tennis Elbow?

Tennis elbow will usually heal on its own if you rest the injured tendon by stopping or changing your activity. If pain increases or the condition continues and is left untreated, a loss of function may occur so it is important to seek medical care. Types of helpful treatment are:

- **Reduce inflammation and pain:** Rest, ice, elevation, and compression (RICE), Nonsteroidal anti-inflammatory drugs (NSAIDs), such as ibuprofen according to package directions, injections of steroids or painkillers to temporarily relieve symptoms

- **Rehabilitation:** Perform range of motion exercises to decrease stiffness and increase flexibility, physical therapy to strengthen the muscles

- **Orthotics:** An elbow strap or wrist splint to restrict the movement of the tendon and protect from further strain

- **Activity Modification:** Improve posture and technique, alternate hands during activities, use a smaller grip on tools or rackets, have a workstation assessment

Nonoperative treatment is successful in about 90 percent of patients with tennis elbow, but in severe cases with symptoms lasting 4–6 months, surgery may be required. The outpatient procedure consists of removing the section of the damaged tendon and repairing the remaining tendon. Surgery is only required in a small amount of patients seen with Tennis elbow, and the success rate of the procedure is very high.

## When Can I Return to Normal Activities?

Returning to regular activities depends on the individual case and extent of the damage to the tendon. People heal at different rates so it is important to not rush recovery and to not push yourself. Although there may be a period of relief, pain may come back, and ending a treatment plan early may increase the chance of reinjury. You may be able to start performing normal levels of activity if:

- The injured elbow is no longer swollen
- The injured elbow feels as strong as the noninjured elbow
- The elbow can be flexed with no trouble
- Bearing weight is no longer painful
- You can grip objects pain-free

## How Can I Prevent Tennis Elbow?

The best way to prevent Tennis elbow is to avoid overuse. If any pain is felt during activity you should stop and rest the elbow. If symptoms arise during activities at work, frequent breaks should be taken.

Tennis elbow can develop from using the wrong equipment, such as a racket that is too heavy, or a golf club that has a grip that is too large. Poor posture and bad technique may also lead to Tennis elbow. To help prevent Tennis elbow it is important to:

- Stretch and warm up before using the upper extremities
- Ice the elbow after activity
- Use alternate hands during activities to prevent overuse
- Strengthen the muscles of the arm, elbow, wrist, and back
- Use correct technique

# Section 32.2

# *Osteochondritis Dissecans of the Elbow (Little League Elbow)*

"Osteochondritis Dissecans of the Elbow (Little League Elbow)," © 2017 Omnigraphics. Reviewed June 2017.

Osteochondritis dissecans (OCD) is an overuse injury that involves damage and detérioration of the articular cartilage that cushions and protects the elbow joint. Ongoing, forceful use of the arm disrupts the blood supply to the cartilage and the underlying subchondral bone, which eventually causes small pieces of cartilage and bone to weaken, crack, break off, and interfere with the function of the elbow joint. OCD is sometimes referred to as Little League Elbow because the injury has been associated with the repetitive stress of pitching a baseball, but it also affects young people who play other sports that place strain on the elbow, such as gymnastics, tennis, and weightlifting. OCD usually affects people between the ages of 10 and 20 whose bones are still growing and thus are more prone to injury. In contrast, adult elbow injuries typically affect ligaments and tendons rather than bones.

## *Causes and Symptoms*

Since OCD of the elbow often affects several members or genera-tions of the same family, some experts believe that the condition has a genetic component that makes some people more likely to develop it. Research also suggests that overuse strain contributes to the devel-opment of the condition. Most adolescents who are treated for OCD of the elbow are active in sports that involve repeated, forceful throwing, hitting, pulling, or landing actions that place stress on the elbow joint, causing the bones to jam into the articular cartilage over and over again. Since the cartilage is immature and the bones are still growing, the repeated impacts can cause damage to the elbow joint.

The symptoms of elbow OCD typically appear gradually and worsen over time. In fact, 80 percent of athletes diagnosed with the condition cannot recall a specific injury to their elbow. The first sign of a prob-lem is usually pain or discomfort while engaging in the activity that is creating repetitive stress on the elbow joint. As the condition worsens, athletes may experience the following additional symptoms:

- aching of the elbow while not playing sports

- sharp pain when bending or straightening the arm

- swelling on the inside of the elbow joint

- stiffness and difficulty straightening the elbow

- grinding, crackling, or popping sounds (crepitus) when moving the elbow joint

- catching or locking of the elbow as loose cartilage or bone chips interfere with joint function.

## Diagnosis

To make a diagnosis of OCD of the elbow, the doctor will take a medical history and conduct a physical examination. The doctor will inquire about the athlete's age and involvement in sports and activities that cause repetitive stress to the elbow joint, such as baseball, tennis, and gymnastics. The doctor will then examine the sore elbow for swelling and tenderness and compare it to the healthy elbow. Next, the doctor will evaluate the range of motion in each elbow and check for crepitus during elbow movement.

The doctor will order diagnostic imaging tests to help determine the condition of the bones and cartilage in the elbow joint. Although X-rays of athletes with elbow OCD sometimes appear normal, they may show irregularities in the elbow joint, such as changes in shape, size, or alignment. X-rays can also show whether the athlete's growth plates remain open and detect the presence of cracks or bone chips. Magnetic resonance imaging (MRI) or computed tomography (CT) scans may also be used to get a more accurate picture of the bones and tissues in the elbow joint, as well as to monitor changes during the healing process.

## Treatment

Treatment of elbow OCD depends on the severity of the condition. Most experts prefer to treat mild cases conservatively, with a combination of rest, bracing, and physical therapy. Younger athletes and those with early cartilage damage that has not progressed to the point of deterioration and tearing are the best candidates for this approach. The athletes are advised to stop engaging in the repetitive action that caused the elbow soreness for around six weeks, although they are usually encouraged to continue exercising to maintain fitness. A baseball pitcher, for instance, might be able to serve as designated hitter or play a position that does not demand much throwing, like first base. Conservative care may also include prescription or over-the-counter anti-inflammatory medications to help relieve pain and swelling, as well as regular application of ice to the elbow. Some experts recommend wearing a hinged brace to support the elbow during the rest period as well as when the athlete resumes activities.

Following a period of complete rest of the affected elbow, athletes must undergo physical therapy to strengthen and stretch muscles and regain range of motion in the joint. A key part of physical therapy for elbow OCD involves activity modification, in which athletes learn methods of changing their body mechanics to improve form and reduce strain on to the elbow. When pain and other symptoms disappear, athletes can make a slow, gradual return to competition. Baseball pitchers, for example, should follow a strict program that gradually increases the number, distance, and effort of throws. Although many young athletes will be tempted to return to action quickly, failure to follow the treatment plan can lead to serious, lifelong elbow conditions like arthritis.

For more severe cases of elbow OCD, the treatment is likely to involve surgery. This approach is often necessary for athletes who continue to experience symptoms after completing six months of conservative treatment, as well as for those who have fragments of cartilage and bone—known as loose bodies—restricting movement of the elbow joint. Procedures used to treat OCD of the elbow may be performed as open surgery through an incision on the outer part of the elbow, or as minimally invasive arthroscopic surgery using an instrument with a tiny camera mounted on the end. The most commonly used surgical techniques include the following:

- Drilling

  For elbow OCD that has not yet produced loose bodies, the surgeon may use a special instrument to drill tiny holes through the damaged articular cartilage and into the healthy layer of bone underneath. Drilling stimulates a healing response in the bone marrow, causing drops of blood to fill the holes and new cartilage to grow in the damaged area.

- Debridement

  This method is generally used when cartilage and bone in the elbow joint is damaged or torn, but remains attached.

The surgeon uses a small instrument to shave away (debride) irritated, loose, or dead tissue from the joint. The surface of the bone is smoothed down until it bleeds, which stimulates the bone marrow to fill in the damaged area.

• Pinning

When advanced OCD has caused pieces of bone or cartilage to detach from the elbow joint, the surgeon may debride the damaged area and then use surgical wires to pin the fragments back in place.

• Grafting

In some cases, the surgeon may attempt to repair an area of damaged articular cartilage in the elbow by replacing it with a graft of tissue transplanted from a different joint. The osteochondral autograft transplantation (OAT) technique involves harvesting healthy plugs of bone and cartilage, usually from the knee joint, and transferring them to the elbow. However, differences between knee and elbow cartilage can make it challenging to match the graft with the shape of the damaged area.

## Recovery and Prevention

Although surgery can relieve pain, provide stability, and increase range of motion in the elbow, few athletes are able to regain peak form afterward. Most young athletes with elbow OCD that is severe enough to require surgery are forced to modify their activities or stop playing high-level sports. The main goal of surgical treatment is to prevent the development of degenerative arthritis in the elbow in adulthood.

Fortunately, there are ways to prevent the development of elbow OCD in young athletes, including the following:

• pay close attention to symptoms and cease activities that cause elbow pain until symptoms subside

• limit pitch counts for young baseball players, and avoid throwing breaking pitches—which cause the most elbow stress—until age 14 for a curveball and 16 for a slider

• avoid specialization in a single sport year-round, and promote cross-training in multiple sports

• emphasize the benefits of resistance training, conditioning, and physical fitness

• teach proper mechanics and form to reduce the risk of injury.

*References*

1. "Adolescent Osteochondritis Dissecans of the Elbow," Orthopod, n.d.

2. "Little League Elbow," Healthy Children, November 21, 2015.

3. "Preferred Treatment for OCD of the Elbow," Active Sport Physiotherapy Clinic, 2014.

4. Savoie III, Felix H. "Osteochondritis Dissecans of the Elbow," *Operative Techniques in Sports Medicine,* 2008.

# Section 32.3

# *Ulnar Collateral Ligament Injuries (Thrower's Elbow)*

"Ulnar Collateral Ligament Injuries (Thrower's Elbow),"
© 2017 Omnigraphics. Reviewed June 2017.

The ulnar collateral ligament (UCL) is a thick, triangular band of connective tissue on the inside of the elbow that links the humerus (upper arm bone) to the ulna (forearm bone on the same side as the pinkie finger). The UCL plays an important role in stabilizing the elbow joint, particularly during overhead motions like throwing a ball. The ligament can become stretched, damaged, or torn from overuse in the repeated, forceful overhead motions that are commonly performed in such sports as baseball, football, volleyball, water polo, cricket, and tennis. As a result, the injury is sometimes called "thrower's elbow." Although minor UCL injuries can heal on their own, surgery is sometimes required to repair tears in the ligament and restore stability to the elbow joint. The UCL reconstruction procedure is often referred to as "Tommy John surgery" after the famous Major League Baseball pitcher who became the first person to undergo it in 1974.

## *Causes*

Repetitive stress from forceful throwing motions is the most common cause of ulnar collateral ligament injuries. Athletes like professional pitchers who throw hard on a regular basis place a great deal of strain on the UCL, causing tiny tears to develop in the soft tissue. These microtears accumulate over time, causing weakness and degeneration of the ligament. Eventually, the UCL may tear, rupture, or "pop," resulting in pain and instability in the elbow joint. Other contributing factors to thrower's elbow may include failure to warm up and cool down properly, poor throwing mechanics or technique, lack of rest between throwing sessions, and use of improper or ill-fitting equipment. In addition to overuse, UCL tears can also be caused by an acute injury, such as falling onto an outstretched hand.

A related condition that develops in adolescents between the ages of 10 and 20 is known as Little League elbow. Since the bones of young athletes are still growing, the type of repetitive throwing motions that place stress on the UCL typically damage the growth plate in the elbow rather than the ligament itself. In advanced cases, pieces of cartilage and bone break off and interfere with movement of the elbow joint.

## Symptoms and Diagnosis

Pain in the elbow when throwing is the first sign of injury to the UCL. The pain may radiate down the forearm into the wrist or hand, and the inside of the elbow may feel tender or appear slightly swollen. If condition progresses to the point where the ligament ruptures, many athletes report hearing a popping sound, which is immediately followed by pain, weakness, and instability in the elbow joint. Finally, some athletes also experience numbness or tingling in the forearm and hand.

To diagnose a UCL injury, a doctor will begin by taking a health history, which will include questions about the athlete's participation in sports and the onset and duration of symptoms. Next, the doctor will conduct a physical examination of the elbow, manipulating it gently to identify the source of pain. One test of elbow strength and stability is the valgus stress test, in which the doctor applies pressure to the outside of the elbow joint while bending the arm. The doctor will also order diagnostic imaging tests, such as magnetic resonance imaging (MRI) or magnetic resonance arthrogram (MRA), to view areas of damage in the elbow joint.

## Treatment

Treatment for the early stages of UCL injury is usually conservative. At the onset of symptoms, the athlete may be advised to rest the elbow for several days, apply ice to the area, take anti-inflammatory medications, and wear an elbow brace or compression sleeve. Once the pain has gone away, the athlete may be urged to perform physical therapy or rehabilitation to improve the strength, flexibility, stability, and range of motion of the elbow joint.

For severe cases, in which the UCL has ruptured, treatment involves surgical reconstruction of the ligament. The surgeon makes an incision on the inside of the elbow, splits and retracts the flexor muscles to reveal the UCL beneath, and replaces the damaged ligament with a tendon taken from the athlete's arm, leg, or foot.

There are two main surgical techniques used to replace the UCL ligament. In the docking technique, the surgeon drills two holes in the ulna and three holes in the medial epicondyle at the end of the humerus. The new tendon is looped through the holes in the ulna, stretched across the elbow joint, and threaded through the bottom hole in the medial epicondyle. Next, sutures attached to the ends of the tendon are passed through the upper holes in the medial epicondyle. The surgeon uses these sutures to pull the tendon tight and adjust its tension to allow a full range of movement in the elbow. When the optimal tension has been achieved, the surgeon ties off the sutures.

In the figure of eight technique, the surgeon drills two holes in the ulna and two holes in the medial epicondyle. The new tendon graft is looped through all four holes in a figure-eight pattern and then sutured together. After surgery, the athlete's elbow is bandaged and placed in a splint for several weeks to protect it while it heals. Although rehabilitation from Tommy John surgery can take more than a year, more than 80 percent of pitchers who undergo it are able to return to their previous level of competition.

## Prevention

The key to preventing UCL injuries is to avoid overuse and repetitive stress of the elbow. Experts recommend taking the following precautions to protect the UCL from damage:

- warm up and stretch before any throwing activity
- perform regular strength and conditioning of the arms, shoulders, and core
- cool down properly following activity
- limit pitch counts and allow recovery time between games
- avoid playing a single sport year round

- pay attention to proper body and throwing mechanics

- cease throwing immediately upon experiencing pain

- seek medical treatment if pain persists following rest, ice, and anti-inflammatory medication.

### References

1. Dikmanis, Andris. "Fitness and Training: Thrower's Elbow," *Baseball Player Magazine,* July 1, 2010.

2. "Physical Therapist's Guide to Ulnar Collatoral Ligament Injury," Move Forward PT, 2017.

3. Walker, Brad. "Throwers Elbow and Throwers Elbow Treatment," Stretch Coach, 2017.

## Section 32.4

# *Ulnar Nerve Entrapment (Cubital Tunnel Syndrome)*

Text in this section is from "Ulnar Nerve Entrapment at the Elbow (Cubital Tunnel Syndrome)," © 1995-2017 American Academy of Orthopaedic Surgeons. Reprinted with permission.

Ulnar nerve entrapment occurs when the ulnar nerve in the arm becomes compressed or irritated.

The ulnar nerve is one of the three main nerves in your arm. It travels from your neck down into your hand, and can be constricted in several places along the way, such as beneath the collarbone or at the wrist. The most common place for compression of the nerve is behind the inside part of the elbow. Ulnar nerve compression at the elbow is called "cubital tunnel syndrome."

Numbness and tingling in the hand and fingers are common symptoms of cubital tunnel syndrome. In most cases, symptoms can be managed with conservative treatments like changes in activities and bracing. If conservative methods do not improve your symptoms, or if the nerve compression is causing muscle weakness or damage in your hand, your doctor may recommend surgery.

## Anatomy

At the elbow, the ulnar nerve travels through a tunnel of tissue (the cubital tunnel) that runs under a bump of bone at the inside of your elbow. This bony bump is called the medial epicondyle. The spot where the nerve runs under the medial epicondyle is commonly referred to as the "funny bone." At the funny bone the nerve is close to your skin, and bumping it causes a shock-like feeling.

Beyond the elbow, the ulnar nerve travels under muscles on the inside of your forearm and into your hand on the side of the palm with the little finger. As the nerve enters the hand, it travels through another tunnel (Guyon's canal).

The ulnar nerve gives feeling to the little finger and half of the ring finger. It also controls most of the little muscles in the hand that help with fine movements, and some of the bigger muscles in the forearm that help you make a strong grip.

## Cause

In many cases of cubital tunnel syndrome, the exact cause is not known. The ulnar nerve is especially vulnerable to compression at the elbow because it must travel through a narrow space with very little soft tissue to protect it.

## Common Causes of Compression

There are several things that can cause pressure on the nerve at the elbow:

- When your bend your elbow, the ulnar nerve must stretch around the boney ridge of the medial epicondyle. Because this stretching can irritate the nerve, keeping your elbow bent for long periods or repeatedly bending your elbow can cause painful symptoms. For example, many people sleep with their elbows bent. This can aggravate symptoms of ulnar nerve compression and cause you to wake up at night with your fingers asleep.

- In some people, the nerve slides out from behind the medial epicondyle when the elbow is bent. Over time, this sliding back and forth may irritate the nerve.

- Leaning on your elbow for long periods of time can put pressure on the nerve.

- Fluid buildup in the elbow can cause swelling that may compress the nerve.

- A direct blow to the inside of the elbow can cause pain, electric shock sensation, and numbness in the little and ring fingers. This is commonly called "hitting your funny bone."

## Risk Factors

Some factors put you more at risk for developing cubital tunnel syndrome. These include:

- Prior fracture or dislocations of the elbow

- Bone spurs/ arthritis of the elbow

- Swelling of the elbow joint

- Cysts near the elbow joint

- Repetitive or prolonged activities that require the elbow to be bent or flexed

## Symptoms

Cubital tunnel syndrome can cause an aching pain on the inside of the elbow. Most of the symptoms, however, occur in your hand.

- Numbness and tingling in the ring finger and little finger are common symptoms of ulnar nerve entrapment. Often, these symptoms come and go. They happen more often when the elbow is bent, such as when driving or holding the phone. Some people wake up at night because their fingers are numb.

- The feeling of "falling asleep" in the ring finger and little finger, especially when your elbow is bent. In some cases, it may be harder to move your fingers in and out, or to manipulate objects.

- Weakening of the grip and difficulty with finger coordination (such as typing or playing an instrument) may occur. These symptoms are usually seen in more severe cases of nerve compression.

- If the nerve is very compressed or has been compressed for a long time, muscle wasting in the hand can occur. Once this happens, muscle wasting cannot be reversed. For this reason, it is important to see your doctor if symptoms are severe or if they are less severe but have been present for more than 6 weeks.

## Home Remedies

There are many things you can do at home to help relieve symptoms. If your symptoms interfere with normal activities or last more than a few weeks, be sure to schedule an appointment with your doctor.

* Avoid activities that require you to keep your arm bent for long periods of time.

* If you use a computer frequently, make sure that your chair is not too low. Do not rest your elbow on the armrest.

* Avoid leaning on your elbow or putting pressure on the inside of your arm. For example, do not drive with your arm resting on the open window.

* Keep your elbow straight at night when you are sleeping. This can be done by wrapping a towel around your straight elbow or wearing an elbow pad backwards.

## Doctor Examination

### Medical History and Physical Examination

Your doctor will discuss your medical history and general health. He or she may also ask about your work, your activities, and what medications you are taking.

After discussing your symptoms and medical history, your doctor will examine your arm and hand to determine which nerve is compressed and where it is compressed. Some of the physical examination tests your doctor may do include:

* Tap over the nerve at the funny bone. If the nerve is irritated, this can cause a shock into the little finger and ring finger—although this can happen when the nerve is normal as well.

* Check whether the ulnar nerve slides out of normal position when you bend your elbow.

* Move your neck, shoulder, elbow, and wrist to see if different positions cause symptoms.

* Check for feeling and strength in your hand and fingers.

## Tests

**X-rays.** These imaging tests provide detailed pictures of dense structures, like bone. Most causes of compression of the ulnar nerve cannot be seen on an x-ray. However, your doctor may take X-rays of your elbow or wrist to look for bone spurs, arthritis, or other places that the bone may be compressing the nerve.

**Nerve conduction studies.** These tests can determine how well the nerve is working and help identify where it is being compressed.

Nerves are like "electrical cables" that travel through your body carrying messages between your brain and muscles. When a nerve is not working well, it takes too long for it to conduct.

During a nerve conduction test, the nerve is stimulated in one place and the time it takes for there to be a response is measured. Several places along the nerve will be tested and the area where the response takes too long is likely to be the place where the nerve is compressed.

Nerve conduction studies can also determine whether the compression is also causing muscle damage. During the test, small needles are put into some of the muscles that the ulnar nerve controls. Muscle damage is a sign of more severe nerve compression.

## Treatment

Unless your nerve compression has caused a lot of muscle wasting, your doctor will most likely first recommend nonsurgical treatment.

### Nonsurgical Treatment

**Non-steroidal anti-inflammatory medicines.** If your symptoms have just started, your doctor may recommend an anti-inflammatory medicine, such as ibuprofen, to help reduce swelling around the nerve.

Although steroids, such as cortisone, are very effective anti-inflammatory medicines, steroid injections are generally not used because there is a risk of damage to the nerve.

**Bracing or splinting.** Your doctor may prescribe a padded brace or splint to wear at night to keep your elbow in a straight position.

**Nerve gliding exercises.** Some doctors think that exercises to help the ulnar nerve slide through the cubital tunnel at the elbow and the Guyon's canal at the wrist can improve symptoms. These exercises may also help prevent stiffness in the arm and wrist.

## Surgical Treatment

Your doctor may recommend surgery to take pressure off of the nerve if:

- Nonsurgical methods have not improved your condition
- The ulnar nerve is very compressed
- Nerve compression has caused muscle weakness or damage

There are a few surgical procedures that will relieve pressure on the ulnar nerve at the elbow. Your orthopaedic surgeon will talk with you about the option that would be best for you.

These procedures are most often done on an outpatient basis, but some patients do best with an overnight stay at the hospital.

**Cubital tunnel release.** In this operation, the ligament "roof" of the cubital tunnel is cut and divided. This increases the size of the tunnel and decreases pressure on the nerve.

After the procedure, the ligament begins to heal and new tissue grows across the division. The new growth heals the ligament, and allows more space for the ulnar nerve to slide through.

Cubital tunnel release tends to work best when the nerve compression is mild or moderate and the nerve does not slide out from behind the bony ridge of the medial epicondyle when the elbow is bent.

**Ulnar nerve anterior transposition.** In many cases, the nerve is moved from its place behind the medial epicondyle to a new place in front of it. Moving the nerve to the front of the medial epicondyle prevents it from getting caught on the bony ridge and stretching when you bend your elbow. This procedure is called an anterior transposition of the ulnar nerve.

The nerve can be moved to lie under the skin and fat but on top of the muscle (subcutaneous transposition), or within the muscle (intermuscular transposition), or under the muscle (submuscular transposition).

**Medial epicondylectomy.** Another option to release the nerve is to remove part of the medial epicondyle. Like ulnar nerve transposition, this technique also prevents the nerve from getting caught on the boney ridge and stretching when your elbow is bent.

## Surgical Recovery

Depending on the type of surgery you have, you may need to wear a splint for a few weeks after the operation. A submuscular transposition usually requires a longer time (3 to 6 weeks) in a splint.

Your surgeon may recommend physical therapy exercises to help you regain strength and motion in your arm. He or she will also talk with you about when it will be safe to return to all your normal activities.

## Surgical Outcome

The results of surgery are generally good. Each method of surgery has a similar success rate for routine cases of nerve compression. If the nerve is very badly compressed or if there is muscle wasting, the nerve may not be able to return to normal and some symptoms may remain even after the surgery. Nerves recover slowly, and it may take a long time to know how well the nerve will do after surgery.

Chapter 33

# Hand Injuries

## *Chapter Contents*

Section 33.1

# *Finger Sprains, Fractures, and Dislocations*

"Finger Sprains, Fractures, and Dislocations,"
© 2017 Omnigraphics. Reviewed June 2017.

## *Anatomy of the Fingers*

The fingers of the hand, also called digits, are important parts of the body made for manipulating and feeling the world around us. Fingers are made up of bones, tendons, nerve fibers and blood vessels. There are a total of 14 bones in the fingers that are called the phalanx (singular) or phalanges (plural): two in the thumb and three each in the remaining digits. These are subdivided into the outermost phalanges or distal phalanges that contain the nails; the intermediate phalanges in the middle of the finger; and the proximal phalanges that attach to the five metacarpal bones of the palm. The thumb lacks an intermediate phalanx.

The multiple joints of the phalanges involving the interphalangeal joints (finger-finger) and metacarpophalangeal joints (finger-hand) provide strength and dexterity to the digits and scope for a wide range of movement. The finger joints are protected by a tough band of connective tissue including the cartilage, ligaments, and tendons. The cartilage and ligaments surround the joint surface and provide cushioning, mechanical strength, and stability to the joints. Tendons attach muscles of the forearm and hand to the digits and facilitate straightening or bending of fingers. Richly innervated with a large number of sensory receptors, the digits are also an important sense organ in the body.

## *Finger Sprains*

Common injuries among athletes who play ball sports, finger sprains are caused by an injury to the ligaments that run alongside the joints. Depending on their severity, finger sprains may be classified as first-degree, second-degree, or third-degree sprains. Diagnosis is based on a thorough physical assessment and medical history. Imaging tests may be ordered to rule out a possible fracture, if the doctor suspects a third degree sprain.

A first degree sprain results from an overstretched ligament and is usually accompanied by localized swelling and pain. While the swelling may restrict finger mobility, the sprain does not compromise the strength of the finger and the athlete may continue to participate in sports. Taping the affected finger to the adjacent finger is usually recommended to prevent further injury during activity.

A second degree sprain involves more damage to the ligament than a first degree and is usually accompanied by a partial tear of the ligament and the joint capsule (a tough connective tissue sac that surrounds the cavity of a movable joint). Pain and swelling is more pronounced as compared to a first degree sprain and movement is considerably limited.

The most severe type of sprain is a third degree sprain, caused by a complete rupture of the ligament. This type of sprain causes severe swelling, pain, laxity and instability of the finger. While some third degree sprains may be associated with a partial or full dislocation of the finger, some others may cause the bone to actually pull away from the joint, a condition called an avulsion fracture.

## Treatment

Treatment for a finger sprain utilizes the principle of P.R.I.C.E. (protection, rest, ice, compression, and elevation) for the first few weeks following injury. Partially torn ligaments may require longer immobilization than mild sprains, while a total ligament rupture may call for surgical intervention. Rehabilitation after surgery focuses on protected movement under the supervision of a physical or occupational therapist.

## Finger Dislocation

A finger dislocation is a joint injury that occurs when the finger is moved beyond its normal range of motion causing the bones of the finger to move apart or sideways. This misalignment usually affects the distal and proximal interphalangeal joints or the metacarpophalangeal joints and may be complicated by soft tissue injury or a bone fracture.

Dislocation of the distal phalangeal joint (closest to the finger nails) usually results from a trauma and is accompanied by an open wound. Injury to the proximal interphalangeal joints is the most common type of finger dislocation seen in both amateur and professional athletes who play ball sports. Often called "jammed finger," this may also occur when a "jamming force" is applied to the fingertip by a striking ball, or when the finger is overstretched, twisted or bent by an opponent while making a grab for the ball.

## Symptoms

Symptoms of a dislocated finger include immediate pain, swelling and obvious deformity of the finger. Numbness and tingling may be associated with nerve damage and discoloration may indicate damage to blood vessel. If a finger dislocation is suspected, immediate medical attention should be sought. The doctor may order an X-ray to rule out a possible fracture. Delay or failure to provide appropriate treatment for a dislocated finger can result in chronic pain, permanent stiffness, and loss of function of the finger joint.

## Treatment

In most cases of uncomplicated finger dislocation, the doctor uses a simple manipulation called "reduction" to realign the dislocated bones. The technique may be performed with or without local anesthesia, and the doctor prescribes anti-inflammatory or pain medications to reduce swelling and pain. Following a reduction, the doctor orders a second X-ray to check if the reduction has been successful. The injured finger is placed in a protective splint or 'buddy taped' to the uninjured, adjoining finger to immobilize it for a few weeks and allow the damaged connective tissues to heal. During the initial phase of treatment, the P.R.I.C.E. regimen (Protection, Rest, Ice, Compression, and Elevation) is advised, while the final phase may involve rehabilitation with physiotherapy to strengthen and improve stability of the affected joint.

## Finger Fracture

A finger fracture results from a break or crack in one or more bones of the finger and is usually caused by an injury to the hand. Stopping a fast-moving ball or breaking a fall with an outstretched hand are common causes of finger fractures involving the phalanges. Symptoms typically include bruising, swelling, and tenderness of the fracture site; deformity of the injured finger; and inability to move the injured finger.

## *Diagnosis and Treatment*

If a finger fracture is suspected, it should be immediately attended to by a doctor. First aid with an ice pack and a temporary splint may reduce pain and prevent further injury. The doctor orders an X-ray to find the type and extent of fracture and then decides on the treatment. Mild fractures are usually treated conservatively by reduction, which may be done under local anesthesia to numb the pain. Antibiotics and tetanus shots may be given to prevent infection in open fractures, and the injured finger is immobilized for 4–6 weeks with a plaster cast or buddy taping with an adjoining finger to help the fracture heal. For severe finger fractures, surgery is the mainstay of treatment. Small devices such as screws, wires or plates are implanted to fix the bone and stabilize the fracture; and follow-up imaging tests are done to evaluate the fracture and the extent of healing. Return to activity is based on the doctor's assessment and should follow rehabilitation under the guidance of a physical therapist.

### *References*

1.  "Finger Fractures," American Academy of Orthopaedic Surgeons, 2013.

2.  "Finger Dislocation," Harvard Health Publications, 2014.

3.  "Broken finger," National Health Service, 2016.

# Section 33.2

# *Thumb Strains (Skier's Thumb)*

Text in this section is from "Skier's/Gamekeeper's Thumb,"
© 2004-2016, Midwest Orthopaedics at Rush, LLC.
By Dr. John J. Fernandez, Dr. Mark S. Cohen and
Dr. Robert Wysocki of the Midwest Orthopaedics at Rush -
Hand, Wrist and Elbow Institute. Reprinted with permission.

## *What Is Skier's/Gamekeeper's Thumb?*

- Skier's thumb, also known as Gamekeeper's thumb, is an injury
  to the ulnar collateral ligament (UCL), which is located in the
  metacarpophalangeal (MCP) joint where the thumb meets the
  hand. The purpose of the UCL is to keep the thumb stable in
  order to pinch objects. An injury to the UCL can be painful and
  result in a loss of function and pinch strength. Most often, these
  injuries are caused by accidents or falls.

- Skier's thumb got its name because this injury frequently happens during skiing accidents during which a person falls and
  doesn't let go of the ski pole. The thumb is jerked away from the
  index finger, stretching or even completely tearing the ulnar collateral ligament.

- It is also called Gamekeeper's thumb because it can be the result
  of a gradual injury due to repetitive trauma to the thumb. Treatment can be more difficult for Gamekeeper's thumb because the
  gradual thinning of the UCL makes it difficult to reattach when
  torn.

## *What Are the Symptoms of Skier's/Gamekeeper's Thumb?*

- Symptoms of Skier's/Gamekeeper's thumb are easily identified.
  They include:

  - Pain at base of thumb

- Swelling at base of thumb
- Difficulty grabbing objects
- Difficulty throwing objects
- Unstable or wobbly thumb at its base
- Bruising at thumb base

## Who Is Most Likely to Get Skier's/Gamekeeper's Thumb?

- Injuries to the thumb UCL can happen to anyone who has an accident during which the thumb is pulled backward or to the side. Athletes who use their hands are more prone to this injury. It is especially common in contact athletes who play football, rugby, and wrestling and have to apply force with their thumb while tackling or grappling.

- Midwest Orthopaedics at Rush physicians are among the top orthopedic specialists in the U.S. Drs. Mark Cohen, John Fernandez and Robert Wysocki are physicians at the Midwest Orthopaedics at Rush Hand, Wrist & Elbow Institute who are known for treating hand injuries utilizing state-of-the-art and minimally invasive techniques.

## How Is Skier's/Gamekeeper's Thumb Diagnosed?

Since this condition involves damage to soft tissue, physicians at Midwest Orthopaedics at Rush (MOR) Hand, Wrist & Elbow Institute will visually examine the affected area, ask patients how the injury occurred, and review symptoms and pain level. X-ray's will determine if this represents strictly a ligament injury or if a piece of bone has pulled off with the ligament, as this difference guides treatment. Special X-ray's may also be obtained with gentle stress on the ligament to actively test the stability of the MCP joint in many cases.

## How Is Skier's/Gamekeeper's Thumb Treated?

- An orthopedic surgeon who specializes in hands should be seen as soon as possible after the thumb is injured to ensure the best possible recovery.

## Non-Surgical Treatment Options

- Ice to reduce swelling
- Acetaminophen or ibuprofen to reduce pain
- Splint or cast
- Typically, partial UCL tears require immobilization with a splint or cast for four to six weeks. If the UCL is completely torn, surgery is usually required, due to the unpredictable healing of complete tears.

## Surgical Treatment Options

- Surgery is usually an outpatient procedure and a patient can go home the same day. During surgery, the nerve in the arm is blocked and numbed, but in some cases a patient may receive general anesthesia. The procedure involves making small incisions through which the ligament or damaged tissue is cleaned and a small suture is used to anchor the ligament to the bone at its original insertion point so it can heal in a proper position. If there is a bone fracture, pins may be inserted to ensure proper alignment and healing. A brace or cast is typically recommended for up to six weeks. Treatments received within a month after the injury occurred have a higher success rate.

## Section 33.3

# Mallet Finger (Baseball Finger)

Text in this section is from "Mallet Finger (Baseball Finger),"
© 1995–2017 American Academy of Orthopaedic Surgeons.
Reprinted with permission.

Mallet finger is an injury to the thin tendon that straightens the end joint of a finger or thumb. Although it is also known as "baseball finger," this injury can happen to anyone when an unyielding object (like a ball) strikes the tip of a finger or thumb and forces it to bend further than it is intended to go. As a result, you are not able to straighten the tip of your finger or thumb on your own.

## Anatomy

Tendons are tissues that connect muscles to bone. The muscles that move the fingers and thumb are located in the forearm. Long tendons extend from these muscles through the wrist and attach to the small bones of the fingers and thumb.

The extensor tendons on the top of the hand straighten the fingers. The flexor tendons on the palm side of the hand bend the fingers.

## Description

In a mallet injury, when an object hits the tip of the finger or thumb, the force of the blow tears the extensor tendon. Occasionally, a minor force such as tucking in a bed sheet will cause a mallet finger.

The injury may rupture the tendon or pull the tendon away from the place where it attaches to the finger bone (distal phalanx). In some cases, a small piece of bone is pulled away along with the tendon. This is called an avulsion injury.

The long, ring, and small fingers of the dominant hand are most likely to be injured.

## Symptoms

The finger is usually painful, swollen, and bruised. The fingertip will droop noticeably and will straighten only if you push it up with your other hand.

### Risk for Infection

It is very important to seek immediate attention if there is blood beneath the nail or if the nail is detached. This may be a sign of a cut in the nail bed, or that the finger bone is broken and the wound penetrates down to the bone (open fracture). These types of injuries put you at risk for infection.

### First Aid

To relieve pain and reduce swelling, apply ice to your finger immediately and keep your hand elevated above your heart.

# Doctor Examination

A mallet finger injury requires medical treatment to ensure the finger regains as much function as possible. Most doctors recommend seeking treatment within a week of injury. However, there have been cases in which treatment was delayed for as long as a month after injury and full healing was still achieved.

## Physical Examination

After discussing your medical history and symptoms, your doctor will examine your finger or thumb. During the examination, your doctor will hold the affected finger and ask you to straighten it on your own. This is called the mallet finger test.

## X-rays

Your doctor will most likely order x-rays of the injury. If a fragment of the distal phalanx was pulled away when the tendon ruptured, or if there is a larger fracture of the bone, it will appear in an x-ray. An x-ray will also show whether the injury pulled the bones of the joint out of alignment.

# Treatment

Mallet finger injuries that are not treated typically result in stiffness and deformity of the injured fingertip. The majority of mallet finger injuries can be treated without surgery.

In children, mallet finger injuries may involve the cartilage that controls bone growth. The doctor must carefully evaluate and treat this injury in children, so that the finger does not become stunted or deformed.

## Nonsurgical Treatment

Most mallet finger injuries are treated with splinting. A splint holds the fingertip straight (in extension) until it heals.

To restore function to the finger, the splint must be worn full time for 8 weeks. This means that it must be worn while bathing, then carefully changed after bathing. As the splint dries, you must keep your injured finger straight. If the fingertip droops at all, healing is disrupted and you will need to wear the splint for a longer period of time.

Because wearing a splint for a long period of time can irritate the skin, your doctor may talk with you about how to carefully check your skin for problems. Your doctor may also schedule additional visits over the course of the 8 weeks to monitor your progress.

For 3 to 4 weeks after the initial splinting period, you will gradually wear the splint less frequently—perhaps only at night. Splinting treatment usually results in both acceptable function and appearance, however, many patients may not regain full fingertip extension.

For some patients, the splinting regimen is very difficult. In these cases, the doctor may decide to insert a temporary pin across the fingertip joint to hold it straight for 8 weeks.

### Surgical Treatment

Your doctor may consider surgical repair if there is a large fracture fragment or the joint is out of line (subluxed). In these cases, surgery is done to repair the fracture using pins to hold the pieces of bone together while the injury heals.

It is not common to treat a mallet finger surgically if bone fragments or fractures are not present. Surgical treatment of the damaged tendon usually requires a tendon graft—tendon tissue that is taken (harvested) from another part of your body—or even fusing the joint straight.

An orthopedic surgeon should be consulted in making the decision to treat this condition surgically.

# Section 33.4

# *Flexor Tendon Injuries*

This section contains text excerpted from the following sources:
Text in this section begins with excerpts from "Management of
Acute Upper Extremity Conditions," U.S. Federal Bureau of Prisons
(BOP), December 2012. Reviewed June 2017; Text under the heading
"Surgery" is excerpted from "Flexor Tendon Injury Rehabilitation
Regime Study," ClinicalTrials.gov, National Institutes
of Health (NIH), June 3, 2017.

Injuries to the flexor tendons of the hand are common. With injuries
that involve flexor tendons, fully defining the pathology is especially
important. Clinical examination is an essential part of the assessment
of any patient who presents with a hand injury. Identification of damaged structures is best performed by an orthopedic surgeon, as several
studies have shown underdiagnosis of hand injuries when examined
by emergency department staff alone.

## *Flexor Tendon Zones*

Many factors influence recovery following flexor tendon injury—
location of injury, in particular. Flexor tendon injuries are traditionally
described as occurring in one of five zones. Zone 1 contains only the
flexor digitorum profundus (FDP). The functional impact of a zone 1
tendon injury is an inability of the patient to flex the distal joint of
the affected finger.

## *Mechanism of Injury*

Flexor tendon lacerations typically are sustained while a person
is either holding an object or attempting to wrest a object from someone else with the finger in a flexed position. Frequently with this
mechanism of injury, there is an associated digital nerve or artery
laceration.

An avulsion or laceration of the flexor digitorum profundus (FDP)
tendon is often overlooked by the patient or dismissed by the provider
as a "sprained" or jammed finger, resulting in a delayed diagnosis. The

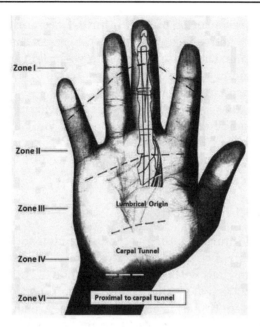

**Figure 33.1.** Flexor Tenon Zone

ring finger is most often involved, and the injury is classically seen in football or rugby players whose fingers are caught in the opponent's jersey, during which time the fingers are forcibly extended while maximal active contraction of the FDP tendon is occurring. There are three types of avulsion of the FDP tendon insertion:

- In a Type I profundus avulsion, the tendon retracts into the palm with loss of its blood/nutritional supply. This type of injury usually results in exquisite tenderness in the palm of the hand at the distal palmar crease.

- Type II profundus avulsion is most often seen, with the end of the injured tendon resting at the proximal interphalangeal (PIP) joint level, its blood supply mostly intact.

- Type III avulsions are associated with a fracture fragment caught in a pulley just below the distal interphalangeal (DIP) joint of the affected finger. Whether the tendon is lacerated or avulsed, surgical reattachment of the tendon ideally should be performed within 7 days, before permanent contracture happens. After 10 days to 2 weeks, the tendon is normally retracted, scarred down, and swollen.

335

The clinical presentation of FDP injuries is remarkable for partial or complete loss of active flexion of the distal joint of the affected finger. In recent avulsions, the patient presents with pain at the DIP joint. Pain is intense along the flexor tendon, radiates to the palm, and can even be experienced in the forearm.

Palpation causes pain, and sometimes ecchymosis/bruising is found at the finger. Active flexion of the DIP joint is impossible. To isolate and test the FDP tendon, hold the PIP joint of the affected finger in extension and have the patient attempt to actively bend the DIP joint.

## Diagnosis and Treatment

All suspected injuries to the profundus tendon should have X-rays taken to determine if there is bony involvement and to rule out a foreign body such as glass with lacerations. In the event that the tendon has been lacerated and at risk for contamination, a tetanus prophylaxis or a booster is given. Broad spectrum antibiotics are also administered. With open wounds, irrigation of the wound is completed along with suturing of the skin.

An assessment of perfusion is performed by assessing capillary refill of the nailbed. Capillary refill that is delayed more than 3 seconds is indicative of a vascular injury. Neurologic status can be quickly assessed using reported perception of light touch and/or sharp/dull. A clean, bulky dressing is applied that includes the forearm and entire hand.

Any suspected tendon injury should be referred to an orthopedic surgeon as quickly as feasible, so that a prompt repair of the tendon(s) can be initiated.

## Surgery

Damaged flexor tendons are repaired surgically with sutures (stitches). After repair, a splint is applied to the fingers, hand and wrist for six to twelve weeks to protect the repair while the tendon heals and regains its normal strength. Most rehabilitation protocols use a splint in which the wrist position is kept straight (neutral) or bent (flexed). Some groups have described splinting with the wrist cocked back (extended) and have made the argument that this may improve outcomes, as experimental data suggests that splinting the hand with the wrist extended increases the range of movement of the repaired flexor tendon (excursion), and therefore reduces the chance of the tendon sticking down to the surrounding tissues (adhesion).

# Part Seven

# Injuries to the Trunk, Groin, Upper Legs, and Knees

Chapter 34

# Trunk and Groin Injuries

## Chapter Contents

# Section 34.1

# *Hematuria*

This section includes text excerpted from "Hematuria (Blood in the Urine)," National Institute of Diabetes and Digestive and Kidney Diseases (NIDDK), July 2016.

## What Is Hematuria?

Hematuria is the presence of blood in a person's urine. The two types of hematuria are

1.  Gross hematuria—when a person can see the blood in his or her urine

2.  Microscopic hematuria—when a person cannot see the blood in his or her urine, yet it is seen under a microscope

## What Is the Urinary Tract?

The urinary tract is the body's drainage system for removing wastes and extra fluid. The urinary tract includes

*   two kidneys

*   two ureters

*   the bladder

*   the urethra

The kidneys are two bean-shaped organs, each about the size of a fist. They are located just below the rib cage, one on each side of the spine. Every day, the kidneys filter about 120 to 150 quarts of blood to produce about 1–2 quarts of urine, composed of wastes and extra fluid. Children produce less urine than adults. The urine flows from the kidneys to the bladder through tubes called ureters. The bladder stores urine until releasing it through urination. When the bladder empties, urine flows out of the body through a tube called the urethra at the bottom of the bladder.

# What Causes Hematuria?

Reasons people may have blood in the urine include:

- vigorous exercise
- infection in the bladder, kidney, or prostate
- trauma
- viral illness, such as hepatitis—a virus that causes liver disease and inflammation of the liver
- sexual activity
- menstruation
- endometriosis—a problem in women that occurs when the kind of tissue that normally lines the uterus grows somewhere else, such as the bladder

More serious reasons people may have hematuria include:

- bladder or kidney cancer
- inflammation of the kidney, urethra, bladder, or prostate—a walnut-shaped gland in men that surrounds the urethra and helps make semen
- blood-clotting disorders, such as hemophilia
- sickle cell disease—a genetic disorder in which a person's body makes abnormally shaped red blood cells
- polycystic kidney disease—a genetic disorder in which many cysts grow on a person's kidneys

# Who Is More Likely to Develop Hematuria?

People who are more likely to develop hematuria may

- do strenuous exercise, such as long-distance running
- have an enlarged prostate
- have urinary stones
- take certain medications, including blood thinners, aspirin and other pain relievers, and antibiotics
- have a bacterial or viral infection, such as streptococcus or hepatitis

341

- have a family history of kidney disease

- have a disease or condition that affects one or more organs

## What Are the Symptoms of Hematuria?

People with gross hematuria have urine that is pink, red, or brown. Even a small amount of blood in the urine can cause urine to change color. In most cases, people with gross hematuria do not have other signs and symptoms. People with gross hematuria that includes blood clots in the urine may have bladder pain or pain in the back.

## How Is Hematuria Diagnosed?

A healthcare professional diagnoses hematuria or the cause of the hematuria with

- a medical history

- a physical exam

  - Digital rectal exam

  - Pelvic exam

- urinalysis

- additional testing

  - Blood test

  - Computed tomography (CT) scan

  - Cystoscopy

  - Kidney biopsy

  - Magnetic resonance imaging (MRI)

## How Is Hematuria Treated?

Healthcare professionals treat hematuria by treating its underlying cause. If no serious condition is causing a patient's hematuria, he or she typically does not need treatment.

## Eating, Diet, and Nutrition

Researchers have not found that eating, diet, and nutrition play a role in causing or preventing hematuria.

# Section 34.2

# *Groin and Perineal Injuries in Athletes*

This section contains text excerpted from the following sources:
Text under the heading "Sportsman's Hernia" is excerpted from "A
Randomised, Blinded Study on Laparoscopic Mesh Reinforcement for
Chronic Groin Pain," ClinicalTrials.gov, U.S. National Institutes of
Health (NIH), March 15, 2010. Reviewed June 2017; Text beginning
with the heading "Symptoms and Diagnosis" is excerpted from
"TEP versus Open Minimal Suture Repair for the Sportsman's
Groin (SPORT)," ClinicalTrials.gov, U.S. National Institutes of
Health (NIH), November 2014; Text beginning with the heading is
"Perineal Injury in Males" excerpted from "Perineal Injury in Males,"
National Institute of Diabetes and Digestive and Kidney Diseases
(NIDDK), March 2014; Text under the heading "Using No-Nose
(Noseless) Bicycle Saddles to Prevent Genital Numbness and Sexual
Dysfunction" is excerpted from "Using No-Nose (Noseless) Bicycle
Saddles to Prevent Genital Numbness and Sexual Dysfunction,"
Centers for Disease Control and Prevention (CDC), March 2, 2017.

## *Sportsman's Hernia*

Chronic groin pain is a frequent cause for referral to general surgeons. In some cases this pain may be due to the presence of a hernia. However, if on clinical examination there is no palpable lump or
bulge, the cause of the pain may be difficult to elucidate. Some of these
patients may have the diagnosis of sportsman's groin. Other names
which have been attached to this condition include Gilmore groin and
sportsman's hernia. These conditions are more commonly associated
with sportsmen and women but those who do not play sport may also
receive this diagnosis. Sportsman's groin is thought to be a syndrome
of weakness of the posterior inguinal wall without a clinically recog-
nizable hernia. Differing explanations for sportsman's groin include
avulsion of the conjoint tendon from the pubic tubercle, weakening
of the transversalis fascia, tears in the internal or external oblique,
superficial inguinal ring dilatation and abnormalities of the rectus
abdominus insertion.

343

## Symptoms and Diagnosis

The prevalence of chronic groin pain in athletes and physically active adults is between 5 and 10 percent. The groin area is vulnerable in contact sports such as soccer, ice hockey, and rugby that require sudden muscle contraction around the hip and lower abdomen, repetitive kicking and side-to-side motion. Common causes for chronic groin pain in such sports include adductor tendonitis, musculus rectus abdominis tendopathy, osteitis pubis or disruption of the posterior wall of inguinal canal, which are all referred to as athletic pubalgia. No exact pathophysiological mechanism for pain has so far been identified in sportsman's hernia (posterior inguinal wall deficiency). A tear of the abdominal wall in posterior inguinal canal or conjoined tendon (tendinopathy), with or without bulging of a hernia, is suggested to be typical of a sportsman's hernia. The tissue damage is similar as in an incipient direct inguinal hernia with or without bulge.

Diagnosis of a sportsman's hernia can only be set in patients having a typical history and having a suspected posterior inguinal wall deficiency on careful clinical examination. Magnetic resonance imaging (MRI) should be performed to exclude other injuries in the groin area. Sometimes ultrasonography (US) would be added in the diagnostic work-up. Although presenting with similar symptoms, the clinical entity of "sportsman's hernia" is exclusively distinct from athletic pubalgia, which includes a more wide range of groin injuries, such as adductor tendonitis and/or inflammation of the pubic symphysis.

## Treatment

Treatment of chronic groin pain is aimed toward its specific pathology. The first line of management includes rest, muscle strengthening and stretching exercises, physiotherapy, anti-inflammatory analgesics, as well as local anesthetic and/or corticosteroid injections. In resistant cases, operative treatment might be considered. Various operative approaches in athlete's pubalgia have been proposed depending on the suspected nature of injury. These operative approaches include open and laparoscopic methods of hernia repair, tenotomy of muscle tendons close to the pubic bone, as well as release or neurectomies of nearby nerves. The results of operative treatment are good to excellent in 70 to 90 percent of patients. There is no evidence-based consensus available to guide surgeons for choosing between various operative treatments of sportsman's hernia/athletic pubalgia. Both conventional open and laparoscopic repairs produce good results, although the latter may allow the patient to an earlier return to full sports activity.

344

Open minimal repair (OMR) technique in local or spinal anesthesia seems to be a promising surgical approach in the treatment of posterior inguinal wall deficiency. This is best described as open minimal repair and involves a small incision into the groin of the affected side. Once the inguinal canal is exposed the back wall is repaired using a simple suture to reinforce the weakness. An one-center analysis of this technique reported full freedom of pain in 91 percent four weeks after operation, full recovery to sports after 2 weeks and good patient's satisfaction in 100 percent. The laparoscopic techniques are reported to give an excellent outcome in 80–90 percent of patients. These methods are more expensive and need to be performed under general anesthesia. The OMR technique is developed solely to strengthen the posterior inguinal wall weakness using nonabsorbable sutures. Endoscopic total extraperitoneal (TEP) technique in general anesthesia is also used for the treatment of Sportsman's hernia/athletic pubalgia and may heal a wider area in groin. TEP utilizes a mesh placed in the preperitoneal space behind the pubic symphysis and posterior inguinal canal.

## Perineal Injury in Males

Perineal injury is an injury to the perineum, the part of the body between the anus and the genitals, or sex organs. In males, the perineum is the area between the anus and the scrotum, the external pouch of skin that holds the testicles. Injuries to the perineum can happen suddenly, as in an accident, or gradually, as the result of an activity that persistently puts pressure on the perineum. Sudden damage to the perineum is called an acute injury, while gradual damage is called a chronic injury.

### Why Is the Perineum Important?

The perineum is important because it contains blood vessels and nerves that supply the urinary tract and genitals with blood and nerve signals. The perineum lies just below a sheet of muscles called the pelvic floor muscles. Pelvic floor muscles support the bladder and bowel.

### What Are the Complications of Perineal Injury?

Injury to the blood vessels, nerves, and muscles in the perineum can lead to complications such as

• bladder control problems

• sexual problems

345

**Bladder control problems.** The nerves in the perineum carry signals from the bladder to the spinal cord and brain, telling the brain when the bladder is full. Those same nerves carry signals from the brain to the bladder and pelvic floor muscles, directing those muscles to hold or release urine. Injury to those nerves can block or interfere with the signals, causing the bladder to squeeze at the wrong time or not to squeeze at all. Damage to the pelvic floor muscles can cause bladder and bowel control problems.

**Sexual problems.** The perineal nerves also carry signals between the genitals and the brain. Injury to those nerves can interfere with the sensations of sexual contact.

Signals from the brain direct the smooth muscles in the genitals to relax, causing greater blood flow into the penis. In men, damaged blood vessels can cause erectile dysfunction (ED), the inability to achieve or maintain an erection firm enough for sexual intercourse. An internal portion of the penis runs through the perineum and contains a section of the urethra. As a result, damage to the perineum may also injure the penis and urethra.

## Common Causes of Acute Perineal Injury

### Straddle Injuries

Straddle injuries result from falls onto objects such as metal bars, pipes, or wooden rails, where the person's legs are on either side of the object and the perineum strikes the object forcefully. These injuries include motorcycle and bike riding accidents, saddle horn injuries during horseback riding, falls on playground equipment such as monkey bars, and gymnastic accidents on an apparatus such as the parallel bars or pommel horse.

In rare situations, a blunt injury to the perineum may burst a blood vessel inside the erectile tissue of the penis, causing a persistent partial erection that can last for days to years. This condition is called high-flow priapism. If not treated, ED may result.

### Impalement

Impalement injuries may involve metal fence posts, rods, or weapons that pierce the perineum. Impalement is rare, although it may occur where moving equipment and pointed tools are in use, such as on farms or construction sites. Impalement can also occur as the result of a fall, such as from a tree or playground equipment, onto something sharp. Impalement injuries are most common in combat situations. If an impalement injury pierces the skin and muscles, the injured person needs immediate medical attention to minimize blood loss and repair the injury.

## What Are the Most Common Causes of Chronic Perineal Injury?

Chronic perineal injury most often results from a job-or sport-related practice—such as bike, motorcycle, or horseback riding—or a long-term condition such as chronic constipation.

Sitting on a narrow, saddle-style bike seat—which has a protruding "nose" in the front—places far more pressure on the perineum than sitting in a regular chair. In a regular chair, the flesh and bone of the buttocks partially absorb the pressure of sitting, and the pressure occurs farther toward the back than on a bike seat. The straddling position on a narrow seat pinches the perineal blood vessels and nerves, possibly causing blood vessel and nerve damage over time. Research shows wider, noseless seats reduce perineal pressure.

Occasional bike riding for short periods of time may pose no risk. However, men who ride bikes several hours a week—such as competitive bicyclists, bicycle couriers, and bicycle patrol officers—have a significantly higher risk of developing mild to severe ED. The ED may be caused by repetitive pressure on blood vessels, which constricts them and results in plaque buildup in the vessels.

Other activities that involve riding saddle-style include motorcycle and horseback riding. Researchers have studied bike riding more extensively than these other activities; however, the few studies published regarding motorcycle and horseback riding suggest motorcycle riding increases the risk of ED and urinary symptoms. Horseback riding appears relatively safe in terms of chronic injury, although the action of bouncing up and down, repeatedly striking the perineum, has the potential for causing damage.

## How Is Perineal Injury Evaluated?

Healthcare providers evaluate perineal injury based on the circumstances and severity of the injury. In general, the evaluation process includes a physical examination and one or more imaging tests.

During a physical examination, the patient lies face-up with legs spread and feet in stirrups. The healthcare provider looks for cuts, bruises, or bleeding from the anus. The healthcare provider may insert a gloved, lubricated finger into the rectum to feel for internal injuries.

To look for internal injuries, the healthcare provider may order one or more imaging tests.

- Computerized tomography (CT)

- Magnetic resonance imaging (MRI)

- Ultrasound

## How Is Perineal Injury Treated?

Treatments for perineal injury vary with the severity and type of injury. Tears or incisions may require stitches. Traumatic or piercing injuries may require surgery to repair damaged pelvic floor muscles, blood vessels, and nerves. Treatment for these acute injuries may also include antibiotics to prevent infection. After a healthcare provider stabilizes an acute injury so blood loss is no longer a concern, a person may still face some long-term effects of the injury, such as bladder control and sexual function problems. A healthcare provider can treat high-flow priapism caused by a blunt injury to the perineum with medication, blockage of the burst blood vessel under X-ray guidance, or surgery.

## How Can Perineal Injury Be Prevented?

Preventing perineal injury requires being aware of and taking steps to minimize the dangers of activities such as construction work or bike riding:

- People should talk with their healthcare provider about the benefits and risks of perineal surgery well before the operation.

- People who play or work around moving equipment or sharp objects should wear protective gear whenever possible.

- People who ride bikes, motorcycles, or horses should find seats or saddles designed to place the most pressure on the buttocks and minimize pressure on the perineum. Many healthcare providers advise bike riders to use noseless bike seats and to ride in an upright position rather than lean over the handlebars. The National Institute for Occupational Safety and Health (NIOSH), part of the Centers for Disease Control and Prevention (CDC), recommends noseless seats for people who ride bikes as part of their job.

- People with constipation should talk with their healthcare provider about whether to take a laxative or stool softener to minimize straining during a bowel movement.

## *Using No-Nose (Noseless) Bicycle Saddles to Prevent Genital Numbness and Sexual Dysfunction*

The National Institute for Occupational Safety and Health (NIOSH) conducted a study to examine the effect of bicycle saddle design on groin pressure. The study found that the traditional sport/racing saddle was associated with more than two times the pressure in the perineal region than the saddles without a protruding nose. There were no significant differences in perineal pressure among the no-nose saddles. Measures of weight distribution on the pedals and handlebars indicated no differences between the traditional saddle and those without protruding noses.

To examine the benefit of saddles without a protruding nose, NIOSH conducted another study where bicycle police officers from five U.S. metropolitan areas used a no-nose saddle for their bicycles exclusively for 6 months. After 6 months, only three of the 90 men remaining in the study had returned to a traditional saddle. The study found a 66 percent reduction in saddle contact pressure in the perineal region, a significant improvement in penis tactile sensation, and a significant improvement in erectile function. The percentage of officers indicating that they experienced numbness to the buttocks, scrotum, or penis decreased from 73 percent while using traditional saddles at the beginning of the study to 18 percent after using no-nose saddles for 6 months.

NIOSH research has focused mostly on police officers, security officers, and emergency medical personnel who use bicycles as part of their work, rather than on recreational/sport bicyclists. However, one study reported that 21 percent of sport cyclists reported genital numbness after a bicycle race and 13 percent reported impotence while other research reported a 61 percent incidence of genital numbness among cyclists and a 19 percent incidence in erectile dysfunction among cyclists riding more than 400 km (249 miles) per week.

There is much less research on female cyclists and effects associated with traditional bicycle saddles. Previous studies found 40–70 percent of female cyclists experience genital numbness with a traditional saddle. NIOSH and researchers from the Albert Einstein College of Medicine-Montefiore Medical Center investigated the relationship between frequent and/or endurance bicycling on neurological and sexual function in women. The study concluded that there is an association between bicycling and decreased genital sensation in competitive female bicyclists. Additional research is warranted to further examine these issues among female cyclists.

Contrary to some cyclists' belief, it is not normal for any part of your body to go numb or lose feeling. Numbness in the groin or genitals is a warning sign that should not be ignored. NIOSH recommends that workers who ride a bicycle as part of their job take the following steps to help prevent sexual and reproductive health problems:

- Use a no-nose saddle for workplace bicycling. Give yourself time to get used to riding with a no-nose saddle. At first, it may seem very different from the saddle you have used in the past. No-nose saddles may not always be available at retail bicycle shops, but they are readily available for purchase through the Internet.

- Seek guidance on proper bicycle fit from a trained bicycle fit specialist. Use of a no-nose saddle may require different saddle height and angle adjustments. Be sure that the no-nose saddle is adjusted according to the manufacturer's instructions.

- Dismount the bicycle when at a standstill. Do not lean against a post or other object to stay seated on the bicycle saddle when you are not riding.

- Dismount the bicycle if you begin to have numbness, tingling, or loss of feeling in any part of your body.

While much of the scientific community has reached a consensus about the association between erectile dysfunction and traditional bicycle saddles, no-nose saddle designs have not been universally embraced by many cyclists.

Chapter 35

# Hip Injuries

## Chapter Contents

## Section 35.1

## *Hip Bursitis*

Text in this section is from "Hip Bursitis," © 1995-2017 American
Academy of Orthopaedic Surgeons. Reprinted with permission.

Bursae, are small, jelly-like sacs that are located throughout the
body, including around the shoulder, elbow, hip, knee, and heel. They
contain a small amount of fluid, and are positioned between bones and
soft tissues, acting as cushions to help reduce friction.

Bursitis is inflammation of the bursa. There are two major bursae
in the hip that typically become irritated and inflamed. One bursa
covers the bony point of the hip bone called the greater trochanter.
Inflammation of this bursa is called trochanteric bursitis.

Another bursa—the iliopsoas bursa—is located on the inside (groin
side) of the hip. When this bursa becomes inflamed, the condition is
also sometimes referred to as hip bursitis, but the pain is located in the
groin area. This condition is not as common as trochanteric bursitis,
but is treated in a similar manner.

### *Symptoms*

The main symptom of trochanteric bursitis is pain at the point of
the hip. The pain usually extends to the outside of the thigh area. In
the early stages, the pain is usually described as sharp and intense.
Later, the pain may become more of an ache and spread across a larger
area of the hip.

Typically, the pain is worse at night, when lying on the affected hip,
and when getting up from a chair after being seated for a while. It also
may get worse with prolonged walking, stair climbing, or squatting.

### *Risk Factors*

Hip bursitis can affect anyone, but is more common in women and
middle-aged or elderly people. It is less common in younger people
and in men.

The following risk factors have been associated with the development of hip bursitis.

- **Repetitive stress (overuse) injury.** This can occur when running, stair climbing, bicycling, or standing for long periods of time.

- **Hip injury.** An injury to the point of your hip can occur when you fall onto your hip, bump your hip, or lie on one side of your body for an extended period of time.

- **Spine disease.** This includes scoliosis, arthritis of the lumbar (lower) spine, and other spine problems.

- **Leg-length inequality.** When one leg is significantly shorter than the other, it affects the way you walk, and can lead to irritation of a hip bursa.

- **Rheumatoid arthritis.** This makes the bursa more likely to become inflamed.

- **Previous surgery.** Surgery around the hip or prosthetic implants in the hip can irritate the bursa and cause bursitis.

- **Bone spurs or calcium deposits.** These can develop within the tendons that attach muscles to the trochanter. They can irritate the bursa and cause inflammation.

## Doctor Examination

To diagnose hip bursitis, the doctor will perform a comprehensive physical examination, looking for tenderness in the area of the point of the hip. He or she may also perform additional tests to rule out other possible injuries or conditions. These tests can include imaging studies, such as X-rays, bone scanning, and magnetic resonance imaging (MRI).

## Treatment

### Nonsurgical Treatment

The initial treatment for hip bursitis does not involve surgery. Many people with hip bursitis can experience relief with simple lifestyle changes, including:

- **Activity modification.** Avoid the activities that worsen symptoms.

- **Non-steroidal anti-inflammatory drugs (NSAIDs).** Ibuprofen, naproxen, piroxicam, celecoxib, and others, may relieve pain and control inflammation. Use NSAIDs cautiously and for limited periods. Talk with your doctor about the NSAIDs you use. NSAIDs may have adverse side effects if you have certain medical conditions or take certain medications.

- **Assistive devices.** Use of a walking cane or crutches for a week or more when needed.

- **Physical therapy.** Your doctor may prescribe exercises to increase hip strength and flexibility. You may do these exercises on your own, or a physical therapist may teach you how to stretch your hip muscles and use other treatments such as rolling therapy (massage), ice, heat, or ultrasound.

- **Steroid injection.** Injection of a corticosteroid along with a local anesthetic may also be helpful in relieving symptoms of hip bursitis. This is a simple and effective treatment that can be done in the doctor's office. It involves a single injection into the bursa. The injection may provide temporary (months) or permanent relief. If pain and inflammation return, another injection or two, given a few months apart, may be needed. It is important to limit the number of injections, as prolonged corticosteroid injections may damage the surrounding tissues.

## Surgical Treatment

Surgery is rarely needed for hip bursitis. If the bursa remains inflamed and painful after all nonsurgical treatments have been tried, your doctor may recommend surgical removal of the bursa. Removal of the bursa does not hurt the hip, and the hip can function normally without it.

A newer technique that is gaining popularity is arthroscopic removal of the bursa. In this technique, the bursa is removed through a small (1/4-inch) incision over the hip. A small camera, or arthroscope, is placed in a second incision so the doctor can guide miniature surgical instruments and cut out the bursa. This surgery is less invasive, and recovery is quicker and less painful.

Both types of surgeries are done on an outpatient (same-day) basis, so an overnight stay in the hospital is not usually necessary. Early studies show arthroscopic removal of the bursa to be quite effective, but this is still being studied.

## Rehabilitation

Following surgery, a short rehabilitation period can be expected. Most patients find that using a cane or crutches for a couple of days is helpful. It is reasonable to be up and walking around the evening after surgery. The soreness from surgery usually goes away after a few days.

## Prevention

Although hip bursitis cannot always be prevented, there are things you can do to prevent the inflammation from getting worse.

* Avoid repetitive activities that put stress on the hips.

* Lose weight if you need to.

* Get a properly fitting shoe insert for leg-length differences.

* Maintain strength and flexibility of the hip muscles.

# Section 35.2

# Hip Flexor Strains

"Hip Flexor Strains," © 2017 Omnigraphics. Reviewed June 2017.

Hip flexors are a group of muscles situated in front of both hip joints. These muscles help to flex or bend your leg and knee up towards your body in activities like high knee kicks or bending at the waist.

## What Is a Hip Flexor Strain?

Hip flexor strain is an injury caused by a stretch or tear of single or multiple hip flexor muscles resulting in pain often in the front side of the groin or hip. When there is a high force or too much of repetitive activities involving hip flexors, there is excessive tension placed on the muscle. This undue muscle tension can result in strain. Strain can range from a small partial tear to a rupture. A partial tear will result in mild pain and minimal loss of function whereas a rupture involves a major disability and episodes of severe pain.

Hip flexor strains can broadly be classified into three types.

1. Grade 1 Hip Flexor Strain—Only a few muscle fibers are torn, resulting in mild pain but not affecting functional ability.

2. Grade 2 Hip Flexor Strain—Significant number of fibers are torn, resulting in moderate loss of function. Grade 2 strains are common with sports injuries.

3. Grade 3 Hip Flexor Strain—Full rupture of muscle fibers, resulting in severe loss of function.

## Causes and Risk Factors

Hip flexor strain is a common injury in sports that involve forceful stretching of muscles and extreme movements at the hip joint. This is commonly seen with a soccer player who performs a long kick, a gymnast who does stretch routines or with a sprinter. An explosive movement combined with inadequate warm-up can lead to a hip flexor strain.

Some risk factors for a hip flexor strain include:

- Inadequate training, poor techniques and repetitive movements can result in chronic overuse injuries of the hip flexors.

- Inadequate recovery from a previous hip injury.

- Poor endurance and fitness levels.

- Lack of proper warm up.

- Lacking flexibility due to muscle tightness around the hip, knee or lower back.

- Poor posture and malalignment of lower limbs.

## Signs and Symptoms

When athletes strain their hip flexors, they usually experience an acute pain or a pulling sensation on the front side of the hip. The pain worsens with movement especially when the thigh is raised against resistance.

With grade 2 or 3 strains, the athlete may experience severe muscle spasms, pain, limping when walking and significant loss of function. Signs of bruising and swelling may be present with grade 2 or 3 hip flexor strains.

## Diagnosis

Your doctor will perform several examinations to diagnose a hip flexor strain. When there are some associated injuries with grade 3 rupture, X-ray, magnetic resonance imaging (MRI), ultrasound, and computed tomography (CT) scan will aid in differential diagnosis and ruling out other potential causes.

## Treatment

As for any acute soft tissue injury, PRICE (protection, rest, immobilization, compression, and elevation) protocol has to be implemented at the earliest possible point.

- Provide adequate rest to the hip flexor muscles and stop all activities that aggravate symptoms. This helps in quick recovery of the hip flexor muscles.

- Apply ice packs to the hip flexor muscles for about 30 minutes every 3 to 4 hours to lessen the pain.

- If an injured athlete has a limp, he or she should use a pair of crutches to prevent stress on the hip muscles during walking.

- If the pain does not subside with rest and ice, nonsteroidal anti-inflammatory medications can be prescribed to control the pain and swelling.

- Once the pain subsides, your physical therapist can prescribe a set of stretching and strengthening exercises for muscles around the hip and thigh. They will also gradually increase your activity levels to the point at which you can begin participating in sports again. Proper adherence to physical therapy will decrease the likelihood of recurrence of hip flexor strain in future.

## When to Call the Doctor

Call your healthcare provider if you do not feel better after a few weeks of treatment.

Chapter 36

# Upper Leg Injuries

## Chapter Contents

Section 36.1

# *Femur Fracture*

Text in this section is from "Femur Shaft Fracture (Broken Thighbone)," © 1995-2017 American Academy of Orthopaedic Surgeons. Reprinted with permission.

Your thighbone (femur) is the longest and strongest bone in your body. Because the femur is so strong, it usually takes a lot of force to break it. Car crashes, for example, are the number one cause of femur fractures.

The long, straight part of the femur is called the femoral shaft. When there is a break anywhere along this length of bone, it is called a femoral shaft fracture.

## *Types of Femoral Shaft Fractures*

Femur fractures vary greatly, depending on the force that causes the break. The pieces of bone may line up correctly or be out of alignment (displaced), and the fracture may be closed (skin intact) or open (the bone has punctured the skin).

Doctors describe fractures to each other using classification systems. Femur fractures are classified depending on:

- The location of the fracture (the femoral shaft is divided into thirds: distal, middle, proximal)

- The pattern of the fracture (for example, the bone can break in different directions, such as cross-wise, length-wise, or in the middle)

- Whether the skin and muscle above the bone is torn by the injury

The most common types of femoral shaft fractures include:

**Transverse fracture.** In this type of fracture, the break is a straight horizontal line going across the femoral shaft.

**Oblique fracture.** This type of fracture has an angled line across the shaft.

**Spiral fracture.** The fracture line encircles the shaft like the stripes on a candy cane. A twisting force to the thigh causes this type of fracture.

**Comminuted fracture.** In this type of fracture, the bone has broken into three or more pieces. In most cases, the number of bone fragments corresponds with the amount of force required to break the bone.

**Open fracture.** If a bone breaks in such a way that bone fragments stick out through the skin or a wound penetrates down to the broken bone, the fracture is called an open or compound fracture. Open fractures often involve much more damage to the surrounding muscles, tendons, and ligaments. They have a higher risk for complications—especially infections—and take a longer time to heal.

## Cause

Femoral shaft fractures in young people are frequently due to some type of high-energy collision. The most common cause of femoral shaft fracture is a motor vehicle or motorcycle crash. Being hit by a car as a pedestrian is another common cause, as are falls from heights and gunshot wounds. A lower-force incident, such as a fall from standing, may cause a femoral shaft fracture in an older person who has weaker bones.

## Symptoms

A femoral shaft fracture usually causes immediate, severe pain. You will not be able to put weight on the injured leg, and it may look deformed—shorter than the other leg and no longer straight.

## Doctor Examination

### Medical History and Physical Examination

It is important that your doctor know the specifics of how you hurt your leg. For example, if you were in a car accident, it would help your doctor to know how fast you were going, whether you were the driver or a passenger, whether you were wearing your seatbelt, and if the airbags went off. This information will help your doctor determine how you were hurt and whether you may be hurt somewhere else.

It is also important for your doctor to know whether you have other health conditions like high blood pressure, diabetes, asthma, or allergies. Your doctor will also ask you about any medications you take.

After discussing your injury and medical history, your doctor will do a careful examination. He or she will assess your overall condition, and then focus on your leg. Your doctor will look for:

- An obvious deformity of the thigh/leg (an unusual angle, twisting, or shortening of the leg)

- Breaks in the skin

- Bruises

- Bony pieces that may be pushing on the skin

After the visual inspection, your doctor will then feel along your thigh, leg, and foot looking for abnormalities and checking the tightness of the skin and muscles around your thigh. He or she will also feel for pulses. If you are awake, your doctor will test for sensation and movement in your leg and foot.

### Imaging Tests

Other tests that will provide your doctor with more information about your injury include:

- **X-rays.** The most common way to evaluate a fracture is with X-rays, which provide clear images of bone. X-rays can show whether a bone is intact or broken. They can also show the type of fracture and where it is located within the femur.

- **Computed tomography (CT) scan.** If your doctor still needs more information after reviewing your X-rays, he or she may order a CT scan. A CT scan shows a cross-sectional image of your limb. It can provide your doctor with valuable information about the severity of the fracture. For example, sometimes the fracture lines can be very thin and hard to see on an X-ray. A CT scan can help your doctor see the lines more clearly.

## Treatment

### Nonsurgical Treatment

Most femoral shaft fractures require surgery to heal. It is unusual for femoral shaft fractures to be treated without surgery. Very young children are sometimes treated with a cast.

## Surgical Treatment

**Timing of surgery.** If the skin around your fracture has not been broken, your doctor will wait until you are stable before doing surgery. Open fractures, however, expose the fracture site to the environment. They urgently need to be cleansed and require immediate surgery to prevent infection.

For the time between initial emergency care and your surgery, your doctor will place your leg either in a long-leg splint or in skeletal traction. This is to keep your broken bones as aligned as possible and to maintain the length of your leg.

Skeletal traction is a pulley system of weights and counterweights that holds the broken pieces of bone together. It keeps your leg straight and often helps to relieve pain.

**External fixation.** In this type of operation, metal pins or screws are placed into the bone above and below the fracture site. The pins and screws are attached to a bar outside the skin. This device is a stabilizing frame that holds the bones in the proper position so they can heal.

External fixation is usually a temporary treatment for femur fractures. Because they are easily applied, external fixators are often put on when a patient has multiple injuries and is not yet ready for a longer surgery to fix the fracture. An external fixator provides good, temporary stability until the patient is healthy enough for the final surgery. In some cases, an external fixator is left on until the femur is fully healed, but this is not common.

**Intramedullary nailing.** Currently, the method most surgeons use for treating femoral shaft fractures is intramedullary nailing. During this procedure, a specially designed metal rod is inserted into the marrow canal of the femur. The rod passes across the fracture to keep it in position.

An intramedullary nail can be inserted into the canal either at the hip or the knee through a small incision. It is screwed to the bone at both ends. This keeps the nail and the bone in proper position during healing. Intramedullary nailing provides strong, stable, full-length fixation.

Intramedullary nails are usually made of titanium. They come in various lengths and diameters to fit most femur bones.

**Plates and screws.** During this operation, the bone fragments are first repositioned (reduced) into their normal alignment. They

363

are held together with special screws and metal plates attached to the outer surface of the bone. Plates and screws are often used when intramedullary nailing may not be possible, such as for fractures that extend into either the hip or knee joints.

## Recovery

Most femoral shaft fractures take 4 to 6 months to completely heal. Some take even longer, especially if the fracture was open or broken into several pieces.

### Weightbearing

Many doctors encourage leg motion early in the recovery period. It is very important to follow your doctor's instructions for putting weight on your injured leg to avoid problems.

In some cases, doctors will allow patients to put as much weight as possible on the leg right after surgery. However, you may not be able to put full weight on your leg until the fracture has started to heal. It is very important to follow your doctor's instructions carefully. When you begin walking, you will most likely need to use crutches or a walker for support.

### Physical Therapy

Because you will most likely lose muscle strength in the injured area, exercises during the healing process are important. Physical therapy will help to restore normal muscle strength, joint motion, and flexibility.

A physical therapist will most likely begin teaching you specific exercises while you are still in the hospital. The therapist will also help you learn how to use crutches or a walker.

## Complications

### Complications from Femoral Shaft Fractures

Femoral shaft fractures can cause further injury and complications.

- The ends of broken bones are often sharp and can cut or tear surrounding blood vessels or nerves.

- Acute compartment syndrome may develop. This is a painful condition that occurs when pressure within the muscles builds to dangerous levels. This pressure can decrease blood flow, which prevents nourishment and oxygen from reaching nerve and muscle cells. Unless the pressure is relieved quickly, permanent disability may result. This is a surgical emergency. During the procedure, your surgeon makes incisions in your skin and the muscle coverings to relieve the pressure.

- Open fractures expose the bone to the outside environment. Even with good surgical cleaning of the bone and muscle, the bone can become infected. Bone infection is difficult to treat and often requires multiple surgeries and long-term antibiotics.

## Complications from Surgery

In addition to the risks of surgery in general, such as blood loss or problems related to anesthesia, complications of surgery may include:

- Infection

- Injury to nerves and blood vessels

- Blood clots

- Fat embolism (bone marrow enters the bloodstream and can travel to the lungs; this can also happen from the fracture itself without surgery)

- Malalignment or the inability to correctly position the broken bone fragments

- Delayed union or nonunion (when the fracture heals slower than usual or not at all)

- Hardware irritation (sometimes the end of the nail or the screw can irritate the overlying muscles and tendons)

# Section 36.2

# *Hamstring Injuries*

This section contains text excerpted from the following sources: Text in this section begins with excerpts from "The Immediate Effect of Kinesio Tape on Hamstring Muscle Length in Female Students of University of Dammam," ClinicalTrials.gov, National Institutes of Health (NIH), March 20, 2017; Text under the heading "Cause and Symptoms of Hamstring Strain" is excerpted from "Sprains and Strains," National Library of Medicine (NLM), National Institutes of Health (NIH), January 3, 2017; Text under the heading "Mechanism of Hamstring Strain" is excerpted from "Acute Hamstring Strains in Danish Elite Soccer—Prevention and Rehabilitation," ClinicalTrials. gov, National Institutes of Health (NIH), November 9, 2007. Reviewed June 2017; Text under the heading "Treatment" is excerpted from "Questions and Answers about Sprains and Strains," National Institute of Arthritis and Musculoskeletal and Skin Diseases (NIAMS), January 2015; Text under the heading "Rehabilitation and Prevention" is excerpted from "Rehabilitation of Acute Hamstring Injuries in Male Athletes," ClinicalTrials.gov, National Institutes of Health (NIH), May 18, 2016; Text under the heading "Hamstring Muscle Stiffness and Knee Joint Stability" is excerpted from "Funded Injury Control Research Centers (ICRCs)," Centers for Disease Control and Prevention (CDC), July 13, 2010. Reviewed June 2017.

The hamstring muscle is an important muscle that affects the performance of almost all activities of daily living. Since this muscle is a large muscle that pass across two major joints (the hip and knee joint), it is more susceptible to become tight and to lose its extensibility.

## *Cause and Symptoms of Hamstring Strain*

A strain is a stretched or torn muscle or tendon. Tendons are tissues that connect muscle to bone. Twisting or pulling these tissues can cause a strain. Strains can happen suddenly or develop over time. Hamstring muscle strains are common injuries in people playing sports. Symptoms include pain, muscle spasms, swelling, and trouble moving the muscle.

## Mechanism of Hamstring Strain

A common soft tissue injury in sports involving sprinting and jumping is the hamstring strain. Not much evidence-based research has been carried out on prevention of hamstring strains. Most studies suggest that hamstring strains occur during the later part of the swing phase when the player is sprinting. In this phase the hamstring muscles are working to decelerate knee extension—that is, the muscle develops tension while lengthening. This means that the muscles change from functioning eccentrically to concentrically. It is hypothesized that it is during this rapid change from eccentric to concentric function that the muscles are most vulnerable to injuries, and that the injuries can be prevented by increasing the eccentric muscle strength in the hamstring.

## Treatment

Treatment for strains can be thought of as having two stages. The goal during the first stage is to reduce swelling and pain. At this stage, healthcare providers usually advise patients to follow a formula of rest, ice, compression, and elevation (R.I.C.E) for the first 24 to 48 hours after the injury. The healthcare provider also may recommend an over-the-counter or prescription medication to help decrease pain and inflammation. Severe strains may require surgery to repair the torn muscle, or tendons. Surgery is usually performed by an orthopaedic surgeon.

## Rehabilitation and Prevention

• Acute hamstring muscle strain injuries represent the most prevalent noncontact muscle injury reported in sports. Despite the high prevalence and a rapidly expanding body of literature investigating hamstring muscle strain injuries, occurrence and re-injury rates have not improved over the last three decades. Therefore, rehabilitation and secondary prevention are of particular concern, and the primary objective of all rehabilitation protocols is to return an athlete to preinjury level as soon as possible with a minimal risk of injury recurrence. There is still a lack of consensus and clinical research regarding the effectiveness of various rehabilitation protocols for acute hamstring injuries in athletes participating in sports with high sprinting demands.

- Eccentric strength training has shown to reduce the risk of both new acute hamstring injuries as well as re-injuries, whereas hamstring exercises being performed at longer muscle-tendon length, preferentially mimicking movements occurring simultaneously at both the knee and hip are reported to be more effective than a protocol containing conventional exercises, and are suggested to be a key strategy in the management of hamstring injuries. However, the preventive effect related to the eccentric training remains unclear and is still debated and the optimal intensity of eccentric training in rehabilitation of acute hamstring strain injuries and prevention of re-injuries is yet unknown.

## Hamstring Muscle Stiffness and Knee Joint Stability

Muscle stiffness has been suggested as a key contributor to joint stability. Certain investigations have evaluated the influence of hamstring muscle stiffness on knee joint stability, and how this factor differs across sex. The hamstrings muscles are capable of limiting the load placed on the Anterior Cruciate Ligament (ACL) potentially reducing injury risk. The ACL is loaded and potentially injured during the arthrokinematic (involuntary) knee joint motion of anterior tibial translation. Anterior tibial translation lengthens the hamstrings, and the hamstrings respond by producing tensile force which resists further lengthening, similar to a rubber band. Muscle stiffness refers to the ratio of change in tensile force to change in muscle length associated with joint motion (A Force/A Length), and a stiffer hamstring group would provide a greater increase in resistive tensile force per unit of muscle lengthening caused by anterior tibial translation, thus enhancing knee joint stability. Additionally, hamstring stiffness is greater in males than in females. Given the potential for heightened hamstring stiffness to shield the ACL from excessive loading, the lesser hamstring stiffness noted in females may contribute to the higher female ACL injury rate. The sex difference in hamstring stiffness and the greater incidence of ACL injury in females suggest that hamstring stiffness plays an important role in defining knee joint stability and ACL injury risk.

Chapter 37

# Knee Injury Basics

## What Do the Knees Do? How Do They Work?

The knee is the joint where the bones of the upper leg meet the bones of the lower leg, allowing hinge-like movement while providing stability and strength to support the weight of the body. Flexibility, strength, and stability are needed for standing and for motions like walking, running, crouching, jumping, and turning.

Several kinds of supporting and moving parts, including bones, cartilage, muscles, ligaments, and tendons, help the knees do their job. Each of these structures is subject to disease and injury. When a knee problem affects your ability to do things, it can have a big impact on your life. Knee problems can interfere with many things, from participation in sports to simply getting up from a chair and walking.

## What Causes Knee Problems?

Knee problems can be the result of injury or disease.

### Injury

Knee injuries can occur as the result of a direct blow or sudden movements that strain the knee beyond its normal range of motion. Sometimes knees are injured slowly over time. Problems with the hips

---

This chapter includes text excerpted from "Knee Problems—Questions and Answers about Knee Problems," National Institute of Arthritis and Musculoskeletal and Skin Diseases (NIAMS), March 2016.

or feet, for example, can cause you to walk awkwardly, which throw off the alignment of the knees and leads to damage. Knee problems can also be the result of a lifetime of normal wear and tear. Much like the treads on a tire, the joint simply wears out over time. This chapter discusses some of the most common knee injuries, but first describes the structure of the knee joint.

### Disease

A number of diseases can affect the knee. The most common is arthritis. Although arthritis technically means "joint inflammation," the term is used loosely to describe many different diseases that can affect the joints. Some of the most common forms of arthritis and their effects on the knees are described a bit later in this chapter.

## What Are the Parts of the Knee?

Like any joint, the knee is composed of bones and cartilage, ligaments, tendons, and muscles. Take a closer look at the different parts of the knee in the Figure 37.1 below.

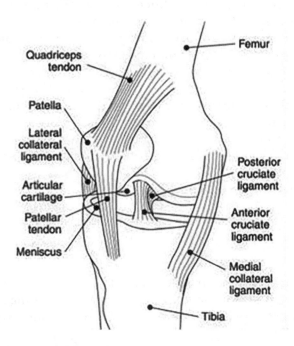

**Figure 37.1.** *Lateral View of the Knee*

## Bones and Cartilage

The knee joint is the junction of three bones: the femur (thigh bone or upper leg bone), the tibia (shin bone or larger bone of the lower leg), and the patella (kneecap). The patella is 2–3 inches wide and 3–4 inches long. It sits over the other bones at the front of the knee joint and slides when the knee moves. It protects the knee and gives leverage to muscles.

The ends of the three bones in the knee joint are covered with articular cartilage, a tough, elastic material that helps absorb shock and allows the knee joint to move smoothly. Separating the bones of the knee are pads of connective tissue called menisci. The menisci are two crescent-shaped discs, each called a meniscus, positioned between the tibia and femur on the outer and inner sides of each knee. The two menisci in each knee act as shock absorbers, cushioning the lower part of the leg from the weight of the rest of the body as well as enhancing stability.

## Muscles

There are two groups of muscles at the knee. The four quadriceps muscles on the front of the thigh work to straighten the knee from a bent position. The hamstring muscles, which run along the back of the thigh from the hip to just below the knee, help to bend the knee.

## Tendons and Ligaments

The quadriceps tendon connects the quadriceps muscle to the patella and provides the power to straighten the knee. The following four ligaments connect the femur and tibia and give the joint strength and stability:

- The medial collateral ligament, which runs along the inside of the knee joint, provides stability to the inner (medial) part of the knee.

- The lateral collateral ligament, which runs along the outside of the knee joint, provides stability to the outer (lateral) part of the knee.

- The anterior cruciate ligament, in the center of the knee, limits rotation and the forward movement of the tibia.

- The posterior cruciate ligament, also in the center of the knee, limits backward movement of the tibia.

The knee capsule is a protective, fiber-like structure that wraps around the knee joint. Inside the capsule, the joint is lined with a thin, soft tissue called synovium.

## How Are Knee Problems Diagnosed?

Doctors diagnose knee problems based on the findings of a medical history, physical exam, and diagnostic tests.

### Medical History

During the medical history, the doctor asks how long symptoms have been present and what problems you are having using your knee. In addition, the doctor will ask about any injury, condition, or health problem that might be causing the problem.

### Physical Examination

The doctor bends, straightens, rotates (turns), or presses on the knee to feel for injury and to determine how well the knee moves and where the pain is located. The doctor may ask you to stand, walk, or squat to help assess the knee's function.

### Diagnostic Tests

Depending on the findings of the medical history and physical exam, the doctor may use one or more tests to determine the nature of a knee problem. Some of the more commonly used tests include:

- **X-ray (radiography).** A procedure in which an X-ray beam is passed through the knee to produce a two-dimensional picture of the bones.

- **Computerized axial tomography (CT) scan.** A painless procedure in which X-rays are passed through the knee at different angles, detected by a scanner, and analyzed by a computer. CT scan images show soft tissues such as ligaments or muscles more clearly than do conventional X-rays. The computer can combine individual images to give a three-dimensional view of the knee.

- **Ultrasound.** A technique that uses sound waves to produce images of the soft tissue structures within and around the knee. A small, hand-held scanner is placed on and around the skin of the knee, which may be moved into different positions throughout the exam.

- **Magnetic resonance imaging (MRI).** A procedure that uses a powerful magnet linked to a computer to create pictures of areas inside the knee. During the procedure, your leg is placed in a cylindrical chamber where energy from a powerful magnet (rather than X-rays) is passed through the knee. An MRI is particularly useful for detecting soft tissue damage.

- **Arthroscopy.** A surgical technique in which the doctor manipulates a small, lighted optic tube (arthroscope) that has been inserted into the joint through a small incision in the knee. Images of the inside of the knee joint are projected onto a television screen.

- **Joint aspiration.** A procedure that uses a syringe to remove fluid buildup in a joint to reduce swelling and relieve pressure. A laboratory analysis of the fluid can determine the presence of a fracture, an infection, or an inflammatory response.

- **Biopsy.** A procedure in which tissue is removed from the body and studied under a microscope.

## What Are Some Common Knee Injuries and Problems?

There are many diseases and types of injuries that can affect the knee. These are some of the most common, along with their diagnoses and treatment.

### Arthritis

There are some 100 different forms of arthritis, rheumatic diseases, and related conditions. Virtually all of them have the potential to affect the knees in some way; however, the following are the most common.

- **Osteoarthritis.** Some people with knee problems have a form of arthritis called osteoarthritis. In this disease, the cartilage gradually wears away and changes occur in the adjacent bone. Osteoarthritis may be caused by joint injury or being overweight. It is associated with aging and most typically begins in people age 50 or older. A young person who develops osteoarthritis typically has had an injury to the knee or may have an inherited form of the disease.

- **Rheumatoid arthritis.** Rheumatoid arthritis, which generally affects people at a younger age than does osteoarthritis, is an autoimmune disease. This means it occurs as a result of the immune system attacking components of the body. In rheumatoid arthritis, the primary site of the immune system's attack is the synovium, the membrane that lines the joint. This attack causes inflammation of the joint. It can lead to destruction of the cartilage and bone and, in some cases, muscles, tendons, and ligaments as well.

- **Other rheumatic diseases.** These include:

  - **Gout.** An acute and intensely painful form of arthritis that occurs when crystals of the bodily waste product uric acid are deposited in the joints.

  - **Systemic lupus erythematosus (lupus).** An autoimmune disease characterized by destructive inflammation of the skin, internal organs, and other body systems, as well as the joints.

  - **Ankylosing spondylitis.** An inflammatory form of arthritis that primarily affects the spine, leading to stiffening and in some cases fusing into a stooped position.

  - **Psoriatic arthritis.** A condition in which inflamed joints produce symptoms of arthritis for patients who have or will develop psoriasis.

  - **Reactive arthritis.** A term describing forms of arthritis that are caused by infectious agents, such as bacteria or viruses. Prompt medical attention is essential to treat the infection and minimize damage to joints, particularly if fever is present.

*Symptoms*

The symptoms are different for the different forms of arthritis. For example, people with rheumatoid arthritis, gout, or other inflammatory conditions may find the knee swollen, red, and even hot to the touch. Any form of arthritis can cause the knee to be painful and stiff.

*Diagnosis*

The doctor may confirm the diagnosis by conducting a careful history and physical examination. Blood tests may be helpful for diagnosing rheumatoid arthritis, but other tests may also be needed.

Analyzing fluid from the knee joint, for example, may be helpful in diagnosing gout. X-rays may be taken to determine loss or damage to cartilage or bone.

### Treatment

Like the symptoms, treatment varies depending on the form of arthritis affecting the knee. For osteoarthritis, treatment is targeted at relieving symptoms and may include pain-reducing medicines such as aspirin or acetaminophen; nonsteroidal anti-inflammatory drugs (NSAIDs) such as ibuprofen; or, in some cases, injections of cortico-steroid medications directly into the knee joint.

### Chondromalacia

Chondromalacia, also called chondromalacia patellae, refers to softening and breakdown of the articular cartilage of the kneecap. This disorder occurs most often in young adults and can be caused by injury, overuse, misalignment of the patella, or muscle weakness. Instead of gliding smoothly across the lower end of the thigh bone, the kneecap rubs against it, thereby roughening the cartilage underneath the kneecap. The damage may range from a slightly abnormal surface of the cartilage to a surface that has been worn away to the bone. Chondromalacia related to injury occurs when a blow to the kneecap tears off either a small piece of cartilage or a large fragment containing a piece of bone (osteochondral fracture).

### Symptoms

The most frequent symptom of chondromalacia is a dull pain around or under the kneecap that worsens when walking down stairs or hills. A person may also feel pain when climbing stairs or when the knee bears weight as it straightens. The disorder is common in runners and is also seen in skiers, cyclists, and soccer players.

### Diagnosis

Your description of symptoms and an X-ray or MRI usually help the doctor make a diagnosis. Although arthroscopy can confirm the diagnosis, it's not performed unless conservative treatment has failed.

*Treatment*

Many doctors recommend that people with chondromalacia perform low-impact exercises that strengthen muscles, particularly muscles of the inner part of the quadriceps, without injuring joints. Swimming, riding a stationary bicycle, and using a cross-country ski machine are examples of good exercises for this condition. If these treatments don't improve the condition, surgery may be indicated.

## Meniscal Injuries (Injuries to the Menisci)

The menisci can be easily injured by the force of rotating the knee while bearing weight. A partial or total tear may occur when a person quickly twists or rotates the upper leg while the foot stays still (for example, when dribbling a basketball around an opponent or turning to hit a tennis ball). If the tear is tiny, the meniscus stays connected to the front and back of the knee; if the tear is large, the meniscus may be left hanging by a thread of cartilage. The seriousness of a tear depends on its location and extent.

*Symptoms*

Generally, when people injure a meniscus, they feel some pain, particularly when the knee is straightened. If the pain is mild, the person may continue moving. Severe pain may occur if a fragment of the meniscus catches between the femur and the tibia. Swelling may occur soon after injury if there is damage to blood vessels. Swelling may also occur several hours later if there is inflammation of the joint lining (synovium). Sometimes, an injury that occurred in the past but was not treated becomes painful months or years later, particularly if the knee is injured a second time. After any injury, the knee may click, lock, feel weak, or give way. Although symptoms of meniscal injury may disappear on their own, they frequently persist or return and require treatment.

*Diagnosis*

In addition to listening to your description of the onset of pain and swelling, the doctor may perform a physical examination and request X-rays or an ultrasound of the knee. An MRI may be recommended to confirm the diagnosis. Occasionally, the doctor may use arthroscopy to help diagnose a meniscal tear.

*Treatment*

If the tear is minor and the pain and other symptoms go away, the doctor may recommend a muscle-strengthening program. The following exercises are designed to build up the quadriceps and hamstring muscles and increase flexibility and strength after injury to the meniscus:

- Warming up the joint by riding a stationary bicycle, then straightening and raising the leg (but not straightening it too much).

- Extending the leg while sitting (a weight may be worn on the ankle for this exercise).

- Raising the leg while lying on the stomach.

- Exercising in a pool (walking as fast as possible in chest-deep water, performing small flutter kicks while holding onto the side of the pool, and raising each leg to 90 degrees in chest-deep water while pressing the back against the side of the pool).

Before beginning any type of exercise program, consult your doctor or physical therapist to learn which exercises are appropriate for you and how to do them correctly, because doing the wrong exercise or exercising improperly can cause problems. A healthcare professional can also advise you on how to warm up safely and when to avoid exercising a joint affected by arthritis. If your lifestyle is limited by the symptoms or the problem, surgery may be indicated.

### Cruciate Ligament Injuries

Cruciate ligament injuries are sometimes referred to as sprains. They don't necessarily cause pain, but they are disabling. The anterior cruciate ligament is most often stretched or torn (or both) by a sudden twisting motion (for example, when the feet are planted one way and the knees are turned another). The posterior cruciate ligament is most often injured by a direct impact, such as in an automobile accident or football tackle.

*Symptoms*

You may hear a popping sound, and the leg may buckle when you try to stand on it.

*Diagnosis*

The doctor may perform several tests to see whether the parts of the knee stay in proper position when pressure is applied in different directions. A thorough examination is essential. An MRI is accurate in detecting a complete tear, but arthroscopy may be the only reliable means of detecting a partial one.

*Treatment*

For an incomplete tear, the doctor may recommend an exercise program to strengthen surrounding muscles. He or she may also prescribe a brace to protect the knee during activity. For a completely torn anterior cruciate ligament in an active athlete and motivated person, the doctor is likely to recommend surgery.

## Medial and Lateral Collateral Ligament Injuries

The medial collateral ligament is more easily injured than the lateral collateral ligament. The cause of collateral ligament injuries is most often a blow to the outer side of the knee that stretches and tears the ligament on the inner side of the knee. Such blows frequently occur in contact sports such as football or hockey.

*Symptoms*

When injury to the medial collateral ligament occurs, you may feel a pop and the knee may buckle sideways. Pain and swelling are common.

*Diagnosis*

A thorough examination is needed to determine the type and extent of the injury. In diagnosing a collateral ligament injury, the doctor exerts pressure on the side of the knee to determine the degree of pain and the looseness of the joint. An MRI is helpful in diagnosing injuries to these ligaments.

*Treatment*

Most sprains of the collateral ligaments will heal if you follow a prescribed exercise program. In addition to exercise, the doctor may recommend ice packs to reduce pain and swelling, and a small sleeve-type brace to protect and stabilize the knee. A sprain may take 2 to 4 weeks to heal. A severely sprained or torn collateral ligament may be accompanied by a torn anterior cruciate ligament, which usually requires surgical repair.

## Tendon Injuries

Knee tendon injuries range from tendinitis (inflammation of a tendon) to a ruptured (torn) tendon. If a person overuses a tendon during certain activities such as dancing, cycling, or running, the tendon stretches and becomes inflamed. Tendinitis of the patellar tendon is sometimes called "jumper's knee" because in sports that require jumping, such as basketball, the muscle contraction and force of hitting the ground after a jump strain the tendon. After repeated stress, the tendon may become inflamed or tear.

### Symptoms

People with tendinitis often have tenderness at the point where the patellar tendon meets the bone. In addition, they may feel pain during running, hurried walking, or jumping. A complete rupture of the quadriceps or patellar tendon is not only painful, but also makes it difficult for a person to bend, extend, or lift the leg against gravity.

### Diagnosis

If there is not much swelling, the doctor will be able to feel a defect in the tendon near the tear during a physical examination. An X-ray will show that the patella is lower than normal in a quadriceps tendon tear and higher than normal in a patellar tendon tear. The doctor may use an ultrasound or MRI to confirm a partial or total tear.

### Treatment

Initially, the treatment for tendinitis involves rest, elevating the knee, applying ice, and taking NSAID medications such as aspirin or ibuprofen to relieve pain and decrease inflammation and swelling. A series of rehabilitation exercises is also useful. If the quadriceps or patellar tendon is completely ruptured, a surgeon will reattach the ends.

Rehabilitating a partial or complete tear of a tendon requires an exercise program that is similar to but less vigorous than that prescribed for ligament injuries. The goals of exercise are to restore the ability to bend and straighten the knee and to strengthen the leg to prevent repeat injury.

## Osteochondritis Dissecans

Osteochondritis dissecans results from a loss of the blood supply to an area of bone underneath a joint surface. It usually involves the knee. The affected bone and its covering of cartilage gradually loosen and cause pain. This problem usually arises spontaneously in an active adolescent or young adult. It may be caused by a slight blockage of a small artery or by an unrecognized injury or tiny fracture that damages the overlying cartilage. A person with this condition may eventually develop osteoarthritis.

Lack of a blood supply can cause bone to break down (osteonecrosis). The involvement of several joints or the appearance of osteochondritis dissecans in several family members may indicate that the disorder is inherited.

### Symptoms

If normal healing doesn't occur, cartilage separates from the diseased bone and a fragment breaks loose into the knee joint, causing weakness, sharp pain, and locking of the joint.

### Diagnosis

An X-ray, MRI, or arthroscopy can determine the condition of the cartilage and can be used to diagnose osteochondritis dissecans.

### Treatment

In most cases, healing occurs after a period of rest and limited activity. Physical therapy can be beneficial. When conservative measures do not help or cartilage fragments are loose, surgery may be indicated.

## What Kinds of Doctors Evaluate and Treat Knee Problems?

After an examination by your primary care doctor, he or she may refer you to a rheumatologist, an orthopaedic surgeon, or both. A rheumatologist specializes in *nonsurgical* treatment of arthritis and other rheumatic diseases. An orthopaedic surgeon, or orthopaedist, specializes in *nonsurgical* and *surgical* treatment of bones, joints, and soft tissues such as ligaments, tendons, and muscles.

## *About Total Knee Replacement*

Joint replacement is becoming more common, and hips and knees are the most commonly replaced joints.

The new joint, called a prosthesis, can be made of plastic, metal, or ceramic materials. It may be cemented into place or uncemented. An uncemented prosthesis is designed so that bones will grow into it.

First made available in the late 1950s, early total knee replacements did a poor job of mimicking the natural motion of the knee. For that reason, these procedures resulted in high failure and complication rates. Advances in total knee replacement technology in the past several years have enhanced the design and fit of knee implants.

Total knee replacement may be indicated when X-rays and other tests show joint damage; when moderate-to-severe, persistent pain does not improve adequately with nonsurgical treatment; and when the limited range of motion in their knee joint diminishes their quality of life.

Most patients appear to experience rapid and substantial reduction in pain, feel better in general, and enjoy improved joint function. Although most total knee replacement surgeries are successful, failure does occur and revision is sometimes necessary.

You may also be referred to a physiatrist. Specializing in physical medicine and rehabilitation, physiatrists seek to restore optimal function to people with injuries to the muscles, bones, tissues, and nervous system.

Minor injuries or arthritis may be treated by an internist (a doctor trained to diagnose and treat nonsurgical diseases) or your primary care doctor.

## *How Can People Prevent Knee Problems?*

Some knee problems, such as those resulting from an accident, cannot be foreseen or prevented. However, people can prevent many knee problems by following these suggestions:

- Before exercising or participating in sports, warm up by walking or riding a stationary bicycle, then do stretches. Stretching the muscles in the front of the thigh (quadriceps) and back of the thigh (hamstrings) reduces tension on the tendons and relieves pressure on the knee during activity.

- Strengthen the leg muscles by doing specific exercises (for example, by walking up stairs or hills or by riding a stationary bicycle). A supervised workout with weights is another way to strengthen the leg muscles that support the knee.

• Avoid sudden changes in the intensity of exercise. Increase the force or duration of activity gradually.

• Wear shoes that fit properly and are in good condition. This will help maintain balance and leg alignment when walking or running. Flat feet or overpronated feet (feet that roll inward) can cause knee problems. People can often reduce some of these problems by wearing special shoe inserts (orthotics).

• Maintain a healthy weight to reduce stress on the knee. Obesity increases the risk of osteoarthritis of the knee.

## What Types of Exercise Are Best for People with Knee Problems?

Ideally, everyone should get three types of exercise regularly:

• Range-of-motion exercises to help maintain normal joint movement and relieve stiffness.

• Strengthening exercises to help keep or increase muscle strength. Keeping muscles strong with exercises, such as walking up stairs, doing leg lifts or dips, or riding a stationary bicycle, helps support and protect the knee.

• Aerobic or endurance exercises to improve function of the heart and circulation and to help control weight. Weight control can be important to people who have arthritis because extra weight puts pressure on many joints. Some studies show that aerobic exercise can reduce inflammation in some joints.

If you already have knee problems, your doctor or physical therapist can help with a plan of exercise that will help the knee(s) without increasing the risk of injury or further damage. As a general rule, you should choose gentle exercises such as swimming, aquatic exercise, or walking rather than jarring exercises such as jogging or high-impact aerobics.

Chapter 38

# Knee Cartilage Injuries

## Chapter Contents

# Section 38.1

# *Patellofemoral Knee Pain (Chondromalacia Patella)*

Text in this section is excerpted from "Patellofemoral Pain,"
© 2017 The American Orthopaedic Society for Sports Medicine.
Reprinted with permission. All rights reserved.

## *What Is Patellofemoral Pain?*

Pain around the front of the knee is often referred to as patellofemoral pain. This pain may be caused by soft cartilage under the kneecap (patella), referred pain from another area such as the back or hip, or soft tissues around the front of the knee.

In athletes, soft tissue pain in the retinaculum (tendon tissue) of the anterior knee (front part) is fairly common. This may come from strain of the tendon—which connects the kneecap to the lower leg bone (patellar tendon) or upper leg bone (quadriceps tendon)—or the retinaculum which supports the kneecap on both the inner and outer sides of the knee.

Some patellofemoral pain is a result of the kneecap being abnormally aligned. If the patella is not correctly aligned, it may come under excessive stress, particularly with vigorous activities. This can also cause excessive wear on the cartilage of the kneecap, which can result in chondromalacia (a condition in which the cartilage softens and may cause a painful sensation in the underlying bone or irritation of the synovium [joint lining]).

## *Treatment of Patellofemoral Pain*

Treatment depends on the specific problem causing the pain. If the soft tissues (retinaculum, tendon, or muscle) are the source of the pain, then stretching can be very helpful to make the support structures more resilient and flexible. One simple stretch for the quadriceps tendon is to lie prone, grab the ankle of the affected leg with one hand and gently pull the heel towards the buttock to stretch the front of the knee. Hamstring stretching (the muscle on the back of the thigh) can also be very helpful to reduce stress on the patellofemoral joint. It is helpful to warm up before stretching, with light activity such as walking or doing calisthenics for several minutes. Hip strengthening exercises have also been shown to reduce patellofemoral pain when done in addition to a stretching program.

Other treatments may involve exercises to build the quadriceps muscle, taping the patella to help with alignment, or using a specially fitted brace which provides support specific to the problem. Using ice and non-steroidal anti-inflammatory medications can also be helpful. It is often necessary to temporarily modify physical activities until the pain decreases.

In more extreme situations, more invasive treatments may be needed. Injection therapy can provide temporary relief of pain. Corticosteroid injections can relieve the inflammation inside the knee, and allow for improved pain relief during a rehabilitation exercise program of stretching and strengthening. Sometimes a specific surgical procedure may be needed to help relieve the pain. If the cartilage under the kneecap is fragmented and causing mechanical symptoms and swelling, arthroscopic removal of the fragments may be helpful. If the patella is badly aligned, however, a surgical procedure may be needed to place the kneecap back into proper alignment, thereby reducing abnormal pressures on the cartilage and supporting structures around the front of the knee.

In some people, particularly those who have had previous knee surgery, there may be a specific painful area in the soft tissue around the patella which may require resection (removal).

## *Controlling or Preventing Patellofemoral Pain*

Good general conditioning is important. Stretching, particularly in the prone position, will keep the supporting structures around the front of the knee flexible and less likely to be irritated with exercise. Proper training, without sudden increases of stress to the front of the knee, will help avoid pain. Weight reduction and activity modification may be necessary in some people.

Section 38.2

## *Osteochondritis Dissecans of the Knee*

This section includes text excerpted from "Osteochondritis Dissecans," Genetic and Rare Diseases Information Center (GARD), National Center for Advancing Translational Sciences (NCATS), February 8, 2015.

Osteochondritis dissecans is a joint condition that occurs when a piece of cartilage and the thin layer of bone beneath it, separates from the end of the bone. If the piece of cartilage and bone remain close to where they detached, they may not cause any symptoms. However, affected people may experience pain, weakness and/or decreased range of motion in the affected joint if the cartilage and bone travel into the joint space. Although osteochondritis dissecans can affect people of all ages, it is most commonly diagnosed in people between the ages of 10 and 20 years. In most cases, the exact underlying cause is unknown. Rarely, the condition can affect more than one family member (called familial osteochondritis dissecans); in these cases, osteochondritis dissecans is caused by changes (mutations) in the *ACAN* gene and is inherited in an autosomal dominant manner. Treatment for the condition varies depending on many factors, including the age of the affected person and the severity of the symptoms, but may include rest; casting or splinting; surgery and/or physical therapy.

### *Symptoms*

The signs and symptoms of osteochondritis dissecans vary from person to person. If the piece of cartilage and bone remain close to where they detached, they may not cause any symptoms. However, affected people may experience the following if the cartilage and bone travel into the joint space:

- Pain, swelling and/or tenderness
- Joint popping
- Joint weakness
- Decreased range of motion

Although osteochondritis dissecans can develop in any joint of the body, the knee, ankle and elbow are most commonly affected. Most people only develop the condition in a single joint.

## Cause

In most cases, the exact underlying cause of osteochondritis dissecans is not completely understood. Scientists suspect that it may be due to decreased blood flow to the end of the affected bone, which may occur when repetitive episodes of minor injury and/or stress damage a bone overtime.

In some families, osteochondritis dissecans is caused by changes (mutations) in the *ACAN* gene. In these cases, which are referred to as familial osteochondritis dissecans, the condition generally affects multiple joints and is also associated with short stature and early-onset osteoarthritis. The *ACAN* gene encodes a protein that is important to the structure of cartilage. Mutations in this gene weaken cartilage, which leads to the various signs and symptoms of familial osteochondritis dissecans.

## Diagnosis

A diagnosis of osteochondritis dissecans is usually suspected based on the presence of characteristic signs and symptoms. Additional testing can then be ordered to confirm the diagnosis. These test may include X-rays, magnetic resonance imaging (MRI) and/or computed tomography (CT scan).

## Treatment

The primary aim of treatment for osteochondritis dissecans is to restore normal function of the affected joint, relieve pain and prevent osteoarthritis. Treatment for the condition varies depending on many factors including the age of the affected person and the severity of the symptoms. In children and young teens, osteochondritis dissecans often heals overtime without surgical treatment. These cases are often managed with rest and in some cases, crutches and/or splinting to relieve pain and swelling.

If nonsurgical treatments are not successful or the case is particularly severe (i.e., the cartilage and bone are moving around within the joint space), surgery may be recommended. Following surgery, physical therapy is often necessary to improve the strength and range of motion of the affected joint.

# Section 38.3

# *Meniscal Injuries*

This section contains text excerpted from the following sources:
Text beginning with the heading "Injuries to the Menisci" is
excerpted from "Knee Problems—Questions and Answers about
Knee Problems," National Institute of Arthritis and Musculoskeletal
and Skin Diseases (NIAMS), March 2016; Text under the heading
"Meniscal Injuries in High School Athletes" is excerpted from
"Epidemiology of Meniscal Injuries in U.S. High School
Athletes from 2007/08-2012/13," Centers for Disease
Control and Prevention (CDC), October 27, 2015.

## *Injuries to the Menisci*

The menisci can be easily injured by the force of rotating the knee
while bearing weight. A partial or total tear may occur when a person
quickly twists or rotates the upper leg while the foot stays still (for
example, when dribbling a basketball around an opponent or turning
to hit a tennis ball). If the tear is tiny, the meniscus stays connected
to the front and back of the knee; if the tear is large, the meniscus
may be left hanging by a thread of cartilage. The seriousness of a tear
depends on its location and extent.

## *Symptoms*

Generally, when people injure a meniscus, they feel some pain,
particularly when the knee is straightened. If the pain is mild, the
person may continue moving. Severe pain may occur if a fragment of
the meniscus catches between the femur and the tibia. Swelling may
occur soon after injury if there is damage to blood vessels. Swelling
may also occur several hours later if there is inflammation of the joint
lining (synovium). Sometimes, an injury that occurred in the past but
was not treated becomes painful months or years later, particularly
if the knee is injured a second time. After any injury, the knee may
click, lock, feel weak, or give way. Although symptoms of meniscal
injury may disappear on their own, they frequently persist or return
and require treatment.

## Diagnosis

In addition to listening to your description of the onset of pain and swelling, the doctor may perform a physical examination and request X-rays or an ultrasound of the knee. An magnetic resonance imaging (MRI) may be recommended to confirm the diagnosis. Occasionally, the doctor may use arthroscopy to help diagnose a meniscal tear.

## Treatment

If the tear is minor and the pain and other symptoms go away, the doctor may recommend a muscle-strengthening program. The following exercises are designed to build up the quadriceps and hamstring muscles and increase flexibility and strength after injury to the meniscus:

- Warming up the joint by riding a stationary bicycle, then straightening and raising the leg (but not straightening it too much).

- Extending the leg while sitting (a weight may be worn on the ankle for this exercise).

- Raising the leg while lying on the stomach.

- Exercising in a pool (walking as fast as possible in chest-deep water, performing small flutter kicks while holding onto the side of the pool, and raising each leg to 90 degrees in chest-deep water while pressing the back against the side of the pool).

Before beginning any type of exercise program, consult your doctor or physical therapist to learn which exercises are appropriate for you and how to do them correctly, because doing the wrong exercise or exercising improperly can cause problems. A healthcare professional can also advise you on how to warm up safely and when to avoid exercising a joint affected by arthritis. If your lifestyle is limited by the symptoms or the problem, surgery may be indicated.

## Meniscal Injuries in High School Athletes

Steady increases in high school athletics participation over the past decade resulted in 7.6 million participants during recent academic years. While many health benefits are associated with participation in sports, interscholastic athletics incurs risk of acute injuries which can have long-term consequences. Meniscal injuries are one such injury, with a reported mean annual incidence rate in the general population of 66–70 per 100,000 people. Concurrently, arthroscopic treatment for meniscal injuries is an extremely common orthopaedic procedure in the United States. Recognition of risk factors for the development of meniscal injuries in youth athletes is essential to preserving the long-term health of the knee as meniscal lesions are associated with a 4–14 times increase in the risk of knee osteoarthritis.

Overall the most commonly reported injury mechanism is a player-player contact, accounting for 41.9 percent of all injuries, followed by noncontact (38.2%). Consistent with previous reports, for most sports, the most common action causing injury was rotation around a planted foot. A study of NBA players reported 31.7 percent of meniscal injuries occurred via a noncontact mechanism. When looking specifically at basketball a certain study demonstrated a higher proportion of noncontact meniscal injuries for both males and females, 42.9 and 45.9 percent, respectively. This suggests younger basketball players, having not yet reached physical maturity, may be more susceptible to injury by rotation around a planted foot.

Meniscal injuries were found to account for 15.1 percent of all knee injuries in high school athletes. While few findings are similar, a certain study analyzed a population that was not age restricted and utilized different clinical surveillance methods, limiting direct comparison.

Meniscal injuries often occur in conjunction with injury to other knee structures. In a study 54 percent of reported meniscal injuries had at least one concomitant knee injury. The most common associated injury was Anterior Cruciate Ligament (ACL) tear (36.9%), which is similar to previous reports observing 36.6 percent of meniscal tears having associated ACL tear.

Meniscal injury patterns among high school athletes vary by gender, sport, and type of exposure. Certain studies clearly defines American football as the greatest sport at risk for meniscus tears in high school athletics. However in gender-comparable sports girls may be at higher risk for meniscal injury. Most athletes with meniscus tears are able to return to sport in season, though often require surgery. Recognizing distinct differences in these injury patterns will help drive evidence-based, targeted injury prevention strategies and efforts.

Chapter 39

# Knee Ligament Injuries

## Chapter Contents

# Section 39.1

# *Anterior Cruciate Ligament (ACL) Injury*

This section contains text excerpted from the following sources: Text
under the heading "An Athlete's Nightmare: Tearing the ACL" is
excerpted from "An Athlete's Nightmare: Tearing the ACL," National
Library of Medicine (NLM), National Institutes of Health (NIH), 2008.
Reviewed June 2017; Text under the heading "Anterior Cruciate
Ligament (ACL) Injury and Its Effects" is excerpted from "Funded Injury
Control Research Centers (ICRCs)," Centers for Disease Control and
Prevention (CDC), July 13, 2010. Reviewed June 2017; Text under the
heading "Long-Term Data Reveal Rate and Risk Factors for Subsequent
Surgeries Following Initial ACL Reconstruction" is excerpted from
"Long-Term Data Reveal Rate and Risk Factors for Subsequent
Surgeries Following Initial ACL Reconstruction," National Institute of
Arthritis and Musculoskeletal and Skin Diseases (NIAMS), December
2013. Reviewed June 2017; Text under the heading "Alternative Warm-
Up Program Reduces Risk of ACL Injuries for Female College Soccer
Players" is excerpted from "Alternative Warm-Up Program Reduces
Risk of ACL Injuries for Female College Soccer Players,"
Centers for Disease Control and Prevention (CDC),
July 25, 2008. Reviewed June 2017.

## *An Athlete's Nightmare: Tearing the ACL*

All too common among athletes, an anterior cruciate ligament
(ACL) injury is usually caused by a sudden deceleration or landing
maneuver with the leg in a vulnerable position. Although ACL injuries
are most often seen in team sports, 70 percent are incurred with little
or no contact with another athlete.

Studies have shown that young female athletes sustain more
ACL injuries than young males. In fact, young women are two to
eight times more likely than their male counterparts to injure that
ligament.

There are many different theories as to why young women suffer
a higher rate of ACL injuries. One thought is that women have more
of a knock-knee alignment. The alignment of women's knees tends to
bend inward when women land. Some researchers believe that this
inward bend may predispose women to ACL injuries.

One of the major reasons any athlete suffers ACL damage is because they land in a flat-footed position, as opposed to landing on the balls of their feet. If the calf muscles are not absorbing the force, and if the knee is not in the proper position, the knee buckles and tears the ACL.

## Anterior Cruciate Ligament (ACL) Injury and Its Effects

Anterior cruciate ligament (ACL) injury typically occurs in the physically active population, and while the incidence of ACL injury is greater in males due to greater exposure to physical activity, the relative risk of injury per exposure is 2 to 8 times greater in females. Furthermore, ACL injury, whether managed surgically or conservatively, substantially increases the risk of developing osteoarthritis, a condition that adversely affects quality of life and may indirectly lead to obesity due to a pain-induced sedentary lifestyle. Prevention, rather than treatment, is the pivotal issue in reducing the public health burden of ACL injury. However, additional research is necessary to establish the appropriate factors to be targeted by injury prevention efforts. Furthermore, the origins of the higher female ACL injury rate have not been clearly established. Muscle stiffness has been suggested as a key contributor to joint stability. The hamstrings muscles are capable of limiting the load placed on the ACL potentially reducing injury risk. The ACL is loaded and potentially injured during the arthrokinematic (involuntary) knee joint motion of anterior tibial translation.

Anterior tibial translation lengthens the hamstrings, and the hamstrings respond by producing tensile force which resists further lengthening, similar to a rubber band. Muscle stiffness refers to the ratio of change in tensile force to change in muscle length associated with joint motion (A Force/A Length), and a stiffer hamstring group would provide a greater increase in resistive tensile force per unit of muscle lengthening caused by anterior tibial translation, thus enhancing knee joint stability. Additionally, hamstring stiffness is greater in males than in females. Given the potential for heightened hamstring stiffness to shield the ACL from excessive loading, the lesser hamstring stiffness noted in females may contribute to the higher female ACL injury rate. The sex difference in hamstring stiffness and the greater incidence of ACL injury in females suggest that hamstring stiffness plays an important role in defining knee joint stability and ACL injury risk.

## Long-Term Data Reveal Rate and Risk Factors for Subsequent Surgeries Following Initial ACL Reconstruction

Nearly one-fifth of patients who undergo knee surgery to reconstruct a torn anterior cruciate ligament (ACL) eventually need to have additional surgery on the same knee, according to research published in *The American Journal of Sports Medicine.* The study, which was funded by the NIH's National Institute of Arthritis and Musculoskeletal and Skin Diseases (NIAMS), also clarified key risk factors associated with the need for subsequent knee surgeries.

Rupture of the knee's ACL is a common sports-related injury. It is associated with other knee problems, such as meniscal tears and knee instability. Over the long-term, it can lead to knee osteoarthritis. Some patients are able to cope with an ACL tear with physical therapy and rest, but most active people undergo surgery to reconstruct the ligament to restore knee function and prevent further tears.

Although ACL reconstructive surgery is common and often successful, the rate and risk factors for subsequent knee surgery is not known until now.

In the Multicenter Orthopaedic Outcomes Network (MOON) study, researchers followed nearly 1,000 people for several years after the patients underwent initial ACL reconstruction. They wanted to determine the rate at which additional surgeries were performed, and to identify specific risk factors that lead to additional surgeries. The median age among patients at their initial surgery was 23.

Six years after surgery, about 19 percent of participants had undergone at least one more surgery on the initial damaged knee. In addition, 10 percent had undergone surgery on the other knee—6.4 percent of these procedures were to reconstruct a ruptured ACL. Patients who had ACL surgery earlier in life were more likely to have subsequent surgeries, a finding that echoes previous research. These young people typically are more athletic and active, and might be less likely to fully comply with postoperative instructions. It's also possible that they have biological differences that predispose them to injury and re-injury.

Patients with ligaments taken from a cadaver to reconstruct their ACL, rather than a ligament from their own bodies, were also more likely to undergo additional surgery. Previous research has suggested that using cadaver-sourced ligaments may lead to an increased risk of immune-incompatibility and could potentially transmit infectious diseases, although the risk for passing on disease is very low. The MOON findings provided further evidence of the possible hazards associated with using them. Unlike other research, however, the researchers did not find that women or those with a higher body mass index were at an increased risk for subsequent surgery.

The results of the MOON study provide patients, parents, health-care providers, coaches and trainers with valuable information about the risks associated with ACL surgery, as well as ways in which patients may reduce their chances for needing subsequent surgery.

## Alternative Warm-Up Program Reduces Risk of ACL Injuries for Female College Soccer Players

The risk of potentially devastating tears to an important knee ligament may be reduced in female college soccer players by an alternative warm-up program that focuses on stretching, strengthening, and improving balance and movements, according to a Centers for Disease Control and Prevention (CDC) study published online in *The American Journal of Sports Medicine*. The program can be done without additional equipment or extensive training that other prevention programs may require.

Female athletes are at greater risk for anterior cruciate ligament (ACL) injuries, compared to males participating in similar activities. The gender difference becomes even greater for noncontact ACL injuries, which occur usually in stopping, turning, or landing from a jump as opposed to colliding with another player or something on the field like the goal post.

The study shows tremendous promise for female collegiate soccer players, especially those with a history of ACL injuries. Enjoying sports is a great way to stay fit. And to stay healthy, coaches, athletic trainers, and athletes are encouraged to consider adapting this program into their routine.

The study explored the effectiveness of the Prevent Injury and Enhance Performance (PEP) program developed by the Santa Monica Orthopedic and Sports Medicine Research Foundation, Santa Monica, Calif. The Foundation conducts research to prevent musculoskeletal and neurologic injuries. The PEP program is designed to help teams prevent noncontact ACL injuries without a significant investment in equipment or time. The session includes warm-up, stretching, strengthening, and sport-specific agility exercises.

The study followed 61 women's soccer teams with 1,435 players in Division I of the National Collegiate Athletic Association (NCAA) for a single season. Twenty-six teams were randomly assigned to use the program and 35 other teams served as a comparison group. Teams participating in the study came from many different regions, conferences and experienced a variety of competitive success.

Researchers noted that while the number of injuries reported in this study was small, the use of the PEP program was effective in reducing the risk of ACL injuries, and the program can be done during regular practice time and without special equipment.

## Section 39.2

# *Posterior Cruciate Ligament (PCL) Injury*

Text in this section is from "Posterior Cruciate Ligament Injuries," © 1995-2017 American Academy of Orthopaedic Surgeons. Reprinted with permission.

The posterior cruciate ligament is located in the back of the knee. It is one of several ligaments that connect the femur (thighbone) to the tibia (shinbone). The posterior cruciate ligament keeps the tibia from moving backwards too far.

An injury to the posterior cruciate ligament requires a powerful force. A common cause of injury is a bent knee hitting a dashboard in a car accident or a football player falling on a knee that is bent.

### *Anatomy*

Two bones meet to form your knee joint: your thighbone (femur) and shinbone (tibia). Your kneecap sits in front of the joint to provide some protection.

Bones are connected to other bones by ligaments. There are four primary ligaments in your knee. They act like strong ropes to hold the bones together and keep your knee stable.

**Collateral ligaments.** These are found on the sides of your knee. The medial collateral ligament is on the inside and the lateral collateral ligament is on the outside. They control the sideways motion of your knee and brace it against unusual movement.

**Cruciate ligaments.** These are found inside your knee joint. They cross each other to form an "X" with the anterior cruciate ligament in front and the posterior cruciate ligament in back. The cruciate ligaments control the back and forth motion of your knee.

The posterior cruciate ligament keeps the shinbone from moving backwards too far. It is stronger than the anterior cruciate ligament and is injured less often. The posterior cruciate ligament has two parts that blend into one structure that is about the size of a person's little finger.

## Description

Injuries to the posterior cruciate ligament are not as common as other knee ligament injuries. In fact, they are often subtle and more difficult to evaluate than other ligament injuries in the knee.

Many times a posterior cruciate ligament injury occurs along with injuries to other structures in the knee such as cartilage, other ligaments, and bone.

Injured ligaments are considered "sprains" and are graded on a severity scale.

**Grade 1 Sprains.** The ligament is mildly damaged in a Grade 1 Sprain. It has been slightly stretched, but is still able to help keep the knee joint stable.

**Grade 2 Sprains.** A Grade 2 Sprain stretches the ligament to the point where it becomes loose. This is often referred to as a partial tear of the ligament.

**Grade 3 Sprains.** This type of sprain is most commonly referred to as a complete tear of the ligament. The ligament has been split into two pieces, and the knee joint is unstable.

Posterior cruciate ligament tears tend to be partial tears with the potential to heal on their own. People who have injured just their posterior cruciate ligaments are usually able to return to sports without knee stability problems.

## Cause

An injury to the posterior cruciate ligament can happen many ways. It typically requires a powerful force.

- A direct blow to the front of the knee (such as a bent knee hitting a dashboard in a car crash, or a fall onto a bent knee in sports)

397

- Pulling or stretching the ligament (such as in a twisting or hyperextension injury)

- Simple misstep

## Symptoms

The typical symptoms of a posterior cruciate ligament injury are:

- Pain with swelling that occurs steadily and quickly after the injury

- Swelling that makes the knee stiff and may cause a limp

- Difficulty walking

- The knee feels unstable, like it may "give out"

## Doctor Examination

During your first visit, your doctor will talk to you about your symptoms and medical history.

During the physical examination, your doctor will check all the structures of your injured knee, and compare them to your non-injured knee. Your injured knee may appear to sag backwards when bent. It might slide backwards too far, particularly when it is bent beyond a 90° angle. Other tests which may help your doctor confirm your diagnosis include X-rays and magnetic resonance imaging (MRI). It is possible, however, for these pictures to appear normal, especially if the injury occurred more than 3 months before the tests.

**X-rays.** Although they will not show any injury to your posterior cruciate ligament, X-rays can show whether the ligament tore off a piece of bone when it was injured. This is called an avulsion fracture.

**MRI.** This study creates better images of soft tissues like the posterior cruciate ligament.

## Treatment

### Nonsurgical Treatment

If you have injured just your posterior cruciate ligament, your injury may heal quite well without surgery Your doctor may recommend simple, nonsurgical options.

**RICE.** When you are first injured, the RICE method—rest, ice, gentle compression and elevation—can help speed your recovery.

**Immobilization.** Your doctor may recommend a brace to prevent your knee from moving. To further protect your knee, you may be given crutches to keep you from putting weight on your leg.

**Physical therapy.** As the swelling goes down, a careful rehabilitation program is started. Specific exercises will restore function to your knee and strengthen the leg muscles that support it. Strengthening the muscles in the front of your thigh (quadriceps) has been shown to be a key factor in a successful recovery.

## Surgical Treatment

Your doctor may recommend surgery if you have combined injuries. For example, if you have dislocated your knee and torn multiple ligaments including the posterior cruciate ligament, surgery is almost always necessary.

**Rebuilding the ligament.** Because sewing the ligament ends back together does not usually heal, a torn posterior cruciate ligament must be rebuilt. Your doctor will replace your torn ligament with a tissue graft. This graft is taken from another part of your body, or from another human donor (cadaver). It can take several months for the graft to heal into your bone.

**Procedure.** Surgery to rebuild a posterior cruciate ligament is done with an arthroscope using small incisions. Arthroscopic surgery is less invasive. The benefits of less invasive techniques include less pain from surgery, less time spent in the hospital, and quicker recovery times.

Surgical procedures to repair posterior cruciate ligaments continue to improve. More advanced techniques help patients resume a wider range of activities after rehabilitation.

## Rehabilitation

Whether your treatment involves surgery or not, rehabilitation plays a vital role in getting you back to your daily activities. A physical therapy program will help you regain knee strength and motion. If you had surgery, physical therapy will begin 1 to 4 weeks after your procedure.

How long it takes you to recover from a posterior cruciate ligament injury will depend on the severity of your injury. Combined injuries often have a slow recovery, but most patients do well over time.

If your injury requires surgery, it may be several weeks before you return to a desk job—perhaps months if your job requires a lot of activity. Full recovery typically requires 6 to 12 months.

Although it is a slow process, your commitment to therapy is the most important factor in returning to all the activities you enjoy.

Chapter 40

# Patellar Tendinitis and Tendinopathy

## What Is a Tendon?

A tendon is a flexible band of fibrous tissue that connects muscles to bones. Tendinitis (also called tendonitis) is inflammation of a tendon. Tendons transmit the pull of the muscle to the bone to cause movement. They are found throughout the body, including the hands, wrists, elbows, shoulders, hips, knees, ankles, and feet. If a person overuses a tendon during activities such as dancing, cycling, or running, it may elongate or undergo microscopic tears and become inflamed. Trying to break a fall may also cause the quadriceps muscles to contract and tear the quadriceps tendon above the knee cap (patella) or the patellar tendon below it. This type of injury is most likely to happen in older people whose tendons tend to be weaker and less flexible. Tendinitis of the patellar tendon is sometimes called jumper's knee because in

This chapter contains text excerpted from the following sources: Text under the heading "What Is a Tendon?" is excerpted from "Questions and Answers about Bursitis and Tendinitis," National Institute of Arthritis and Musculoskeletal and Skin Diseases (NIAMS), February 2017; Text under the heading "Cause and Mechanism of Injury" is excerpted from "Exercise Therapy for Patellar Tendinopathy Evaluated with Advanced UTE-MRI," ClinicalTrials.gov, National Institutes of Health (NIH), February 13, 2017; Text beginning with the heading "Symptoms" is excerpted from "Knee Problems—Questions and Answers about Knee Problems," National Institute of Arthritis and Musculoskeletal and Skin Diseases (NIAMS), March 2016.

sports that require jumping, such as basketball, the muscle contraction and force of hitting the ground after a jump strain the tendon. After repeated stress, the tendon may become inflamed or tear.

## Cause and Mechanism of Injury

Patellar tendinopathy is a clinical condition of gradually progressive activity-related pain at the insertion of the patellar tendon at the apex patellae. Prolonged repetitive stress of the knee-extensor apparatus can lead to this common overuse tendinopathy in athletes from different sports, resulting in pain and impaired performance in athletes. High prevalence rates have been reported in jumping sports such as volleyball and basketball (45% and 32% in elite athletes, respectively). Symptoms can be long-standing if not treated appropriately in the initial stages.

Tendinopathy is a widely accepted, generic term that encompasses any abnormal condition of a tendon. Clinical symptoms include activity-related pain associated with tenderness, localized swelling and impaired performance. Histopathologically, tendinopathy is characterized by structural disorganization of the tendon collagen that alters the loading capacity of a specific tendon.

## Symptoms

People with tendinitis often have tenderness at the point where the patellar tendon meets the bone. In addition, they may feel pain during running, hurried walking, or jumping. A complete rupture of the quadriceps or patellar tendon is not only painful, but also makes it difficult for a person to bend, extend, or lift the leg against gravity.

## Diagnosis

If there is not much swelling, the doctor will be able to feel a defect in the tendon near the tear during a physical examination. An X-ray will show that the patella is lower than normal in a quadriceps tendon tear and higher than normal in a patellar tendon tear. The doctor may use an ultrasound or magnetic resonance imaging (MRI) to confirm a partial or total tear.

## Treatment

Initially, the treatment for tendinitis involves rest, elevating the knee, applying ice, and taking nonsteroidal anti-inflammatory drug

(NSAID) medications such as aspirin or ibuprofen to relieve pain and decrease inflammation and swelling. A series of rehabilitation exercises is also useful. If the quadriceps or patellar tendon is completely ruptured, a surgeon will reattach the ends.

Rehabilitating a partial or complete tear of a tendon requires an exercise program that is similar to but less vigorous than that prescribed for ligament injuries. The goals of exercise are to restore the ability to bend and straighten the knee and to strengthen the leg to prevent repeat injury.

Chapter 41

# Dislocated Patella

## The Patella

Patella, or the knee cap, is located in front of the knee. It is shaped like a shield, with the apex pointing downwards. As the knee bends and straightens, the patella glides up and down the patellofemoral groove, the indentation at the front of the thigh bone or femur. The patella is attached to the quadriceps, or thigh muscle, via the quadriceps tendon. This arrangement increases the leverage from quadriceps when the knee is straightened.

## What Is Patella Dislocation?

Normally, the patella lies within the patellofemoral groove and slides vertically within it. When the patella moves or is moved to the outside of this groove onto the bony head of the femur (lateral femoral condyle), patella dislocation occurs. Partial dislocation, known as subluxation of the patella, happens when the knee cap moves partially out of its position in the groove. A patella dislocation is different from dislocation of the knee joint, which is a much more severe traumatic injury.

When the patella dislocates, it also stretches the muscles and ligaments present on the inner side of the knee, causing damage.

---

"Dislocated Patella," © 2017 Omnigraphics. Reviewed June 2017.

## Causes of Patella Dislocation

Several factors can cause patella dislocation. Trauma to the knee primarily causes dislocation, often by sudden twisting or a direct blow. The following are the other risk factors which can predispose to patella dislocation:

- Past history of patella dislocation or subluxation.

- Hyperlaxity, or abnormally wide range of motion of the soft tissues around the patella. Hyperlaxity is generally a condition associated with inherited diseases, such as Marfan syndrome, etc.

- Maltracking of the patella in the patellafemoral groove. Maltracking occurs when the quadriceps are of unequal strength and the patella is pulled out of the groove to the side of the stronger muscle.

- Shallow femoral groove.

- Weaker quadriceps muscles, especially vastus medialis, the inner quadriceps muscle.

- Tight muscles, ligaments and other soft tissue structures on the outer side of the knee.

- During running, over pronation of the feet, where the feet roll in, puts significant lateral stress on the patella. Rolling in of the feet causes the leg to turn inwards and causes the patella to dislocate outwards as the quadriceps contract.

- Individuals with a greater "Q-angle" are at a greater risk for patellar dislocations. The "Q-angle" is formed by envisioning a circle around the patella, the line of pull of the quad muscle forms the tail of the "Q." If the tail of the "Q" is more than 25 degrees off of the center of the quad-patella-patellar tendon line of pull, it is considered an abnormally high "Q-angle."

Studies have shown that after the initial dislocation, incidence of recurring dislocations is around 40 percent. Patellar dislocations are commonly seen in soccer, weight lifting, running, football, baseball, and basketball players. In the United States, the prevalence of patellar dislocation is about 3 million knee injuries annually.

## Symptoms

Symptoms will depend on how much the patella has moved out of the groove and how much damage has happened to the soft tissues. The general symptoms are:

- Obvious deformity around the knee joint.
- Inability to straighten the knee joint.
- Extreme pain around knee cap until it is relocated.
- Acute and rapid swelling around the knee joint.
- Tenderness around the knee cap.
- Feeling of giving way and knee buckling when trying to stand.

## How Is Patella Dislocation Diagnosed?

Your doctor will do an examination, looking for signs of patella dislocation, associated muscle and ligament damage, movement in the knee joint, and tenderness. They will ask you how the injury occurred and about specific symptoms.

To confirm the diagnosis and identify damaged structures surrounding the kneecap or to the patella joint surface, an X-ray, ultrasound, or magnetic resonance imaging (MRI) may also be done.

## Treatment

### Immediate Treatment

If the patella remains dislocated, the athlete has to be taken to the emergency room. Pain medication will be given to the athlete to relax his or her knee muscles, and gentle pressure will be applied to move the kneecap back into place. This process is called a "reduction."

### Nonsurgical Treatment

- **RICE.** Apply RICE (rest, ice, compression, and elevation) principles to the injured knee. Ice can be applied for 10 to 15 minutes every hour initially reducing to 2 or 3 times a days as swelling and symptoms reduce.

- **Immobilization.** Your doctor may recommend a patella stabilizing brace for 3 to 4 weeks. This stabilizes the knee while it heals.

- **Weightbearing.** Your doctor may recommend using crutches for walking for the first week or two after the injury. This will reduce the load on the patella and enhance the healing process.

- **Physical therapy.** Once the knee has started to heal, your physical therapist will recommend specific exercises that will strengthen the thigh muscles holding the knee joint in place.

After the first dislocation, the patella often remains looser, or more unstable, than it was before the injury. The soft tissue structures are stretched and the patella may dislocate again. Ongoing exercises to strengthen quadriceps muscles in the thigh will prevent future patellar dislocations.

### Surgical Treatment

The type of surgery will depend on the cause of the dislocation. Arthroscopic surgeries are usually performed to reconstruct and strengthen the ligaments that hold the patella in place.

Complex surgical procedures are required for repeated dislocation caused by a congenital or other bone deformity.

## Return to Sport with Patella Dislocations

Once an athlete has sustained a patella dislocation, there is always increased instability around the kneecap due to the residual weakness and loss of balance as a result of the injury. It is important to follow your physiotherapist's advice, who will design a customized exercise program to help you return to sports and to your previous level of function.

### References

1. "Kneecap Dislocation," U.S. National Library of Medicine (NLM), 2017.

2. "Patellar Dislocation and Instability in Children (Unstable Kneecap)," American Academy of Orthopaedic Surgeons (AAOS), 2014.

3. "Patella Dislocation," Virtual Sports Injury Clinic, 2013.

4. "Patella Dislocation," Physio Works, 2013.

Chapter 42

# Other Overuse
# Knee Injuries

## Chapter Contents

# Section 42.1

## *Iliotibial (IT) Band Friction Syndrome*

This section includes text excerpted from "Knee Problems—Questions and Answers about Knee Problems," National Institute of Arthritis and Musculoskeletal and Skin Diseases (NIAMS), March 2016.

Iliotibial band syndrome is an inflammatory condition caused when a band of tissue rubs over the outer bone (lateral condyle) of the knee. Although iliotibial band syndrome may be caused by direct injury to the knee, it is most often caused by the stress of long-term overuse, such as sometimes occurs in sports training and, particularly, in running.

### *Symptoms*

A person with this syndrome feels an ache or burning sensation at the side of the knee during activity. Pain may be localized at the side of the knee or radiate up the side of the thigh. A person may also feel a snap when the knee is bent and then straightened. Swelling is usually absent, and knee motion is normal.

### *Diagnosis*

The diagnosis of this disorder is typically based on the symptoms, such as pain at the outer bone, and exclusion of other conditions with similar symptoms.

### *Treatment*

Usually, iliotibial band syndrome disappears if the person reduces activity and performs stretching exercises followed by muscle-strengthening exercises. In rare cases when the syndrome doesn't disappear, surgery may be necessary to split the tendon so it isn't stretched too tightly over the bone.

Section 42.2

# *Plica Syndrome*

This section includes text excerpted from "Knee Problems—Questions and Answers about Knee Problems," National Institute of Arthritis and Musculoskeletal and Skin Diseases (NIAMS), March 2016.

Plica syndrome occurs when plicae (bands of synovial tissue) are irritated by overuse or injury. Synovial plicae are the remains of tissue pouches found in the early stages of fetal development. As the fetus develops, these pouches normally combine to form one large synovial cavity. If this process is incomplete, plicae remain as four folds or bands of synovial tissue within the knee. Injury, chronic overuse, or inflammatory conditions are associated with this syndrome.

## *Symptoms*

Symptoms of plica syndrome include pain and swelling, a clicking sensation, and locking and weakness of the knee.

## *Diagnosis*

Because the symptoms are similar to those of some other knee problems, plica syndrome is often misdiagnosed. Diagnosis usually depends on excluding other conditions that cause similar symptoms.

## *Treatment*

The goal of treatment for plica syndrome is to reduce inflammation of the synovium and thickening of the plicae. The doctor usually prescribes medicine to reduce inflammation. People are also advised to reduce activity, apply ice and an elastic bandage to the knee, and do strengthening exercises. If treatment fails to relieve symptoms, the doctor may recommend arthroscopic or open surgery to remove the plicae.

# Part Eight

# Injuries to the Lower Legs, Ankles, and Feet

# Chapter 43

# *Leg Stress Fractures*

A stress fracture is a tiny crack that appears in a bone. It often results from repetitive strain placed on the weight-bearing bones of the legs and feet by athletes running or training for other sports. As the leg muscles become fatigued, they can no longer absorb all of the shock from impact with the ground. The excess load is transferred to the bones, which may create stress fractures. More than half of all stress fractures affect the lower legs, particularly the tibia and fibula (shin bones), while another third affect the feet, especially the tarsal, navicular, and metatarsal bones. The femur, pelvis, and spine account for most other stress fractures, although some athletes who participate in sports that involve forceful overhand throwing may develop stress fractures in the arms.

## *Causes and Risk Factors*

The most common cause of stress fractures is repetitive stress from the feet striking a hard surface while running or jumping. As a result, stress fractures often affect distance runners, track and field athletes, tennis players, basketball players, dancers, gymnasts, and military recruits. Some factors that may increase the risk of stress fractures include rapidly increasing in the duration or intensity of training, changing to an unfamiliar surface, wearing worn-out shoes or other improper equipment, using poor biomechanics, and allowing insufficient rest time between workouts or competitions. Some studies

"Leg Stress Fractures," © 2017 Omnigraphics. Reviewed June 2017.

suggest that a diet low in calcium can also make people more vulnerable to stress fractures.

Although stress fractures can affect anyone, women and girls are statistically more likely to experience them than men and boys. Doctors attribute this gender difference to the "female athlete triad," which is comprised of three conditions that sometimes occur together in elite female athletes: eating disorders (such as anorexia or bulimia); infrequent or absent menstrual periods (amenorrhea); and loss of bone mass (osteoporosis). Eating disorders combined with excessive training can cause significant weight loss, which decreases production of the hormone estrogen and leads to amenorrhea. Low estrogen, in turn, reduces the body's ability to process calcium, which leads to osteoporosis. The combination of these factors increases the risk of stress fractures.

## Symptoms and Diagnosis

The main symptom of stress fractures is pain during activity that becomes less noticeable with rest. A lower-leg stress fracture in its early stages is often referred to as "shin splints," a generalized pain in the shin bone that appears during or after an intense training session. The pain occurs as the muscles tug repeatedly on the points where they are attached to the tibia. Over time, the constant pulling from overuse of the muscles can cause a tiny crack to form in the bone. When fractures begin to appear, the pain will usually worsen and become concentrated in a smaller area.

Diagnosis of a stress fracture typically involves taking X-rays of the affected area. If the fractures are too small to appear on traditional X-rays, the doctor may follow up with additional diagnostic imaging tests, such as magnetic resonance imaging (MRI) or computed tomography (CT) scans.

## Treatment

The main treatment for stress fractures is rest. Athletes must take time off from the sport or activity that caused the problem in order to give the fracture a chance to heal. The length of time required depends on the bone that has sustained the injury. Most bones require four to six weeks, but some may require eight weeks or more. In many cases, the bone is immobilized in a cast or brace to provide stability during the healing process, and the athlete must use crutches or special shoe inserts in order to reduce stress on the bone. Some studies suggest that using an electrical bone stimulator device can speed the healing process.

It is important to avoid returning to action before the bone is fully healed, because re-injury to the same area can lead to chronic problems that resist treatment. In many cases, athletes can maintain their fitness level through cross-training activities that do not aggravate the stress fracture, such swimming, biking, or training on an elliptical machine.

## Prevention

The following suggestions can help athletes prevent stress fractures:

- If an activity causes pain, stop and rest for a few days until the pain subsides.

- Rather than concentrating on a single sport, use cross-training to accomplish fitness goals.

- Start new activities slowly and increase the duration and intensity gradually over time.

- Use proper equipment and replace running shoes often.

- Eat a healthy diet that is high in calcium and vitamin D.

### References

1. Fullem, Brian. "A Stress Fracture Primer," *Runner's World,* April 2000.

2. Patel, Deepak S., Matt Roth, and Neha Kapil. "Stress Fractures: Diagnosis, Treatment, and Prevention," *American Family Physician,* January 1, 2011.

3. "Stress Fractures," Ortho Info, October 2007.

Chapter 44

# Medial Tibial Stress Syndrome (Shin Splints)

Medial tibial stress syndrome, commonly called shin splints, is characterized by inflammation of the muscles, tendons, and bone tissue around the tibia, the larger of the two bones in the lower leg below the knee. Although most common among runners, shin splints can be caused by any vigorous sports activity or a sudden increase in the intensity of your training routine. Shin splints may also be caused by hyperpronation of the foot. Commonly called "flat feet," hyperpronation causes an individual's weight to shift from the heel to the forefeet. This in turn, places a stress on the muscles, tendons, and ligaments of the foot, shin, and knee and precipitates overuse injuries in high impact sports such as running, basketball, and soccer.

## Risk Factors

Runners, gymnasts, and military recruits are most commonly affected by shin splints, but even walkers can develop shin splints, especially if they walk too much, or too fast. Athletes who start a new program and those who rapidly increase the duration and intensity of activity are also at risk for developing shin splints. Certain preexisting conditions such as weak core muscles and muscle imbalance can also trigger shin splints as can flat feet and high foot arches. Training on

"Medial Tibial Stress Syndrome (Shin Splints)," © 2017 Omnigraphics. Reviewed June 2017.

hard, uneven surfaces, such as concrete or wearing improper, worn out shoes that do not provide arch support can also cause shin splints or exacerbate the condition.

## Symptoms

Tenderness and pain along the shin bone in one or both legs caused by inflammation of the periosteum (the connective tissue sheath around the tibia) and the soft tissues surrounding it are typical of a shin splint. What begins as a dull, diffuse ache in the lower leg during exercise and improves considerably with cessation of activity may progress to sharp, severe pain which persists even during inactivity. In extreme cases, untreated shin splints can lead to stress fractures of the tibia. This may show up as acute, focal pain that makes it difficult to continue any activity.

## Diagnosis

A shin splint is usually diagnosed on the basis of a physical examination and medical history. However, the doctor may order imaging tests to eliminate other possible causes including peripheral vascular disease, exertional compartment syndrome, or tendinitis. If the doctor suspects the shin splint has progressed to a stress fracture, he may order magnetic resonance imaging (MRI) to evaluate the extent of tibial injury and any associated soft tissue injury.

## Treatment

Conservative treatment options for shin splints include rest and ice. Rest is regarded as the most important treatment during the acute phase of injury and depending on the severity of condition, patients may be advised cessation of activity for 2–6 weeks. NSAIDs (nonsteroidal anti-inflammatory drugs) and Acetaminophen are prescribed for pain relief. Applying an ice pack for 15–20 minutes at a time is advised several times a day. An elastic compression bandage around the shin may also be useful in bringing down the swelling.

The second phase of treatment focuses on modifying training routines and correcting biomechanical abnormalities such as flat foot. Physical therapists and podiatrists can also work with athletes to formulate an appropriate rehabilitation plan to enable their return to sports. The plan can involve low-impact exercises; gait retraining; proper technique; and correct warm-up routines. Return to activity at a lower level intensity is the most important aspect of a proper rehabilitation plan. Calf exercises to strengthen the calf muscles and prevent muscle fatigue improve endurance. Cross-training exercises such as swimming and cycling can also be added to the rehab regimen. At the same time care should be taken to scale back any activity that exacerbates the condition.

## Athletic Footwear and Orthotics

Appropriate footwear may be required to reduce load on the shin, and some athletes, especially those with excessive pronation or fallen arches, may benefit from custom-made orthotics which can help stabilize the foot and ankle.

## Surgery

The majority of shin splint cases are cured or improve significantly with conservative treatment, and surgery is considered only in cases that do not benefit from conservative management. Fasciotomy, in which an incision is made in the fascia—the tissue covering the calf muscle sheath—can be helpful when the shin splint is caused by a damaged fascia. Surgery may also be used to treat shin splints caused by the inflammation of the periosteum, and the procedure involves stripping of the periosteum.

If the shin splint has progressed to a high risk stress fracture, surgery with intramedullary nail placement (a metal rod placed in the cavity of a bone) is considered. Returning to sports after surgery usually takes many months. The surgeon has to determine, with the help of imaging tests, if the fracture has healed before he or she can allow the athlete to bear weight. An extensive rehabilitation program to rebuild strength and regain full weight bearing precedes the athlete's gradual return to sports.

### References

1.  "Shin Splints," American Academy of Orthopaedic Surgeons (AAOS), 2012.

2.  "Shin Splints," Mayo Clinic, 2016.

3.  "Medial Tibial Stress Syndrome: Conservative Treatment Options," National Library of Medicine (NLM), 2009.

Chapter 45

# Achilles Tendon Injuries

## What Is Achilles Tendon?

The Achilles tendon, the largest tendon in the human body, lies at the back of the ankle and links the calf muscles to the heel bone. When the muscles contract, the tendon tightens and pulls on the heel, enabling us to point our toes and stand on tiptoe. The Achilles tendon is also used for all types of motion, such as walking, running and jumping. It can withstand large stresses, but a sudden strain can cause a tear or rupture. Many injuries occur in middle age while participating in recreational sports like tennis, volleyball or basketball. Achilles tendon ruptures are serious injuries that typically require surgery and many weeks of recovery.

## Achilles Tendinitis

Achilles tendon injuries involve an irritation, stretch, or tear to the tendon connecting the calf muscle to the back of the heel. Achilles tendinitis is a common overuse injury, but can also be caused by tight

This chapter contains text excerpted from the following sources: Text under the heading "What Is Achilles Tendon?" is excerpted from "Sex Differences in Achilles Tendon Properties May Explain Why Ruptures Occur More Often in Men," National Institute of Arthritis and Musculoskeletal and Skin Diseases (NIAMS), December 2016; Text beginning with the heading "Achilles Tendinitis" is excerpted from "Questions and Answers about Bursitis and Tendinitis," National Institute of Arthritis and Musculoskeletal and Skin Diseases (NIAMS), February 2017.

or weak calf muscles or any condition that causes the tendon to become less flexible and more rigid, such as reactive arthritis or normal aging. Achilles tendon injuries can happen to anyone who regularly participates in an activity that causes the calf muscle to contract, like climbing stairs or using a stair-stepper, but are most common in middle-aged "weekend warriors" who may not exercise regularly. Among professional athletes, most Achilles injuries seem to occur in quick-acceleration or jumping sports like football, tennis, and basketball, and almost always end the season's competition for the athlete.

Achilles tendinitis can be a chronic condition. It can also cause what appears to be a sudden injury. Tendinitis is the most common factor contributing to Achilles tendon tears. When a tendon is weakened by age or overuse, trauma can cause it to rupture. These injuries can be so sudden and agonizing that they have been known to bring down charging professional football players in shocking fashion.

## How Is the Condition Diagnosed?

Diagnosis of tendinitis begins with a medical history and physical examination. The patient will describe the pain and circumstances in which pain occurs. The location and onset of pain, whether it varies in severity throughout the day, and the factors that relieve or aggravate the pain are all important diagnostic clues. Therapists and physicians will use manual tests called selective tissue tension tests to determine which tendon is involved, and then will palpate (a form of touching the tendon) specific areas of the tendon to pinpoint the area of inflammation. X-rays do not show tendons or bursae, but may be helpful in ruling out bone problems or arthritis. In the case of a torn tendon, X-rays may help show which tendon is affected. The doctor may also use magnetic resonance imaging (MRI) to confirm a partial or total tear. MRIs detect both bone and soft tissues like muscles, tendons and their coverings (sheaths), and bursae.

To rule out infection, the doctor may remove and test fluid from the inflamed area.

## What Kind of Healthcare Professional Treats This Condition?

A primary care physician or a physical therapist can treat the common causes of tendinitis. Complicated cases or those resistant to conservative therapies may require referral to a specialist, such as an orthopaedist or rheumatologist.

## How Is Tendinitis Treated?

Treatment focuses on healing the injured tendon. The first step in treating this condition is to reduce pain and inflammation with rest, compression, elevation, and anti-inflammatory medicines such as aspirin, naproxen, or ibuprofen. Ice may also be used in acute injuries, but most cases of tendinitis are considered chronic, and ice is not helpful. When ice is needed, an ice pack can be applied to the affected area for 15 to 20 minutes every 4 to 6 hours for 3 to 5 days. Longer use of ice and a stretching program may be recommended by a healthcare provider.

Activity involving the affected joint is also restricted to encourage healing and prevent further injury.

Protective devices, such as foot orthoses, may temporarily reduce stress to the affected tendon and facilitate quicker healing times, while allowing general activity levels to continue as usual. Gentle stretching and strengthening exercises are added gradually. Massage of the soft tissue may be helpful. These may be preceded or followed by use of an ice pack. If there is no improvement, the doctor may inject a corticosteroid medicine into the area surrounding the inflamed bursa or tendon. Although corticosteroid injections are a common treatment, they must be used with caution because they may lead to weakening or rupture of the tendon. If there is still no improvement after 6 to 12 months, the doctor may perform either arthroscopic or open surgery to repair damage and relieve pressure on the tendons and bursae. After surgery the patient will wear a cast or brace or immobilizing device for 3 to 6 weeks and use crutches. For a partial tear, the doctor might apply a cast without performing surgery.

Chapter 46

# Ankle Injuries

## Chapter Contents

# Section 46.1

# *Ankle Sprains*

This section contains text excerpted from the following sources:
Text in this section begins with excerpts from "Ankle Injuries and
Disorders," U.S. National Library of Medicine (NLM), National
Institutes of Health (NIH), March 17, 2016; Text under the heading
"Risk Factors" is excerpted from "Balance Problems after Unilateral
Lateral Ankle Sprains," U.S. Department of Veterans Affairs (VA),
December 2006. Reviewed June 2017; Text beginning with the
heading "Symptoms" is excerpted from "Protocols for Injuries to
the Foot and Ankle," Rhode Island Judiciary, U.S. Department of
Justice (DOJ), May 5, 2009. Reviewed June 2017.

Your ankle bone and the ends of your two lower leg bones make up
the ankle joint. Your ligaments, which connect bones to one another,
stabilize and support it. Your muscles and tendons move it. The most
common ankle problems are sprains and fractures. A sprain is an
injury to the ligaments. It may take a few weeks to many months to
heal completely.

## *Risk Factors*

Ankle sprains are the most common acute pathology seen in athletic
activities. Up to one-sixth of all time lost from sports is because of this
type of injury. Sixteen percent of all sports injuries are ankle ligament
sprains. The cost for treatment and rehabilitation of these injuries is
significant. Reducing the incidence of ankle ligament injuries depends
on identifying the conditions under which such injuries occur (e.g.,
extrinsic variables, such as height and ankle-specific measures, that
might predispose athletes to such injuries). Many researchers have
reported that individuals with a history of ankle sprains are more
susceptible to subsequent ankle sprains or chronic ankle instability.
Studies show that over 73 percent of ankle sprains occur in ankles
that had previously been sprained. Therefore, previously sprained
ankles must have some risk factors that cause them to be recurrently
sprained. Numerous factors and mechanisms are thought to contribute to this increased ankle sprain occurrence. Some of these factors

are instability, muscle weakness, limited mobility of the ankle joint, problems related to footwear, and damage to the proprioceptors in the ligaments of the ankle.

## Symptoms

The patient typically presents acutely after an accident or fall with immediate pain and swelling at the injury site, with often the inability to ambulate. Obtaining an accurate history is important, in particular the mechanism of injury. Ankle sprains typically occur after an inversion of the foot ("rolling in," "rolled over"). The patient complains of pain and inability to ambulate.

## Diagnosis

Radiography: Three view X-rays (AP, Mortise, and Lateral) should be obtained of the ankle to evaluate for injury. Stress views and weight bearing views can often be helpful to evaluate for gross ligamentous instability. Repeat X-rays 2–3 weeks after injury can be helpful in identifying stress fractures or unstable ligamentous injuries in those patients who fail to improve after a period of activity modification.

## Treatment Based On Injury Type

### Anatomy of the Ankle

Stability of the ankle is made possible by both bony congruence (the fit of the talus within the distal tibia and fibula) as well as by the integrity of the ligaments, muscles, and tendons which surround the ankle. The ligaments and bones represent the static stabilizers (as they are fixed) and the muscles and tendons represent the dynamic stabilizers (as they move). The lateral side of the ankle is stabilized by the lateral collateral ligament (LCL) complex, the fibula and syndesmosis, and the peroneal tendons. The LCL complex consists of the anterior talo-fibular ligament, the calcaneo-fibular ligament, and the posterior talo-fibular ligament. The medial side of the ankle is stabilized by the deltoid ligament, the medial malleolus, the posterior tibial tendon, flexor digitorum longus tendon, and the flexor hallucis longus tendon. The deltoid ligament consists of superficial and deep layers which work in concert to stabilize the medial side of the ankle.

## *Grading of Ankle Sprains*

The most common ligament injured in the typical inversion ankle sprain is the anterior talo-fibular ligament, followed by the calcaneo-fibular ligament, the posterior talo-fibular ligament, and finally the deltoid ligament.

Ankle sprains are graded 1–3.

Acute surgical repair is NOT indicated, even with MRI confirmed complete ligament rupture. Patients with clinical ankle instability after months of rehabilitation MAY warrant surgical reconstruction.

1. **Grade 1 Sprain:** Microtearing of the collateral ligaments about the ankle, without any appreciable ankle joint laxity on exam. Treated with RICE protocol (Rest, Ice, Compressive Dressing (splint), Elevation). Typically resolves within 1–2 weeks.

2. **Grade 2 Sprain:** Complete tearing of some of the collateral ligaments of the ankle, with some laxity noted on physical exam. Treated with RICE protocol, immobilization with an ankle brace or CAM walker boot, and early mobilization with Physical Therapy. Typically resolved in 2–4 weeks.

3. **Grade 3 Sprain:** Complete rupture of the collateral ligaments of the ankle (usually medial or lateral side), with gross instability on examination. Acute surgical repair is NOT indicated. Treatment requires immobilization in a short leg cast or CAM walker boot for 2–3 weeks, followed by 3–6 weeks of Physical Therapy. Grade 3 sprains can potentially go on to gross instability that requires long-term bracing, rehabilitation, or surgical reconstruction.

## *Chronic Ankle Instability*

Ankles which are chronically unstable after 2–3 months of rehabilitation and bracing warrant further workup with stress X-rays and/or MRI to evaluate for intra-articular Osteochondral defects. Based on functional complaints, physical exam, and diagnostic tests, reconstructive surgery may be required for functional recovery. Postoperatively, patients are typically immobilized with a cast or CAM walker for 4–6 weeks, followed by a functional rehabilitation and Proprioceptive training program for another 4–6 weeks.

## *Return to Activity*

For all of the above, return to sedentary work is possible as early as 1–2 weeks after injury or reconstructive surgery. Return to full function is based on completion of a functional rehabilitation and Proprioceptive training program.

# Section 46.2

# *Ankle Instability*

Text in this section is from "Ankle Instability," © 2017 American Orthopaedic Foot & Ankle Society®. Reprinted with permission.

## *Overview*

Ankle sprains are among the most common musculoskeletal ailments treated. The incidence in the general public is 2.15 per 1000 persons per year. While the vast majority of patients go on to heal without long term sequelae, some may go on to develop chronic ankle instability. Ankle instability is a debilitating condition incorporating recurrent sprains, persistent pain and repeated instances of giving way. The condition is multifactorial with contributions from static alignment, muscle weakness, poor proprioception, and ligamentous injury. When left untreated, this condition decreases one's level of function and quality of life with the potential to lead to arthritis and chronic pain.

## *Anatomy*

The ankle joint consists of the articulation between the tibia, fibula and dome of the talus. The high degree of congruency confers stability to the ankle but the complex interplay between the surrounding ligaments, as well as the overall alignment of the foot and ankle, is critical to stability. The lateral ligament complex includes the anterior talofibular ligament (ATFL), the calcaneofibular ligament (CFL), and the posterior talofibular ligament (PTFL) while medially stability is imparted by the deltoid ligament.

## Biomechanics

Ankle stability relies on both osseous, ligamentous and tendinous structures. Static stabilizers are the osseus and ligamentous structures. Tendons provide dynamic stabilization, namely the peroneal tendons as they relate to lateral instability. The congruency of the ankle joint imparts a high degree of stability. Malalignment of the ankle due to hindfoot valgus or cavovarus has been correlated with ankle instability however it is at the level of the ligaments that primary stability occurs. The ATFL primarily resists translational laxity of the talus in the sagittal plane. It has been demonstrated that the ATFL has the lowest threshold for failure and thus is the most commonly injured ligament. The CFL resists excessive supination at both the mortise and the subtalar joint. The PTFL is a robust ligament with a broad surface conferring a high tensile strength. It provides resistance to inversion and internal rotation. Injury to the PTFL is the least likely to occur.

## Pathogenesis

Ankle instability arises from the same mechanism as that of simple ankle sprains. The lateral ligament complex – in particular the ATFL and CFL – are vulnerable to inversion injuries. Most patients go on to heal with limited long term sequelae however some patients exhibit chronic symptoms related to functional and mechanical changes produced by an acute injury. Mechanical factors contributing to instability include attenuation of ligaments resulting in laxity, synovial changes and degenerative changes. Functional factors contributing to instability include alteration in proprioception, neuromuscular control, postural control and the resultant strength deficits after sustaining an ankle sprain. The end result is a propensity for recurrent ankle sprains, persistent pain, and muscular weakness.

## Clinical Presentation

Patients with ankle arthritis present with pain and swelling. In general, one should investigate for a history of trauma, particularly since the soft tissue complications after surgery are related to either previous injury or surgery. Patients should be asked about the history of an open fracture or postoperative infection. It is also important to note multiple sprains or fracture and whether patients have a feeling of instability in the ankle joint.

432

Patients with ankle instability present with persistent pain, recurrent sprains, and a feeling of giving way. Patients should be queried about a history of ankle sprains, previous treatment of their ankle, and any surgical interventions performed.

A thorough physical exam is 96% sensitive and 84% specific in the diagnosis of chronic instability. Overall alignment should be discerned in weight bearing fashion as well as a thorough neurovascular exam to look for any underlying cause of instability. Lateral sided ankle tenderness, range of motion, and provocative tests including anterior drawer testing and the talar tilt test aid in the diagnosis. Physical examination should include specific assessment for hindfoot alignment, equinus contracture and generalized signs of hypermobility (such as Beighton's). Testing proprioception with a Romberg test is helpful for diagnosis as well as guiding treatment.

## Imaging Studies

Plain films of the ankle are the first line for imaging studies. Weight-bearing radiographs are imperative to assess the overall alignment of the ankle and foot. Stress radiographs comparing the affected side to the unaffected sign are the gold standard in diagnosis mechanical stability. A difference of >3mm in anterior drawer and >3 degrees on talar tilt is significant for instability. While plain films are limited in assessing the soft tissue, osseous pathology including fractures and arthritis can be seen.

Ultrasound can be utilized to diagnose tears in the ATFL and CFL although this modality is highly user dependent and studies suggest a thorough physical exam is superior in both specificity and sensitivity.

MRI is a useful adjunct in assessing the soft tissue structures as well as chondral injury. Without dynamic imaging studies MRI is limited in making a diagnosis of instability but changes in ligamentous morphology can be appreciated. There is utility for MRI in preoperative planning for patients who fail conservative management.

## Treatment

After a diagnosis of ankle instability is established, non-operative treatment is the first line of therapy. Strength training and proprioception instruction are used, focusing on taking the ankle through a full range of normal motion. A number of different braces are available to stabilize the ankle however none address the underlying pathology of ankle instability. A role for bracing may exist in conjunction with rehabilitation as demands on the ankle are increased.

If after a course of adequate rehabilitation instability still exists, surgical intervention may be warranted. Numerous surgical treatments exist but can be grossly categorized as either an anatomic repair or tenodesis stabilization.

The goal of anatomic repair is to restore normal anatomy and biomechanics while maintaining ankle motion. The modified Brostrom repair is the most commonly utilized anatomic repair. Imbrication of the ATFL and CFL are followed by fortification with a mobilized portion of the inferior extensor retinaculum.

Tenodesis stabilization restricts laxity and pathologic motion but ignores the underlying ligamentous pathology causing the instability. Stabilization is achieved at the expense of altering normal ankle and hindfoot biomechanics. The Christman-Snook procedure involves weaving a split peroneus brevis tendon through the calcaneus and talus, attempting to replicate the path of the ATFL and CFL. By splitting the peroneus brevis, it is felt some of its function is maintained. The Evans procedure involves tenodesis of the peroneus brevis to longus proximally with rerouting of the entire distal peroneus brevis tendon through a drill hole in the distal fibula. More recently described tendon autograft and allograft reconstruction techniques attempt to restore stability conferred by the ATFL and CFL while maintaining motion and avoiding sacrifice of dynamic stabilizers.

The role for arthroscopy in ankle instability has been expanding. Arthroscopy allows for the treatment of numerous conditions seen in conjunction with ankle instability including osteochondral lesions of the talus, impingement, loose bodies, adhesions, chondromalacia, and osteophytes. There has also been enthusiasm for arthroscopic repair of both the ATFL and CFL.

## *Conclusion*

Ankle sprains are among the most common musculoskeletal injuries sustained. While the vast majority go on to heal without complication, a subset of patients will go on to develop pain, recurrent sprains and a feeling of the ankle give way—all hallmarks of chronic ankle instability. While ankle instability can be a debilitating condition, knowledge of the pathology, altered biomechanics and an understanding of the treatment algorithm allows for high levels of patient satisfaction when appropriately treated.

# Section 46.3

# *Ankle Fractures*

Text in this section is from "Ankle Fractures," © 2017 American
Orthopaedic Foot & Ankle Society®. Reprinted with permission.

## Overview

Ankle fractures are one of the more common injuries encountered
by orthopaedic surgeons and can represent a significant burden in
terms of morbidity. The primary concern with these injuries is the
long-term risk of post-traumatic arthritis in the ankle. While there are
controversies about both diagnosis and treatment for some of these
injuries, ensuring the maintenance or restoration of normal anatomy
can help to reduce the risk of arthritis.

## Anatomy

The fibula and tibia come together to form the ankle mortise and
articulate with the talus. The majority of the stability of the ankle
with weight-bearing is conferred by the very congruent bony anatomy.
However, ligaments play a role in stability as well, as the large deltoid
ligament medially provides a broad connection between the medial
malleolus and the talus. On the lateral side the tibio-fibular articulation, or syndesmosis, is stabilized by the anterior and posterior inferior
tibio-fibular ligaments (AITFL and PITFL respectively), as well as
the interosseous ligament and, to a lesser degree, the interosseous
membrane extending proximally. These syndesmotic ligaments can
be injured in some ankle fractures.

## Classification

Fractures of the distal tibia and fibula as they articulate with the
talus are loosely characterized by the mechanism of injury in the sense
that rotational ankle fractures are thought of separately from axial
loading or pilon fracture type injuries. That being said, there is clearly
some overlap between the two general grouping of injuries, and some

435

injuries are hard to cleanly fit into one category. This summary will focus more on the rotational type injuries and what overlap they may have with axial loading injuries.

Ankle fractures as they are traditionally classified by Lauge-Hansen fall into a couple of different categories. Supination-external rotation (SER) fractures represent the majority of these injuries, with the supination describing the position of the foot and external rotation the applied force. In this scenario, however, it is the foot that typically remains planted while the leg internally rotates relative to the foot. The injury will often proceed in a progressive manner in which injury begins anteriorly and then proceeds clockwise around the ankle. Pronation-external rotation (PER) fractures typically begin medially and then proceed clockwise with a primary difference being that the syndesmosis is often disrupted and the fibula fracture is often a Weber C, "high" fibula fracture. Both of these fractures will often have some degree of posterior malleolus fracture in which the intact posterior-inferior tibio-fibular ligament (PITFL) pulls off a piece of bone.

Supination adduction (SAD) fractures and pronation abduction (PAB) fractures are injuries that typically proceed just in the coronal plane and do not involve rotation. SAD fractures proceed from lateral to medial and start with a low fibula fracture and then the talus can be driven into the medial shoulder of the plafond, creating a characteristic vertical medial malleolar fracture that can often have articular impaction. PAB fractures proceed from medial to lateral with fracture of the medial malleolus and then often a characteristic "high" fibula fracture with comminution. The rotational fractures and PAB injuries can also injure the syndesmosis with those injuries that have "high" fibula fractures being perhaps more likely to have syndesmotic disruption. The rotational fractures, and indeed any of these fractures, can also be influenced by the relative plantarflexion of the ankle. Posterior pilon variants in which there is some degree of posterior comminution have been described. These fractures can extend more medial or have an entirely separate posteromedial piece than the typical posterior malleolus fracture that is posterolateral.

## Clinical Presentation/Exam

Ankle fractures represent a broad spectrum of injury and fitting that into a single clinical presentation is not possible. That being said, patients will typically have swelling, bruising, and global pain about the ankle. Swelling will often not reach its zenith until about 72 hours after injury. The usual physical examination will be limited by pain, and palpating specific structures (i.e. the deltoid ligament) has been shown not to correlate well with injury. Therefore, especially in distal fibular fractures in which it is difficult to tell if there is a medial injury (SER 4 equivalent fractures), external rotation stress radiographs can assist with clarifying the extent of injury.

## Imaging

Plain radiographs with three views of the ankle will provide the most information as the initial diagnostic procedure. A CT scan may also be indicated, especially if there is a posterior malleolar fracture present on X-ray, as the size of the posterior malleolar bone fragment can be very difficult to accurately predict from a plain radiograph. MRI perhaps has less utility for most ankle fractures, although some surgeons suggest that it can provide insight into the ligamentous status of the injured ankle. As noted above, stress radiographs are warranted if there is suspicion of a syndesmosis injury.

## Decision for Surgery

The goal of ankle surgery is restoration of normal anatomy if possible. Approximately 70% of people with ankle arthritis have a history of significant ankle injury. This risk is thought to be related to two things: the impaction at the time of the injury and the possibility of malunion leading to uneven articular loading. The impaction at the time of the injury is a function of the injury itself and cannot be changed with or without surgery. Malunion, however, can often be avoided by fixing the injury surgically. However, we do not operate on all ankle fractures. Ultimately, the decision comes down to whether the injury is felt to have sufficient instability that there is risk of any displacement with treatment by closed means. From a practical standpoint most bimalleolar and trimalleolar fractures are unstable, and, therefore, will benefit from surgical treatment. Rarely, patients will have these injuries (i.e. bimalleolar or trimalleolar fractures) that do not show any displacement, and these injuries can be treated nonoperatively. For isolated distal fibula fractures, as above, a manual radiographic stress test is often performed to assess the structural integrity of the deltoid ligament with medial opening necessitating surgical fixation.

Two areas of fairly intense debate amongst surgeons have been the posterior malleolus and the syndesmosis. The two are related to some degree in the sense that the fractured posterior malleolus almost always has an attached, intact PITFL, which is the posterior component of the syndesmosis and its stoutest constituent. Perhaps the principle difficulty with the syndesmosis simply lies in diagnosing insufficiency of the syndesmotic ligament complex. To be sure, certain fractures alert surgeons to the potential for injury, although the reality is that the surgeon often does not know whether the syndesmosis is unstable until intraoperative stress tests are performed. Even the intraoperative stress test can be somewhat subjective, and one must keep in mind that syndesmotic instability can occur in any plane. For the posterior malleolus many surgeons rely on the size of the fragment as the decision point for whether the fragment should be fixed. However, when a syndesmotic injury is present, the need for syndesmotic screws can sometimes be obviated by fixing the posterior malleolus fracture and reestablishing the PITFL.

## Treatment

Once the decision for surgery is made, treatment most often consists of fixing the bony injuries. In a fibula fracture with deltoid ligament insufficiency, the fibula alone is often all that is fixed, providing a lateral buttress to hold the talus underneath the plafond. Repair of the deltoid ligament during the same surgery is controversial. In a bimalleolar fracture most surgeons will fix both the medial and lateral malleoli. In a trimalleolar fracture the medial and lateral malleoli will also be fixed, but fixation of the posterior malleolus is controversial as above. If a syndesmotic injury is present, screws or strong suture that hold the tibia and fibula together, are often required. However, as above, these screws may be obviated if the PITFL can be reestablished.

Post-operative treatment typically involves a period of non-weight-bearing, with a majority of surgeons favoring at least 6 weeks, although there is little consensus about what time period is most appropriate. With syndesmotic injury the time period is often extended to some degree. Once the patient is removed from the post-operative splint and prior to weight-bearing, the patient is allowed to work on ROM exercises, which help provide the cartilage with nutrition and can potentially decrease intraarticular scar tissue.

## Conclusion

Ankle fractures as a whole represent a significant potential cause of morbidity. However, with timely and appropriate treatment, long term sequelae can often be avoided, and the patient can return to his or her previous lifestyle without restriction.

Chapter 47

# Injuries to the Feet

## Chapter Contents

# Section 47.1

# *Plantar Fasciitis (Heel Spurs)*

"Plantar Fasciitis (Heel Spurs)," © 2017 Omnigraphics.
Reviewed June 2017.

The plantar facia is a ligament that runs along the bottom of the foot, from the heel to the base of the toes. It provides support to the arch and helps absorb shock from walking, running, or jumping. Plantar fasciitis is a condition in which the plantar fascia becomes irritated and inflamed, causing pain in the heel. It is very common, affecting about 10 percent of all people at some point in their lives. Although it occurs most frequently among middle-aged people—especially women—it can also be related to overuse or repetitive stress among younger people who are active in sports.

## *Causes*

Plantar fasciitis occurs when the ligament is subjected to strain or injury. The following situations increase the risk of developing the condition:

- having orthopedic issues like high arches or flat feet

- wearing shoes that are worn out, fit poorly, or have insufficient cushioning or arch support

- standing, walking, or running on hard surfaces for long periods of time

- rapidly increasing the intensity, distance, or duration of physical activity

- being overweight or experiencing sudden weight gain, such as during pregnancy

- using poor biomechanics or having an abnormal walking or running gait

- having tight Achilles tendons or calf muscles.

## Symptoms and Diagnosis

Pain on the bottom of the foot, usually on or just in front of the heel, is the most common symptom of plantar fasciitis. Many people find that the pain is most intense first thing in the morning, when they get out of bed and try to walk. Although the pain generally gets better during the day, it may grow worse again following physical activity. Stiffness in the foot may make it difficult to climb stairs or stand on tiptoes. The condition may affect only one foot or both feet at the same time.

To diagnose plantar fasciitis, the doctor will take a medical history, including questions about the symptoms the patient is experiencing, any injuries to the foot or heel, and the physical activities the patient engages in regularly. The doctor will also conduct a physical examination of the feet, checking for redness, swelling, and tenderness in the plantar fascia when flexing the foot or pointing the toe. In some cases, the doctor will also order diagnostic imaging tests, such as an X-ray or magnetic resonance imaging (MRI) scan, to rule out other types of foot injuries that could cause similar symptoms, such as a fracture.

## Treatment

Many people see improvement in the symptoms of plantar fasciitis by using some combination of the following conservative approaches to treatment:

- Avoid activities that cause pain—such as standing or running on hard surfaces—for several weeks;

- Reduce inflammation by applying ice to the heel regularly and taking anti-inflammatory medications;

- Gently stretch the feet and Achilles tendons several times per day, beginning first thing in the morning before getting out of bed;

- Wear well-fitting shoes with cushioned soles and good arch support.

If conservative treatment approaches do not relieve symptoms, there are a few medical treatments available for plantar fasciitis. However, most of these treatments are relatively unproven, so they are mainly tried in difficult cases. For instance, a podiatrist can provide orthotic shoe inserts or heel cups to support the arches or correct other foot problems that may be contributing to the condition. The doctor may also provide a splint to be worn overnight that holds the Achilles tendon and plantar fascia in a slightly stretched position. In some cases, the patient may be fitted with a walking brace or cast to cushion, protect, and rest the plantar fascia.

For patients with severe heel pain that continues for more than six months despite conservative treatments, the doctor may try an experimental approach called extracorporeal shock-wave therapy, which involves using an ultrasound device to deliver high-energy sound waves to the plantar fascia to promote healing. A steroid injection may also help relieve heel pain, although this treatment approach carries the risk of rupturing the plantar fascia. Surgery is considered the treatment of last resort for plantar fasciitis. The procedure involves partially detaching or releasing the plantar fascia from the heel bone and removing any bony growths known as heel spurs that may be present. Potential complications include weakness in the arch of the foot, damage to nerves in the foot, and loss of foot function.

## Recovery and Prevention

Fortunately, most people recover from plantar fasciitis with rest and conservative treatment, although it may take several months for the symptoms to resolve. Physical therapy can speed the recovery process by stretching and strengthening muscles in the feet and lower legs, as well as correcting foot and gait problems that may have contributed to the condition.

Left untreated, however, plantar fasciitis can lead to chronic heel pain and a related condition called heel spurs. As the plantar fascia ligament is overstretched and irritated, the heel bone may respond by building up calcium deposits at the point where it attaches. Over time, these bony protrusions can erode the fatty tissue lining the bottom of the heel. Heel spurs can cause stabbing pain, damage to the foot, and gait changes that may in turn cause injury to the ankles, knees, hips, or back. It is important to note that plantar fasciitis is not typically caused by heel spurs, though, and that heel spurs are painless for most people.

The following steps can help prevent the development of plantar fasciitis:

- Wear shoes with cushioned heels and good arch support;

- Replace running shoes regularly;

- Warm up properly and stretch the Achilles tendon before exercise;

- Avoid prolonged standing, walking, or running on hard surfaces;

- Lose weight if needed.

### References

1. Case-Lo, Christine. "Plantar Fasciitis," Healthline, February 16, 2016.

2. Imm, Nick. "Heel and Foot Pain (Plantar Fasciitis)," *Patient,* February 2, 2016.

3. "Plantar Fasciitis: Topic Overview," WebMD, 2015.

# Section 47.2

# *Metatarsalgia*

"Metatarsalgia," © 2017 Omnigraphics. Reviewed June 2017.

The metatarsals are five long bones that form the arch in the middle of the foot. They connect to the toe bones at the ball of the foot. Metatarsalgia is a condition in which the heads of the metatarsal bones near the toe joints rub together, putting pressure on nerves and causing pain and inflammation in the ball of the foot. It is sometimes referred to as a stone bruise because the stabbing pain may resemble having a rock in the shoe. Metatarsalgia often develops as an overuse injury in athletes who participate in sports that involve running and jumping, although it can also affect people who have underlying foot issues or wear improperly fitting shoes.

## Causes and Risk Factors

Several different activity and lifestyle factors appear to be related to the development of metatarsalgia. In addition, certain physical traits and medical conditions appear to increase people's risk. Some of the most common causes and risk factors include the following:

- participating in high-impact sports, such as distance running or dance;

- wearing shoes that fit poorly, lack support and cushioning, or place pressure on the ball of the foot, such as high heels, pointy or box-toe shoes, and cleats or spikes;

- having feet with high arches or a second toe that is longer than the big toe;

- having deformities of the feet, such as hammertoes or bunions;

- being overweight;

- reaching middle age, when the pad of fat that protects the ball of the foot naturally becomes thinner and provides less protection from impact;

- developing stress fractures in the metatarsals, which can lead to metatarsalgia when people adjust the weight distribution in their feet to compensate;

- having inflammatory conditions such as gout or rheumatoid arthritis;

- having diabetes, which can irritate nerves in the feet;

- developing Morton's neuroma, a condition in which fibrous tissue grows between the metatarsal heads.

## Symptoms and Diagnosis

The main symptom of metatarsalgia is pain in the ball of the foot. The pain may be described as sharp, shooting, aching, burning, or like having a rock in the shoe. It typically becomes worse upon standing, walking, running, jumping, or flexing the feet. Walking barefoot on a hard surface may be particularly painful. Some people also experience numbness or tingling in the toes. The symptoms typically appear gradually and get worse over time, until the pain makes it difficult for athletes to compete to their level of ability.

To diagnose metatarsalgia, the doctor will begin by asking questions about the patient's symptoms, lifestyle and activities, and usual footwear. The doctor may also watch the patient walk on a treadmill to assess their normal gait and determine whether the placement of the feet is putting excess pressure on the metatarsal heads. The doctor may order blood tests to see whether the patient has an underlying medical condition that increases the risk of metatarsalgia, such as gout, diabetes, or arthritis. Finally, the doctor is likely to order diagnostic imaging tests such as X-rays or a magnetic resonance imaging (MRI) scan to check for stress fractures or structural problems in the foot.

## Treatment

Most cases of metatarsalgia respond to conservative methods of treatment, such as the following:

* taking a break from high-impact sports and other activities that cause pain, and switch to low-impact cross-training options like swimming or bicycling to maintain fitness;
* applying ice to the affected foot several times per day;
* elevating the foot whenever possible to reduce swelling;
* taking anti-inflammatory medications to relieve pain and swelling;
* avoiding wearing high heels or shoes that do not fit properly;
* replacing running shoes regularly;
* using metatarsal pads, shock-absorbing insoles, or arch supports to relieve pressure on the metatarsal bones and improve foot function.

For severe cases of metatarsalgia that do not improve with conservative treatment, a doctor may try a steroid injection to help alleviate pain and inflammation. Surgery is considered a treatment of last resort for the condition. Procedures used to treat metatarsalgia may involve reshaping the metatarsal bones, releasing or removing irritated nerves between the metatarsal bones, or correcting other foot deformities that may be contributing to the condition, such as hammertoes or bunions. Left untreated, metatarsalgia can cause alterations in foot placement or gait that can lead to future problems with the ankles, knees, hips, or back.

## References

1. "Metatarsalgia," Mayo Clinic, November 4, 2016.

2. "Metatarsalgia," WebMD, 2017.

3. Nordqvist, Christian. "Metatarsalgia: Causes, Symptoms, and Treatments," *Medical News Today,* June 18, 2015.

Section 47.3

# *Sesamoiditis and Sesamoid Fracture*

"Sesamoiditis and Sesamoid Fracture," © 2017
Omnigraphics. Reviewed June 2017.

A sesamoid is a special type of bone that is embedded within a muscle or tendon rather than connected to another bone at a joint. Sesamoid bones appear in several parts of the human body, including the hand, wrist, knee, and foot. There are two sesamoid bones located on the underside of the ball of the foot—one on each side of the first metatarsal bone where it meets the big toe. They are embedded in the flexor hallucis brevis tendon, which helps control the up-and-down motion of the big toe. As the tendon slides over the smooth surface of the sesamoid bones, it acts like a pulley to enable the big toe to push off the ground and absorb impact from the ground while walking or running.

The sesamoid bones in the foot are vulnerable to several types of injury:

- Sesamoiditis is an overuse injury that is common among athletes who engage in sports and activities that put constant pressure or repeated force on the forefoot, such as running, dancing, or squatting in the catcher position in baseball. The rubbing of the tendon on the sesamoid bones causes irritation and chronic inflammation.

- Sesamoid fracture is when one or both of the sesamoid bones in the foot are broken. An acute sesamoid fracture may occur due to a traumatic injury, such as falling from a height and landing on the ball of the foot, while a chronic sesamoid fracture may occur due to repetitive stress.

Turf toe is a soft tissue injury of the big toe that sometimes affects the sesamoid bones or the flexor hallucis brevis tendon. It typically occurs due to traumatic hyperextension of the big toe, and it often affects athletes who play sports on grass, like football or soccer.

## Symptoms and Diagnosis

The main symptom of sesamoid injury is pain in the ball of the foot at the base of the big toe. In sesamoiditis, the pain is likely to appear gradually over time and become worse with activity. In a sesamoid fracture, the pain is more likely to appear suddenly and be accompanied by swelling, bruising, and limited range of motion of the big toe. In turf toe, the pain and swelling may tend to affect the toe itself more than the ball of the foot.

To diagnose a sesamoid injury, the doctor will examine the foot for signs of inflammation and tenderness and assess the range of motion in the big toe. An X-ray is usually performed to check for a sesamoid fracture. In some cases, however, X-rays may not aid in diagnosis because the patient has bipartite sesamoid bones, meaning that the bones are naturally divided into two pieces. Since the sesamoid bones are so small, it can be difficult to distinguish between bipartite sesamoid bones and a sesamoid fracture. The radiologist is likely to concentrate on the edges of the bones, which tend to be smooth in a bipartite sesamoid and jagged in a fractured sesamoid. An X-ray of the other foot can also be used for comparison. Finally, the doctor may order blood tests to check for underlying medical conditions that can cause pain and inflammation in the feet, such as arthritis or gout.

## Treatment

Sesamoiditis usually improves after several weeks of conservative, noninvasive treatment. Athletes are typically advised to take a break from physical activities that cause pain, apply ice to the bottom of the foot, and use anti-inflammatory medication to relieve pain and swelling. It may also be helpful to wear low-heeled shoes with stiff soles and to insert a cushioning pad made of felt or foam rubber to reduce pressure on the ball of the foot and big toe. The toe may also be immobilized with athletic tape in a downward-bending or flexed position to promote healing.

Treatment for sesamoid fracture usually involves immobilization of the foot in a walking cast or removable fracture brace for six to eight weeks. To reduce swelling, the doctor may inject a steroid medication into the metatarsophalangeal joint at the base of the big toe.

If this conservative treatment fails to relieve pain and restore function to the foot, surgery may be necessary. The most common procedure used to treat a sesamoid fracture is sesamoidectomy, or surgical removal of the broken sesamoid bones. Surgery is considered a last resort, however, due to the risk of complications—such as damage to the soft tissues or joint capsule of the metatarsophalangeal joint—that can affect foot function. Removal of the sesamoid bones can also result in misalignment of the foot and the development of an uncomfortable foot deformity called a bunion. These large, bony lumps on the side of the foot occur when weakness in the joint causes the big toe to twist toward the middle of the foot.

### References

1. "Sesamoid Injuries," American Orthopaedic Foot and Ankle Society, 2017.

2. "Sesamoid Injuries in the Foot," Foot Health Facts, 2017.

3. Swierzewski, John J. "Sesamoiditis," Remedy's Health Communities, December 31, 1999.

## Section 47.4

# *Fifth Metatarsal Fracture*

"Fifth Metatarsal Fracture," © 2017 Omnigraphics.
Reviewed June 2017.

The metatarsals are a group of five long bones located in the fore-foot. They connect the articulating bones of the mid- and hind-foot to the phalanges (toe bones) and constitute an important weight-bearing structure. The five metatarsals are numbered from the big toe as the first, second, third, fourth and fifth metatarsal, each consisting of a body or shaft, a proximal base, and a distal head. Fractures of the metatarsal are quite common, often resulting from trauma or direct injury, such as dropping a heavy object on the foot or kicking something hard. Fractures can also result from chronic overuse or repetitive stress injury, commonly associated with high-impact sports, such as soccer, football, or running.

The fifth metatarsal, the bone that connects to the little toe, is the most commonly fractured metatarsal. Injury can occur at any point along the length of the bone and usually results from inversion (movement that tilts the foot toward the midline of the body) or dorsiflexion (backward bending of the foot). Depending on the extent and mechanism of the injury, metatarsal fractures may be closed or open. In a closed fracture, the overlying skin is intact, and there is no open wound. An open fracture, on the other hand, is accompanied by damage to skin and soft tissue and is usually associated with risk of infection. Fractures of the fifth metatarsal can also be categorized as displaced or nondisplaced. In a nondisplaced fracture, the bone maintains its alignment despite being broken into fragments. In contrast, a displaced fracture results in an incorrect alignment of the bone fragments making it more difficult to treat.

## Types of Metatarsal Fracture

Three types of fractures can occur in the fifth metatarsal:

- **Avulsion fracture.** This type of fracture usually occurs at the base of the fifth metatarsal. A violent force may cause the tendon or ligament that attaches to the base of the metatarsal to pull away a fragment from the main bone. Also called the "dancer's fracture," avulsion fractures may co-occur with ankle sprains, and ankle fractures and may need to be evaluated alongside ankle injuries to avoid a missed diagnosis. Symptoms can include ecchymosis (discoloration of skin from hemorrhage underneath), soft tissue swelling, and pain at the base of the metatarsal. Nondisplaced avulsion fractures are generally treated conservatively, and the prognosis is usually good. Displaced avulsion fractures, by and large, require surgical intervention.

- **Jones fracture.** Named after the English surgeon and Father of Modern Orthopedics, Sir Robert Jones, a Jones fracture is the most complex of the fifth metatarsal fractures and occurs within 1.5 cm of the tuberosity (a rounded bump at the end of the bone). This type of injury is ascribed to an acute trauma caused by sudden pivot-shifting with the heel off the ground and is commonly experienced in sports such as basketball, football, and tennis. Typical symptoms of Jones Fracture include the sudden onset of pain, swelling, and weight-bearing difficulty. In addition to difficulty walking, there is pain associated with other types of increased activity. One of the most significant factors that affects the treatment outcome for Jones fracture is the poor blood supply to the injured area. Some parts of the fifth metatarsal have poor vascularity and therefore a propensity for delayed healing.

- **Stress fracture.** Stress fractures are the least common type of the fifth metatarsal fractures and are precipitated by fatigue or repetitive stress, especially in young athletes. These fractures are often the result of poor conditioning, but improper technique and equipment are also risk factors for this type of injury. In those starting out a new exercise regimen, doing too much too soon can raise the risk of stress fractures significantly. Experienced athletes are also at risk when they tend to overdo training or play without giving their body a chance to recover. Although the exact mechanism of stress fractures of the fifth metatarsal remains unclear, it is believed that prolonged muscle fatigue transmits excessive forces to the surrounding bone, thereby reducing its stress-bearing capacity. Stress fractures can result in significant morbidity for athletes if diagnosis and treatment are delayed. The symptoms usually present as pain for weeks or months, with the intensity of pain increasing with weight-bearing activity.

## Diagnosis

As with any type of fracture, physical examination and patient history are the first steps in diagnosis. Physical examination focuses on external signs of injury; palpation for assessing the point of greatest pain, and neurovascular evaluation. Patient history would typically include the cause of the injury, as well as the onset and duration of symptoms.

## Imaging Tests

Radiography is the mainstay of diagnosis of fifth metatarsal injuries. While most fractures show up on X-rays, some of them may require CT (computed tomography) or MRI (magnetic resonance imaging) scans for further assessment. Metatarsal stress fractures are generally more difficult to investigate than other types of fractures, as they often don't show up on X-rays, particularly in the early stages. Consequently, a bone scan or MRI may be needed to make a stress-fracture diagnosis.

## *Treatment*

The symptoms, location, and extent of injury will determine the type of treatment for fractures of the fifth metatarsal. Typically, nonsurgical intervention is considered for nondisplaced fractures, including weight-bearing protection in a cast or CAM (controlled ankle movement) boot. Crutches may also be used to take the weight off the injured foot. Pain usually subsides within eight weeks following injury. Surgical intervention is considered for displaced fractures or those that fail to heal following conservative treatment. Surgery is generally the preferred treatment option for Jones and stress fractures in athletes who are looking for a quick return-to-play without much weight-bearing restriction. The gold standard in surgical treatment involves fixation of an intramedullary screw. With this procedure, a small incision is made on the outer side of the foot, and the fractured pieces of the bones are aligned. A hole is then drilled through the metatarsal shaft, and a surgical screw is inserted through the two ends of the fractured bone to stabilize the fracture. In some cases, the procedure may be accompanied by bone grafting to hasten bone union and reduce the risk of refracture.

### *References*

1. "Fractures of the Fifth Metatarsal," American College of Foot and Ankle Surgeons (ACFAS), n.d.

2. Johnson, Julie, MD. "Fifth Metatarsal Fractures," American Orthopaedic Foot & Ankle Society (AOFAS), June 2015.

3. Strayer, Scott M., MC, Steven G. Greece, MD, and Michael J. Petrizzi, MD. "Fractures of the Proximal Fifth Metatarsal," American Academy of Family Physicians (AAFP), May 1, 1999.

4. Bowes, Julia, MD and Richard Buckley, MD. "Fifth Metatarsal Fractures and Current Treatment," National Center for Biotechnology Information (NCBI), December 18, 2016.

Section 47.5

## *Stress Fractures of the Foot*

Text in this section is from "Stress Fractures of the Foot and Ankle," © 1995-2017 American Academy of Orthopaedic Surgeons. Reprinted with permission.

A stress fracture is a small crack in a bone, or severe bruising within a bone. Most stress fractures are caused by overuse and repetitive activity, and are common in runners and athletes who participate in running sports, such as soccer and basketball.

Stress fractures usually occur when people change their activities— such as by trying a new exercise, suddenly increasing the intensity of their workouts, or changing the workout surface (jogging on a treadmill vs. jogging outdoors). In addition, if osteoporosis or other disease has weakened the bones, just doing everyday activities may result in a stress fracture.

The weight-bearing bones of the foot and lower leg are especially vulnerable to stress fractures because of the repetitive forces they must absorb during activities like walking, running, and jumping.

Refraining from high impact activities for an adequate period of time is key to recovering from a stress fracture in the foot or ankle. Returning to activity too quickly can not only delay the healing process but also increase the risk for a complete fracture. Should a complete fracture occur, it will take far longer to recover and return to activities.

### *Description*

Stress fractures occur most often in the second and third metatarsals in the foot, which are thinner (and often longer) than the adjacent first metatarsal. This is the area of greatest impact on your foot as you push off when you walk or run.

Stress fractures are also common in the calcaneus (heel); fibula (the outer bone of the lower leg and ankle); talus (a small bone in the ankle joint); and the navicular (a bone on the top of the midfoot).

Many stress fractures are overuse injuries. They occur over time when repetitive forces result in microscopic damage to the bone. The repetitive force that causes a stress fracture is not great enough to cause an acute fracture—such as a broken ankle caused by a fall. Overuse stress fractures occur when an athletic movement is repeated so often, weight-bearing bones and supporting muscles do not have enough time to heal between exercise sessions.

Bone is in a constant state of turnover—a process called remodeling. New bone develops and replaces older bone. If an athlete's activity is too great, the breakdown of older bone occurs rapidly—it outpaces the body's ability to repair and replace it. As a result, the bone weakens and becomes vulnerable to stress fractures.

## Cause

The most common cause of stress fractures is a sudden increase in physical activity. This increase can be in the frequency of activity—such as exercising more days per week. It can also be in the duration or intensity of activity—such as running longer distances.

Even for the non athlete, a sudden increase in activity can cause a stress fracture. For example, if you walk infrequently on a day-to-day basis but end up walking excessively (or on uneven surfaces) while on a vacation, you might experience a stress fracture. A new style of shoes can lessen your foot's ability to absorb repetitive forces and result in a stress fracture.

Several other factors—from your training regimen to your diet—can increase your risk for a stress fracture.

### Bone Insufficiency

Conditions that decrease bone strength and density, such as osteoporosis, and certain long-term medications can make you more likely to experience a stress fracture-even when you are performing normal everyday activities. For example, stress fractures are more common in the winter months, when Vitamin D is lower in the body.

Studies show that female athletes are more prone to stress fractures than male athletes. This may be due, in part, to decreased bone density from a condition that doctors call the "female athlete triad." When a girl or young woman goes to extremes in dieting or exercise, three interrelated illnesses may develop: eating disorders, menstrual dysfunction, and premature osteoporosis. As a female athlete's bone mass decreases, her chances for getting a stress fracture increase.

## *Poor Conditioning*

Doing too much too soon is a common cause of stress fracture. This is often the case with individuals who are just beginning an exercise program-but it occurs in experienced athletes, as well. For example, runners who train less over the winter months may be anxious to pick up right where they left off at the end of the previous season. Instead of starting off slowly, they resume running at their previous mileage. This situation in which athletes not only increase activity levels, but push through any discomfort and do not give their bodies the opportunity to recover, can lead to stress fractures.

## *Improper Technique*

Anything that alters the mechanics of how your foot absorbs impact as it strikes the ground may increase your risk for a stress fracture. For example, if you have a blister, bunion, or tendonitis, it can affect how you put weight on your foot when you walk or run, and may require an area of bone to handle more weight and pressure than usual.

## *Change in Surface*

A change in training or playing surface, such as a tennis player going from a grass court to a hard court, or a runner moving from a treadmill to an outdoor track, can increase the risk for stress fracture.

## *Improper Equipment*

Wearing worn or flimsy shoes that have lost their shock-absorbing ability may contribute to stress fractures.

## Symptoms

The most common symptom of a stress fracture in the foot or ankle is pain. The pain usually develops gradually and worsens during weight-bearing activity. Other symptoms may include:

- Pain that diminishes during rest
- Pain that occurs and intensifies during normal, daily activities
- Swelling on the top of the foot or on the outside of the ankle
- Tenderness to touch at the site of the fracture
- Possible bruising

## First Aid

See your doctor as soon as possible if you think that you have a stress fracture in your foot or ankle. Ignoring the pain can have serious consequences. The bone may break completely.

Until your appointment with the doctor, follow the RICE protocol. RICE stands for rest, ice, compression, and elevation.

- **Rest.** Avoid activities that put weight on your foot. If you have to bear weight for any reason, make sure you are wearing a very supportive shoe. A thick-soled cork sandal is better than a thin slipper.

- **Ice.** Apply ice immediately after the injury to keep the swelling down. Use cold packs for 20 minutes at a time, several times a day. Do not apply ice directly on your skin.

- **Compression.** To prevent additional swelling, lightly wrap the area in a soft bandage.

- **Elevation.** As often as possible, rest with your foot raised up higher than your heart.

In addition, nonsteroidal anti-inflammatory drugs, or NSAIDs, such as ibuprofen or naproxen can help relieve pain and reduce swelling.

## Doctor Examination

### Physical Examination

Your doctor will discuss your medical history and general health. He or she will ask about your work, your activities, your diet, and what medications you are taking. It is important that your doctor is aware of your risk factors for stress fracture. If you have had a stress fracture before, your doctor may order a full medical work-up with laboratory tests to check for nutritional deficiencies such as low calcium or Vitamin D.

After discussing your symptoms and health history, your doctor will examine your foot and ankle. During the examination, he or she will look for areas of tenderness and apply gentle pressure directly to the injured bone. Often, the key to diagnosing a stress fracture is the patient's report of pain in response to this pressure. Pain from a stress fracture is typically limited to the area directly over the injured bone and is not generalized over the whole foot.

## Imaging Tests

Your doctor may order imaging tests to help confirm the diagnosis.

**X-rays.** X-rays provide images of dense structures, such as bone. Since a stress fracture starts as a tiny crack, it is often difficult to see on a first X-ray. The fracture may not be visible until several weeks later when it has actually started to heal. After a few weeks, a type of healing bone called callus may appear around the fracture site. In many cases, this is the point at which the fracture line actually becomes visible in the bone.

**Other imaging studies.** If your doctor suspects a stress fracture but cannot see it on an X-ray, he or she may recommend a bone scan or a magnetic resonance imaging (MRI) scan. Although a bone scan is less specific than an MRI in showing the actual location of the stress fracture, both of these types of studies are more sensitive than X-rays and can detect stress fractures earlier.

## Treatment

The goal of treatment is to relieve pain and allow the fracture to heal so that you are able to return to your activities. Following your doctor's treatment plan will help you return to activities faster and prevent further damage to the bone.

Treatment will vary depending on the location of the stress fracture and its severity. The majority of stress fractures are treated nonsurgically.

### Nonsurgical Treatment

In addition to the RICE protocol and anti-inflammatory medication, your doctor may recommend that you use crutches to keep weight off your foot until the pain subsides. Other recommendations for nonsurgical treatment may include:

**Modified activities.** It typically takes from 6 to 8 weeks for a stress fracture to heal. During that time, switch to activities that place less stress on your foot and leg. Swimming and cycling are good alternative activities. However, you should not resume any type of physical activity that involves your injured foot or ankle-even if it is low impact-without your doctor's recommendation.

**Protective footwear.** To reduce stress on your foot and leg, your doctor may recommend wearing protective footwear. This may be a stiff-soled shoe, a wooden-soled sandal, or a removable short-leg fracture brace shoe.

**Casting.** Stress fractures in the fifth metatarsal bone (on the outer side of the foot) or in the navicular or talus bones take longer to heal. Your doctor may apply a cast to your foot to keep your bones in a fixed position and to remove the stress on your involved leg.

### Surgical Treatment

Some stress fractures require surgery to heal properly. In most cases, this involves supporting the bones by inserting a type of fastener. This is called internal fixation. Pins, screws, and/or plates are most often used to hold the small bones of the foot and ankle together during the healing process.

## Recovery

In most cases, it takes from 6 to 8 weeks for a stress fracture to heal. More serious stress fractures can take longer. Although it can be hard to be sidelined with an injury, returning to activity too soon can put you at risk for larger, harder-to-heal stress fractures and an even longer down time. Reinjury could lead to chronic problems and the stress fracture might never heal properly.

Once your pain has subsided, your doctor may confirm that the stress fracture has healed by taking X-rays. A computed tomography (CT) scan can also be useful in determining healing, especially in bones where the fracture line was initially hard to see.

Once the stress fracture has healed and you are pain free, your doctor will allow a gradual return to activity. During the early phase of rehabilitation, your doctor may recommend alternating days of activity with days of rest. This gives your bone the time to grow and withstand the new demands being placed upon it. As your fitness level improves, slowly increase the frequency, duration, and intensity of your exercise.

## Prevention

The following guidelines can help you prevent stress fractures in the future:

- **Eat a healthy diet.** A balanced diet rich in calcium and Vitamin D will help build bone strength.

- **Use proper equipment.** Old or worn running shoes may lose their ability to absorb shock and can lead to injury. In general, athletic shoes should have a softer insole, and a stiffer outer sole.

- **Start new activity slowly.** Gradually increase your time, speed, and distance. In most cases, a 10 percent increase per week is appropriate.

- **Cross train.** Vary your activities to help avoid overstressing one area of your body. For example, alternate a high-impact sport like running with lower-impact sports like swimming or cycling.

- **Add strength training to your workout.** One of the best ways to prevent early muscle fatigue and the loss of bone density that comes with aging is to incorporate strength training. Strength-training exercises use resistance methods like free weights, resistance bands, or your own bodyweight to build muscles and strength.

- **Stop your activity if pain or swelling returns.** Rest for a few days. If the pain continues, see your doctor.

Chapter 48

# Toe Injuries

## Chapter Contents

# Section 48.1

# *Turf Toe*

Text in this section is from "Turf Toe," © 2017 American College of
Foot and Ankle Surgeons (ACFAS). Reprinted with permission.

## *What Is Turf Toe?*

Turf toe is a sprain of the big toe joint resulting from injury during
sports activities. The injury usually results from excessive upward
bending of the big toe joint. The condition can be caused from either
jamming the toe or from repetitive injury when pushing off repeatedly
when running or jumping. Although this injury is most commonly
reported in football players, participants in soccer, basketball, wrestling, gymnastics and dance also are at risk.

## *Causes*

The name "turf toe" comes from the fact that this injury is especially common among athletes who play on artificial turf. When playing sports on artificial turf, the foot can stick to the hard surface,
resulting in jamming of the big toe joint. There has been some indication that less-supportive flexible shoes worn on artificial turf are
also to blame.

## *Symptoms*

- The signs and symptoms of turf toe can include pain, swelling
  and limited joint movement.

- If turf toe is caused by repetitive actions that cause injury, the
  signs and symptoms will usually begin slowly and can gradually
  worsen. Turf toe can also be caused by a direct injury leading
  to damage of the bone beneath the cartilage. If direct injury is
  the cause, the signs and symptoms may begin suddenly and get
  worse over a 24-hour period.

## Diagnosis

To arrive at a diagnosis, the foot and ankle surgeon will obtain your medical history and examine your foot. X-rays are typically ordered to rule out any broken bone. Other advanced imaging studies may also be helpful for proper diagnosis.

## Treatment

Initial treatments include rest, ice, compression, and elevation. (RICE), as well as a change to less-flexible footwear. Operative treatment is reserved for individuals with severe cases and prolonged pain.

# Section 48.2

# *Toe and Forefoot Fractures*

Text in this section is from "Toe and Forefoot Fractures,"
© 1995-2017 American Academy of Orthopaedic Surgeons.
Reprinted with permission.

Fractures of the toes and forefoot are quite common. Fractures can result from a direct blow to the foot—such as accidentally kicking something hard or dropping a heavy object on your toes. They can also result from the overuse and repetitive stress that comes with participating in high-impact sports like running and basketball.

Although fracturing a bone in your toe or forefoot can be quite painful—it rarely requires surgery. In most cases, a fracture will heal with rest and a change in activities.

## Anatomy

The forefoot has 5 metatarsal bones and 14 phalanges (toe bones). There are 3 phalanges in each toe—except for the first toe, which usually has only 2.

All the bones in the forefoot are designed to work together when you walk. A fracture, or break, in any of these bones can be painful and impact how your foot functions.

## Description

Toe and forefoot fractures often result from trauma or direct injury to the bone. Fractures can also develop after repetitive activity, rather than a single injury. This is called a "stress fracture."

Fractures may either be "non-displaced," where the bone is cracked but the ends of the bone are together, or "displaced," where the end of the broken bones have partially or completely separated.

Fractures can also be divided into "closed fractures" where the skin is not broken and "open fractures" where the skin is broken and the wound extends down to the bone.

Open fractures are particularly serious because, once the skin is broken, bacteria can enter the wound and cause infection in the bone. Immediate treatment is required to prevent infection.

## Symptoms

The most common symptoms of a fracture are pain and swelling. Other symptoms may include:

- Bruising or discoloration that extends to nearby parts of the foot

- Pain with walking and weight bearing

## First Aid

If you think you have a fracture, it is important to see your doctor as soon as possible. A fracture that is not treated can lead to chronic foot pain and arthritis and affect your ability to walk.

While you are waiting to see your doctor, you should do the following:

- Apply ice to help reduce swelling.

- Elevate your foot as much as possible.

- Limit weight bearing.

- Lightly wrap your foot in a soft compressive dressing.

# Doctor Examination

## Physical Examination

When you see your doctor, he or she will take a history to find out how your foot was injured and ask about your symptoms. Your doctor will then examine your foot and may compare it to the foot on the opposite side.

During the exam, he or she will look for:

- Swelling

- Tenderness over the fracture site

- Bruising or discoloration—your foot may be red or ecchymotic ("black and blue")

- Deformity

- Skin abrasions or open wounds

- Loss of sensation—an indication of nerve injury

## Imaging Studies

Your doctor will also order imaging studies to help diagnose the fracture.

**X-rays.** X-rays provide images of dense structures, such as bone. An x-ray can usually be done in your doctor's office.

Most fractures can be seen on a routine plain x-ray. A stress fracture, however, may start as a tiny crack in the bone and may not be visible on a first x-ray.

In many cases, a stress fracture cannot be seen until several weeks later when it has actually started to heal and a type of healing bone called "callus" appears around the fracture site.

**Magnetic Resonance Imaging (MRI) scans.** If your doctor suspects a stress fracture but cannot see it on a plain x-ray, he or she may recommend an MRI scan. This type of study uses a magnetic field and radio waves to create a computerized image of your foot.

More sensitive than an x-ray, an MRI can detect changes in the bone that may indicate a fracture. Unlike an x-ray, there is no radiation with an MRI. The study takes 40 minutes to do, however, and has to be scheduled separately from your doctor's visit.

# Treatment

Treatment for a toe or forefoot fracture depends upon:

- The location of the injury
- The type of fracture

## *Fractures of the Toes*

Even though toes are very small, injuries to the toes can often be quite painful.

A fracture of the toe may result from a direct injury, such as dropping a heavy object on the front of your foot, or from accidentally kicking or running into a hard object. A fracture may also result if you accidentally hit the side of your foot on a piece of furniture on the ground—and your toes are twisted or pulled sideways or in an awkward direction.

The proximal phalanx is the toe bone that is closest to the metatarsals. Because it is the longest of the toe bones, it is the most likely to fracture.

A fractured toe may become swollen, tender and discolored. If the bone is out of place, your toe will appear deformed.

### *Treatment*

Most broken toes can be treated symptomatically. For several days it may be painful to bear weight on your injured toe. As your pain subsides, however, you can begin to bear weight as you are comfortable. During this time, it may be helpful to wear a wider than normal shoe.

"Buddy taping" your broken toe to an adjacent toe can also sometimes help relieve pain.

If the bone is out of place and your toe appears deformed, it may be necessary for your doctor to manipulate or "reduce" the fracture. This procedure is most often done in the doctor's office. You will be given a local anesthetic to numb your foot, then your doctor will manipulate the fracture back into place and straighten your toe.

## *Metatarsal Fractures*

The metatarsals are the long bones between your toes and the middle of your foot. Each metatarsal has the following four parts:

- Head—which makes a joint with the base of the toe
- Neck—the narrow area between the head and the shaft

- Shaft—the long part of the bone

- Base—which makes a joint with the midfoot

Fractures can occur in any part of the metatarsal, but most often occur in the neck or shaft of the bone.

Like toe fractures, metatarsal fractures can result from either a direct blow to the forefoot or from a twisting injury.

Some metatarsal fractures are stress fractures. Stress fractures are small cracks in the surface of the bone that may extend and become larger over time.

Stress fractures are typically caused by repetitive activity or pressure on the forefoot. They are common in runners and athletes who participate in high-impact sports such as soccer and basketball.

A stress fracture can also come from a sudden increase in physical activity or a change in your exercise routine.

*Treatment*

Most metatarsal fractures can be treated with an initial period of elevation and limited weight bearing. This is followed by gradual weight bearing, as tolerated, in a cast or walking boot. Surgery is not often required.

However, if you have fractured several metatarsals at the same time and your foot is deformed or unstable, surgery is necessary.

During the procedure, your doctor will make an incision in your foot, then insert pins or plates and screws to hold the bones in place while they heal. This is called "internal fixation."

Surgery may be delayed for several days to allow the swelling in your foot to go down. If you have an open fracture, however, your doctor will perform surgery immediately

*Fifth Metatarsal Fractures*

The fifth metatarsal is the long bone on the outside of your foot. Injuries to this bone may be different than fractures of the first four metatarsals.

Most commonly, the fifth metatarsal fractures through the base of the bone. This usually occurs from an injury where the foot and ankle are twisted downward and inward.

In this type of injury, the tendon that attaches to the base of the fifth metatarsal may stretch and pull a fragment of bone away from the base. Since the fragment is pulled away from the rest of the bone, this type of injury is called an "avulsion fracture."

An avulsion fracture is also sometimes called a "ballerina fracture" or "dancer's fracture" because of the "pointe" position that ballet dancers assume when they are up on their toes.

Another type of fifth metatarsal fracture is a horizontal or transverse fracture through the junction of the base and shaft of the bone. This is sometimes called a "Jones fracture." Since the blood supply to this area is poor, Jones fractures are more prone to difficulties in healing.

*Treatment*

Most fifth metatarsal fractures can be treated with weight bearing as comfortable in a walking boot. If an avulsion fracture results in a large displaced fracture fragment, however, open reduction and internal fixation with plates and screws may be necessary.

Because of its location on the bone, a Jones fracture may take longer to heal. In some cases, a Jones fracture may not heal at all, a condition called "nonunion." When this happens, surgery is often required to treat the fracture.

## Recovery

Healing of a broken toe may take from 4 to 8 weeks.

Metatarsal fractures usually heal in 6 to 8 weeks, but may take longer. Your doctor will take follow-up x-rays to make sure that the bone is properly aligned and healing. Even with proper healing, your foot may be swollen for several months and it may be hard to find a comfortable shoe.

Your doctor will tell you when it is safe to resume activities and return to sports. If you experience any pain, however, you should stop your activity and notify your doctor. Returning to activities too soon can put you at risk for re-injury.

# Part Nine

# Diagnosis, Treatment, and Rehabilitation of Sports Injuries

Chapter 49

# Imaging and Diagnostic Tests

## Chapter Contents

# Section 49.1

# *Arthrogram*

This section includes text excerpted from "Arthrogram
with MRI or CT Scan," U.S. Department of Veterans
Affairs (VA), July 2013. Reviewed June 2017.

An arthrogram is a test that uses X-rays to obtain a series of images of a joint after a contrast material (such as a dye, water, air, or a combination of these) has been injected into the joint. This allows the radiologist to see the soft tissue structures of your joint, such as tendons, ligaments, muscles, cartilage, and your joint capsule. These structures are not seen on a plain X-ray without contrast material. A special type of X-ray, called fluoroscopy, is used to take pictures of the joint.

An arthrogram is used to check a joint to find out what is causing your symptoms or problem with your joint. An arthrogram may be more useful than a regular X-ray because it shows the surface of soft tissues lining the joint as well as the bones of the joint. This test can be done on your hip, knee, or shoulder.

Other tests, such as magnetic resonance imaging (MRI) and computed tomography (CT), give different information about a joint. They may be used with an arthrogram or when an arthrogram does not provide a clear picture of the joint.

## *Why Is an Arthrogram Done?*

An arthrogram is used to find the cause of ongoing, unexplained joint pain, swelling, or abnormal movement of your joint. It may be done alone, before, or as part of other tests, such as MRI, or a CT.

## *An Arthrogram Is Used To*

- Find problems in your joint capsule, ligaments, cartilage (including tears, degeneration, or disease), and the bones in the joint. In your shoulder, it may be used to help find rotator cuff tears or a frozen shoulder.

- Find abnormal growths or fluid-filled cysts.

- Confirm that a needle has been placed correctly in your joint before joint fluid analysis, a test in which a sample of joint fluid is removed with a thin needle.

- Check needle placement before a painkilling injection, such as a corticosteroid injection.

## How to Prepare

Tell your doctor before your arthrogram if you:

- Are or might be pregnant.

- Are allergic to any type of contrast material.

- Are allergic to iodine. The dye used for an arthrogram may contain iodine.

- Are allergic to any medicines, including anesthetics.

- Have ever had a serious allergic reaction (anaphylaxis) from any substance, such as a bee sting or eating shellfish.

- Have bleeding problems or are taking blood-thinning medicines.

- Have a known infection in or around your joint. The dye may make your infection worse.

You will be asked to sign a consent form before the test. Talk to your doctor about any concerns you have regarding the need for the test, its risks, how it will be done, or what the results will mean.

## How It Is Done

An arthrogram is done by a doctor who specializes in interpreting X-rays (radiologist).

- You will be asked to remove your clothing and put on a gown.

- The technologist will then take two images of your joint (either your hip, shoulder, or knee)

- The radiologist will clean the skin over your joint with a special soap and will drape your joint with sterile towels.

- A local anesthetic is used to numb the skin and tissues over the joint.

- A needle is then placed into your joint area.

- Joint fluid may be removed so that more contrast material (such as dye or air) can be put into the joint.

- A sample of joint fluid may be sent to a lab to be looked at under a microscope.

- The fluoroscope shows that the needle is placed correctly in your joint.

- The dye or air is then put through the needle into your joint.

- The joint may be injected with both dye and air (double-contrast arthrogram).

- The needle will be removed after the injection of contrast.

- You may be asked to move your joint around to help the dye or air spread inside your joint.

- Images from the fluoroscope show if the dye has filled your entire joint.

- Hold as still as possible while the X-rays are being taken unless your doctor tells you to move your joint through its entire range of motion.

- The X-rays need to be taken quickly, before the dye spreads to other tissues around your joint.

- An arthrogram usually takes about 30–60 minutes.

- If you are having a CT scan or MRI after an arthrogram you will then be transferred to that area for additional imaging.

- After the arthrogram, rest your joint for about 12 hours.

- Do not do any strenuous activity for 1–2 days.

- Use ice for any swelling and use pain medicine for any pain.

- If a bandage or wrap is put on your joint following an arthrogram, you will be told how long to use it.

## How It Feels

- You will feel a prick and sting when the numbing agent is given. You may feel tingling, pressure, pain, or fullness in your joint as the dye is put in.

472

- The X-ray table may feel hard and the room may be cool.

- You may have some mild pain, tenderness, and swelling in your joint after the test. Ice packs and nonprescription pain relievers, used as the package directs, may help you feel more comfortable. You may also hear a grating, clicking, or cracking sound when you move your joint. This is normal and goes away in about 24 hours. If you have ongoing pain, tenderness, or swelling of the joint, tell your doctor.

## *Risks of an Arthrogram*

You can have a few problems from an arthrogram, such as:

- Joint pain for more than 1 or 2 days.

- An allergic reaction to the dye (usually within the first 5 minutes after the dye/contrast is given).

- Rarely, damage to the structures inside your joint or bleeding in the joint may occur.

- Infection in the joint.

There is always a slight risk of damage to cells or tissue from being exposed to any radiation, including the low levels of radiation used for this test. But the risk of damage from the X-rays is usually very low compared with the potential benefits of the test.

Section 49.2

# *Bone Scan and Bone Density Test*

This section contains text excerpted from the following sources:
Text under the heading "Bone Scan" is excerpted from "Procedures/
Diagnostic Tests," Clinical Center, National Institute of Health
(NIH), February 19, 2017; Text under the heading "Bone Density
Test" is excerpted from "Get a Bone Density Test," Office of Disease
Prevention and Health Promotion (ODPHP), U.S. Department of
Health and Human Services (HHS), July 1, 2016.

## Bone Scan

A bone scan helps your doctor find out if there is a tumor, infection,
or other abnormality in your bone. This scan is a safe, effective, and
painless way to make pictures of your bones. For this scan, you will
be given a compound containing a small amount of radioactivity. This
compound is used only for diagnostic purposes. The scan is done in the
nuclear medicine department.

### Preparation

There is no special preparation for this scan. You may eat and drink
whatever you like.

### Procedure

• In the morning, a small amount of the compound (radioisotope)
will be given to you by vein. You may then go back to your room.

• After the injection, try to drink extra glasses of water over
the next few hours. This will help your body rid itself of the
radioactivity.

• Please return to the diagnostic imaging section at the time
scheduled for you by the appointment clerk: about 2 1/2 to 3
hours after the injection.

• Once you are in the imaging room, you will rest on a firm table
with your head flat. During the scan, you will lie on your back.

- While you are in this position, a sensitive machine (called a scanner) will record the radiation given off by the radioisotope. Lie very still. Many pictures will be taken as the scanner moves from your head to your toes. After the scan, more pictures will be taken of your head and hands. Stay very still while these pictures are being taken.

### After the Procedure

There are no side effects, and the scan is painless. The only sensation you will feel will be the injection of the radioisotope in your vein.

If you have questions about the procedure, please ask. Your nurse and doctor are ready to assist you at all times.

### Special Instructions

- Because it uses radioactivity, this scan is not performed in pregnant women. *If you are pregnant or think you might be pregnant, please inform your doctor immediately so that a decision can be made about this scan.*

- *Also, please inform your doctor immediately if you are breastfeeding.* Some scans can be performed in breastfeeding women if they are willing to stop breastfeeding for a while.

## Bone Density Test

A bone density test measures how strong your bones are. The test will tell you if you have osteoporosis, or weak bones.

- If you are a woman age 65 or older, schedule a bone density test.

- If you are a woman age 50–64, ask your doctor if you need a bone density test.

If you are at risk for osteoporosis, your doctor or nurse may recommend getting a bone density test every 2 years.

Men can get osteoporosis, too. If you are a man over age 65 and you are concerned about your bone strength, talk with your doctor or nurse.

### What Is Osteoporosis?

Osteoporosis is a bone disease. It means your bones are weak and more likely to break. People with osteoporosis most often break bones in the hip, spine, and wrist.

There are no signs or symptoms of osteoporosis. You might not know you have the disease until you break a bone. That's why it's so important to get a bone density test to measure your bone strength.

### *What Happens during a Bone Density Test?*

A bone density test is like an X-ray or scan of your body. A bone density test doesn't hurt. It only takes about 15 minutes.

### *Am I at Risk for Osteoporosis?*

Anyone can get osteoporosis, but it's most common in older women. The older you are, the greater your risk for osteoporosis.

These things can also increase your risk for osteoporosis:

• Hormone changes (especially for women who have gone through menopause)

• Not getting enough calcium and Vitamin D

• Taking certain medicines

• Smoking cigarettes or drinking too much alcohol

• Not getting enough physical activity

### *What If I Have Osteoporosis?*

If you have osteoporosis, you can still slow down bone loss. Finding and treating it early can keep you healthier and more active—and lower your chances of breaking a bone.

Depending on the results of your bone density test, you may need to:

• Add more calcium and vitamin D to your diet

• Exercise more to strengthen your bones

• Take medicine to stop bone loss

Your doctor can tell you what steps are right for you. It doesn't matter how old you are—it's not too late to stop bone loss!

### *Take Action!*

Take these steps to protect your bone health.

*Schedule a Bone Density Test*

Ask your doctor if you are at risk for osteoporosis and find out when to start getting bone density tests.

*What about Cost?*

Screening for osteoporosis is covered under the Affordable Care Act (ACA), the healthcare reform law passed in 2010. Depending on your insurance plan, you may be able to get screened at no cost to you.

## Take Action: Calcium and Vitamin D

*Get Enough Calcium*

Getting enough calcium helps keep your bones strong. Good sources of calcium include:

- Low-fat or fat-free milk, cheese, and yogurt
- Almonds
- Broccoli and greens
- Tofu with added calcium
- Orange juice with added calcium
- Calcium pills

*Get Enough Vitamin D*

Vitamin D helps your body absorb (take in) calcium. You need both vitamin D and calcium for strong bones.

Your body makes vitamin D when you are out in the sun. You can also get vitamin D from:

- Salmon or tuna
- Fat-free or low-fat milk and yogurt with added vitamin D
- Breakfast cereals and juices with added vitamin D
- Vitamin D pills

## Get Active

Physical activity can help slow down bone loss. Weight-bearing activities (like running or doing jumping jacks) help keep your bones strong.

- Aim for 2 hours and 30 minutes a week of moderate aerobic activity. If you are new to exercise, start with 10 minutes of activity at a time.

- Do strengthening activities at least 2 days a week. These include lifting weights or using resistance bands (long rubber strips that stretch).

- Find an exercise buddy or go walking with friends. You will be more likely to stick with it if you exercise with other people.

### Take Action: Healthy Habits

If you have a health condition or a disability, be as active as you can be. Your doctor can help you choose activities that are right for you.

*Stay Away from Cigarettes and Alcohol*

Smoking cigarettes and drinking too much alcohol can weaken your bones.

If you drink alcohol, drink only in moderation. This means no more than 1 drink a day for women and no more than 2 drinks a day for men.

*Take Steps to Prevent Falls*

Falls can be especially serious for people with weak bones. You can make small changes to lower your risk of falling, like doing exercises that improve your balance. For example, try walking backwards or standing up from a sitting position without using your hands.

# Section 49.3

# *Computed Tomography (CT) Scan*

This section includes text excerpted from "Computed Tomography (CT) Scans and Cancer," National Cancer Institute (NCI), July 16, 2013. Reviewed June 2017.

## *What Is Computed Tomography?*

Computed tomography (CT) is an imaging procedure that uses special X-ray equipment to create detailed pictures, or scans, of areas inside the body. It is also called computerized tomography and computerized axial tomography (CAT).

The term *tomography* comes from the Greek words *tomos* (a cut, a slice, or a section) and *graphein* (to write or record). Each picture created during a CT procedure shows the organs, bones, and other tissues in a thin "slice" of the body. The entire series of pictures produced in CT is like a loaf of sliced bread—you can look at each slice individually (2-dimensional pictures), or you can look at the whole loaf (a 3-dimensional picture). Computer programs are used to create both types of pictures.

Most modern CT machines take continuous pictures in a helical (or spiral) fashion rather than taking a series of pictures of individual slices of the body, as the original CT machines did. Helical CT has several advantages over older CT techniques: it is faster, produces better 3-D pictures of areas inside the body, and may detect small abnormalities better. The newest CT scanners, called multislice CT or multidetector CT scanners, allow more slices to be imaged in a shorter period of time.

In addition to its use in cancer, CT is widely used to help diagnose circulatory (blood) system diseases and conditions, such as coronary artery disease (atherosclerosis), blood vessel aneurysms, and blood clots; spinal conditions; kidney and bladder stones; abscesses; inflammatory diseases, such as ulcerative colitis and sinusitis; and injuries to the head, skeletal system, and internal organs. CT can be a life-saving tool for diagnosing illness and injury in both children and adults.

479

## What Can a Person Expect during a CT Procedure?

During a CT procedure, the person lies very still on a table, and the table passes slowly through the center of a large X-ray machine. With some types of CT scanners, the table stays still and the machine moves around the person. The person might hear whirring sounds during the procedure. At times during a CT procedure, the person may be asked to hold their breath to prevent blurring of the images.

Sometimes, CT involves the use of a contrast (imaging) agent, or "dye." The dye may be given by mouth, injected into a vein, given by enema, or given in all three ways before the procedure. The contrast dye highlights specific areas inside the body, resulting in clearer pictures. Iodine and barium are two dyes commonly used in CT.

In very rare cases, the contrast agents used in CT can cause allergic reactions. Some people experience mild itching or hives (small bumps on the skin). Symptoms of a more serious allergic reaction include shortness of breath and swelling of the throat or other parts of the body. People should tell the technologist immediately if they experience any of these symptoms, so they can be treated promptly. Very rarely, the contrast agents used in CT can also cause kidney problems in certain patients. These kidney problems usually do not have any symptoms, but they can be detected by running a simple test on a blood sample.

CT does not cause any pain. However, lying in one position during the procedure may be slightly uncomfortable. The length of a CT procedure depends on the size of the area being scanned, but it usually lasts only a few minutes to half an hour. For most people, the CT is performed on an outpatient basis at a hospital or a radiology center, without an overnight hospital stay.

Some people are concerned about experiencing claustrophobia during a CT procedure. However, most CT scanners surround only portions of the body, not the whole body. Therefore, people are not enclosed in a machine and are unlikely to feel claustrophobic.

Women should let their healthcare provider and the technologist know if there is any possibility that they are pregnant, because radiation from CT can harm a growing fetus.

## What Is Total, or Whole-Body, CT?

Total, or whole-body, CT creates pictures of nearly every area of the body—from the chin to below the hips. This procedure, which is used routinely in patients who already have cancer, can also be used in people who do not have any symptoms of disease. However, whole-body CT has not been shown to be an effective screening method for healthy people. Most abnormal findings from this procedure do not indicate a serious health problem, but the tests that must be done to follow up and rule out a problem can be expensive, inconvenient, and uncomfortable. In addition, whole-body CT can expose people to relatively large amounts of ionizing radiation—about 12 mSv (millisieverts), or four times the estimated average annual dose received from natural sources of radiation. Most doctors recommend against whole-body CT for people without any signs or symptoms of disease.

## What Is Combined PET/CT?

Combined PET/CT uses two imaging methods, CT and positron emission tomography (PET), in one procedure. CT is done first to create anatomic pictures of the organs and structures in the body, and then PET is done to create colored pictures that show chemical or other functional changes in tissues.

Different types of positron-emitting (radioactive) substances can be used in PET. Depending on the substance used, different kinds of chemical or functional changes can be imaged. The most common type of PET procedure uses an imaging agent called FDG (a radioactive form of the sugar glucose), which shows the metabolic activity of tissues. Because cancerous tumors are usually more metabolically active than normal tissues, they appear different from other tissues on a PET scan. Other PET imaging agents can provide information about the level of oxygen in a particular tissue, the formation of new blood vessels, the presence of bone growth, or whether tumor cells are actively dividing and growing.

Combining CT and PET may provide a more complete picture of a tumor's location and growth or spread than either test alone. The combined procedure may improve the ability to diagnose cancer, to determine how far a tumor has spread, to plan treatment, and to monitor response to treatment. Combined PET/CT may also reduce the number of additional imaging tests and other procedures a patient needs.

## Is the Radiation from CT Harmful?

Some people may be concerned about the amount of radiation they receive during CT. CT imaging involves the use of X-rays, which are a form of ionizing radiation. Exposure to ionizing radiation is known to increase the risk of cancer. Standard X-ray procedures, such as routine chest X-rays and mammography, use relatively low levels of ionizing radiation. The radiation exposure from CT is higher than that from standard X-ray procedures, but the increase in cancer risk from one CT scan is still small. Not having the procedure can be much more risky than having it, especially if CT is being used to diagnose cancer or another serious condition in someone who has signs or symptoms of disease.

The widespread use of CT and other procedures that use ionizing radiation to create images of the body has raised concerns that even small increases in cancer risk could lead to large numbers of future cancers. People who have CT procedures as children may be at higher risk because children are more sensitive to radiation and have a longer life expectancy than adults. Women are at a somewhat higher risk than men of developing cancer after receiving the same radiation exposures at the same ages.

People considering CT should talk with their doctors about whether the procedure is necessary for them and about its risks and benefits. Some organizations recommend that people keep a record of the imaging examinations they have received in case their doctors don't have access to all of their health records.

## What Are the Risks of CT Scans for Children?

Radiation exposure from CT scans affects adults and children differently. Children are considerably more sensitive to radiation than adults because of their growing bodies and the rapid pace at which the cells in their bodies divide. In addition, children have a longer life expectancy than adults, providing a larger window of opportunity for radiation-related cancers to develop.

Individuals who have had multiple CT scans before the age of 15 were found to have an increased risk of developing leukemia, brain tumors, and other cancers in the decade following their first scan. However, the lifetime risk of cancer from a single CT scan was small— about one case of cancer for every 10,000 scans performed on children.

In talking with healthcare providers, three key questions that the parents can ask are: why is the test needed? Will the results change the treatment decisions? Is there an alternative test that doesn't involve radiation? If the test is clinically justified, then the parents can be reassured that the benefits will outweigh the small long-term risks.

# Section 49.4

# *Magnetic Resonance Imaging (MRI)*

This section includes text excerpted from "MRI (Magnetic Resonance Imaging)," U.S. Food and Drug Administration (FDA), November 7, 2016.

Magnetic resonance imaging (MRI) is a medical imaging procedure for making images of the internal structures of the body. MRI scanners use strong magnetic fields and radio waves (radiofrequency energy) to make images. The signal in an MR image comes mainly from the protons in fat and water molecules in the body.

During an MRI exam, an electric current is passed through coiled wires to create a temporary magnetic field in a patient's body. Radio waves are sent from and received by a transmitter/receiver in the machine, and these signals are used to make digital images of the scanned area of the body. A typical MRI scan last from 20–90 minutes, depending on the part of the body being imaged.

For some MRI exams, intravenous (IV) drugs, such as gadolinium-based contrast agents (GBCAs) are used to change the contrast of the MR image. Gadolinium-based contrast agents are rare earth metals that are usually given through an IV in the arm.

## *Uses*

MRI gives healthcare providers useful information about a variety of conditions and diagnostic procedures including:

- abnormalities of the brain and spinal cord

- abnormalities in various parts of the body such as breast, prostate, and liver

- injuries or abnormalities of the joints

- the structure and function of the heart (cardiac imaging)

- areas of activation within the brain (functional MRI or fMRI)

- blood flow through blood vessels and arteries (angiography)

- the chemical composition of tissues (spectroscopy)

In addition to these diagnostic uses, MRI may also be used to guide certain interventional procedures.

## Benefits and Risks

### Benefits

An MRI scanner can be used to take images of any part of the body (e.g., head, joints, abdomen, legs, etc.), in any imaging direction. MRI provides better soft tissue contrast than CT (computed tomography) and can differentiate better between fat, water, muscle, and other soft tissue than CT (CT is usually better at imaging bones). These images provide information to physicians and can be useful in diagnosing a wide variety of diseases and conditions.

### Risks

MR images are made without using any ionizing radiation, so patients are not exposed to the harmful effects of ionizing radiation. But while there are no known health hazards from temporary exposure to the MR environment, the MR environment involves a strong, static magnetic field, a magnetic field that changes with time (pulsed gradient field), and radiofrequency energy, each of which carry specific safety concerns:

- The strong, static magnetic field will attract magnetic objects (from small items such as keys and cell phones, to large, heavy items such as oxygen tanks and floor buffers) and may cause damage to the scanner or injury to the patient or medical professionals if those objects become projectiles. Careful screening of people and objects entering the MR environment is critical to ensure nothing enters the magnet area that may become a projectile.

- The magnetic fields that change with time create loud knocking noises which may harm hearing if adequate ear protection is not used. They may also cause peripheral muscle or nerve stimulation that may feel like a twitching sensation.

- The radiofrequency energy used during the MRI scan could lead to heating of the body. The potential for heating is greater during long MRI examinations.

The use of gadolinium-based contrast agents (GBCAs) also carries some risk, including side effects such as allergic reactions to the contrast agent.

Some patients find the inside of the MRI scanner to be uncomfortably small and may experience claustrophobia. Imaging in an open MRI scanner may be an option for some patients, but not all MRI systems can perform all examinations, so you should discuss these options with your doctor. Your doctor may also be able to prescribe medication to make the experience easier for you.

To produce good quality images, patients must generally remain very still throughout the entire MRI procedure. Infants, small children, and other patients who are unable to lay still may need to be sedated or anesthetized for the procedure. Sedation and anesthesia carry risks not specific to the MRI procedure, such as slowed or difficult breathing, and low blood pressure.

## Patients with Implants, External and Accessory Devices

The MR environment presents unique safety hazards for patients with implants, external devices and accessory medical devices. Examples of implanted devices include artificial joints, stents, cochlear implants, and pacemakers. An external device is a device that may touch the patient like an external insulin pump, a leg brace, or a wound dressing. An accessory device is a nonimplanted medical device (such as a ventilator, patient monitor) that is used to monitor or support the patient.

- The strong, static magnetic field of the MRI scanner will pull on magnetic materials and may cause unwanted movement of the medical device.

- The radiofrequency energy and magnetic fields that change with time may cause heating of the implanted medical device and the surrounding tissue, which could lead to burns.

- The magnetic fields and radiofrequency energy produced by an MRI scanner may also cause electrically active medical devices to malfunction, which can result in a failure of the device to deliver the intended therapy.

- The presence of the medical device will degrade the quality of the MR image, which may make the MRI scan uninformative or may lead to an inaccurate clinical diagnosis, potentially resulting in inappropriate medical treatment.

Therefore patients with implanted medical devices should not receive an MRI exam unless the implanted medical device has been positively identified as MR Safe or MR Conditional. An MR Safe device is nonmagnetic, contains no metal, does not conduct electricity and poses no known hazards in all MR environments. An MR Conditional device may be used safely only within an MR environment that matches its conditions of safe use. Any device with an unknown MRI safety status should be assumed to be MR Unsafe.

## Adverse Events

Adverse events for MRI scans are very rare. Millions of MRI scans are performed in the United States every year, and the FDA receives around 300 adverse event reports for MRI scanners and coils each year from manufacturers, distributors, user facilities, and patients. The majority of these reports describe heating and/or burns (thermal injuries). Second degree burns are the most commonly reported patient problem. Other reported problems include injuries from projectile events (objects being drawn toward the MRI scanner), crushed and pinched fingers from the patient table, patient falls, and hearing loss or a ringing in the ear (tinnitus). The U.S. Food and Drug Administration (FDA) has also received reports concerning the inadequate display or quality of the MR images.

## What Patients Should Know before Having an MRI Exam

Before your MRI exam, you will likely be asked to fill out a screening questionnaire. The International Society for Magnetic Resonance in Medicine (ISMRM) has a sample patient screening form available on its website. For your safety, answering the questionnaire accurately is extremely important. In particular, make sure you notify the MRI technologist or radiologist if you have any implanted medical devices, such as stents, knee or hip replacements, pacemakers, or drug pumps. Also be sure to tell the technologist if you have any tattoos or drug patches as these can cause skin irritation or burns during the exam. The medical team will need to make sure that these devices can safely enter the MR environment.

Some devices are MR Safe or MR Conditional, meaning that they can be safely used in the MR environment under specific conditions. If you have an implant card for your device, bring it with you to your MRI exam so that you can help the doctor or the MRI technologist identify what type of device you have.

The space where you will lay in an MRI scanner to have your images taken can be a tight fit for some people, especially larger individuals. If you believe that you will feel claustrophobic, tell the MRI technologist or your doctor.

The MRI scanner will make a lot of noise as it takes images. This is normal. You should be offered earplugs and/or headphones to make the noise sound less loud. You may also be able to listen to music through the headphones to make the MRI exam more enjoyable.

If your exam includes a contrast agent, the MRI technologist will place a small intravenous (IV) line in one of your arms. You may feel some coldness when the contrast agent is injected. Be sure to notify the technologist if you feel any pain or discomfort.

Remember, your doctor has referred you to have an MRI because he or she believes the scan will provide useful information. If you have any questions about your procedure, don't be afraid to ask.

### *Questions to Ask Your Doctor*

- "What information will the MRI scan provide? How might this change my treatment options?"

- "Is there any reason why I shouldn't have an MRI scan?" (If you have any implanted devices (such as a pacemaker, stents, an insulin pump, or an artificial joint), be sure your doctor knows about them.)

- "Will my exam involve contrast agent? What additional information will using the contrast agent provide?"

### *Questions to Ask the MRI Technologist*

- "How long can I expect my scan to last?"

- "Can I listen to music during my MRI scan? Can I choose the music?"

- "Where is the call button I can use to let you know if there is a problem?"

# Section 49.5

# *Ultrasound*

This section includes text excerpted from "Ultrasound,"
National Institute of Biomedical Imaging and
Bioengineering (NIBIB), July 2016.

## *What Is Medical Ultrasound?*

Medical ultrasound falls into two distinct categories: diagnostic and therapeutic.

Diagnostic ultrasound is a noninvasive diagnostic technique used to image inside the body. Ultrasound probes, called transducers, produce sound waves that have frequencies above the threshold of human hearing (above 20KHz), but most transducers in current use operate at much higher frequencies (in the megahertz (MHz) range). Most diagnostic ultrasound probes are placed on the skin. However, to optimize image quality, probes may be placed inside the body via the gastrointestinal tract, vagina, or blood vessels. In addition, ultrasound is sometimes used during surgery by placing a sterile probe into the area being operated on.

Diagnostic ultrasound can be further subdivided into anatomical and functional ultrasound. Anatomical ultrasound produces images of internal organs or other structures. Functional ultrasound combines information such as the movement and velocity of tissue or blood, softness or hardness of tissue, and other physical characteristics, with anatomical images to create "information maps." These maps help doctors visualize changes/differences in function within a structure or organ.

Therapeutic ultrasound also uses sound waves above the range of human hearing but does not produce images. Its purpose is to interact with tissues in the body such that they are either modified or destroyed. Among the modifications possible are: moving or pushing tissue, heating tissue, dissolving blood clots, or delivering drugs to specific locations in the body. These destructive, or ablative, functions are made possible by use of very high-intensity beams that can destroy diseased or abnormal tissues such as tumors. The advantage of using ultrasound therapies is that, in most cases, they are noninvasive. No incisions or cuts need to be made to the skin, leaving no wounds or scars.

## How Does It Work?

Ultrasound waves are produced by a transducer, which can both emit ultrasound waves, as well as detect the ultrasound echoes reflected back. In most cases, the active elements in ultrasound transducers are made of special ceramic crystal materials called piezoelectrics. These materials are able to produce sound waves when an electric field is applied to them, but can also work in reverse, producing an electric field when a sound wave hits them. When used in an ultrasound scanner, the transducer sends out a beam of sound waves into the body. The sound waves are reflected back to the transducer by boundaries between tissues in the path of the beam (e.g., the boundary between fluid and soft tissue or tissue and bone). When these echoes hit the transducer, they generate electrical signals that are sent to the ultrasound scanner. Using the speed of sound and the time of each echo's return, the scanner calculates the distance from the transducer to the tissue boundary. These distances are then used to generate two-dimensional images of tissues and organs.

During an ultrasound exam, the technician will apply a gel to the skin. This keeps air pockets from forming between the transducer and the skin, which can block ultrasound waves from passing into the body.

## What Is Ultrasound Used For?

**Diagnostic ultrasound.** Diagnostic ultrasound is able to noninvasively image internal organs within the body. However, it is not good for imaging bones or any tissues that contain air, like the lungs. Under some conditions, ultrasound can image bones (such as in a fetus or in small babies) or the lungs and lining around the lungs, when they are filled or partially filled with fluid. One of the most common uses of ultrasound is during pregnancy, to monitor the growth and development of the fetus, but there are many other uses, including imaging the heart, blood vessels, eyes, thyroid, brain, breast, abdominal organs, skin, and muscles. Ultrasound images are displayed in either 2D, 3D, or 4D (which is 3D in motion).

**Functional ultrasound.** Functional ultrasound applications include Doppler and color Doppler ultrasound for measuring and visualizing blood flow in vessels within the body or in the heart. It can also measure the speed of the blood flow and direction of movement. This is done using color-coded maps called color Doppler imaging. Doppler ultrasound is commonly used to determine whether plaque build-up inside the carotid arteries is blocking blood flow to the brain.

Another functional form of ultrasound is elastography, a method for measuring and displaying the relative stiffness of tissues, which can be used to differentiate tumors from healthy tissue. This information can be displayed as either color-coded maps of the relative stiffness; black-and white maps that display high-contrast images of tumors compared with anatomical images; or color-coded maps that are overlayed on the anatomical image. Elastography can be used to test for liver fibrosis, a condition in which excessive scar tissue builds up in the liver due to inflammation.

Ultrasound is also an important method for imaging interventions in the body. For example, ultrasound-guided needle biopsy helps physicians see the position of a needle while it is being guided to a selected target, such as a mass or a tumor in the breast. Also, ultrasound is used for real-time imaging of the location of the tip of a catheter as it is inserted in a blood vessel and guided along the length of the vessel. It can also be used for minimally invasive surgery to guide the surgeon with real-time images of the inside of the body.

**Therapeutic or interventional ultrasound.** Therapeutic ultrasound produces high levels of acoustic output that can be focused on specific targets for the purpose of heating, ablating, or breaking up tissue. One type of therapeutic ultrasound uses high-intensity beams of sound that are highly targeted, and is called High Intensity Focused Ultrasound (HIFU). HIFU is being investigated as a method for modifying or destroying diseased or abnormal tissues inside the body (e.g., tumors) without having to open or tear the skin or cause damage to the surrounding tissue. Either ultrasound or MRI is used to identify and target the tissue to be treated, guide and control the treatment in real time, and confirm the effectiveness of the treatment. HIFU is currently the U.S. Food and Drug Administration (FDA)-approved test for the treatment of uterine fibroids, to alleviate pain from bone metastases, and most recently for the ablation of prostate tissue. HIFU is also being investigated as a way to close wounds and stop bleeding, to break up clots in blood vessels, and to temporarily open the blood brain barrier so that medications can pass through.

## *Are There Risks?*

Diagnostic ultrasound is generally regarded as safe and does not produce ionizing radiation like that produced by X-rays. Still, ultrasound is capable of producing some biological effects in the body under specific settings and conditions. For this reason, the FDA requires that diagnostic ultrasound devices operate within acceptable limits. The FDA, as well as many professional societies, discourage the casual use of ultrasound (e.g., for keepsake videos) and recommend that it be used only when there is a true medical need.

Chapter 50

# Medications for Sports Injuries

The treatment and prevention of injuries related to sports and exercise is an integral part of sports medicine. While medication is a small part of the overall treatment plan, it plays an important role in the immediate management of pain and inflammation associated with sport injuries. But the causes and effects of the injury should be assessed properly to make an accurate diagnosis and create an appropriate treatment plan. Medications can range from simple pain-relieving liniment to potent corticosteroids and can be used to treat a variety of conditions resulting from acute and chronic injuries. Some athletes are prescribed medicines to treat specific conditions, such as asthma, diabetes, cough, and skin infections. Nutritional supplements and performance-enhancing substances are also sometimes used by athletes to improve health and athletic results.

The main classes of medication used to treat sports injuries include analgesics, anti-inflammatories, and antibiotics. A number of other medications are provided as a first line of treatment by coaches, primary care physicians, or emergency departments. Many athletes take to self-medication, which may have deleterious effects in terms of both efficacy in treating the injury and side effects.

"Medications for Sports Injuries," © 2017 Omnigraphics. Reviewed June 2017.

## Analgesics

These are medications, taken as tablets or quick-acting injections, that are used to control pain and inflammation at the site of injury. They work by blocking pain signals to the brain or by altering the way the brain interprets the pain signals. While these medicines do not treat the underlying condition causing the pain, they are widely used in sports to relieve both acute and chronic pain associated with injuries. Studies indicate that many athletes resort to self-medication for pain in order to continue their participation in sports. This does not allow adequate time for healing and may have serious consequences. Absence of pain resulting from medication use can mask the actual injury and push athletes to overexert, thereby increasing the risk of aggravating the injury.

There are two main classes of analgesics:

- **Narcotic pain medications.** Also known as opioids, these are strong analgesics used to control moderate to severe pain that does not respond to other analgesics. Medications in this category include natural narcotics, such as morphine and codeine, as well as synthetic drugs, such as Dilaudid, Demerol, and Vicodin. Opioid usage needs to be closely supervised by physicians, as it carries a high risk for drug tolerance, dependence, and abuse. Opioids can also be extremely dangerous if taken in combination with tranquilizers or alcohol.

- **Nonnarcotic pain medications.** These are the most commonly used over-the-counter analgesics. Acetaminophen, marketed as the Tylenol brand, among others, is the most popular nonnarcotic pain medication used to relieve mild to moderate pain. Recognized as safe, and having minimal side effects or drug interactions, acetaminophen is often administered in combination with nonsteroidal anti-inflammatory drugs (NSAIDs) for effective pain relief.

## Anti-Inflammatory Medications

These medications are primarily used to treat to treat inflammation (the body's response to injury and infection) associated with sports injuries. There are two classes of anti-inflammatory medications: steroidal and nonsteroidal.

- **Steroidal anti-inflammatories.** Medications generally prescribed in this class consist of synthetic hormones: cortisones or corticosteroids. Popularly known as "cortisone shots," these drugs are used to reduce pain and inflammation and treat a variety of musculoskeletal conditions, such as bursitis, herniated disc, and tendon injuries. Their use, however, is controlled under the WADA (World Anti-Doping Agency) code and requires a therapeutic use exemption (TUE). Prednisone, hydrocortisone, and dexamethasone are some of the commonly used drugs in this class, and these are available as pills, creams, inhalers or injectables.

* **Nonsteroidal anti-inflammatories.** These drugs have been widely used in sports medicine to treat inflammation accompanying injury or after surgery. Generally recognized as safe, these nonprescription drugs also work well as pain relievers in low doses. NSAIDs work by blocking enzymes in the body that help make prostaglandins, a group of naturally occurring lipids that play a key role in the inflammatory response and cause pain, fever and inflammation. The enzyme, called cyclooxygenase, or COX, occurs in two forms: COX-1 and COX-2. While the former protects the stomach lining and helps maintain kidney function, the latter is produced in response to joint injury and inflammation. Traditional NSAIDs, such as aspirin and ibuprofen, block the actions of both COX-1 and COX-2.

Long-term use of traditional NSAIDs offers some protection against heart disease by preventing blood clots, but the downside is damage to the stomach lining. The new-generation NSAIDs, the "COX-2 inhibitors," named for the enzyme they inhibit, includes drugs such as celecoxib (Celebrex), which are believed to be less damaging to the gastrointestinal system than traditional NSAIDs. While NSAIDs have become a staple drug for sports injuries, high doses and prolonged use can cause not only gastrointestinal problems (ulcers, bleeding), but also side effects like exacerbation of allergies and renal impairment.

## Antibiotics

Antibiotics are used to treat lacerations and open wounds that are associated with sports injuries. While antibiotics cannot treat viral infections, they are widely used as a prophylactic measure to prevent secondary infections or to treat them when they occur. In the last few decades, the indiscriminate use of antibiotics has become a matter of concern for all, including the athletic community. There has

495

been an alarming increase in antibiotic-resistant strains of common bacteria, such as the *Staphylococcus aureus* known as methicillin-resistant *Staphylococcus aureus* (MRSA), an organism that can cause life-threatening illness in bones, surgical wounds, blood, heart, and lungs. Studies have also shown the association between fluoroquinolones (a broad-spectrum antibiotic) and tendon injuries, and the FDA has issued a warning regarding the increased risk of tendon rupture with fluoroquinolone use. Sports physicians frequently overprescribe antibiotics to prevent or resolve infection and ensure early return to play. This may lead to adverse consequences that can compromise health and performance. Thus, it is important to consider a proper antibiotic regimen for athletes based on the specific pathogen, dosing frequency, and allergies, if any. Athletes should also ensure that they run through the full course of antibiotics and report to their physician if the infection or symptoms worsen.

## Other Over-the-Counter (OTC) Medications

In recent years, there has been an overwhelming increase in the use of supplements and OTC medications by sports and fitness buffs. A staggering variety of sports supplements, also called ergogenic aids, are available over-the-counter, and these do not require U.S. Food and Drug Administration (FDA) approval. While some of these supplements, such as vitamins and minerals, may not be harmful, using them for purposes other than what they are intended for may cause more harm than good. Also, the fact that some of these products are natural (herbs or botanicals) may provide a false sense of security to users who tend to overlook any potential toxicity associated with the product. Despite being produced according to the standard manufacturing practices outlined by the FDA, many of these OTC medications contain ingredients that may not be listed on the label, and caution should be exercised while using these products. Glucosamine, chondroitin sulfate, and methylsulfonylmethane are examples of supplements that have received increasing attention in recent years. While some early studies have shown them to be beneficial in treating pain and degenerative conditions of the musculoskeletal system, further studies are required to substantiate them.

### References

1. "Use of Medicines in Sports," American Academy of Pediatrics (AAP), November 21, 2015.

2. Batten, George B., MD. "The Role of Medications in the Treatment of Sports-Related Injuries," Tri-Valley Orthopedic Specialists, Inc., n.d.

3. Shile, Marlana Jean. "Dangers of Pain Medication Use in Athletes," Sutter Health, Palo Alto Medical Foundation, October 2013.

4. "What Are NSAIDs?" American Academy of Orthopaedic Surgeons (AAOS), January 2009.

Chapter 51

# Specialized Surgical Treatments and Therapy

## Chapter Contents

# Section 51.1

# *Arthroscopic Surgery*

"Arthroscopic Surgery," © 2017 Omnigraphics. Reviewed June 2017.

Arthroscopy is a minimally invasive surgical technique used to evaluate, diagnose, and treat or repair a variety of joint-related conditions. Literally translated, arthroscopy means "looking into the joint." Surgeons insert a tiny, fiberoptic camera through a small incision and use it to examine the interior structure of the joint. Images are greatly magnified and displayed on a television screen.

Initially used as a diagnostic tool prior to performing traditional open surgery, arthroscopy has rapidly gained popularity as a standalone medical procedure. Since it is most often performed on an outpatient basis, it is less stressful for patients and offers faster recovery times than traditional surgeries. In addition, advancements in medical instrumentation and fiberoptic technology have enabled surgeons to use it to treat an expanding array of conditions.

## *Indications for Arthroscopy*

Arthroscopy is one of the final steps in the process of diagnosing and treating joint injuries and diseases. The process begins with a complete medical history and physical examination of the patient, and then it involves noninvasive imaging tests such as X-rays, magnetic resonance imaging (MRI), or computed tomography (CT). After reviewing the results of these tests, an orthopedic surgeon may recommend an arthroscopic procedure for one of the following problems:

- **Unexplained joint pain.** Arthroscopy can be used to determine the causes of joint pain that cannot be explained using conventional diagnostic tools.

- **Synovitis.** This condition, which is characterized by inflammation of the synovial membrane lining the cavities of joints, can often be treated through arthroscopy.

- **Removal of loose pieces of bone or cartilage.** Fragments arising from arthritis, injury, or other causes can be easily removed through arthroscopy.

- **Arthritis.** Arthroscopy cannot completely cure arthritis, but it may be used to repair damaged joints and relieve symptoms associated with it.

- **Biopsies.** Arthroscopy can be used to collect samples and analyze the characteristics of synovial fluid in order to diagnose joint disease. Arthroscopy is also used to obtain cartilage tissue for use in cartilage transplant procedures.

- **Meniscal injury.** The meniscus is a crescent-shaped cartilage that distributes weight and reduces friction in the knee, wrist, and other joints. Damage to the meniscus—which can occur suddenly from a traumatic injury or gradually from normal wear and tear—can result in pain, swelling, and impaired joint function. Meniscal repair is one of the most common types of arthroscopic procedures, and it leads to improvement in symptoms for many patients.

- **Ligament repair.** Arthroscopy is often used to diagnose, repair, or reconstruct torn or damaged ligaments.

## The Arthroscopic Procedure

Arthroscopy may be performed under general, spinal, or local anesthesia, depending on the joint being treated and the type of problem being investigated. The orthopedic surgeon makes a small incision in the skin of the affected joint and inserts a pencil-sized instrument called an arthroscope. The arthroscope is fitted with a small lens and a light source to illuminate the interior structure of the joint. The arthroscope is also equipped with a fiberoptic camera that transmits images onto a screen. If the initial examination of the joint reveals the need for a corrective procedure, the surgeon makes additional incisions as needed to insert other miniature medical instruments.

## Recovery after Arthroscopy

As a minimally invasive procedure, arthroscopic surgery causes significantly less trauma to the soft tissues of the joint than traditional open surgery. As a result, it offers a faster recovery time. The small arthroscopic incisions heal quickly, and the operative dressing is usually removed within a couple of days. The joint itself may take several weeks to recover, depending on the overall health of the patient and the procedure involved. In patients who require complex surgical procedures to correct extensive damage to cartilage and ligaments, recovery may take several months. Prior to discharge from the hospital, the healthcare provider generally provides the patient with explicit instructions on the type of activities to avoid, as well as the rehabilitative activities to undertake in order to speed recovery and improve postoperative joint function.

## Risks Involved in Arthroscopy

Arthroscopy is generally considered a safe and effective medical procedure. Although most people who undergo it will experience some discomfort and swelling, these symptoms are typically short-lived. Many patients can return to work and resume normal activities within a few weeks. Serious complications are rare, affecting less than one percent of cases, and may include the following:

- **Postoperative infection.** If an infection develops within the joint, the patient will experience swelling, pain, and fever.

- **Nerve damage.** When an arthroscopic procedure damages a nerve, the patient may experience numbness and tingling sensations around the joint.

- **Hemorrhage.** A small amount of bleeding is normal in arthroscopic procedures, but excessive bleeding may require treatment in a hospital setting.

- **Equipment or implant failure.** Arthroscopic instruments are tiny and fragile, and they occasionally break during surgery. In these instances, the procedure may be extended, or a second surgery may be required. Likewise, the implants and components the surgeon uses to hold the joint in place (including pins, screws, rods, plates, and suture anchors) may break, leaving loose pieces floating around inside the joint. Since these fragments can rub against and damage surrounding tissues, they may need to be removed in a second surgery.

- **Deep-vein thrombosis (DVT).** DVT occurs when a blood clot forms in a vein following surgery. In rare cases, the blood clot may break away and pass through the bloodstream to the lungs, where it can obstruct the blood supply and create a dangerous

condition called pulmonary embolism. Most surgeons take precautions to reduce the risk of DVT, such as administering blood
thinners and getting the patients up and moving as soon as possible after surgery.

### References

1.  NHS Choices. "Arthroscopy," Gov.UK, 2015.

2.  Waller, C.S. "Knee Arthroscopy," May 2010.

3.  Wilkerson, Rick. "Arthroscopy," American Academy of Ortho-
    paedic Surgeons, May 2010.

## Section 51.2

# *Anterior Cruciate Ligament (ACL) Repair*

This section contains text excerpted from the following sources: Text
in this section begins with excerpts from "Surgical Guideline for
Work-Related Knee Injuries 2016," Washington State Department
of Labor & Industries (Washington L&I), July 2016; Text under the
heading "Risk Factors for Subsequent Surgeries Following Initial
ACL Reconstruction" is excerpted from "Rate and Risk Factors for
Surgeries Following Initial ACL Reconstruction," National Institute
of Arthritis and Musculoskeletal and Skin Diseases (NIAMS),
December 2013. Reviewed June 2017.

Reconstruction of the anterior cruciate ligament (ACL) involves
the use of an anatomically positioned autograft or allograft to restore
function to a torn or ruptured ligament. The ACL functions to prevent
the tibia from sliding forward relative to the femur. It also prevents
excessive knee extension, varus and valgus movements, and tibial rotation. An intact ACL protects the menisci from sheering forces during
movements such as landing from a jump, pivoting, or decelerating from
a run. Injuries to the ACL most often occur during twisting or pivoting
in sports or high intensity activities that do not involve contact.

## ACL Reconstruction

ACL reconstruction (usually done arthroscopically) is considered when all the following criteria are met

1. Patient reports a feeling of instability or "giving way" OR

2. Pain and effusion that limits normal function AND

3. Positive Lachman's sign OR

4. Positive pivot shift OR

5. Positive anterior drawer

**Please note:** pain alone is not an indication for surgery.

## The Treatment Plan Includes

1. Physical therapy

2. Functional bracing

3. Activity modification

A torn ACL will not heal independently, leaving the patient with a permanent patholaxity. Chronic instability leads to a higher rate of late meniscal tears. Approximately half of all ACL injuries have concomitant damage to menisci or articular cartilage. Surgery for meniscal injury is increased with nonoperative patients who choose to return to high level activity.

## Risk Factors for Subsequent Surgeries Following Initial ACL Reconstruction

Nearly one-fifth of patients who undergo knee surgery to reconstruct a torn anterior cruciate ligament (ACL) eventually need to have additional surgery on the same knee, according to recent research published in the *American Journal of Sports Medicine*. The study, which was funded by the NIH's National Institute of Arthritis and Musculoskeletal and Skin Diseases (NIAMS), also clarified key risk factors associated with the need for subsequent knee surgeries.

Rupture of the knee's ACL is a common sports-related injury. It is associated with other knee problems, such as meniscal tears and knee instability. Over the long-term, it can lead to knee osteoarthritis. Some patients are able to cope with an ACL tear with physical therapy and rest, but most active people undergo surgery to reconstruct the ligament to restore knee function and prevent further tears.

"Although ACL reconstructive surgery is common and often successful, we have not known the rate and risk factors for subsequent knee surgery until now," said senior author Kurt Spindler, M.D., of Vanderbilt University

In the Multicenter Orthopaedic Outcomes Network (MOON) study, Spindler and his colleagues followed nearly 1,000 people for several years after the patients underwent initial ACL reconstruction. They wanted to determine the rate at which additional surgeries were performed, and to identify specific risk factors that lead to additional surgeries. The median age among patients at their initial surgery was 23.

Six years after surgery, about 19 percent of participants had undergone at least one more surgery on the initial damaged knee. In addition, 10 percent had undergone surgery on the other knee—6.4 percent of these procedures were to reconstruct a ruptured ACL. Patients who had ACL surgery earlier in life were more likely to have subsequent surgeries, a finding that echoes previous research. "These young people typically are more athletic and active, and might be less likely to fully comply with postoperative instructions," said Dr. Spindler. "It's also possible that they have biological differences that predispose them to injury and re-injury," he added.

Patients with ligaments taken from a cadaver to reconstruct their ACL, rather than a ligament from their own bodies, were also more likely to undergo additional surgery. Previous research has suggested that using cadaver-sourced ligaments may lead to an increased risk of immune-incompatibility and could potentially transmit infectious diseases, although the risk for passing on disease is very low. The MOON findings provided further evidence of the possible hazards associated with using them. Unlike other research, however, the researchers did not find that women or those with a higher body mass index were at an increased risk for subsequent surgery.

The results of the MOON study provide patients, parents, healthcare providers, coaches and trainers with valuable information about the risks associated with ACL surgery, as well as ways in which patients may reduce their chances for needing subsequent surgery.

# Section 51.3

# *Cartilage Repair and Restoration*

This section contains text excerpted from the following sources:
Text in this chapter begins with excerpts from "T846.01: CBER
BLA Clinical Review Memorandum," U.S. Food and Drug
Administration (FDA), September 1, 2016; Text under the heading
"Stem Cells in Cartilage Regeneration" is excerpted from "Filling the
Holes—Meeting the Challenges of Engineering Quality," National
Institute of Biomedical Imaging and Bioengineering (NIBIB),
May 31, 2011. Reviewed June 2017.

Millions of people suffer from joint pain caused by damaged cartilage,
the lubricating tissue found on the ends of bones in various places in the
body, including joints. The main sources of cartilage damage are sports
injuries and arthritis. In arthritis, joint cartilage permanently wastes
away, making even simple movements very painful. For many patients,
relief comes only from total joint replacement, a surgical procedure that
carries risks, including blood clots and nerve injury. An alternative to
total joint replacement is cartilage repair. Being slippery, cartilage is particularly difficult to repair. Currently available adhesives for such repair
have limitations. Synthetic adhesives are not highly compatible with
tissues, and their biological counterparts—which are compatible with
tissues—do not have sufficient binding strength to work on cartilage.

Surgical techniques designed to repair damaged cartilage can
relieve pain and restore knee function. Most importantly, surgery can
delay or prevent the onset of arthritis. Most candidates for articular
cartilage restoration are young adults with a single injury, or lesion.
Older patients, or those with many lesions in one joint, are less likely
to benefit from available surgical approaches.

The most common procedures for knee cartilage repair and/or restoration are:

- Microfracture

- Drilling

- Abrasion Arthroplasty

- Autologous Chondrocyte Implantation (ACI)

- Osteochondral Autograft Transplantation (OAT)

- Osteochondral Allograft (OCA) Transplantation

The microfracture procedure is intended to stimulate the marrow to provide "an enriched environment for tissue regeneration." Microfracture begins with debridement of the cartilage defect down to the subchondral bone including the calcified layer of cartilage. The procedure is then taken a step further, whereby an awl is used to pierce the subchondral bone at regular anatomical intervals. The prepared lesion provides a pool that helps hold the marrow clot. Microfracture results in the development of fibrocartilage at the site of the procedure. Fibrocartilage is a mixture of fibrous and cartilaginous tissue, the latter consisting of both type I and type II collagen. Fibrocartilage is tough and has some elasticity, but is not an adequate replacement for the smooth hyaline cartilage normally present in joint surfaces. Fibrocartilage is less durable, less resilient and less able to withstand shock and shearing forces, compared to native articular hyaline cartilage. Retrospective magnetic resonance imaging (MRI) analysis of 80 patients showed that microfracture led to bony overgrowth in nearly 50 percent of the patients reviewed. Moreover, clinical improvement after microfracture is not consistently observed: about 25 percent of patients treated with microfracture reported no or minimal relief in pain and symptoms within the first 12–24 months of treatment and clinical improvement can wane after 24 months.

Drilling, like microfracture, stimulates the production of a mixture of smooth hyaline cartilage and fibrous scar-like tissue. Multiple holes are made through the injured area in the subchondral bone with a surgical drill or wire. The subchondral bone is penetrated to create a healing response. Drilling can be done with an arthroscope. It is less precise than microfracture and the heat of the drill may cause injury to some of the tissues.

Abrasion arthroplasty is similar to drilling. Instead of drills or wires, high speed burrs are used to remove the damaged cartilage and reach the subchondral bone. Abrasion arthroplasty can be done with an arthroscope.

Autologous chondrocyte implantation (ACI) is a two-step procedure. First, healthy cartilage tissue is removed from a nonweight-bearing area of the bone. The chondrocytes from cartilage tissue are cultured and increase in number over a 3- to 5-week period. An open surgical procedure, or arthrotomy, is then done to implant the newly grown cells. First, the cartilage defect is prepared for debridement. A layer of periosteum is sewn over the area. This cover is sealed with fibrin glue. The newly grown cells are then injected into the defect under the periosteal cover. ACI is most useful for younger patients who have single defects larger than 2 cm in diameter.

In osteochondral autograft transplantation, cartilage (and bone) tissue is transferred from one part of the joint to another (non-weight-bearing). The graft is taken as a cylindrical plug of cartilage and subchondral bone. It is then matched to the surface area of the defect and impacted into place. Osteochondral autograft is used for smaller cartilage defects. This is because the healthy graft tissue can be taken only from a limited area of the same joint. The procedure can be performed arthroscopically. If a cartilage defect is too large for an autograft, a cadaveric allograft may be considered. Like an autograft, it is a block of cartilage and bone. In the laboratory it is sterilized and prepared. It is tested for any possible disease transmission. Allografts are typically implanted through an open incision.

The long-term outcomes of osteochondral autograft and allograft procedures are not known precisely, as there are no clinical data from randomized and well controlled studies.

## *Stem Cells in Cartilage Regeneration*

Once damaged, cartilage heals very slowly, if at all. Researchers have been exploring various cell-based techniques to promote cartilage regeneration. Transplantation of patients' own cartilage-producing cells—called chondrocytes—has been tried in the clinic to repair small defects in cartilage. However, the technique has not achieved widespread use because it is difficult to collect sufficient numbers of chondrocytes from patients and grow them in the lab. "The chondrocytes in the arthritic joint are usually [of] inferior quality. In addition, cartilage produced by chondrocytes in culture is weaker than the native tissue. As quality chondrocytes are a sparse commodity, the researchers turned to mesenchymal stem cells (MSCs) found in the bone marrow. Like plant seedlings that sprout with the right combination of water, light, and temperature, stem cells can be coaxed to transform into specific cell types given the right factors. Depending on the cues they receive, MSCs have the potential to give rise to bone cells, cartilage cells, or fat cells. Ongoing clinical trials are exploring direct injection of MSCs to repair damaged cartilage.

Chapter 52

# Sports Physical Therapy

## Learning about Physical Therapy

According to the World Confederation for Physical Therapy (WCPT), physical therapy (PT) is concerned with maximizing quality of life and movement potential within the health spheres of promotion, prevention, treatment/intervention, and rehabilitation. The goal of physical therapy is to promote physical, psychological, emotional, and social well-being. Sports physical therapy is the specialized branch of physiotherapy that deals with injury prevention, management, and return to play.

## Sports Physical Therapist

A sports physical therapist (PT) is a licensed and certified professional who demonstrates advanced competencies in the promotion of safe participation in physical activity, provides advice, and prescribes rehabilitation and training plans. This will help the athlete restore optimal function contributing to the enhancement of sports performance and prevent future injuries.

Sports PTs are often the first responders at training and competition sites when injuries happens. They also work with sports clubs, teams, private and state-run hospitals or clinics, and recreational sports facilities.

---

"Sports Physical Therapy," © 2017 Omnigraphics. Reviewed June 2017.

509

# Prehabilitation

Prehabilitation is all about prevention of injuries. The sports PT performs a preventive injury risk assessment and trains the athlete to prevent the problem before it happens. There are three phases of prehabilitation:

1.  Assess an uninjured player for posture, flexibility, agility, muscle strength, joint alignment, core stability, and movement pattern.

2.  Identify risks involved in the sport itself.

3.  Consider other details, such as the player's position in the sport.

Prehabilitation exercises are sport- and athlete-specific. For example, a short-distance runner will have a different athletic requirement than a long-distance running athlete.

## Early Injury Treatment

Sports PTs treat injuries early using the R.I.C.E. (Rest, Ice, Compression, and Elevation) method to relieve pain, reduce swelling, and promote faster healing. Injured athletes should follow these four steps immediately after the injury occurs and continue for at least 48 hours. They should also avoid H.A.R.M (Heat, Alcohol, Running or Exercise, and Massage) in the first 48 to 72 hours of injury for faster recovery.

## Stretching Exercises

Stretching exercises lengthen the muscles, along with their respective tendons, so that a normal muscle length-tension ratio is maintained for optimal performance. Stretching promotes flexibility, allowing the athlete to use the full range of motion in a particular joint effectively.

A proper warm-up and a dynamic stretching program are the best ways to prepare for any sport. It is like warming up a car engine before it can roar down the street. Many studies have shown that a proper warm-up and a stretching regimen can reduce the incidence of sports injuries significantly.

A period of exercise cool down is also needed after playing a sport. About 5 to 10 minutes of static stretching of the muscles will prevent DOMS (Delayed Onset Muscle Soreness).

## Strengthening Exercises

Generally, strengthening exercises are known to bulk up the muscles, enabling the lifting heavy weights. Depending on the treatment goals, sport, or function, your physiotherapist will be able to prescribe a specific set of strengthening exercises. The components of muscle strength are power, endurance, and speed of contraction, and each needs to be built up through strength training.

## Supportive Taping and Strapping

Taping is usually done by physiotherapists for the following benefits:

• pain relief

• to improve joint stability

• to reduce injury recurrence

• to enhance the athlete's confidence

Based on the assessment, your physiotherapist can decide to use one of three types of tape:

1. Rigid strapping tape—This is the most commonly used one and is also known as "sports tape" or "athletic tape."

2. Elastic strapping tape—This is used when less support is needed.

3. Kinesiology tape—This is an improved version of elastic tape, which acts dynamically, assisting the muscle function.

## Core Strengthening and Stability

The spine is an inherently unstable part of the body, with a lot of mobility, especially in the lower back. The small, deep core muscles connect one vertebra to another. They are the main structures that support, control, and move the lower spine. As they are small and ideally located, they require less energy to do the job of stabilizing the spine during varied sports activities. A physiotherapist will be able to assess the strength and prescribe specific core-strengthening exercises.

## Electrotherapy and Local Modalities

Electrotherapy and local modalities help in pain relief and enhance the healing process using physical energies, such as electrical, sound, light, magnetic, and temperature. The modalities will have short-term benefits and help the therapist introduce exercises and progress with them.

Electrotherapy modalities include:

- ultrasound

- laser

- transcutaneous electrical nerve stimulation (TENS)

Local modalities include:

- ice

- heat

## Sports Massage

Sports massage is a very effective adjunct treatment for soft tissue injuries, so regular massage sessions form part of athletes' injury prevention strategy. This also has plenty of benefits—not only physical but also physiological and psychological benefits. A massage can improve general body condition, prevent loss of mobility, cure and restore mobility to injured soft tissue, enhance performance, and extend the overall life of your sporting career.

### References

1. Russell, Zoe. "What Is Sports Physiotherapy?" Physioworks. com, August 20, 2016.

2. "What Is a Sports Physical Therapist?" SPA Project, n.d.

3. "Treatment & Therapies," Virtual Sports Injury Clinic, n.d.

# Part Ten

# Sports Injuries in Children and Young Athletes

Chapter 53

# Children and Sports Injuries

## Chapter Contents

# Section 53.1

## Sport and Recreation Safety for Children

This section includes text excerpted from "Sports and Recreation-Related Injuries," Centers for Disease Control and Prevention (CDC), February 23, 2011. Reviewed June 2017.

As people's participation in organized sport activity increases, so does the rate of sports-related injuries. Recreational activities, including sports, account for an estimated 3.2 million visits to emergency rooms each year for children aged 5–14 years. Injuries from organized and unorganized sports account for 775,000 emergency room visits annually for children in this same age group. Sports-related injuries are the leading cause of emergency room visits in 12–17-year-olds.

### Who's at Risk?

Because playing sports involves a certain amount of risk, those who play are at a higher risk for sports-related injuries. Twice as many males as females suffer sports-related injuries. This is due, in part, to the types of sports males and females play. Collision or contact sports have higher injury rates—football, basketball, baseball and soccer account for about 80 percent of all sports-related emergency room visits for children between 5 and 14 years of age. While teens and young adults experience injuries related to the force they can generate and the intensity of play, children in this age group are less proficient at assessing risks and have less coordination, slower reaction times and less accuracy than adults. Children between 5 and 14 years old account for almost 40 percent of all sports-related injuries.

When it comes to recreational activities, another group "at risk" for injuries includes adults who have been "out of practice" for a particular sport or are not accustomed to physical activity. Adults sometimes overestimate their abilities to undertake a new exercise program and push themselves to the point of injury.

## Can It Be Prevented?

Estimates suggest that half of all childhood sports-related injuries can be prevented, and steps can be taken to reduce risks in all types of recreational activities:

- To avoid unnecessary injuries, all children and adolescents should have a physical exam before starting new sports activities.

- Participate in activities that are supervised by an experienced or trained coach who understands and enforces game rules.

- If starting a new exercise program, set realistic goals and start with frequencies and intensities appropriate to your current physical condition (based on consultation with your physician) and injury-history.

- Ensure that playing fields and environments are safe and well-maintained (e.g., well-maintained playing fields free of tripping hazards, holes, exposed sprinklers, broken glass).

- Make sure you are properly outfitted for the sport in which you plan to participate—proper protective gear (helmet, shin guards, knee pads); shoes that fit well and are appropriate for the sport; clothing that is not too loose so it won't become tangled. In some sports, mouth guards and face protection can help prevent traumas to the face, head, eyes, and mouth, which are among the most common types of injuries.

- Stretch and warm-up before playing.

- Do not "play through" pain. If you are injured, see your doctor. Follow all the doctor's orders for recovery, and get the doctor's OK before returning to play. Playing again too soon can lead to a more serious and long-lasting injuries.

- Have a first aid kit available at all times.

- Learn skills to prevent injuries specific to your sport (e.g., learn how to safely stop or fall while inline skating).

- For children's team sports, be sure to match and group children based on skill level, weight and physical maturity especially for contact sports.

# Section 53.2

# *Playground Injuries*

This section contains text excerpted from the following sources: Text under the heading "Outdoor Home Playground Safety Checklist" is excerpted from "Outdoor Home Playground Safety Handbook," U.S. Consumer Product Safety Commission (CPSC), August 17, 2005. Reviewed June 2017; Text under the heading "Burn Safety Awareness on Playgrounds: Thermal Burns from Playground Equipment" is excerpted from "Burn Safety Awareness on Playgrounds," U.S. Consumer Product Safety Commission (CPSC), April 26, 2012. Reviewed June 2017.

## *Outdoor Home Playground Safety Checklist*

**Supervision:** Be sure to always supervise children on play equipment.

**Surfacing:** Install a protective surface under and around play equipment to reduce the likelihood of serious head injuries.

- For most play equipment, install protective surfacing 6 feet in all directions beyond the equipment.

- For swings, extend protective surfacing in front and back of the swing to a distance that is twice the height of the bar from which the swing is suspended.

- For tire swings, install protective surfacing outward from the swing equal to the suspension chain plus 6 feet.

**Types of Surfacing:** Carpeting and thin mats are not adequate as protective surfacing. Maintain at least 9 inches of loose-fill material or use an ASTM F1292 rated material at the depth required for the equipment height.

- Use wood mulch/chips, shredded rubber mulch, or engineered wood fiber for equipment up to 8 feet high;

- Use sand, pea gravel, or mulch products listed above for play equipment up to 5 feet high; or

- Use surface mats tested to provide impact protection equal to or greater than the height of the play equipment.

**Equipment Maintenance:** Periodically check nuts, bolts, caps, swing seats, suspension ropes, chains, and cables and replace as necessary. Maintain loose-fill surfacing and surface mats.

**Opening:** Eliminate openings that can trap a child's head or neck, such as openings in guardrails or ladders. Openings should be smaller than 3½ inches to prevent entry of a small child's body, or larger than 9 inches to allow a child's head and body to slide completely through.

**Ropes:** Never attach jump ropes, clotheslines, pet leashes, or cords of any kind to play equipment. Anchor any climbing ropes at both ends. Remove drawstrings from children's clothes. Children can strangle on these.

**Anchors:** Bury or cover anchors with adequate surfacing material to prevent tripping. Play equipment should not tip over.

**Guardrails or Barriers:** Make sure that platforms and ramps over 30 inches high have guardrails or barriers to prevent falls.

**Repair:** Repair sharp points or edges on equipment that can cause injuries.

**Upkeep of Hardware:** Replace missing hardware, eliminate protruding bolts, and close "S" hooks that can cause injuries.

## Burn Safety Awareness on Playgrounds: Thermal Burns from Playground Equipment

The U.S. Consumer Product Safety Commission (CPSC) wants you to be aware of the risk of thermal burns from playground equipment. You may remember the metal slides of your youth and how they could get very hot in the summer sun. But what you may not realize is that today's newer materials, such as plastics and rubbers, also have the potential to become hot enough to burn a child's skin.

## Doesn't It Have to Be Hot outside in Order for a Child to Receive a Burn?

Surprisingly, no! The weather does not have to be hot in order for equipment to heat up and cause burns. Even in mild weather, as long as the equipment or surfacing is in direct sunlight for an extended period of time, there is a risk of sustaining a thermal burn injury. In fact, one reported incident occurred on a 74°F day and resulted in a child receiving serious second-degree burns from a plastic slide.

## *I Only Have to Worry about Metal Slides, Right?*

No. Metal is not the only material that can cause thermal burns. Because it is known that bare (uncoated) metal slides can cause severe burns, many pieces of metal playground equipment have either been replaced with plastic equipment or coated with heat-reducing paint— yet burns still occur on playgrounds.

## *What Should I Watch For?*

- Uncoated metal equipment, or metal equipment where the heat-reducing coating has rubbed off
- Slides, swings, or other equipment that a child may sit on
- Dark-colored plastics and rubbers, especially the surfacing under and around the playground equipment
- Asphalt and concrete surfaces near playgrounds

## *Who Is Most at Risk?*

A child of any age can be burned by a hot surface; however, children 2 years old and younger are most at risk for two reasons:

1. A young child's skin is more susceptible to burning because it is thinner and more delicate.

2. Young children have not yet learned to react by removing themselves from the hot surface. Unlike the reflex that happens when a child touches a very hot surface with their hand, a young child who is sitting or standing on the hot surface may scream from the pain of burning, but they may not know to move from the location that is burning them.

## *What Can I Do?*

- **Always be aware** of the sun and weather conditions, and **do not assume** that the equipment is safe because the air temperature is not very high.

- **Always check the temperature** of the equipment and surfacing before letting your children play on the playground.

- Remember, a young child's skin will burn faster than your own. If it feels hot to your hand, it may be too hot for a child's bare skin.

- Because some materials transfer heat more slowly than others, these materials may not feel hot with a quick touch.

- Always dress your child in **appropriate clothing** for the playground (e.g., shoes, pants).

- Remember that playground equipment, as well as **playground surfacing**, may cause burns.

- Several incidents have involved a child running barefoot across the playground.

- **Always** watch your children while on the playground. Supervision can help to prevent some incidents.

## *Where Can I Report an Injury or Burn?*

If your child is injured on the playground, first seek medical attention, if necessary, then:

- Call the park owner or operator, which is often your local parks and recreation department or school system, and notify them of the injury.

- Report the incident to CPSC by calling 800-638-2772 or logging on to www.SaferProducts.gov.

- Call the manufacturer (if known), and notify them of the injury.

Chapter 54

# Sports Physicals

You already know that playing sports helps keep you fit. You also know that sports are a fun way to socialize and meet people. But you might not know why it's so important to get a sports physical at the beginning of your sports season.

## What Is a Sports Physical?

In the sports medicine field, the sports physical exam is known as a preparticipation physical examination (PPE). The exam helps determine whether it's safe for you to participate in a certain sport. Most states actually require that kids and teens have a sports physical before they can start a new sport or begin a new competitive season. But even if a sports physical isn't required, doctors still highly recommend getting one.

The two main parts to a sports physical are the medical history and the physical exam.

### Medical History

This part of the exam includes questions about:

- serious illnesses among family members
- illnesses that you had when you were younger or may have now, such as asthma, diabetes, or epilepsy

Text in this chapter is © 1995-2017. The Nemours Foundation/KidsHealth®. Reprinted with permission.

- previous hospitalizations or surgeries

- allergies (to insect bites, for example)

- past injuries (including concussions, sprains, or bone fractures)

- whether you've ever passed out, felt dizzy, had chest pain, or had trouble breathing during exercise

- any medications that you are on (including over-the-counter medications, herbal supplements, and prescription medications)

The medical history questions are usually on a form that you can bring home, so ask your parents to help you fill in the answers. If possible, ask both parents about family medical history.

Answer the questions as well as you can. Try not to guess the answers or give answers you think your doctor wants.

Looking at patterns of illness in your family is a good way to consider possible conditions you may have. Most sports medicine doctors believe the medical history is the most important part of the sports physical exam, so take time to answer the questions carefully. It's unlikely that your answers will prevent you from playing your sports.

### Physical Examination

During the physical part of the exam, the doctor will usually:

- record your height and weight

- take a blood pressure and pulse (heart rate and rhythm)

- test your vision

- check your heart, lungs, abdomen, ears, nose, and throat

- evaluate your posture, joints, strength, and flexibility

Although most of the exam will be the same for males and females, if a person has started or already gone through puberty, the doctor may ask girls and guys different questions. For example, if a girl is heavily involved in a lot of active sports, the doctor may ask her about her period and diet to make sure she doesn't have something like female athlete triad (poor nutrition, irregular or absent periods, and weak bones).

A doctor will also ask questions about use of drugs, alcohol, or dietary supplements, including steroids or other "performance enhancers" and weight-loss supplements, because these can affect a person's health.

At the end of your exam, the doctor will either fill out and sign a form if everything checks out OK or, in some cases, recommend a follow-up exam, additional tests, or specific treatment for medical problems.

## Why Is a Sports Physical Important?

A sports physical can help you find out about and deal with health problems that might interfere with your participation in a sport. For example, if you have frequent asthma attacks but are a starting forward in soccer, a doctor might be able to prescribe a different type of inhaler or adjust the dosage so that you can breathe more easily when you run.

Your doctor may even have some good training tips and be able to give you some ideas for avoiding injuries. For example, he or she may recommend certain stretching or strengthening activities, that help prevent injuries. A doctor also can identify risk factors that are linked to specific sports. Advice like this will make you a better, stronger athlete.

## When and Where Should I Go for a Sports Physical?

Some people go to their own doctor for a sports physical; others have one at school. During school physicals, you may go to half a dozen or so "stations" set up in the gym; each one is staffed by a medical professional who gives you a specific part of the physical exam.

If your school offers the exam, it's convenient to get it done there. But even if you have a sports physical at school, it's a good idea to see your regular doctor for an exam as well. Your doctor knows you—and your health history—better than anyone you talk to briefly in a gym.

If your state requires sports physicals, you'll probably have to start getting them when you're in seventh grade. Even if sports physicals aren't required by your school or state, it's still smart to get them if you participate in school sports. And if you compete regularly in a sport before ninth grade, you should begin getting these exams even earlier.

Getting a sports physical once a year is usually adequate. If you're healing from a major injury, like a broken wrist or ankle, however, get checked out after it's healed before you start practicing or playing again.

You should have your physical about 6 weeks before your sports season begins so there's enough time to follow up on something, if necessary. Neither you nor your doctor will be very happy if your sports physical is the day before baseball practice starts and it turns out there's something that needs to be taken care of before you can suit up.

## What If There's a Problem?

What happens if you don't get the OK from your own doctor and have to see a specialist? Does that mean you won't ever be able to letter in softball or hockey? Don't worry if your doctor asks you to have other tests or go for a follow-up exam—it could be something as simple as rechecking your blood pressure a week or two after the physical.

Your doctor's referral to a specialist may help your athletic performance. For example, if you want to try out for your school's track team but get a slight pain in your knee every time you run, an orthopedist or sports medicine specialist can help you figure out what's going on. Perhaps the pain comes from previous overtraining or poor running technique. Maybe you injured the knee a long time ago and it never totally healed. Or perhaps the problem is as simple as running shoes that don't offer enough support. Chances are, a doctor will be able to help you run without the risk of further injury to the knee by giving you suggestions or treatment before the sports season begins.

It's very unlikely that you'll be disqualified from playing sports. The ultimate goal of the sports physical is to make sure you're safe while playing sports, not to stop you from playing. Most of the time, a specialist won't find any reason to prevent you from playing your sport.

## Do I Still Have to Get a Regular Physical?

In a word, yes. It may seem like overkill, but a sports physical is different from a standard physical.

The sports physical focuses on your well-being as it relates to playing a sport. It's more limited than a regular physical, but it's a lot more specific about athletic issues. During a regular physical, however, your doctor will address your overall well-being, which may include things that are unrelated to sports. You can ask your doctor to give you both types of exams during one visit; just be aware that you'll need to set aside more time.

Even if your sports physical exam doesn't reveal any problems, it's always to monitor yourself when you play sports. If you notice changes in your physical condition—even if you think they're small, such as muscle pain or shortness of breath—be sure to mention them to a parent or coach. You should also inform your phys-ed teacher or coach if your health needs have changed in any way or if you're taking a new medication.

Just as professional sports stars need medical care to keep them playing their best, so do teenage athletes. You can give yourself the same edge as the pros by making sure you have your sports physical.

Chapter 55

# *Preventing Children's Sports Injuries*

Taking part in sports and recreation activities is an important part of a healthy, physically active lifestyle for kids. But injuries can, and do, occur. More than 2.6 million children 0–19 years old are treated in the emergency department each year for sports and recreation-related injuries.

Thankfully, there are steps that parents can take to help make sure kids stay safe on the field, the court, or wherever they play or participate in sports and recreation activities.

## *Childhood Sports Injuries: A Common and Serious Problem*

Although sports participation provides numerous physical and social benefits, it also has a downside: the risk of sports-related injuries. According to the Centers for Disease Control and Prevention (CDC), more than 2.6 million children 0–19 years old are treated in the emergency department each year for sports and recreation-related injuries.

This chapter contains text excerpted from the following sources: Text in this chapter begins with excerpts from "Child Safety and Injury Prevention," Centers for Disease Control and Prevention (CDC), March 14, 2017; Text beginning with the heading "Childhood Sports Injuries: A Common and Serious Problem" is excerpted from "Preventing Musculoskeletal Sports Injuries in Youth: A Guide for Parents," National Institute of Arthritis and Musculoskeletal and Skin Diseases (NIAMS), September 2016.

These injuries are by far the most common cause of musculoskeletal injuries in children treated in emergency departments. They are also the single most common cause of injury-related primary care office visits.

## The Most Common Musculoskeletal Sports-Related Injuries in Kids

Although sports injuries can range from scrapes and bruises to serious brain and spinal cord injuries, most fall somewhere between the two extremes. Here are some of the more common types of injuries.

### Sprains and Strains

A sprain is an injury to a ligament, one of the bands of tough, fibrous tissue that connects two or more bones at a joint and prevents excessive movement of the joint. An ankle sprain is the most common athletic injury.

A strain is an injury to either a muscle or a tendon. A muscle is a tissue composed of bundles of specialized cells that, when stimulated by nerve messages, contract and produce movement. A tendon is a tough, fibrous cord of tissue that connects muscle to bone. Muscles in any part of the body can be injured.

### Growth Plate Injuries

In some sports accidents and injuries, the growth plate may be injured. The growth plate is the area of developing tissues at the end of the long bones in growing children and adolescents. When growth is complete, sometime during adolescence, the growth plate is replaced by solid bone. The long bones in the body include:

- the long bones of the hand and fingers (metacarpals and phalanges)
- both bones of the forearm (radius and ulna)
- the bone of the upper leg (femur)
- the lower leg bones (tibia and fibula)
- the foot bones (metatarsals and phalanges).

If any of these areas becomes injured, it's important to seek professional help from an orthopaedic surgeon, a doctor who specializes in bone injuries.

## Repetitive Motion Injuries

Painful injuries such as stress fractures (a hairline fracture of the bone that has been subjected to repeated stress) and tendinitis (inflammation of a tendon) can occur from overuse of muscles and tendons. Some of these injuries don't always show up on X-rays, but they do cause pain and discomfort. The injured area usually responds to rest, ice, compression, and elevation (R.I.C.E). Other treatments can include crutches, cast immobilization, and physical therapy.

## Preventing and Treating Musculoskeletal Injuries

Injuries can happen to any child who plays sports, but there are some things that can help prevent and treat injuries.

### Prevention

• Enroll your child in organized sports through schools, community clubs, and recreation areas that are properly maintained. Any organized team activity should demonstrate a commitment to injury prevention. Coaches should be trained in first aid and cardiopulmonary resuscitation (CPR), and should have a plan for responding to emergencies. Coaches should be well versed in the proper use of equipment, and should enforce rules on equipment use.

• Organized sports programs may have adults on staff who are certified athletic trainers. These individuals are trained to prevent, recognize, and provide immediate care for athletic injuries.

• Make sure your child has—and consistently uses—proper gear for a particular sport. This may reduce the chances of being injured.

• Make warm-ups and cool-downs part of your child's routine before and after sports participation. Warm-up exercises make the body's tissues warmer and more flexible. Cool-down exercises loosen muscles that have tightened during exercise.

• Make sure your child has access to water or a sports drink while playing. Encourage him or her to drink frequently and stay properly hydrated. Remember to include sunscreen and a hat (when possible) to reduce the chance of sunburn, which is a type of injury to the skin. Sun protection may also decrease the chances of malignant melanoma—a potentially deadly skin cancer—or other skin cancers that can occur later in life.

531

- Learn and follow safety rules and suggestions for your child's particular sport. You'll find some more sport-specific safety suggestions below.

## Treatment

Treatment for sports-related injuries will vary by injury. But if your child suffers a soft tissue injury (such as a sprain or strain) or a bone injury, the best immediate treatment is easy to remember: RICE (rest, ice, compression, elevation) the injury. Get professional treatment if any injury is severe. A severe injury means having an obvious fracture or dislocation of a joint, prolonged swelling, or prolonged or severe pain.

## Keep Kids Exercising

It's important that kids continue some type of regular exercise after the injury heals. Exercise may reduce their chances of obesity, which has become more common in children. It may also reduce the risk of diabetes, a disease that can be associated with a lack of exercise and poor eating habits. Exercise also helps build social skills and provides a general sense of well-being. Sports participation is an important part of learning how to build team skills.

As a parent, it is important for you to encourage your children to be physically active. It's also important to match your child to the sport, and not push him or her too hard into an activity that he or she may not like or be capable of doing. Teach your children to follow the rules and to play it safe when they get involved in sports, so they'll spend more time having fun in the game and be less likely to be sidelined with an injury. You should be mindful of the risks associated with different sports and take important measures to reduce the chance of injury.

## Sport-Specific Safety Information

Here are some winning ways to help prevent an injury from occurring.

### Basketball

- **Common injuries and locations:** Sprains, strains, bruises, fractures, scrapes, dislocations, cuts, injuries to teeth, ankles, and knees. (Injury rates are higher in girls, especially for the anterior cruciate ligament or ACL, the wide ligament that limits rotation and forward movement of the shin bone.)

532

- **Safest playing with:** Eye protection, elbow and knee pads, mouth guard, athletic supporters for males, proper shoes, water. If playing outdoors, wear sunscreen and, when possible, a hat.

- **Injury prevention:** Strength training (particularly knees and shoulders), aerobics (exercises that develop the strength and endurance of heart and lungs), warm-up exercises, proper coaching, use of safety equipment.

## Track and Field

- **Common injuries:** Strains, sprains, scrapes from falls.

- **Safest playing with:** Proper shoes, athletic supporters for males, sunscreen, water.

- **Injury prevention:** Proper conditioning and coaching.

## Football

- **Common injuries and locations:** Bruises, sprains, strains, pulled muscles, tears to soft tissues such as ligaments, broken bones, internal injuries (bruised or damaged organs), concussions, back injuries, sunburn. Knees and ankles are the most common injury sites.

- **Safest playing with:** Helmet, mouth guard, shoulder pads, athletic supporters for males, chest/rib pads, forearm, elbow, and thigh pads, shin guards, proper shoes, sunscreen, water.

- **Injury prevention:** Proper use of safety equipment, warm-up exercises, proper coaching techniques and conditioning.

## Baseball and Softball

- **Common injuries:** Soft tissue strains, impact injuries that include fractures caused by sliding and being hit by a ball, sunburn.

- **Safest playing with:** Batting helmet; shin guards; elbow guards; athletic supporters for males; mouth guard; sunscreen; cleats; hat; detachable, "breakaway bases" rather than traditional, stationary ones.

- **Injury prevention:** Proper conditioning and warm-ups.

*Soccer*

- **Common injuries:** Bruises, cuts and scrapes, headaches, sunburn.

- **Safest playing with:** Shin guards, athletic supporters for males, cleats, sunscreen, water.

- **Injury prevention:** Aerobic conditioning and warm-ups, and—when age appropriate—proper training in "heading" (that is, using the head to strike or make a play with the ball).

*Gymnastics*

- **Common injuries:** Sprains and strains of soft tissues.

- **Safest playing with:** Athletic supporters for males, safety harness, joint supports (such as neoprene wraps), water.

- **Injury prevention:** Proper conditioning and warm-ups.

## Treat Injuries with "RICE"

**Rest:** Reduce or stop using the injured area for at least 48 hours. If you have a leg injury, you may need to stay off of it completely.

**Ice:** Put an ice pack on the injured area for 20 minutes at a time, four to eight times per day. Use a cold pack, ice bag, or a plastic bag filled with crushed ice that has been wrapped in a towel.

**Compression:** Ask your child's doctor about elastics wraps, air casts, special boots, or splints that can be used to compress an injured ankle, knee, or wrist to reduce swelling.

**Elevation:** Keep the injured area elevated above the level of the heart to help decrease swelling. Use a pillow to help elevate an injured limb.

Chapter 56

# Overtraining Burnout in Young Athletes

## Overtraining Syndrome[1]

Are you the type of athlete that has a need to always practice, weight lift, or do some kind of cardiovascular workout? Does your mind tell you that training and training and more training will make you feel better? Do you also tell yourself that rest or sitting around is bad for you? If you answered yes, you might have what is known as overtraining syndrome, "staleness," or "burnout."

## Risk Factors[1]

Overtraining occurs when there is a continuous, excessive overload of exercise without proper rest and proper nutrition. Many people fail to adapt to the stress sustained during high intensity training because they don't give their bodies enough time to adapt and recuperate. A poorly designed program consisting of a rapid increase in volume and intensity, consistently high volume training, and insufficient time for

This chapter includes text excerpted from documents published by two public domain sources. Text under headings marked 1 are excerpted from "Feeling 'Stale' from Overtraining," National Aeronautics and Space Administration (NASA), n.d. Reviewed June 2017; Text under heading marked 2 is excerpted from "Exercise and Bone Health for Women: The Skeletal Risk of Overtraining," National Institute of Arthritis and Musculoskeletal and Skin Diseases (NIAMS), May 2016.

rest and recovery can lead to the body shutting down. Other factors that will increase your chances for developing overtraining syndrome are frequent competition, pre-existing medical conditions, poor diet, environmental stress, and psychosocial stress.

## The Skeletal Risk of Overtraining in Female Athletes[2]

Girls and women who engage in rigorous exercise regimens or who try to lose weight by restricting their eating are at risk for these health problems. They may include serious athletes, "gym rats" (who spend considerable time and energy working out), and girls and women who believe "you can never be too thin."

Some athletes see amenorrhea (the absence of menstrual periods) as a sign of successful training. Others see it as a great answer to a monthly inconvenience. And some young women accept it blindly, not stopping to think of the consequences. But missing your periods is often a sign of decreased estrogen levels. And lower estrogen levels can lead to osteoporosis, a disease in which your bones become brittle and more likely to break.

Usually, bones don't become brittle and break until women are much older. But some young women, especially those who exercise so much that their periods stop, develop brittle bones, and may start to have fractures at a very early age. Some 20-year-old female athletes have been said to have the bones of an 80-year-old woman. Even if bones don't break when you're young, low estrogen levels during the peak years of bone-building, the preteen and teen years, can affect bone density for the rest of your life. And studies show that bone growth lost during these years may never be regained.

Broken bones don't just hurt—they can cause lasting physical malformations. Have you noticed that some older women and men have stooped postures? This is not a normal sign of aging. Fractures from osteoporosis have left their spines permanently altered.

## Signs of Burnout[1]

With all these factors and living in a world filled with stress, how do you know if you have this syndrome? There are many signs and symptoms with overtraining, but the primary element is the unpredicted drop in performance. A person can train and compete at the same level as they are use to, but they will have greater difficulty in maintaining the performance. Other signs and symptoms include excessive muscle fatigue, increased resting heart rate, trouble sleeping, depression, anxiety, increased weight loss, frequent injuries, and illnesses.

## Treatment[1]

Overtraining syndrome is not something that is hard to treat. First off, it is always wise to consult a physician if it is suspected. This can rule out any disease or illness that can be caused by overtraining. Recovery will take at least two weeks depending on how severe the case is. Your activities should be extremely limited, if not discontinued during this time frame, and proper rest and nutrition should be given. A diet of low fat and high carbohydrates is recommended because of the depleted glycogen level over the period of time.

## Prevention[1]

Early recognition will prevent any damages that could affect the body. To prevent overtraining from occurring, have an alternative workout schedule with proper rest for the body in between. Training should alternate from a heavy workday to a light workday. Good nutrition complete with complex carbohydrates, fruits, vegetables, and protein should be part of the diet. Proper hydration is a must! A person exercising should take in at least 8 servings, 12 fl oz. each, of water per pound lost. Increases in training should be progressed slowly so the body has time to adapt. To increase in training, one should use the 10% rule. The 10% rule is an increase of 10% in either intensity, duration or volume in one workout session at a time. Intensity, duration, and volume should not be increased at the same time. Most importantly, educating yourself about proper exercise is a key. And listen to you body... It will tell you when it's had enough!

Chapter 57

# Growth Plate Injuries

## What Is the Growth Plate?

The growth plate, also known as the epiphyseal plate or physis, is the area of growing tissue near the ends of the long bones in children and adolescents. Each long bone has at least two growth plates: one at each end. The growth plate determines the future length and shape of the mature bone. When growth is complete—sometime during adolescence—the growth plates close and are replaced by solid bone.

Because the growth plates are the weakest areas of the growing skeleton—even weaker than the nearby ligaments and tendons that connect bones to other bones and muscles—they are vulnerable to injury. Injuries to the growth plate are called fractures.

## Who Gets Growth Plate Injuries?

Growth plate injuries can occur in growing children and adolescents. In a child, a serious injury to a joint is more likely to damage a growth plate than the ligaments that stabilize the joint. Trauma that would cause a sprain in an adult might cause a growth plate fracture in a child.

Growth plate fractures occur twice as often in boys as in girls, because girls' bodies mature at an earlier age than boys. As a result,

This chapter includes text excerpted from "Growth Plate Injuries—Questions and Answers about Growth Plate Injuries," National Institute of Arthritis and Musculoskeletal and Skin Diseases (NIAMS), May 2014.

their bones finish growing sooner, and their growth plates are replaced by stronger, solid bone.

Growth plate injuries often occur in competitive sports such as football, basketball, or gymnastics, or as a result of recreational activities such as biking, sledding, skiing, or skateboarding.

Fractures can result from a single traumatic event, such as a fall or automobile accident, or from chronic stress and overuse. Most growth plate fractures occur in the long bones of the fingers (phalanges) and the outer bone of the forearm (radius). They are also common in the lower bones of the leg (the tibia and fibula).

## What Causes Growth Plate Injuries?

Growth plate injuries can be caused by an event such as a fall or blow to the limb, or they can result from overuse. For example, a gymnast who practices for hours on the uneven bars, a long-distance runner, and a baseball pitcher perfecting his curveball can all have growth plate injuries.

Although many growth plate injuries are caused by accidents that occur during play or athletic activity, growth plates are also susceptible to other disorders, such as bone infection, that can alter their normal growth and development. Other possible causes of growth plate injuries include the following:

- **Child abuse.** Fractures are common among physically abused children, and growth plate injuries are prevalent because the growth plate is the weakest part of the bone.

- **Injury from extreme cold (for example, frostbite).** Exposure to extreme cold can damage the growth plate in children and result in short, stubby fingers or premature degenerative arthritis (breakdown of the joint cartilage).

- **Radiation and medications.** Research has suggested that chemotherapy given for childhood cancers may negatively affect bone growth. Prolonged use of steroids for inflammatory conditions such as juvenile idiopathic arthritis can also harm bone growth.

- **Neurological disorders.** Children with certain neurological disorders that result in sensory deficit or muscular imbalance are prone to growth plate fractures, especially at the ankle and knee. Children who are born with insensitivity to pain can have similar types of injuries.

- **Genetics.** The growth plates are where many inherited disorders that affect the musculoskeletal system appear. Scientists are beginning to understand the genes and gene mutations involved in skeletal formation, growth, and development. This new information is raising hopes for improving treatment for children who are born with poorly formed or improperly functioning growth plates.

- **Metabolic disease.** Disease states such as kidney failure and hormone disorders can affect the growth plates and their function. The bone growth of children with long-term conditions of this kind may be negatively affected.

## How Are Growth Plate Fractures Diagnosed?

A child who has persistent pain, or pain that affects athletic performance or the ability to move and put pressure on a limb, should never be allowed or expected to "work through the pain." Whether an injury is acute or due to overuse, it should be evaluated by a doctor, because some injuries, if left untreated, can cause permanent damage and interfere with proper growth of the involved limb.

The doctor will begin the diagnostic process by asking about the injury and how it occurred and by examining the child. The doctor will then use X-rays to determine if there is a fracture, and if so, the type of fracture. Often the doctor will X-ray not only the injured limb but the opposite limb as well. Because growth plates have not yet hardened into solid bone, neither the structures themselves nor injuries to them show up on X-rays. Instead, growth plates appear as gaps between the shaft of a long bone, called the metaphysis, and the end of the bone, called the epiphysis. By comparing X-rays of the injured limb to those of the noninjured limb, doctors can look for differences that indicate an injury.

Very often the X-ray is negative, because the growth plate line is already there, and the fracture is undisplaced (the two ends of the broken bone are not separated). The doctor can still diagnose a growth plate fracture on clinical grounds because of tenderness of the plate. Children do get ligament strains if their growth plates are open, and they often have undisplaced growth plate fractures.

Other tests doctors may use to diagnose a growth plate injury include magnetic resonance imaging (MRI), computed tomography (CT), and ultrasound.

Because these tests enable doctors to see the growth plate and areas of other soft tissue, they can be useful not only in detecting the presence of an injury, but also in determining the type and extent of the injury.

## What Are the Different Types of Growth Plate Injuries?

Since the 1960s, the Salter-Harris classification, which divides most growth plate fractures into five categories based on the type of damage, has been the standard. The categories are as follows:

### Type I: Fracture through the Growth Plate

The epiphysis is completely separated from the end of the bone or the metaphysis, through the deep layer of the growth plate. The growth plate remains attached to the epiphysis. The doctor has to put the fracture back into place if it is significantly displaced. Type I injuries generally require a cast to protect the plate as it heals. Unless there is damage to the blood supply to the growth plate, the likelihood that the bone will grow normally is excellent.

### Type II: Fracture through the Growth Plate and Metaphysis

This is the most common type of growth plate fracture. It runs through the growth plate and the metaphysis, but the epiphysis is not involved in the injury. Like type I fractures, type II fractures may need to be put back into place and immobilized. However, the growth plate fracture heals a great deal, especially in younger children. If it is not too displaced, the doctor may not need to put it back into position. In this case, it will strengthen with time.

### Type III: Fracture through Growth Plate and Epiphysis

This fracture occurs only rarely, usually at the lower end of the tibia, one of the long bones of the lower leg. It happens when a fracture runs completely through the epiphysis and separates part of the epiphysis and growth plate from the metaphysis. Surgery is sometimes necessary to restore the joint surface to normal. The outlook or prognosis for growth is good if the blood supply to the separated portion of the epiphysis is still intact and if the joint surface heals in a normal position.

## Type IV: Fracture Through Growth Plate, Metaphysis, and Epiphysis

This fracture runs through the epiphysis, across the growth plate, and into the metaphysis. Surgery is frequently needed to restore the joint surface to normal and to perfectly align the growth plate. Unless perfect alignment is achieved and maintained during healing, prognosis for growth is poor, and angulation (bending) of the bone may occur. This injury occurs most commonly at the end of the humerus (the upper arm bone) near the elbow.

## Type V: Compression Fracture Through Growth Plate

This uncommon injury occurs when the end of the bone is crushed and the growth plate is compressed. It is most likely to occur at the knee or ankle. Prognosis is poor, since premature stunting of growth is almost inevitable.

A newer classification, called the Peterson classification, adds a type VI fracture, in which a portion of the epiphysis, growth plate, and metaphysis is missing. This usually occurs with open wounds or compound fractures, and often involves lawnmowers, farm machinery, snowmobiles, or gunshot wounds. All type VI fractures require surgery, and most will require later reconstructive or corrective surgery. Bone growth is almost always stunted.

## What Kind of Doctor Treats Growth Plate Injuries?

For all but the simplest injuries, your child's doctor will probably refer him or her to an orthopaedic surgeon (a doctor who specializes in bone and joint problems in children and adults) for treatment. Some problems may require the services of a pediatric orthopaedic surgeon, who specializes in injuries and musculoskeletal disorders in children.

## How Are Growth Plate Injuries Treated?

Treatment for growth plate injuries depends on the type of injury. In all cases, treatment should be started as soon as possible after injury and will generally involve a mix of the following:

### Immobilization

The affected limb is often put in a cast or splint, and the child is told to limit any activity that puts pressure on the injured area.

## *Manipulation or Surgery*

If the fracture is displaced (meaning the ends of the injured bones no longer meet as they should), the doctor will have to put the bones or joints back in their correct positions, either by using his or her hands (called manipulation) or by performing surgery. Sometimes the doctor needs to fix the break and hold the growth plate in place with screws or wire. After the procedure, the bone will be set in place (immobilized) so it can heal without moving. This is usually done with a cast that encloses the injured growth plate and the joints on both sides of it. The cast is left in place until the injury heals, which can take anywhere from a few weeks to 2 or more months for serious injuries. The need for manipulation or surgery depends on the location and extent of the injury, its effect on nearby nerves and blood vessels, and the child's age.

## *Strengthening and Range-of-Motion Exercises*

These are exercises designed to strengthen the muscles that support the injured area of the bone and to improve or maintain the joint's ability to move in the way that it should. Your child's doctor may recommend these after the fracture has healed. A physical therapist can work with your child and his or her doctor to design an appropriate exercise plan. Long-term followup is usually necessary to monitor the child's recuperation and growth.

## Will the Affected Limb of a Child with a Growth Plate Injury Still Grow?

Most growth plate fractures heal without any lasting effect. Whether an arrest of growth occurs depends on the treatment provided, and the following factors, in descending order of importance:

- **Severity of the injury.** If the injury causes the blood supply to the epiphysis to be cut off, growth can be stunted. If the growth plate is shifted, shattered, or crushed, the growth plate may close prematurely, forming a bony bridge or "bar." The risk of growth arrest is higher in this setting. An open injury in which the skin is broken carries the risk of infection, which could destroy the growth plate.

- **Age of the child.** In a younger child, the bones have a great deal of growing to do; therefore, growth arrest can be more serious, and closer surveillance is needed. It is also true, however, that younger bones have a greater ability to heal.

- **Which growth plate is injured.** Some growth plates, such as those in the region of the knee, are more involved in extensive bone growth than others.

- **Type of fracture.** Of the six fracture types described earlier, types IV, V, and VI are the most serious.

The most frequent complication of a growth plate fracture is premature arrest of bone growth. The affected bone grows less than it would have without the injury, and the resulting limb could be shorter than the opposite, uninjured limb. If only part of the growth plate is injured, growth may be lopsided and the limb may become crooked.

Growth plate injuries at the knee have the greatest risk of complications. Nerve and blood vessel damage occurs most frequently there. Injuries to the knee have a much higher incidence of premature growth arrest and crooked growth.

Chapter 58

# Developmental Diseases and Sports Injuries

## Chapter Contents

Section 58.1

## *Osgood-Schlatter Disease*

This section includes text excerpted from "Knee Problems—Questions
and Answers about Knee Problems," National Institute of Arthritis
and Musculoskeletal and Skin Diseases (NIAMS), March 2016.

Osgood-Schlatter disease is a condition caused by repetitive stress
or tension on part of the growth area of the upper tibia (the apoph-
ysis). It is characterized by inflammation of the patellar tendon and
surrounding soft tissues at the point where the tendon attaches to
the tibia. The disease may also be associated with an injury in which
the tendon is stretched so much that it tears away from the tibia and
takes a fragment of bone with it. The disease most commonly affects
active young people, particularly boys between the ages of 10 and 15,
who play games or sports that include frequent running and jumping.

### Symptoms

People with this disease experience pain just below the knee joint
that usually worsens with activity and is relieved by rest. A bony bump
that is particularly painful when pressed may appear on the upper
edge of the tibia (below the kneecap). Usually, the motion of the knee
is not affected. Pain may last a few months and may recur until the
child's growth is completed.

### Diagnosis

Osgood-Schlatter disease is most often diagnosed by the symptoms.
An X-ray may be normal, or show an injury, or, more typically, show
that the growth area is in fragments.

### Treatment

Osgood-Schlatter disease is temporary and the pain usually
goes away without treatment. Applying ice to the knee when pain
begins helps relieve inflammation and is sometimes used along with

stretching and strengthening exercises. The doctor may advise you to limit participation in vigorous sports. Children who wish to continue moderate or less stressful sports activities may need to wear knee pads for protection and apply ice to the knee after activity. If there is a great deal of pain, sports activities may be limited until the discomfort becomes tolerable.

# Section 58.2

# *Sever's Disease*

Text in this section is © 1995-2017. The Nemours Foundation/ KidsHealth®. Reprinted with permission.

Although the name might sound pretty frightening, Sever's disease is really a common heel injury that occurs in kids. It can be painful, but is only temporary and has no long-term effects.

## *About Sever's Disease*

Sever's disease, also called calcaneal apophysitis, is a painful bone disorder that results from inflammation (swelling) of the growth plate in the heel. A growth plate, also called an epiphyseal plate, is an area at the end of a developing bone where cartilage cells change over time into bone cells. As this occurs, the growth plates expand and unite, which is how bones grow.

Sever's disease is a common cause of heel pain in growing kids, especially those who are physically active. It usually occurs during the growth spurt of adolescence, the approximately 2-year period in early puberty when kids grow most rapidly. This growth spurt can begin any time between the ages of 8 and 13 for girls and 10 and 15 for boys. Sever's disease rarely occurs in older teens because the back of the heel usually finishes growing by the age of 15, when the growth plate hardens and the growing bones fuse together into mature bone.

Sever's disease is similar to Osgood-Schlatter disease, a condition that affects the bones in the knees.

## Causes

During the growth spurt of early puberty, the heel bone (also called the calcaneus) sometimes grows faster than the leg muscles and tendons. This can cause the muscles and tendons to become very tight and overstretched, making the heel less flexible and putting pressure on the growth plate. The Achilles tendon (also called the heel cord) is the strongest tendon that attaches to the growth plate in the heel. Over time, repeated stress (force or pressure) on the already tight Achilles tendon damages the growth plate, causing the swelling, tenderness, and pain of Sever's disease.

Such stress commonly results from physical activities and sports that involve running and jumping, especially those that take place on hard surfaces, such as track, basketball, soccer, and gymnastics.

Sever's disease also can result from standing too long, which puts constant pressure on the heel. Poor-fitting shoes can contribute to the condition by not providing enough support or padding for the feet or by rubbing against the back of the heel.

Although Sever's disease can occur in any child, these conditions increase the chances of it happening:

- **pronated foot** (a foot that rolls in at the ankle when walking), which causes tightness and twisting of the Achilles tendon, thus increasing its pull on the heel's growth plate

- **flat or high arch**, which affects the angle of the heel within the foot, causing tightness and shortening of the Achilles tendon

- **short leg syndrome** (one leg is shorter than the other), which causes the foot on the short leg to bend downward to reach the ground, pulling on the Achilles tendon

- **overweight or obesity**, which puts weight-related pressure on the growth plate

## Signs and Symptoms

The most obvious sign of Sever's disease is pain or tenderness in one or both heels, usually at the back. The pain also might extend to the sides and bottom of the heel, ending near the arch of the foot.

A child also may have these related problems:

- swelling and redness in the heel

- difficulty walking

- discomfort or stiffness in the feet upon awaking
- discomfort when the heel is squeezed on both sides
- an unusual walk, such as walking with a limp or on tiptoes to avoid putting pressure on the heel

Symptoms are usually worse during or after activity and get better with rest.

## Diagnosis

A doctor can usually tell that a child has Sever's disease based on the symptoms reported. To confirm the diagnosis, the doctor will probably examine the heels and ask about the child's activity level and participation in sports. The doctor might also use the squeeze test, squeezing the back part of the heel from both sides at the same time to see if doing so causes pain. The doctor might also ask the child to stand on tiptoes to see if that position causes pain.

Although imaging tests such as X-rays generally are not that helpful in diagnosing Sever's disease, some doctors order them to rule out other problems, such as fractures. Sever's disease cannot be seen on an X-ray.

## Treatment

The immediate goal of treatment is pain relief. Because symptoms generally worsen with activity, the main treatment for Sever's disease is rest, which helps to relieve pressure on the heel bone, decreasing swelling and reducing pain.

As directed by the doctor, a child should cut down on or avoid all activities that cause pain until all symptoms are gone, especially running barefoot or on hard surfaces because hard impact on the feet can worsen pain and inflammation. The child might be able to do things that do not put pressure on the heel, such as swimming and biking, but check with a doctor first.

The doctor might also recommend that a child with Sever's disease:

- perform foot and leg exercises to stretch and strengthen the leg muscles and tendons
- elevate and apply ice (wrapped in a towel, not applied directly to the skin) to the injured heel for 20 minutes two or three times per day, even on days when the pain is not that bad, to help reduce swelling

- use an elastic wrap or compression stocking that is designed to help decrease pain and swelling

- take an over-the-counter medicine to reduce pain and swelling, such as acetaminophen (Tylenol) or ibuprofen (Advil, Motrin)

**Note:** Children should not be given aspirin for pain due to the risk of a very serious illness called Reye syndrome.

In very severe cases, the doctor might recommend that the child wear a cast for anywhere from 2 to 12 weeks to immobilize the foot so that it can heal.

## *Recovery and Recurrence*

One of the most important things to know about Sever's disease is that, with proper care, the condition usually goes away within 2 weeks to 2 months and does not cause any problems later in life. The sooner Sever's disease is addressed, the quicker recovery is. Most kids can return to physical activity without any trouble once the pain and other symptoms go away.

Although Sever's disease generally heals quickly, it can recur if long-term measures are not taken to protect the heel during a child's growing years. One of the most important is to make sure that kids wear proper shoes. Good quality, well-fitting shoes with shock-absorbent (padded) soles help to reduce pressure on the heel. The doctor may also recommend shoes with open backs, such as sandals or clogs, that do not rub on the back of the heel. Shoes that are heavy or have high heels should be avoided. Other preventive measures include continued stretching exercises and icing of the affected heel after activity.

If the child has a pronated foot, a flat or high arch, or another condition that increases the risk of Sever's disease, the doctor might recommend special shoe inserts, called orthotic devices, such as:

- heel pads that cushion the heel as it strikes the ground

- heel lifts that reduce strain on the Achilles tendon by raising the heel

- arch supports that hold the heel in an ideal position

If a child is overweight or obese, the doctor will probably also recommend weight loss to decrease pressure on the heel.

The risk of recurrence goes away on its own when foot growth is complete and the growth plate has fused to the rest of the heel bone, usually around age 15.

# Chapter 59

# *Return to Play*

A question that is often asked by injured athletes and their coaches and parents is, "When can sports resume?" Return to play (RTP) decisions are frequently controversial, and there can be differences of opinion between healthcare providers and others. But there are specific policies in place for certain sports and specific injuries that can help guide athletes in making the right decision on RTP. The process has to be clearly understood by the athletes and families so that they can work with their doctor and physical therapist in RTP decisions.

Injuries mostly occur at the vulnerable structures of the body, like ligaments, tendons, and bones. If the athlete returns to the sport before full recovery, the injury can easily become worse. A mild sprain could become severe; a stress fracture can turn into a complete fracture; or a mild concussion might result in secondary brain injury or even death.

## *Recovery from Sports Injuries*

An athlete should follow a seven-step treatment and rehabilitation program before returning to play:

1. **Encourage complete healing.** Healing time can vary depending on the site, severity, and type of injury. A ligament sprain may take 2 to 4 weeks to heal, whereas a leg fracture will take 8 to 12 weeks. Swelling, if any, has to come down fully. During this time, an athlete can keep him- or herself fit by doing some exercises (working the uninjured limb) or activities like swimming that will not put stress on the injured area.

---

"Return to Play," © 2017 Omnigraphics. Reviewed June 2017.

This should be done under the guidance of a physician or a physical therapist.

2. **Restore pain-free full range of motion.** For most of the healing time, the injured part will be immobilized using a splint or a cast, which can result in reduced range of motion in the joint or muscle. Before returning to play, the athlete should achieve full pain-free range in the joint by doing range-of-motion exercises prescribed by the physical therapist. A good rule to follow: no return to sports if there is any limited motion in a joint.

3. **Regain muscle strength.** Due to the rest and immobilization following injury, the muscles around the injured part will weaken. This reduction in muscle strength needs to be improved before returning to play. The trainer or physical therapist will prescribe progressive resistance exercises for the gradual return of optimal muscle strength required for the sport.

4. **Regain normal stride.** There should be no limping present with running and walking before returning to play. If present, the cause needs to reassessed and managed.

5. **Regain endurance.** Athletes can continue general conditioning exercises with cross training during the recovery phase. Using an alternative exercise allows maintenance of good cardiovascular fitness while not interfering with the healing process. Activities like swimming, running in water, biking, and rowing are excellent alternative exercises to help maintain endurance.

6. **Regain sport-specific skills.** The athlete should be able to perform the specific actions required for the sport effectively. The agility, balance, and flexibility required must be fully restored, both to ensure performance and to reduce the chance of re-injury. For example, retraining a knee injury in football should involve the ability to run, stop, change directions, and jump.

7. **Regain confidence.** When an injury keeps an athlete out of competition, it can result in a lot of psychological stress. The athlete needs to work to regain full confidence in his or her performance levels. Returning to play too soon may increase the risk of re-injury, new injury, depression, or poor performance.

Working closely with sports medicine experts can help ensure that the injured athlete recovers fully by following the program advised by them. Even though there will be tremendous pressure on the athlete to resume as soon as possible, his or her health and safety must be given top priority. Therefore, a systematic recovery protocol has to be strictly followed every day, at all levels of play, from recreational players to elite athletes.

## Psychological Factors in Successful Return to Sport after Injury

A great deal of scientific evidence proves that psychological factors play a major role in an injured athlete's successful return to competition. This needs to be taken into consideration during injury rehabilitation, so that the athlete stays calm, focused, and motivated before returning to play.

The following are examples of some of the psychological factors that can affect an injured athlete:

- **Emotions shift over time.** As rehabilitation protocols progress, the athlete feels more positive (confidence and readiness) with lessened negative emotions associated with the initial injury, such as anger, depression and anxiety.

- **Positive psychological response.** An athlete's ability to cope with the stress of injury greatly influences recovery and progression through the rehab program. Staying motivated is crucial, and a positive psychological response is associated with faster return to play after injury.

- **Negative psychological response.** If an athlete has a negative outlook on the injury and rehab, the chances of returning to sports can be decreased, and the risk of re-injury is higher if he or she does return. A negative psychological response usually results in a poor outcome.

- **Fear.** This can remain a noticeable emotion at the time athletes return to play. But there have been reports of athletes who have successfully returned to sports describing an associated dissipation of fear by actually testing the injured body part through returning to play.

- **External pressures.** There can be considerable pressure on an injured athlete to return too soon. The athlete feels pressured to maintain his or her spot on the team and to avoid letting the team and the coach down. When an athlete yields to this pressure and returns to sports prematurely, he or she may subsequently increase the risk of re-injury.

## Recommendations

The following recommendations can further help ensure that athletes are fully prepared to return to play following an injury:

- **Psychological screening.** During rehab, proper screening of athletes needs to be carried out to identify the risk of developing negative psychological responses. Strategies should be developed to address such issues as fear, lack of confidence, and motivation.

- **Performance expectations.** Realistic performance goals should be set. Visual imagery methods can be used during the entire rehab process to build confidence, self-esteem, and a sense of competence.

- **Support.** There has to be constant support from coaches, teammates, parents, and others so that athletes do not perceive the external pressure to return to play too soon.

Psychological readiness usually increases as athletes progress through the rehabilitation process. However, if an athlete's psychological readiness before competition is low, waiting a little longer before returning to the playing field may be the safest course of action.

### References

1. "When is an Athlete Ready to Return to Play?" American Academy of Pediatrics (AAP), November 21, 2015.

2. "Return to Play after Sports Injury," Momsteam.com, n.d.

3. Onate, James A., PhD, ATC, and John Black, J.D. "Return-To-Participation Considerations Following Sports Injury," National Federation of State High School Associations, November 10, 2015.

# Part Eleven

# Additional Help and Information

Chapter 60

# Glossary of Terms Related to Sports Injuries

**acromioclavicular (AC) joint:** The joint of the shoulder located between the acromion (part of the scapula that forms the highest point of the shoulder) and the clavicle (collarbone).

**aerobic physical activity:** Aerobic (or endurance) physical activities use large muscle groups (back, chest, and legs) to increase heart rate and breathing for an extended period of time.

**analgesics:** Medications designed to relieve pain. Analgesics include both prescription and over-the-counter products.

**anterior cruciate ligament:** A ligament in the knee that crosses from the underside of the femur to the top of the tibia. The ligament limits rotation and the forward movement of the tibia.

**arthritis:** Inflammation of a joint or joints in the body.

**arthrogram:** A diagnostic test in which a contrast fluid is injected into the shoulder joint and an X-ray is taken to view the fluid's distribution in the joint. Leaking of fluid into an area where it does not belong may indicate a tear or opening.

**arthroscopic surgery:** Repairing the interior of a joint by inserting a microscope-like device and surgical tools through small cuts rather than one large surgical cut.

---

This glossary contains terms excerpted from documents produced by several sources deemed reliable.

**awkward posture:** Deviation from the natural or "neutral" position of a body part. A neutral position is one that puts minimal stress on the body part.

**biopsy:** A procedure in which tissue is removed from the body and studied under a microscope.

**body mechanics education:** Education that emphasizes how best to align the musculoskeletal system during work and other activities to reduce abnormal joint stress, muscle strain, and fatigue.

**bone scan:** A technique for creating images of bones on a computer screen or on film.

**bursa:** A small sac of tissue located between a bone and other moving structures such as muscles, skin, or tendons. The bursa contains a lubricating fluid that allows these structures to glide smoothly.

**bursitis:** Inflammation or irritation of a bursa.

**carpal tunnel:** An opening inside the wrist through which the median nerve and several tendons pass. The tunnel is formed by the wrist bones and a dense ligament.

**carpal tunnel syndrome (CTS):** A condition in which there is pressure on the median nerve in the carpal tunnel. The nerve gets squeezed when the tendons swell.

**cartilage:** A tough, elastic material that covers the ends of the bones where they meet to form a joint. In the knee, cartilage helps absorb shock and allows the joint to move smoothly.

**cervical spine:** The upper portion of the spine closest to the skull. The cervical spine comprises seven vertebrae.

**cervical vertebrae:** Seven small irregular bones in the neck that support and allow head movement.

**computerized tomography (CT) scan:** A painless procedure in which X-rays are passed through the body at different angles, detected by a scanner, and analyzed by a computer. This produces a series of clear cross-sectional images (slices) of the tissues on a computer screen. CT scan images show soft tissues such as ligaments or muscles more clearly than conventional X-rays. The computer can combine individual images to give a three-dimensional view.

**contact stress:** Pressure on one specific area of the body (such as the forearms or sides of the fingers) that can inhibit nerve function and blood flow in that area.

**corticosteroids:** Synthetic preparations of cortisol, which is a hormone produced by the body. Corticosteroids block the immune system's production of substances that trigger allergic and inflammatory responses. These drugs may be injected directly into the inflammation site. Generally, symptoms improve or disappear within several days.

**cumulative trauma disorder (CTD):** An injury that develops over a period of time because of repeated stress on a specific body part, such as the back, hand, wrist, or forearm. Muscles and joints are stressed, tendons are inflamed, nerves are pinched, and/or the flow of blood is restricted.

**disorder:** A medical condition in which some body function does not work as it should.

**epicondylitis:** A painful and sometimes disabling swelling of the tissues of the elbow.

**exercise:** A type of physical activity that is planned and structured.

**fatigue:** A condition that results when the body cannot provide enough energy for the muscles to perform a task.

**flexibility:** The range of motion possible at a joint. Flexibility exercises enhance the ability of a joint to move through its full range of motion.

**force:** The amount of physical effort needed to do a task.

**glenohumeral joint:** The joint where the rounded upper portion of the humerus (upper arm bone) joins the glenoid (socket in the shoulder blade). This is commonly referred to as the shoulder joint.

**hamstring:** Prominent tendons at the back of the knee. Each knee has a pair of hamstrings that connect to the muscles that flex the knee.

**herniated disk:** A potentially painful problem in which the hard outer coating of the spinal disk is damaged, allowing the disk's jelly-like center to leak and cause irritation to adjacent nerves.

**iliotibial band syndrome:** An inflammatory condition in the knee caused by the rubbing of a band of tissue over the outer bone (lateral condyle) of the knee. Although iliotibial band syndrome may be caused by direct injury to the knee, it is most often caused by the stress of long-term overuse, which sometimes results from sports training.

**impingement syndrome:** When the rotator cuff becomes inflamed and thickened, it may get trapped under the acromion, resulting in shoulder pain or loss of motion.

**inflammation:** The characteristic reaction of tissue to injury or disease. It is marked by four signs: swelling, redness, heat, and pain.

**intervertebral discs:** Discs that sit between the bones of the spinal column (vertebrae) in the back and neck.

**joint:** A junction where two bones meet. Most joints are composed of cartilage, joint space, the fibrous capsule, the synovium, and ligaments.

**lateral collateral ligament:** The ligament that runs along the outside of the knee joint. It provides stability to the outer (lateral) part of the knee.

**ligament:** A tough band of connective tissue that connects bones to bones.

**lumbar spine:** The lower portion of the spine. The lumbar spine comprises five vertebrae.

**magnetic resonance imaging (MRI):** A procedure that uses a powerful magnet linked to a computer to create pictures of areas inside the body.

**medial collateral ligament:** The ligament that runs along the inside of the knee joint, providing stability to the outer (medial) part of the knee.

**median nerve:** The main nerve passing through the carpal tunnel in the wrist.

**meniscus:** A pad of connective tissue that separates the bones of the knee. The menisci are divided into two crescent-shaped discs (lateral and medial) positioned between the tibia and femur on the outer and inner sides of each knee.

**muscle:** A tissue that has the ability to contract, producing movement or force. There are three types of muscle: striated muscle, which is attached to the skeleton; smooth muscle, which is found in such tissues as the stomach and blood vessels; and cardiac muscle, which forms the walls of the heart.

**musculoskeletal disorders (MSDs):** A group of conditions that involve the nerves, tendons, muscles, and supporting structures such as intervertebral discs.

**musculoskeletal system:** The soft tissues and bones in the body. The parts of the musculoskeletal system are bones, muscles, tendons, ligaments, cartilage, nerves, and blood vessels.

**nerves:** Cordlike fibers that carry the signals controlling body movement and allowing senses like sight and touch to work.

**nonsteroidal anti-inflammatory drugs (NSAIDs):** A class of medications that ease pain and inflammation and are available over-the-counter or with a prescription.

**orthopedic surgeon:** A doctor who has been trained in the nonsurgical and surgical treatment of bones, joints, and soft tissues such as ligaments, tendons, and muscles.

**osteochondritis dissecans:** A condition that results from a loss of the blood supply to an area of bone underneath a joint surface. The condition usually involves the knee. In osteochondritis dissecans, the affected bone and its covering of cartilage gradually loosen and cause pain.

**patella:** The bone that sits over the other bones at the front of the knee joint and slides when the leg moves. Commonly referred to as the kneecap, the patella protects the knee and gives leverage to muscles.

**plica syndrome:** A syndrome that occurs when plicae (bands of synovial tissue) are irritated by overuse or injury. Synovial plicae are the remains of tissue pouches found in the early stages of fetal development.

**quadriceps muscle:** The large muscle at the front of the thigh.

**range of motion:** The extent to which a joint can move freely and easily.

**repetitive stress injury (RSI):** An injury caused by working in the same awkward position, or repeating the same stressful motions, over and over.

**RICE:** An acronym for rest, ice, compression, and elevation. These are the four steps often recommended for treating musculoskeletal injuries.

**risk factor:** An action and/or condition that may cause an injury or illness, or make it worse. Examples related to ergonomics include forceful exertion, awkward posture, and repetitive motion.

**rotator cuff:** A set of muscles and tendons that secures the arm to the shoulder blade and permits rotation of the arm.

**sciatica:** Pain felt down the back and outer side of the thigh. The usual cause is a herniated disc that is pressing on a nerve root.

**soft tissues:** Tissues that connect, support, or surround other structures and organs of the body.

**sprain:** Overstretching or overexertion of a ligament, resulting in a tear or rupture of the fibers in the ligament.

**strain:** An injury caused by a muscle, tendon, or ligament stretching.

**stress:** Demand (or "burden") on the human body caused by something outside of the body.

**tendonitis:** Inflammation or irritation of a tendon.

**tendons:** Fibrous cords that connect muscle to bone.

**tenosynovitis:** Inflammation of the lining of the sheath that surrounds a tendon.

**transcutaneous electrical nerve stimulation (TENS):** A technique that uses a small battery-operated unit to send electrical impulses to the nerves to block pain signals to the brain.

**trigger finger:** A common term for tendinitis or tenosynovitis that cause painful locking of the finger(s) while flexing them.

**X-ray (radiography):** A procedure in which an X-ray (high-energy radiation with waves shorter than those of visible light) beam is passed through the body to produce a two-dimensional picture of the bones. X-rays are often used in diagnosing musculoskeletal problems.

Chapter 61

# Directory of Resources Related to Sports Injuries

## General Organizations and Resources

*American Academy of Family Physicians (AAFP)*
11400 Tomahawk Creek Pkwy
Leawood, KS 66211-2680
Toll-Free: 800-274-2237
Phone: 913-906-6000
Fax: 913-906-6075
Website: www.aafp.org

*American Academy of Orthopaedic Surgeons (AAOS)*
9400 W. Higgins Rd.
Rosemont, IL 60018
Phone: 847-823-7186
Fax: 847-823-8125
Website: www.aaos.org
E-mail: custserv@aaos.org

---

Resources in this chapter were compiled from several sources deemed reliable; all contact information was verified and updated in June 2017.

*American Academy of Pediatrics (AAP)*
141 N.W. Point Blvd.
Elk Grove Village, IL 60007-1098
Toll-Free: 800-433-9016
Phone: 847-434-4000
Fax: 847-434-8000
Website: www.aap.org

*American Academy of Physical Medicine and Rehabilitation (AAPM&R)*
9700 W. Bryn Mawr Ave.
Ste. 200
Rosemont, IL 60018
Toll-Free: 877-227-6799
Phone: 847-737-6000
Website: www.aapmr.org
E-mail: info@aapmr.org

*American Association of Neurological Surgeons (AANS)*
5550 Meadowbrook Dr.
Rolling Meadows, IL 60008-3852
Toll-Free: 888-566-AANS (888-566-2267)
Phone: 847-378-0500
Fax: 847-378-0600
Website: www.aans.org
E-mail: info@aans.org

*American Chiropractic Association (ACA)*
1701 Clarendon Blvd.
Ste. 200
Arlington, VA 22209
Phone: 703-276-8800
Fax: 703-243-2593
Website: www.acatoday.org
E-mail: memberinfo@acatoday.org

*American College of Sports Medicine (ACSM)*
401 W. Michigan St.
Indianapolis, IN 46202-3233
Phone: 317-637-9200
Fax: 317-634-7817
Website: www.acsm.org

**American Council on Exercise (ACE)**
4851 Paramount Dr.
San Diego, CA 92123
Toll-Free: 888-825-3636
Phone: 858-576-6500
Fax: 858-576-6564
Website: www.acefitness.org
E-mail: support@acefitness.org

**The American Medical Athletic Association (AMAA)**
4405 E.W. Hwy
Ste. 405
Bethesda, MD 20814
Toll-Free: 800-776-2732
Phone: 301-913-9517
Fax: 301-913-9520
Website: www.amaasportsmed.org

**The American Medical Society for Sports Medicine (AMSSM)**
4000 W. 114th St.
Ste. 100
Leawood, KS 66211
Phone: 913-327-1415
Fax: 913-327-1491
Website: www.amssm.org
E-mail: office@amssm.org

**American Orthopaedic Society for Sports Medicine (AOSSM)**
9400 W. Higgins Rd., Ste. 300
Rosemont, IL 60018
Toll-Free: 877-321-3500
Phone: 847-292-4900
Fax: 847-292-4905
Website: www.sportsmed.org
E-mail: aossm@aossm.org

**American Osteopathic Academy of Sports Medicine (AOASM)**
2424 American Ln.
Madison, WI 53704
Phone: 608-443-2477
Fax: 608-443-2474
Website: www.aoasm.org

**American Physical Therapy Association (APTA)**
1111 N. Fairfax St.
Alexandria, VA 22314-1488
Toll-Free: 800-999-2782
Phone: 703-684-APTA (703-684-2782)
Fax: 703-684-7343
TDD: 703-683-6748
Website: www.apta.org
E-mail: Research-dept@apta.org

**American Running Association (ARA)**
4405 E.W. Hwy
Ste. 405
Bethesda, MD 20814
Phone: 800-776-2732
Fax: 301-913-9520
Website: www.americanrunning.org

**Centers for Disease Control and Prevention (CDC)**
Division of Nutrition, Physical Activity, and
Obesity (DNPAO)
1600 Clifton Rd.
Atlanta, GA 30329-4027
Toll-Free: 800-CDC-INFO (800-232-4636)
Toll-Free TTY: 888-232-6348
Website: www.cdc.gov/nccdphp/dnpao/index.html
E-mail: cdcinfo@cdc.gov

**Consumer Product Safety Commission (CPSC)**
4330 E. W. Hwy
Bethesda, MD 20814
Toll-Free: 800-638-2772
Phone: 301-504-7923
Fax: 301-504-0124; 301-504-0025
TTY: 301-595-7054
Website: www.cpsc.gov

**Gatorade Sports Science Institute (GSSI)**
617 W. Main St.
Barrington, IL 60010
Toll-Free: 800-616-GSSI (800-616-4774)
Website: www.gssiweb.com

## HSHS St. John's Hospital
800 E. Carpenter St.
Springfield, IL 62769
Toll-Free: 888-477-4221
Phone: 217-544-6464
Website: www.st-johns.org

## Hughston Health Alert (HHA)
Hughston Foundation
6262 Veterans Pkwy
Columbus, GA 31908-9517
Toll-Free: 800-331-2910
Phone: 706-324-6661
Website: www.hughston.com
E-mail: webmaster@hughston.com

## National Athletic Trainers' Association (NATA)
1620 Valwood Pkwy, Ste. 115
Carrollton, TX 75006
Toll-Free: 800-879-6282
Phone: 214-637-6282
Fax: 214-637-2206
Website: www.nata.org

## National Center for Sports Safety (NCSS)
2316 First Ave. S.
Birmingham, AL 35233
Toll-Free: 866-508-NCSS (866-508-6277)
Phone: 205-329-7535
Website: www.sportssafety.org
E-mail: info@SportsSafety.org

## National Institute of Arthritis and Musculoskeletal and Skin Diseases (NIAMS)
1 AMS Cir.
Bethesda, MD 20892-3675
Toll-Free: 877-22-NIAMS (877-226-4267)
Phone: 301-495-4484
Fax: 301-718-6366
TTY: 301-565-2966
Website: www.niams.nih.gov
E-mail: NIAMSinfo@mail.nih.gov

*National Strength and Conditioning Association (NSCA)*
1885 Bob Johnson Dr.
Colorado Springs, CO 80906
Toll-Free: 800-815-6826
Phone: 719-632-6722
Fax: 719-632-6367
Website: www.nsca-lift.org
E-mail: nsca@nsca-lift.org

*President's Council on Fitness, Sports & Nutrition (PCFSN)*
1101 Wootton Pkwy, Ste. 560
Rockville, MD 20852
Phone: 240-276-9567
Fax: 240-276-9860
Website: www.fitness.gov
E-mail: fitness@hhs.gov

*University of Pittsburgh Medical Center (UPMC) Sports Medicine*
200 Lothrop St.
Pittsburgh, PA 15213-2582
Toll-Free: 800-533-UPMC (800-533-8762)
Phone: 412-647-UPMC (412-647-8762)
Website: www.upmc.com

## Children and Sports Injuries

*Kidshealth.org*
The Nemours Foundation
Website: www.kidshealth.org

*Safe Kids Worldwide*
1255 23rd St. N.W., Ste. 400
Washington, DC 20037-1151
Phone: 202-662-0600
Fax: 202-393-2072
Website: www.safekids.org

# Dental Injuries

*Academy for Sports Dentistry (ASD)*
118 Faye St.
P.O. Box 364
Farmersville, IL 62533
Toll-Free: 800-273-1788
Phone: 217-241-6747
Fax: 217-529-9120
Website: www academyforsportsdentistry.org

*American Dental Association (ADA)*
211 E. Chicago Ave.
Chicago, IL 60611-2678
Phone: 312-440-2500
Website: www.ada.org

# Exercise-Induced Asthma

*Exercise-Induced Asthma American Academy of Allergy, Asthma, & Immunology (AAAAI)*
555 E. Wells St.
Ste. 1100
Milwaukee, WI 53202-3823
Phone: 414-272-6071
Website: www.aaaai.org
E-mail: info@aaaai.org

*American College of Allergy, Asthma, & Immunology (ACAAI)*
85 W. Algonquin Rd.
Ste. 550
Arlington Heights, IL 60005
Phone: 847-427-1200
Fax: 847-427-9656
Website: www.acaai.org
E-mail: mail@acaai.org

**American Lung Association (ALA)**
55 W. Wacker Dr.
Ste. 1150
Chicago, IL 60601
Toll-Free: 800-LUNGUSA (800-548-8252)
Phone: 202-785-3355
Website: www.lung.org
E-mail: info@lung.org

**Asthma and Allergy Foundation of America (AAFA)**
8201 Corporate Dr.
Ste. 1000
Landover, MD 20785
Toll-Free: 800-7-ASTHMA (800-727-8462)
Website: www.aafa.org
E-mail: info@aafa.org

## Eye Injuries

**Coalition to Prevent Sports Eye Injuries**
5 Summit Ave.
Hackensack, NJ 07601
Toll-Free: 866-265-3582
Fax: 201-621-4352
Website: www.sportseyeinjuries.com

**Prevent Blindness**
211 W. Wacker Dr.
Ste. 1700
Chicago, IL 60606
Toll-Free: 800-331-2020
Website: www.preventblindness.org
E-mail: info@preventblindness.org

## Facial Injuries

**American Academy of Otolaryngology—Head and Neck Surgery (AAO-HNS)**
1650 Diagonal Rd.
Alexandria, VA 22314-2857
Phone: 703-836-4444
Website: www.entnet.org

# Foot Injuries

*American Academy of Podiatric Sports Medicine (AAPSM)*
3121 N.E. 26th St.
Ocala, FL 34470
Phone: 352-620-8562
Website: www.aapsm.org
E-mail: info@aapsm.org

*American Orthopaedic Foot & Ankle Society (AOFAS)*
Orthopaedic Foot & Ankle Foundation
9400 W. Higgins Rd., Ste. 220
Rosemont, IL 60018-4975
Toll-Free: 800-235-4855
Phone: 847-698-4654
Website: www.aofas.org
E-mail: PRCinfo@aofas.org

*American Podiatric Medical Association (APMA)*
9312 Old Georgetown Rd.
Bethesda, MD 20814-1621
Phone: 301-581-9200
Website: www.apma.org

# Hand Injuries

*American Society for Surgery of the Hand (ASSH)*
822 W. Washington Blvd.
Chicago, IL 60607
Phone: 312-880-1900
Fax: 847-384-1435
Website: www.assh.org
E-mail: info@assh.org

# Skin Conditions

*American Academy of Dermatology (AAD)*
930 E. Woodfield Rd.
Schaumburg, IL 60173
Toll-Free: 866-503-SKIN (866-503-7546)
Phone: 847-240-1280
Fax: 847-240-1859
Website: www.aad.org

## Spinal Cord Injuries

*Christopher & Dana Reeve Foundation*
636 Morris Tpke
Ste. 3A
Short Hills, NJ 07078
Toll-Free: 800-225-0292
Phone: 973-379-2690
Website: www.christopherreeve.org
E-mail: TeamReeve@ChristopherReeve.org

*North American Spine Society (NASS)*
7075 Veterans Blvd.
Burr Ridge, IL 60527
Toll-Free: 866-960-6277
Phone: 630-230-3600
Fax: 630-230-3700
Website: www.spine.org

# Index

# Index

Page numbers followed by 'n' indicate a footnote. Page numbers in *italics* indicate a table or illustration.

586

numbness, *continued*
  repetitive motion disorders 31
  sciatica 249
  shoulder dislocation 273
  spondylolisthesis 220
  sprain 20
  traditional bicycle saddles 349
  ulnar collateral ligament injury 314
  wrist fractures 301
nutritional supplements
  traumatic brain injury 185
  safety considerations 493

## O

occupational therapists, spinal injury
  rehabilitation 238
OCD *see* osteochondritis dissecans
Office of Dietary Supplements (ODS)
  publication
    calcium 73n
Office of Disease Prevention and
  Health Promotion (ODPHP)
  publications
    bone density test 474n
    eye injury prevention 201n
    heat illness 156n
    winter sports injuries 143n
Office on Women's Health (OWH)
  publication
    female athlete triad 73n
Omnigraphics
  publications
    arm fractures 290n
    arthroscopic surgery 500n
    cold weather safety 161n
    collarbone injuries 283n
    dislocated patella 405n
    fifth metatarsal fracture 448n
    finger injuries 324n
    hip flexor strains 355n
    jaw injuries 198n
    leg stress fractures 415n
    little league elbow 309n
    medications for sports
      injuries 493n
    metatarsalgia 443n
    plantar fasciitis 440n
    resistance training safety 151n

Omnigraphics
  publications, *continued*
    return to play 553n
    scaphoid fractures 296n
    sesamoiditis and sesamoid
      fracture 446n
    shin splints 419n
    sports injury prevention 91n
    sports physical therapy 509n
    thrower's elbow 313n
    wrist fractures 300n
open fracture
  arm 290
  finger 327
  leg injury 361
  metatarsals 449
opioids
  anabolic steroids 87
  analgesics 251, 494
orthotics
  athletic footwear and
    orthotics 421
  preventing knee problems 382
  shoe qualities to avoid 100
  tennis elbow treatment 307
orthopedic surgeons
  arthroscopy 500
  defined 563
  flexor tendon injuries 334
  mallet injury 333
  skier's/gamekeeper's thumb 329
Osborne Head & Neck Institute
  publication
    cauliflower ear 204n
Osgood-Schlatter disease
  overview 548–9
  Sever disease 549
osteochondritis dissecans
  defined 563
  described 380
  elbow 309
  knees 386
  "Osteochondritis Dissecans"
    (GARD) 386n
  "Osteochondritis Dissecans of the
    Elbow (Little League Elbow)"
    (Omnigraphics) 309n
osteonecrosis, osteochondritis
  dissecans 380

594

pulmonary embolism, arthroscopic
surgery 503

**Q**

q-angle, patella dislocation 406
quadriceps muscle
  defined 563
  knee injury 371
  patella dislocation 406
  tendon 401
quadriceps tendon
  dislocated patella 405
  patellofemoral pain 384
  tendon injuries 379
  tendons and ligaments 371
quadriplegia, spinal cord injury 230
"Questions and Answers about
  Bursitis and Tendinitis" (NIAMS)
  401n, 423n
"Questions and Answers about
  Sprains and Strains" (NIAMS) 366n

**R**

racquetball, tennis elbow 306
radiculopathy
  anticonvulsants 252
  lower back pain 211
  sciatica 250
radius
  arm fractures 290
  growth plate injuries 530, 540
  wrist fractures 300
range of motion, defined 563
range of motion exercises
  growth plate injury 544
  knee problems 382
  return to play 554
  tennis elbow 307
"Rate and Risk Factors for
  Surgeries Following Initial ACL
  Reconstruction" (NIAMS) 503n
reduction
  arm fractures 291
  metatarsal fractures 466
  pain prevention 215
  patella dislocation 407
  patellofemoral pain 385
  return to play 554

reduction, *continued*
  shoulder dislocation 274
  spinal cord injuries 231
  wrist fractures 302
refracture, metatarsal fracture 451
regulations, cervical fractures 226
rehabilitation
  biceps tendon injuries 282
  hamstring strain 367
  hip bursitis 355
  injury prevention 92
  posterior cruciate ligament (PCL)
    injury 399
  recovery from sports injuries 553
  shoulder dislocation 274
  spinal cord injuries 237
  sports injuries 12
  sports physical therapy 509
  sprains and strains 23
  tennis elbow 307
  traumatic brain injury 185
"Rehabilitation of Acute Hamstring
  Injuries in Male Athletes"
  (NIH) 366n
re-injury
  anterior cruciate ligament 394
  hamstring injuries 367
  leg stress fractures 417
  metatarsal fractures 466
  repetitive motion disorders 32
  return to play 554
  turf toe 460
repetitive injury *see* re-injuries
repetitive motion disorders (RMD),
  overview 31–2
"Repetitive Motion Disorders
  Information Page" (NINDS) 31n
repetitive stress injury (RSI)
  defined 563
  metatarsal fracture 448
  *see also* overuse injuries
resection, patellofemoral pain 385
resistance training
  osteochondritis dissecans 312
  overview 151–4
  *see also* strengthening exercises
"Resistance Training Safety"
  (Omnigraphics) 151n

stingers, overview 246–8
straddle injuries, defined 346
strains
 defined 564
 hamstring 366
 hip flexor 355
 overview 17–24
 thumb 328
 *see also* sprains
strapping, physiotherapy 511
strengthening exercise,
 rehabilitation 12
stress, defined 564
stress fractures
 described 6
 feet 452
 legs 415
 metatarsalgia 444
 running 138
 shin splints 420
 tennis 135
"Stress Fractures of the Foot and
 Ankle" (American Academy of
 Orthopaedic Surgeons) 452n
stretching
 ACL injury 395
 brachial plexus injuries 246
 bursitis 28
 concussion 187
 injury prevention 93
 knee problems 381
 patellofemoral pain 384
 thumb strain 328
 winter sports 143
subacromial impingement syndrome
 (SIS), described 270
subluxation
 described 260
 patella 405
sudden cardiac arrest (SCA),
 overview 33–43
sunburn, skin cancer 52
supination adduction (SAD) fractures,
 ankle fractures 436
supplements
 amenorrheic women 76
 examples 496
 traumatic brain injury 185

"Surgical Guideline for Work-Related
 Knee Injuries 2016" (Washington
 L&I) 503n
surgical procedures
 arm fractures 292
 back pain 213
 brachial plexus injuries 248
 sciatica 250
 posterior cruciate ligament (PCL)
 injury 399
 ulnar nerve entrapment 321
swimmer's shoulder
 overuse injuries 153
 tendinitis 26
syndesmosis, ankle anatomy 435
syndesmosis injury, ankle
 fracture 437
synovial fluid, frozen shoulder 261
synovial membrane, shoulder
 structure 258
synovitis, described 500
synovium, arthritis 374

**T**

tai chi *see* balancing exercise
taping, finger sprains 325
TBI *see* traumatic brain injury
"T846.01: CBER BLA Clinical Review
 Memorandum" (FDA) 506n
temporomandibular joints (TMJ), jaw
 injuries 198
tenderness, growth plate fracture 541
tendinitis
 common shoulder problems 257
 knee tendon injuries 379
 repetitive motion injuries 531
 rotator cuff disease 265
 *see also* tendinosis
tendinopathy, overview 401–3
tendinosis, knee injuries 4
tendon injuries, cortisone shots 495
tendonitis
 defined 564
 rotator cuff 265
tendons
 defined 564
 described 25